THE FATHERS
OF THE CHURCH

A NEW TRANSLATION

VOLUME 48

THE FATHERS
OF THE CHURCH

A NEW TRANSLATION

THE HOMILIES
OF SAINT JEROME

Volume I
(1-59 On The Psalms)

Translated by
SISTER MARIE LIGUORI EWALD, I.H.M.

Marygrove College
Detroit, Michigan

THE CATHOLIC UNIVERSITY OF AMERICA PRESS
Washington, D.C.

NIHIL OBSTAT:

REVEREND HARRY A. ECHLE

Censor Librorum

IMPRIMATUR:

✠PATRICK A. O'BOYLE

Archbishop of Washington

December 4, 1963

The *nihil obstat* and *imprimatur* are official declarations that a book or pamphlet is free of doctrinal or moral error. No implication is contained therein that those who have granted the *nihil obstat* and the *imprimatur* agree with the content, opinions, or statements expressed.

Library of Congress Catalog Card No.: 64-13360

Copyright © 1964 by
THE CATHOLIC UNIVERSITY OF AMERICA PRESS, INC.

To

SISTER M. HONORA

CONTENTS

HOMILIES

HOMILIES

INTRODUCTION

I

IN 385, ST. JEROME, sick at heart, fled the cruel calumnies of Rome, and after a year's pilgrimage, sought refuge in the Holy Land. These years were not only the happiest period of his life, but also the most productive and earned for him the title he most coveted, 'vir ecclesiasticus.' From his monastic retreat at Bethlehem, his voice was to resound throughout the Christian world as its undisputed oracle, 'the spiritual director as well as moral and intellectual conscience of half the West.'[1] The Church, too, was to preserve that voice and honor that instruction with the immortal laurel of 'Doctor Maximus in Exponendis Sacris Scripturis.'

Jerome's first years at Bethlehem were a veritable paradise in which the Ciceronian and Christian, as Moricca has happily commented, seemed at last reconciled.[2] His letters to Rusticus and to Marcella reflect the serenity that calmed his turbulent heart after his hasty departure from Rome, the city of his love and learning, that had become to him the sinful confusion of Babylon. From Bethlehem he writes to Marcella: 'In Christ's humble cottage there is only rustic simplicity; except for the chanting of psalms, silence is perfect. Wherever you go, the husbandman sings the alleluia over his plough; the toiling harvester refreshes himself with the psalms; the vine dresser prunes his vine to a song of David. These are the popular

---

1 F. Cavallera, 'The Personality of St. Jerome,' *A Monument to St. Jerome* (ed. F. X. Murphy, New York 1952) 26.
2 U. Moricca, *San Girolamo* (Il Pensiero Cristiano 1-2, ed. G. Minozzi, Milano 1922) 1.45.

songs of this country; the love songs of the shepherd's whistle; the lyrics of the farmer as he tills the soil with devotion.'[3]

Jerome's literary output from 386 to 420 was incredible. 'He was constantly immersed in study and in books; continually occupied in reading and writing, he permitted himself no rest day or night,' so remarked Sulpicius Severus in his *Dialogues*[4] after his friend, Postumianus, prolonged his visit for six months with the saintly monk whom he admired so much.

With the help of Origen's Hexaplar text, Jerome again took up his revision of the Old Latin Bible from the Septuagint, beginning with the Psalter, because the revision undertaken in Rome at the urgency of Pope Damasus had been newly corrupted. After this second version, known as *Psalterium Gallicanum*, came the Book of Job, the books of Solomon— Proverbs, Ecclesiastes, Canticle of Canticles—and Paralipomenon. Except for the Psalter and Job, all that remains of these are their prefaces and a few fragments.[5]

Before Jerome had finished this tremendous work, between 389 and 395, he dedicated himself to the mission of translating the entire Bible from the original Hebrew and Aramaic, a labor which was to occupy him until 405 or 406. The first books he undertook were Samuel and Kings, followed by the sixteen prophets and the Psalter, which must have been completed before 392-393 because they are mentioned in *De viris illustribus* which was written in 392-393. Then came the Book of Job and, after 393, Esdra, Nehemia, Paralipomenon; in 398, the books of Solomon. After that, the five books of the Pentateuch were followed by Josua, Judges, Ruth, Esther. Tobias and Judith he translated from the difficult Aramaic,

---

3 Letter 46.12; cf. Letter 43; 125.8.
4 1.9, PL 20.190.
5 Moricca, *op. cit.*, 46; cf. G. Grützmacher, *Hieronymus. Eine biographische Studie zur alten Kirchengeschichte* 1-3 (Studien zur Geschichte der Theologie und der Kirche, ed. Bonwentsch und Seeberg, 6.3, Leipzig 1901, Berlin 1906, 1908) 2.91-92; L. Hartmann, 'St. Jerome as an Exegete,' *A Monument to St. Jerome* 41; A. Penna, *S. Gerolamo* (Roma 1949) 156-158, 438-439.

and parts of Esdra and Daniel. Whenever he was tempted to
turn back from this stupendous venture, his rabbi teacher—
perhaps Bar-anina—urged him on by the frequent repetition
of 'labor improbus omnia vincit.'[6] Sometime before 398, he
went back to his revision of the Itala text of the New Testament and brought to an end the work he had all but completed in Rome.[7]

Apart from his translations, he tackled exegetical works
with renewed vigor. In 387-388, for Paula and Eustochium,
he composed his commentaries on St. Paul's letters to Philemon, the Galatians, the Ephesians, and Titus. In 388 or 389,
he completed the *Commentary on Ecclesiastes* which he had
begun in Rome at Blesilla's suggestion. From 391 to 406, he
produced commentaries on the twelve minor prophets; by
397, on the ten visions of Isaia; in 398, on the Gospel of St.
Matthew; between 391 and 392, on the Psalms. In the last
years of his life, came the four major prophets, a work incomplete at the time of his death.[8]

To the years 386-391 belong Jerome's translation of the
thirty-nine homilies of Origen on the Gospel of St. Luke and
the treatise of Dismus the Blind on the Holy Spirit, work
likewise begun in Rome but left unfinished when Pope
Damasus who had requested it died. These same years saw
the completion of many treatises on Hebrew questions on
Genesis, on Hebrew names and places, the lives of the desert
fathers, Hilarion and Malchus, and in 392-393 the *De viris
illustribus*.[9]

That Jerome's early serenity suffered a gradual but definite
decline is evident in many of his letters[10] and especially in his
devastating replies to heretics. 'I have never spared heretics;

---

6 Moricca, *op. cit.*, 44-45; cf. *Praefatio in Danielem Prophetam*, PL
   28.1358. Cf. Penna, *op. cit.*, 438-439 for chronology.
7 Grützmacher, *op. cit.*, 1.99-102.
8 Penna, *op. cit.*, 438-439; Moricca, *op. cit.*, 47.
9 Penna, *loc. cit.*; Moricca, *op. cit.*, 48-49.
10 Cf. especially Letter 84 to Pammachius and Oceanus; 50 to Damnio;
   48 to Pammachius.

I have spent all my zeal in making the enemies of the Church my own,' wrote the 'vir ecclesiasticus' in his prologue to *Against the Pelagians*.[11] Toward 393-394, came his mordant attack on Jovinian for his treatise against virginity and monastic life; in 396, against John of Jerusalem; in 401, against Rufinus; in 406, against Vigilantius. From 397 to 405, he engaged in controversy with St. Augustine, and last of all, came his quarrels with the Pelagians that plagued him from 415 to his death on September 30, 420.[12]

St. Jerome's arduous intellectual labor was subject to constant interruption by his frequent illnesses and exacting duties as the spiritual director of many monks and nuns. In his zeal, when already an old man, he opened a school near the monastery for the children of Roman officials and exiles in Palestine. Such strenuous industry in biblical scholarship and personally demanding activities would have been enough to sap the energy, strength, and resources of a most extraordinary man, but it was not enough for Jerome. Visitors and letters reached him from all parts of the Christian world. Africa, Spain, Gaul, Italy, Pannonia, the lands of the Goths,[13] all claimed the attention of the willing monk, whether in letter or in person, seeking direction, enlightenment, conviction, knowledge, solutions to knotty problems, and answers to perplexing questions. Truly a man of the Church, he gave all that he had, all that he could summon, to quiet a conscience, correct an error; deliver a censure; clarify a dogma, supply an interpretation; inspire a saint, rebuke a sinner, awaken a conscience; silence a heretic, down an opponent.

---

11 *Against the Pelagians* 1, Prologue 2, PL 23.519.
12 Moricca, *op. cit.*, 51-80; Penna *op. cit.*, 438-439.
13 Cavallera, *op. cit.*, 27; cf. Letter 46.10.

II

Rufinus and Melania had already set Jerome and Paula the example of founding a monastery for monks and a convent for religious women in Jerusalem. Life in that modern city with its modern entertainment, theatre, baths, and circus, was anything but peaceful. Jerusalem was the terminus of pilgrims and merchants from everywhere, the destination of pilgrims from Brittany and France who met there with bishops of Persia and solitaries from India. The monastery of the Ascension on the Mount of Olives was kept busy servicing Bishop John of Jerusalem.[14]

In 386, therefore, Jerome and Paula chose the peace and quiet of Bethlehem for their solitude. With money from the sale of his patrimony, and with the help of Paula, Jerome built a monastery that was completed in 389.[15] The cloister for men was in a secluded spot outside the city, connected with the main highway by a tiny road. From his monastery, he could see the Basilica of the Nativity,[16] adjacent to which was Paula's convent. Along the main highway was a third building, the hospice for pilgrims erected by Paula because 'Mary and Joseph had not been able to find hospitality.'[17]

Jerome left to Paula the care of the nuns and took upon himself the direction of the monks. His cell was in a grotto near where Christ was born and to it he transported his library. He spared no expense nor fatigue in the zeal and enthusiasm with which he procured treasures of sacred and profane manuscripts.[18] Here, he fully enjoyed his desire for asceticism and a monk's freedom from episcopal ties. In the desert of Chalcis where he had spent five years, from 374 to 379, he had already experienced the hermit's life. From the quarrels among the

---

14 P. Antin, *Essai sur saint Jérôme* (Paris 1951) 97-98.
15 Moricca, *op. cit.*, 44; cf. Letter 66.14.
16 *Against John of Jerusalem* 42, PL 23.411.
17 Letter 108.14.
18 Moricca *op. cit.*, 44.

solitaries there, he had acquired his repugnance for the
hermitage as a breeding place for pride, and had gathered
much first-hand experience that would prove fruitful in the
future guidance of his monks.[19] Even at Rome, he had not
lived as the secluded monk, but as a distinguished director
of souls and the very busy counselor of Pope Damasus.

Gradually both monasteries increased in the number of
subjects. Women were attracted by the example and virtues
of Paula and Eustochium. From the beginning, they were
divided into three groups with separate living quarters according to social rank, all subject, however, to the same discipline.
They assembled daily in an oratory where they chanted psalms,
sang hymns, and prayed according to the hours that later
became known as the canonical hours: Lauds at dawn, Terce
at nine, Sext at noon, Vespers at sunset; at midnight they rose
to pray again. The remaining time, they gave to reading the
Bible from which they memorized a passage every day; studied
the psalms and performed the works of the monastery; engaged
in manual labor and needlework.[20]

There is no documentary evidence on the various daily
observances of Jerome's monastic retreat. Without binding
himself to any particular form of monasticism, Jerome had
always been in sympathy with the work of the great founder
of monastic or cenobitical life, St. Pachomius, whose rule he
later translated.[21]

In the Pachomian monastery, work consisted chiefly in
cultivating the palm and in making mats and other such
articles. Jerome admired that kind of employment and recom-
mended it to those desiring to embrace the monastic life. To
Rusticus he wrote: 'Always find some work to do, never let
the devil find you idle . . . weave baskets of reeds . . . Hoe the
soil and plot out your garden. . . .'[22]

---

19 Cf. Letter 125.9-10; 16-17. Homily 95 on Obedience.
20 Cf. Letter 108.20.
21 Penna, op. cit., 124.
22 Letter 125.11.

Some of the monks may have engaged in gardening and fruit culture much as the Cistercians do today, but it is certain that Jerome never did. In fact, from his intellectual and moral pre-occupation, he often looked with envy upon the humble work of the brethren who found in such labor great ascetical help, in freedom from criticism and maligning from others.[23] Grütz-macher suggests that the occupation of other monks may have been transcribing books because in one of his sermons, Jerome chides the brethren for quarreling over a pen after having given up all their worldly possessions.[24]

As in all ancient monasteries, the monk who asked for ad-mittance took no oath nor made a vow. He simply pledged himself to persevere in his purpose (*propositum*) and to obey a superior, usually called abbot by the Syrians. This manifested resolution (*propositum*) to lead the monastic life, however, strictly bound the individual. Any subsequent regret or deser-tion was considered detestable perjury. 'It was within your power to make the promise,' Jerome impersonates the Lord as saying. 'You made it and you became Mine. I do not intend to give up what is My own; you do not have the liberty to release yourself from your promise. Yours it was to promise, it is not yours to release yourself.'[25]

The life of the monk was a succession of ascetical practices and manual works. The first embraced primarily the Psalter; assistance at liturgical functions; and the observance of defi-nite prescriptions regarding fasting; retirement from the world and the abandonment of all worldliness; prayer, study, and mortification. Jerome and his disciples chanted the psalms at the regular hours. On festal days, the nuns participated with the monks in liturgical solemnities at the Basilica of the Nativity. There the local clergy ordinarily officiated, but on special festivals, the bishop of Jerusalem presided with his

---

23 Cf. *In Job iuxta LXX praefatio*, PL 29.61.
24 Grützmacher, *op. cit.*, 3 (Berlin 1908) 150.
25 Penna, *op. cit.*, 125; cf. Homily 96 on the Persecution of the Christians.

clergy for the joint communities. On greater feasts, the monks went to the Anastasis at Jerusalem. Whether on Sundays or on feasts, the bishop or a priest, and Jerome preached upon the significance of a particular anniversary or expounded a definite text from Scripture.[26]

With their rigorously enforced enclosure, the life of these monks must have been exemplary,[27] for even in the writings of Jerome's enemies, as Rufinus and Palladius, there is no implication of anything reprehensible. In a bitter conflict between the monastery and the diocesan bishop, the secular clergy of the city remained on good terms with the monks.[28] The Sabinian episode is an isolated exception, of special interest because of the insight it affords into the heart of the 'irascible hermit' who could roar like a lion and bleat like a lamb. Jerome's letter is a cry of sincere grief over an offense against God, and a marvelous exhortation to repentance. Penna calls it a precious document of the profile of the saintly man. The director of the monks is a father who admonishes, exhorts, and pardons even the vulgar offense. It is the heart of Jerome exalted by grace.[29]

Every day, the solicitous abbot expounded the Septuagint Bible to his monks, especially the psalms, to arouse the quarrelsome to do good and to inspire all with zest and courage, as he himself states in his *Apologia* against Rufinus.[30] Very different from the fighting, vehement, and impetuous Jerome, is the Jerome of these sermons. With tenderness and constancy, he exhorts his monks to virtue; urges them to show themselves worthy of their profession; to renounce not only worldly

---

26 Penna, *op. cit.*, 125, 123; cf. Letter 22.37; 107.9; Homily 41 on Psalm 119, p. 300. Cf. *S. Silviae peregrinatio* 25 (ed. P. Geyer, CSEL 39.74 lines 20-22). 'Because it is the custom here that all the priests who are present, as many as wish, preach and after all of them the bishop . . . there is a great delay in the services . . .'
27 Cf. Letter 46.10. 'Of all the ornaments of the Church our monks and virgins are the best.'
28 Letter 82.11. Cf. *Against John of Jerusalem* 39.42; Penna, *op. cit.*, 126-127, 236.
29 Penna, *op. cit.*, 287-289; cf. Letter 147.
30 2.24, PL 23.468.

pleasure and earthly joys, but also spitefulness and the disputes bound at times to arise even among generous and well-meaning men.[31]

These homilies represent only one phase of the exceedingly full life of the 'Oracle of the Christian world,' a homely one but dear to Jerome's heart because it was forming souls for Christ. Very different were his listeners from their elite prototype in Rome, women of spiritual development and ascetic perfection, of intelligence and culture. His audience was now mixed Orientals and Latins with catechumens and novices. As only about ninety-six of these sermons have come down to us, many must be lost if Jerome gave daily exhortations. Lacking in eloquence, they are not a work of the Hieronymean carefully polished style. Their value as documents, however, lies precisely in the fact that they are not finished products and appear in the natural and intimate form in which they were uttered—and recorded in shorthand by some monk without, perhaps, even the knowledge of the preacher. Often unadorned, syntactically and grammatically inaccurate, with not a few errors in biblical citations, they clearly reflect their spontaneous character. When we review the extensive and intense enterprises that taxed the mind, heart, and strength of Jerome during his entire life at Bethlehem, these shortcomings are readily understandable. It was normal that he should preach extempore; that he should go to his preaching, moreover, from an interruption to his studies with his mind absorbed in his writings, but alert and attentive, nevertheless, to the needs of his monks. Jerome's own stricture on his commentaries, 'Dicto quodcum in buccam venerit,'[32] applies only too well to his sermons.

Contentwise, they are simple exegetical expositions of the psalms with an all too patent penchant for allegory. They are full of human interest, character traits, community foibles and troubles, geographical and ethnical observations, historical

---

31 Penna, *op. cit.*, 287.
32 *Commentary on Galatians* 3, PL 26.427.

and linguistic notations. Although they lack the depth and loftiness of a St. Augustine, Larbaud[33] finds them full of human interest and learning. Schade[34] observes that a few, such as Homily 69 on Psalm 91, with its discussion on the Trinity and demonstration of the Socratic axiom that the wise man knows that he does not know, are too deeply theological in thought to be impromptu. Penna,[35] however, finds new evidence of the sensitive and responsive soul that Jerome concealed under a harsh exterior. He is touched by Jerome's tender regard for tiny creatures, for the young, the inexperienced; by his many descriptions of minute plants and animals whose perfection and beauty filled him with wonder.

With the help of some of his monks, Jerome prepared catechumens for baptism, a duty very dear to him. All his life he had a special predilection for the young and the little ones. For little Paula, the daughter of Laeta, and Pacatula, the daughter of Gaudentius, he had prepared a special program of Christian education in their tenderest years.[36] He was not content, however, to give wise rules for the education of the young, but broke his heavy studies in Hebrew and the difficult solution of some puzzling biblical problem, by taking up again his Vergil, Cicero, and other favorite authors to teach Latin to the children in Bethlehem. Rufinus used this fact to upbraid Jerome because of the promise made in his famous dream. Penna prefers to interpret this humble work of the erudite monk as another manifestation of his love for the simple and innocent, and a 'praiseworthy attempt to engraft into the new Christian culture whatever the ancient pagan wisdom possessed of the beautiful and the good.'[37]

His affection for the young must have influenced, too, the

---

33 V. Larbaud, *Sous l'invocation de saint Jérôme* (Paris 1946) 32.
34 L. Schade, *Des heiligen Kirchenvaters Eusebius Hieronymus. Ausgewählte-historische homiletische und dogmatische-Schriften.* BKV 1 (1914) 199.
35 Penna, *op. cit.*, 128.
36 Cf. Letter 107; 128.
37 Penna, *op. cit.*, 128. Cf. *Apologia* 2.8, PL 21.592.

selection of Bethlehem for his monastic life. From among the places sanctified by the Redeemer, Jerome chose Bethlehem, where he could contemplate in rapture the tiny Man-God. 'All the places are holy and venerable, where Christ was born, where He was crucified, where He rose and where as victor He ascended into heaven; but this place is fittingly more venerable. . . . Here a poor little Child is born, an Infant is laid in a manger, "because there was no room for them in the inn." '[38] Again, after recalling the crying of the divine Babe, Jerome exclaims, 'O, if only I were permitted to look upon that manger in which the Lord lay! Now, as an honor to Christ we have taken away the manger of clay and have replaced it with a crib of silver, but more precious to me is the one that has been removed.'[39] From the constant thought of the crib and the poverty of the Infant Jesus and of the rejection of Mary and Joseph in Bethlehem, came the generous hospitality exercised by Jerome and Paula for an extraordinary number of strangers and pilgrims.

III

It is to the tireless research of Dom Germain Morin, O.S.B., of the Abbey of Maredsous in Belgium, that we owe the discovery and identification on the basis of internal and external criticism of almost one hundred Hieronymean homilies.

With the help of eight Carolingian manuscripts, eighth and ninth century, Morin was able to reclaim fifty-nine homilies on the Psalms, hidden for centuries in a pseudo-Jerome document known as the *Breviary of St. Jerome on the Psalms;* ten on the Gospel of St. Mark, concealed for a long time among the Latin homilies ascribed falsely to St. John Chrysostom;

---

38 Homily 44 on Psalm 131, p. 329.
39 Homily 88 on the Birth of the Lord.

ten more on various subjects, found badly mutilated with interpolations in the appendices of St. John Chrysostom and St. Augustine. Four more codices, Italian, from the tenth to the sixteenth century, yielded Morin an additional fourteen homilies constituting an alternate series on the Psalms. He amended and published two more on Isaia, along with a few fragments in Greek on the Psalms. All these appear with a critical apparatus, lexical, and other indices, in *Anecdota Maredsolana* III 2-3 (Maredsous, 1895-1903).

Because of inferiority in style and content, these homilies had been excluded from critical editions since the sixteenth century and ascribed to Jerome's apocryphal writings.

The ten homilies on St. Mark, Morin found among the works of St. John Chrysostom in the Latin editions of the sixteenth century. When Erasmus had edited the pseudo-Chrysostom, he had noted a striking resemblance in certain passages to the known writings of St. Jerome that he had published in nine volumes just ten years before. Four centuries later, Morin had been able to verify their true author.[40]

The Homily 84 on St. Mark 13.32, 33 and 14.3-6 closes with the words: 'we have made these comments on the Gospel, and most opportunely has the fourteenth psalm been read. It is now time to discuss it.' These same words begin Homily 5 on Psalm 14 preached during Lent to the catechumens: 'The fourteenth psalm has been read opportunely.' The two homilies are really one sermon preached by St. Jerome.[41]

The second testimony is the witness of St. Augustine who wrote to Fortunatus not later than 413 in Letter 148:[42] 'Lest I delay too long in calling other authorities to your attention, I shall confine myself to saintly Jerome. . . . When that very

---

40 G. Morin, 'Les monuments de la prédication de S. Jérôme,' *Études, Textes, Découvertes* 1 (Anecdota Maredsolana—Seconde Série. Maredsous 1913) 220-293.
41 Morin, *op. cit.*, 225.
42 G. Morin, *S. Hieronymi Presbyteri Tractatus sive Homiliae in Psalmos, in Marci Evangelium aliaque varia Argumenta* (ed. E. Dekkers *Corpus Christianorum* 78.2 Turnhout 1958) 'Praefatio' VIII.

learned man in Scripture was expounding the Psalm where it says: "Understand, you senseless ones among the people; and, you fools, when will you be wise? Shall he who shaped the ear not hear? or he who formed the eye not see?" Among other things he said: "This passage opposes especially the Anthropomorphites who say that God has the same human form and members that we have. They say, for example, that God has eyes: the eyes of the Lord behold all things; the hands of the Lord have made all things. 'Adam heard the footsteps of the Lord walking in the garden,' says Holy Writ. Naturally they hear these words and collate human weaknesses with the magnificence of God. But I say that God is all eye; He is all hand; He is all foot. He is all eye because He sees everything; He is all hand because He is the maker of everything; He is all foot because He is everywhere. Consider again, therefore, the words: 'Shall he who shaped the ear not hear? or he who formed the eye not see?' Scripture did not say, Shall He who shaped the ear not Himself have an ear? It did not say, Shall He not therefore have eyes? But what did it say? 'Shall he who shaped the ear not hear? or he who formed the eye not see?' He produced the parts of the body; He gave them their efficient powers." ' Augustine has quoted most accurately from Jerome's Homily 22 on Psalm 93.

Cassiodorus is twice a witness in his edition on the Psalter. In the Preface where he treats of the influence of the Holy Spirit on the prophets, he mentions St. Jerome's exposition of the text in which St. Mark says of John, 'he saw the heavens opened':[43] 'We must likewise note that the Holy Spirit has been given to the blessed prophet in such a way that at times He departs from him offended by the infirmity of the flesh and the contradiction of sin. He returns, however, when once again the prophet is ready to receive Him. This is in total agreement with blessed Jerome who, in expounding on St. Mark's Gospel where the Evangelist says of John: "he saw the

---

43 Morin, *op. cit.,* IX.

heavens opened and the Spirit as a dove, descending and remaining upon him," developed this point with such cogency
that no one would presume to dispute him.' Most critics believed that this work of St. Jerome had been lost, but Morin
found it in the apocryphal writings of St. John Chrysostom.
It corresponds to Homily 75 on the Beginning of the Gospel
of St. Mark 1.1-12: 'Notice that it says remaining, abiding con-
tinuously, never departing. . . . The Holy Spirit descended
upon Christ and remained; He descends upon men, assuredly,
but does not remain. Furthermore, in the scroll of Ezechiel
. . . almost after every twenty or thirty verses, it says regularly:
"The word of the Lord came to the prophet Ezechiel." Someone may ask: Why is that so frequently repeated in the
prophecy? Because the Holy Spirit certainly descended upon
the prophet, but again withdrew from him. Whenever it says
"the word came," it indicates that the Holy Spirit departed
from him and came back again to him.' Again, in his exposition on Psalm 41, Cassiodorus says:[44] 'We ought to recall
what the blessed Jerome says about these names: "I have
gone through the entire Psalter with considerable care and
nowhere do I find that the Sons of Core have sung anything
sad. There is always the note of joy and happiness in their
songs, always scorn for the worldly and passing, ardent longing
for the heavenly and the eternal. Their spirit is, therefore,
in keeping with the significance of their name." ' These words
are found verbatim in the beginning of Homily 92 on Psalm
41 to the Neophytes.

The last witness is no other than Jerome himself who,
toward the close of the alternate Homily 61 on Psalm 15,
says:[45] 'It is also important to observe that where we read:
"You will fill me with joy," Theodotion said "Seven joys"
and "In your presence the delights at your right hand for
the Victor"; and Aquila and Symmachus have rendered, "Full-
ness of joys with your presence," or "in your presence." Is

44 *Ibid.*
45 *Ibid.* X.

someone asking why Theodotion said "seven" instead of "full-ness"? The answer is obvious to anyone who has even a slight knowledge of Hebrew. The word, SABA, as we have already indicated in the *Book on Hebrew Questions,* has four different meanings: fullness, satiety, oath, seven.'

Following the guidance of such great witnesses, Morin made a sample study of the familiar expressions in the homilies that would be characteristic of the preacher speaking extempore. Hieronymean phrases and sayings accumulated so rapidly that Morin had no difficulty drawing up a list and setting up a gauge to test and measure individual homilies. He has annotated so completely his text with references to parallel marks of expression, style, and content in the other writings of St. Jerome, that he has left very little question of their authorship. He does not, however, pretend that his work is complete and invites others to continue where he has left off.[46]

Other inquiries, moreover, await investigation and other problems clarification. There is the question of the proximate year of delivery of the homilies. Morin sets it as 401-402; other scholars permit a greater leeway—394 to 413.[47] The extreme limit is suggested by the letter of St. Augustine written about 413 in which he referred to the sermon of St. Jerome. In the sermons themselves, there is reference to the Apostate Emperor Julian (c. 363) and the destruction of the Serapeum in Alexandria (c. 389); an allusion to the Origenist controversy (c. 394), and the error of the Anthropomorphites, who were denounced by Theodolphus of Alexandria in a Paschal Letter of 398. In a homily where Jerome speaks of the true Church as being where the true faith was, even when the heretics possessed the church buildings fifteen or twenty years before, Morin sees a reference to the Edict of Theodosius ordering the Anti-Nicenes of the whole empire to restore the

46 *Ibid.* X-XI.
47 Cf. Penna, *op. cit.,* 439; Grützmacher, *op. cit.,* 1.89-90; J. Steinmann, *Saint Jerome and His Times* (Notre Dame, Indiana 1959) 327.

churches to the Catholics, January 10, 381; hence, that sermon may have been preached in 401.[48]

There are further problems: whether the talks were delivered in Greek; their precise value to scholars of the Bible, of ecclesiastical antiquities, of liturgical documents, of the fundamentals of doctrine, of philological disciplines. 'We have already touched upon all these matters in both of our earlier publications,' Morin says. 'The field now lies wide open for further careful investigation in which we hope that our indices will be of some use.'[49] To the scholar who will take upon himself the task of setting up families of manuscripts with their archetype, Morin bequeaths the examination of nine more codices dating from the ninth to the fifteenth century.[50]

From his exhaustive study of the whole collection of homilies, Dom Morin has confirmed his conclusion of their Hieronymean authorship from the following facts. (1) The homilies were preached in a church during liturgical services. 'We are in a church,' the priest says in Homily 45 on Psalm 132, 'but how many saints there are in the desert!' He mentions, also, that they had come to read or sing, sometimes with the Alleluia, the very psalm that he intended to expound. (2) Many were preached on Sundays, but the one on Psalm 6 was postponed until Wednesday because of the illness of the preacher. There are sermons for Christmas day, the feast of the Dedication, the feast of the Apostles Peter and Paul, and a series for Lent. (3) It is obvious that the preacher is a monk and his hearers are monks to whom he spoke frankly of their faults against fraternal charity, as in Homily 41 on Psalm 119: 'We are called monks. . . . We pray at the third hour, at the sixth, at the ninth; we say vespers at sunset; we rise in the middle of the night, then we pray again at cock crow. . . . We

---

48 Morin, 'Les monuments' 233-234.
49 Morin, S. Hieronymi Tractatus, 'Praefatio' XI. For the problem of the alternate series of homilies on the psalms in its possible relation to the lost sermons of the De viris illustribus 135, PL 23.738, cf. 'Les monuments' 289-293.
50 Morin, Tractatus, 'Praefatio' XVIII-XIX.

have given up our property, abandoned our country, renounced the world; and in the monastery we quarrel over a
reed pen!' He draws attention to their restlessness, resentment,
complaints, and other such failings, and reminds them of their
obligation and the virtues of their state in life. In Homily 87
on the beginning of St. John he says: 'Realize your nobility,
monks! John is the first of our calling. He is a monk.' In the
one on Psalm 14 and the last two on St. Mark, he is obviously
addressing catechumens who after baptism would continue to
serve the Lord in the monastery. (4) The preacher is evidently
a Westerner who delivered his sermons in both Greek and
Latin, but more often in Latin; sometimes at Bethlehem, other
times at Jerusalem. His love and preference for Bethlehem is
undisguised, as in Homily 44 on Psalm 131. (5) Throughout,
there is evidence of the characteristic style of St. Jerome:
familiar phrases and expressions, the flair for allegorical interpretation that is found in all his known writings, his letters,
treatises, and commentaries. Inferior in quality to the best
of his work, they do contain striking passages worthy of
Hieronymean eloquence at its best, as well as Hieronymean
indignation against the heretics, Tatian, Marcion, Manichaeus,
Novatian, Arius, and all guilty of an Arian spirit. There is also
his scorn for Plato, Aristotle, Zeno, Epicurus, Porphyry, who
could not compare in wisdom with humble fishermen. His
enthusiasm for Holy Scripture, of which for him every word
contains a mystery, radiates from every one of the sermons.
All are Christ-centered, all reflect his great love for the Man-
God, and his longing to communicate that love to his subjects.
(6) The preacher gives evidence of a thorough knowledge of
the Hebrew and the Greek versions of Scripture found in the
Hexapla of Origen. His quotations from the Hebrew Psalter,
moreover, agree remarkably with the text of the *Psalterium
iuxta Hebraeos*.[51]

In the many faults, weaknesses, imperfections of the sermons,

---

51 Morin, 'Les monuments' 231-245; 252-254.

Morin finds no particular difficulty. The inferiority of style, the many lapses of memory, inexact citations, occasional lack of good taste, the socialistic attitude toward wealth, the constant preoccupation with allegory, are all so many evidences of their impromptu nature. Not destined for publication, they were intended for simple monks; their tone, as we would expect under such circumstances, is almost colloquial. The abbot of the monastery has one purpose, the formation of simple and rough men into monks dedicated to prayer, mortification, retirement, in the humble service of Christ. Time and again, he deliberately speaks in as simple language as possible, and endeavors to express his thoughts so simply that the least experienced might understand. He frequently anticipates a problem that might arise in the minds of the less learned and less sophisticated. Sick most of the time, hindered with many tasks, engrossed with much intense intellectual labor that was a drain on his mind and soul and emotions, an old man with more than a full life, he had one desire, to form Christ in his monks, to help them find and know Him in the Old Testament as well as the New. Everything he sees is Christ-centered as he strives to impart his own Christ-centered spirituality to them. He brought to his sermons all the wealth of his biblical studies, so that text after text crowded in upon his thoughts at the echo of a word or the association of an idea. It all came so fast that he was bound to err. Often he could not escape the particular passage of Scripture with which he had been working and brought it to bear upon whatever he was saying. He never shirked his duty; never missed a single infraction on the part of the monks; was always cognizant of what they were doing, saying, even thinking! His vigilance in the midst of his studies, writings, problems, griefs, and troubles is indeed amazing, yet he found time with manifest generosity for all the spiritual and corporal works of mercy.

The homilies have been rejected from the writings of St. Jerome because of the many defects that can by no means escape the experienced critic. These imperfections, glaring though they may be, are not a scandal to and do not constitute a doubt for Morin. Minor lapses of eloquence are usual to the most skilled writer when suddenly called upon to speak impromptu; the corruption of Hebrew words the scribes themselves contributed as they took down the saintly abbot's words. Jerome alone, however, is responsible for assigning scriptural texts to the wrong author or book and for risking inexact detail; for duplicating biblical incidences and confusing references; for his surprising inconsistencies in the mystical interpretation of Hebrew names and words. Not even his written works are totally free from such flaws, however, and Morin reminds us that no matter how great or learned a man Jerome was, nevertheless, he was still a man and fallible.[52]

In the translation of the homilies that follows, from *S. Hieronymi Presbyteri Tractatus sive Homiliae in Psalmos, in Marci Evangelium aliaque varia Argumenta,* the Morin text has been used as it appears in the seventy-eighth volume of the Christian Corpus: *Corpus Christianorum LXXVIII S. Hieronymi Presbyteri Opera Pars II. Opera Homiletica.* The 'New Migne,' as the Corpus has been called, is planned to embrace volumes one to ninety-six of the *Patrologia Latina* under the direction of Dom Eligius Dekkers of the Priory of Steenbrugge, Belgium. For this edition of the *Homilies of St. Jerome,* the editors have collated three additional manuscripts noted in the *Repertorio Biblico Medii Aevi:* the sixth century ancient Parisian Codex 2235; the Latin Codex, *Guelferbytanum Gudianum* 269, of the seventh century for the homilies on Psalms 7 and 9; and the very old Codex *Lugdunensem* 604 (521) for the homily on Exodus at the Easter Vigil. They have added also a few emendations in the critical apparatus recorded by Vincent Bulhart in the *Thesaurus Linguae Latinae.* They have indicated preferred new variant readings in the notes by an asterisk.

---

52 Morin, *S. Hieronymi Tractatus,* 'Praefatio' XII-XIII; 'Les monuments' 245-255.

The Morin text itself has not in any way been altered, but two sermons have been included because of their apparent genuinity, one delivered on Epiphany, edited by B. Capelle; the other, on the first Sunday of Lent, edited by L. Fraipont. Certain items, some questionable, in *Anecdota Maredsolana* III.2-3 have been excluded, such as from III.2 a Fragment on the Book of Numbers, really the work of Rufinus; and the Homily on Psalm 50 reckoned among the spurious. From Part III.3 there are six omissions: two homilies on Isaia that are to be incorporated in Vol. LXXIII of this collection with St. Jerome's Commentary on Isaia; Greek fragments on the Psalms revealed to be the work of Origen, Athanasius, Eusebius, Basil, Gregory of Nyssa, Didymus, and Theodoretus Cyrus by J. Waldis in *Hieronymi Graeca in Psalmos Fragmenta, Monasterii* 1908; the *Expositiunculae in Evangelium* of Bishop Arnobius that will be found among his other works in Volume LXXV of the Christian Corpus; *De monogramma XPI,* considered spurious by J. Haussleiter in Volume XLIX of the CSEL, 1916; and last of all, the *Fides S. Hieronymi presbyteri* which Andreas Wilmart attributes to Gregory Illiberitanus (*Bulletin de littérature ecclésiastique,* VII, 1906, p. 298; *Revue bénédictine,* XXX, 1913, pp. 274-275).[53]

All references to Jerome's other writings in the footnotes of the Homilies have been confined to Migne. Because of the great discrepancy in the column numbers of the PL edition, before and after the great fire, the Vallarsi section numbers have been inserted after the column number. The translations of passages from Scripture in the Homilies are taken or adapted from the CCD version where that translation exists; otherwise, from the Challoner-Rheims version.

Volume one of the Homilies contains St. Jerome's regular series on the Psalms, a total of fifty-nine sermons. Volume two comprises fifteen homilies constituting an alternate series on the Psalms, Homilies 60-74; ten on the Gospel of St. Mark, Homilies 75-84; and twelve on various topics, Homilies 85-96.

53 *Ibid.,* 'Praefatio' XXI-XXII; VII.

SELECT BIBLIOGRAPHY

Texts:

S. *Eusebius Hieronymus,* ed. J. P. Migne, in *Patrologia Latina* 23-29 (Paris 1845-1890).

S. *Hieronymi Presbyteri Opera.* Pars II *Opera homiletica,* ed. E. Dekkers, in *Corpus Christianorum* 78 (Turnhout 1958).

Morin, Dom G. S. *Hieronymi Presbyteri Tractatus sive Homiliae in Psalmos, in Marci Evangelium aliaque varia Argumenta,* in Anecdota Maredsolana 3.2-3. (Maredsous 1895-1903.)

Secondary Sources:

Antin, P. *Essai sur saint Jérôme* (Paris 1951).

Cavallera, F. 'The Personality of St. Jerome,' in *A Monument to St. Jerome,* ed. F. X. Murphy (New York 1952) 15-34.

Grützmacher, G. *Hieronymus. Eine biographische Studie zur alten Kirchengeschichte,* 1-3. Studien zur Geschichte der Theologie und der Kirche, ed. Bowentsch und Seeberg, 6.3 (Leipzig 1901, Berlin 1906-1908).

Hartmann, L. 'St. Jerome as an Exegete,' in *A Monument to St. Jerome,* ed. F. X. Murphy (New York 1952) 37-81.

Larbaud, V. *Sous l'invocation de saint Jérôme* (Paris 1946).

Moricca, U. *San Girolamo.* Il Pensiero Cristiano 1-2, ed. G. Minozzi (Milano 1922).

Morin, G. 'Les monuments de la prédication de S. Jérôme,' in *Études, Textes, Découvertes* 1. Anecdota Maredsolana, Seconde Série (Maredsous 1913) 220-293.

Penna, A. S. *Gerolamo* (Rome 1949, Barcelona 1952).

Schade, L. *Des heiligen Kirchenvaters Eusebius Hieronymus. Ausgewählte historische homiletische und dogmatische Schriften.* Bibliothek der Kirchenvater, 2 Reihe (Munchen 1914-1937).

Steinmann, J. *St. Jerome and His Times,* tr. R. Matthews (Notre Dame, Indiana 1959).

SAINT JEROME

HOMILIES
ON THE PSALMS

HOMILY 1

ON PSALM 1

T HE PSALTER IS LIKE a stately mansion that has only one key to the main entrance. Within the mansion, however, each separate chamber has its own key. Even though the great key to the grand entrance is the Holy Spirit, still each room without exception has its own smaller key. Should anyone accidentally confuse the keys and throw them out and then want to open one of the rooms, he could not do so until he found the right one. Similarly, the psalms are each like single cells, every one with its own proper key. The main entrance to the mansion of the Psalter is the first psalm which begins with the words: 'Happy the man who follows not the counsel of the wicked.'

Some commentators think that the key to this first psalm must be the person of Christ our Lord, interpreting 'the happy man' to be the man, Christ.[1] They mean well,[2] of course, but such an interpretation certainly shows a lack of experience and knowledge, for if that happy man is Christ, and Christ gave the law, how can the words: 'But delights in the law of the Lord,' apply to Christ? Besides, how can Christ be compared to a tree where it says: 'He is like a tree planted near running water'? For if Christ is compared to a tree, He is less than the tree since in a comparison the thing compared is less than that to which it is compared; hence, the tree would

---

1 Cf. *Commentarioli in psalmos* 1.3.
2 Cf. *Commentary on Isaia* 17.7, PL 24.176 (195).

3

be greater than the Lord who is compared to it.[3] Do you see, then, that the psalm cannot refer to the person of the Lord, but rather refers in general to the just man? I grant that there are many who, with some reason, I think, apply the words of the Psalm to Joseph; I mean Joseph of Arimathea, who did not follow the counsel of the Jews, who did not stand in the way of sinners, and who did not sit in the company of the Pharisees. Nevertheless, what others choose to interpret in a particular way as referring to Joseph, we shall take to apply in a general way to the just man.[4]

'Happy the man who follows not the counsel of the wicked.' In Genesis, we read how Adam was cursed: 'Cursed be the ground because of you;'[5] but the first malediction pronounced against man is absolved and replaced with a benediction. The Old Law lays down, as it were, only one condition of blessedness; the Gospel, on the other hand, announces simultaneously eight beatitudes.[6] 'Happy the man who follows not the counsel of the wicked.' Happy the man, not any man, but the man who has reached the perfection of the manhood of Christ: 'Who follows not the counsel of the wicked.'

Here, Scripture describes the three usual ways of committing sin: we entertain sinful thoughts; we commit sin in act; or we teach what is sinful. First, we entertain a sinful thought; then, after we have reflected upon it, we convert that thought into action. When we commit sin, moreover, we multiply sin by teaching others to do what we have done. 'Happy the man who follows not the counsel of the wicked'—who thinks no evil; 'nor has stood in the way of sinners'[7]—who does no evil; 'nor sits in the company of the insolent'—who has not taught others to sin. He has not consorted with the scornful, 'nor has stood in the way of sinners.'

---

3 Cf. *Against Jovinian* 1.3, PL 23.223 (239). 'When the lesser is equated with the greater, the greater suffers from the comparison while the lower profits.'
4 Cf. *Commentarioli in ps.* 1.12; cf. Letter 53.3, PL 22.542 (273).
5 Gen. 3.17.
6 Matt. 5.3-12; Luke 6.20-23.
7 Cf. Ps. 1.1.

It is difficult for one not to sin. John the Evangelist says,
in fact, that anyone who denies that he has sinned is a liar.[8]
If, therefore, we all sin, what do the words mean, 'nor has
stood in the way of sinners'? If we all sin, no one is happy,
except, of course, the one who has not sinned. But we all sin,
every last one of us, and so no one is blessed.

Consider, however, just what the Scripture says: 'nor has
stood in the way of sinners.' Scripture did not say happy the
man who has not sinned, but rather, happy the man who has
not persevered in sin. 'Nor has stood in the way of sinners.'
Yesterday I committed sin. I am not happy. If, however, I
do not remain in the state of sin, but withdraw from sin, I
become happy once more. 'Nor sits in the company of the
insolent.' Why does it say 'sits' in this verse and 'has stood'
in the preceding one? For this reason: just as he who has
not stood—persisted—in sin is happy, so he who has not sat
—persisted—in evil doctrine is happy. What does that mean?
You see yourselves that the three determinants of beatitude
consist in not thinking evil, in not persevering in sin, and in
not teaching evil. This is really what the Prophet Amos says:
'For three crimes and for four, I will not revoke my word,
says the Lord.'[9] Moreover, he says this same thing eight times.
Now, this is what he actually is saying: you have entertained
sin, I have pardoned you; you have done evil, I have forgiven
you; you have not repented of your sins, I have excused you:
did you also have to teach evil? What the Scripture implies
is this: For three sins and for four, I shall not be angered
against you, says the Lord.[10]

'And meditates on his law day and night.' The psalmist has
already mentioned three things one must not do: follow the
counsel of the wicked; stand in the way of sinners; sit in the

---

8 Cf. 1 John 1.8.
9 Cf. Amos 1.3, 6, 9, 11, 13; 2.1, 4, 6; 9.8-14; cf. Letter 147.3, PL 22.1197
   (1087); 53.8, PL 22.546 (277); 130.8, PL 22.1115 (985); Commentary on
   Amos 1.5, PL 25.996 (228).
10 Cf. Isa. 57.16, Jer. 3.12; Ezech. 16.42; 33.11; Ps. 102.9; cf. likewise
   Amos 9.

company of the insolent. These three things we must not do, but there are also two things that we must do, for it will not be sufficient for us to shun evil unless we seek good.[11] 'But delights in the law of the Lord.' The psalm does not say fears the law, but delights in the law. There are many who observe the law through fear, but fear as a motive for action is far from meritorious. 'But delights in the law of the Lord'— wholeheartedly he obeys the Lord's command.

'And meditates on his law day and night.' Mere words cannot express adequately what the mind conceives. 'But delights in the law of the Lord.' Some one may say: 'Look, I want to obey the law of God, and so because I want to obey, I am happy.' But consider the words that follow. It is not enough to want the law of God, but one must meditate on His law day and night. 'Meditate day and night.' Someone else may object: 'This is too much for human nature to endure, for one must walk, and drink, and eat, and sleep, and perform all the other necessities of life. How, then, meditate on the law of God day and night, and especially since the Apostle says: "Pray without ceasing"?[12] How can I be praying during the time that I am sleeping?'

Meditation on the law does not consist in reading, but in doing, just as the Apostle says in another place: 'Whether you eat or drink, or do anything else, do all for the glory of God.'[13] Even if I merely stretch forth my hand in almsgiving, I am meditating on the law of God; if I visit the sick, my feet are meditating on the law of God; if I do what is prescribed, I am praying with my whole body what others are praying with their lips. The Jews, indeed, prayed with their lips, but our prayer is works. So there are three things we must not do; two things we must do. What reward does one merit who follows these injunctions?

'He is like a tree planted near running water, that yields its

---

11 Cf. *Commentarioli in ps.* 33; cf. Letter 125.14, PL 22.1080 (941).
12 1 Thess. 5.17.
13 1 Cor. 10.31; cf. Letter 127.4, PL 22.1089 (953).

fruit in due season, and whose leaves never fade.' There are many who interpret these words very simply to mean that just as a tree, if planted near water, will take root and grow and not wither away because it has enough moisture, so in like manner one who meditates on the law of God will derive strength and life from his meditation. This is their simple interpretation. But we shall combine spiritual things with spiritual things[14] and read of the tree of life that was planted in Paradise, the tree of life and the tree of the knowledge of good and evil. This tree of life was planted in the Garden of Eden and in Eden there rose a river that separated into four branches. . . .[15] Likewise we read in Solomon[16]—if one accepts that book as Solomon's, for he speaks there of wisdom (Christ the power of God and the wisdom of God)[17]—so then, as I was saying, where Solomon says: 'She is a tree of life to those who grasp her,'[18] he is speaking of wisdom. Now, if wisdom is the tree of life, Wisdom itself, indeed, is Christ. You understand now that the man who is blessed and holy is compared to this tree, that is, he is compared to Wisdom. Consequently, you see, too, that the just man, that blessed man who has not followed in the counsel of the wicked—who has not done that but has done this—is like the tree that is planted near running water. He is, in other words, like Christ, inasmuch as He 'raised us up together, and seated us together in heaven.'[19] You see, then, that we shall reign together with Christ in heaven; you see, too, that because this tree has been planted in the Garden of Eden, we have all been planted there together with Him.

'He is like a tree planted near running water.' Indeed, it is from that fountainhead that all rivers take their rise. 'That

---

14 1 Cor. 2.13.
15 Gen. 2.9, 10.
16 Cf. Letter 54.16, PL 22.559 (293); *Commentary on Zacharia* 12.9, PL 25.1513 (902); *on Osee* 7.8-10, PL 25.878 (75).
17 1 Cor. 1.24.
18 Prov. 3.18.
19 Eph. 2.6.

yields its fruit in due season.' This tree does not yield fruit
in every season, but in the proper season. This is the tree that
does not yield its fruit in the present day, but in the future,
that is, on the day of judgment. This is the tree that bears
blossoms now, that buds forth now, and promises fruits for
the future. This tree bears twofold: it produces fruit and it
produces foliage. The fruit that it bears contains the meaning
of Scripture; the leaves, only the words. The fruit is in the
meaning; the leaves are in the words. For that reason, whoever
reads Sacred Scripture, if he reads merely as the Jews read,
grasps only the words. If he reads with true spiritual insight,
he gathers the fruit.

'And whose leaves never fade.' The leaves of this tree are
by no means useless. Even if one understands Holy Writ only
as history, he has something useful for his soul. We read in
the Apocalypse of John (a book which, although rejected in
these regions,[20] we ought nevertheless to know, because it is
accepted and held as canonical throughout the West, and in
other Phoenician provinces, and in Egypt, for the ancient
churchmen, including Irenaeus,[21] Polycarp, Dionysius,[22] and
other Roman expounders of Sacred Scripture, among whom
is holy Cyprian, accept and interpret it): 'Behold, I saw a
throne set up, and one Lamb and a tree alongside a river,
and on both sides of the river was that tree.'[23] This means
that the tree was both on this side and on that side of the
river. 'And this tree,' he says, 'bore fruit and was yielding its
twelve fruits for the year according to each month. And it
had leaves, too, and the leaves for the healing of the nations.'[24]

'I saw,' he says, 'a single throne set up.' We believe in the
Father, and the Son, and the Holy Spirit, that is true, and
that they are a Trinity; nevertheless the kingship is one. 'I
saw a single throne set up, and I saw a single Lamb standing

20 Cf. Letter 129.3, PL 22.1103 (971).
21 Cf. *Lives of Illustrious Men* 9, PL 23.655 (845).
22 *Ibid.* 69, PL 23.718 (911).
23 Cf. Apoc. 22.1-3; 4.2.
24 Cf. Apoc. 22.2.

in the presence of the throne.'[25] This refers to the Incarnation of the Savior. Scripture says: 'Behold the lamb of God, who takes away the sin of the world!'[26] 'And there was a fountain of water coming forth from beneath the middle of the throne.'[27] Notice that it is from the midst of the throne that there issues forth a river of graces. That river does not issue forth from the throne unless the Lamb is standing before it,[28] for unless we believe in the Incarnation of Christ, we do not receive those graces.

A tree, he says, one lofty tree had been set up. He did not say trees, but only one tree. If there is but one tree, how can it be on both sides of the river? If he had said, I saw trees, it would have been possible for some trees to be on one side of the river and other trees on the other side. Actually, one tree is said to be on both sides of the river. One river comes forth from the throne of God—the grace of the Holy Spirit—and this grace of the Holy Spirit is found in the river of the Sacred Scriptures. This river, moreover, has two banks, the Old Testament and the New Testament, and the tree planted on both sides is Christ. During the year, this tree yields twelve fruits, one for each month, but we are unable to receive the fruits except through the apostles. If one approaches the tree through the apostles, he must receive the fruit; he gathers the fruit from the Sacred Scriptures; he grasps the divine meaning abiding within the words. If, therefore, one comes to this tree through the apostles, he gathers its fruit just as we have said. If, indeed, he cannot pluck the fruit, it is because he is still too weak; he is not yet a disciple, but belongs to the throng; he is an outsider, a stranger from the nations. Because he cannot pluck the fruit, he plucks only words, the leaves for the healing of the nations, for it is written: 'and the leaves are for the healing of the nations.' One who belongs to the nations, who is not a disciple, who is as yet only one of

25 Cf. Apoc. 5.6.
26 John 1.29.
27 Cf. Apoc. 22.1.
28 Cf. Apoc. 7.17.

the crowd, gathers only leaves from the tree; he receives from Scripture plain words for a healing remedy. Briefly, then, the Scripture says: 'and the leaves of the tree are for the healing of the nations'; in other words, the leaves are medicine. Why have we digressed on the Apocalypse? Simply because of that tree 'that yields its fruit in due season, and whose leaves never fade. Whatever he does, prospers.'

We have discussed the happiness of the just man. We spoke of his reward. Because of the three things he did not do and the two things he did do, he was compared to the tree in the Garden of Eden, to Christ, who is Wisdom. We have said all this about the holy man.

Now let us see what Scripture says about the sinner, the wicked man. 'Not so the wicked.' Those universal rewards the just man receives, the wicked man will not receive. 'Not so the wicked.' The psalmist did not say, not so the sinners, for if he had said 'sinners,' we would all then be excluded from reward. 'Not so the wicked.' There is a difference between the wicked and sinners.[29] The wicked deny God altogether; the sinner acknowledges God and in spite of his acknowledgment commits sin. 'Not so the wicked.' In some manuscripts, the words, 'Not so,' are repeated, 'Not so the wicked, not so,' but in the Hebrew there is no such repetition.

We have spoken of the holy man and his likeness to the tree planted near running water. Now for the wicked man, it is exactly the opposite. As the just man is compared to the tree, the wicked man is compared to dust. He who is just is compared to a tree in the Garden of Eden; he who is wicked is compared to dust which the wind drives away. Dust may come from the soil but has ceased to be soil. The wicked are 'like dust which the wind drives away.'[30] Holy Writ says the wicked man will be so unhappy that he is not even dust from the earth. Dust does not seem to have any substance, but it

---

29 Cf. *Commentary on Isaia* 28.23-29, PL 24.327 (386); *Against the Pelagians* 1.28, PL 23.544 (724).
30 Cf. Ps. 1.4.

does, of course, have a kind of existence of its own. There is
no body to it, yet what substance it does have is really by way
of punishment. It is scattered here and there and is never in
any one place; wherever the wind sweeps it, there its whole
force is spent. The same is true of the wicked man. Once he
has denied God, he is led by delusion wherever the breath of
the devil sends him.

Since we have already discussed at length the just man and
his likeness to the tree, also the wicked man and his likeness,
and have talked about the present world, it remains for us
to meditate on the future life and on eternity. 'Therefore in
judgment the wicked shall not stand, nor shall sinners, in the
assembly of the just.' In the Gospel according to John, we
read: 'He who believes in me is not judged; but he who does
not believe in me is already judged.'[31] Who is left to be judged
if both he who believes will not be judged and he who does
not believe is already judged? Who will be judged on the day
of judgment?

Let us reflect upon the one who stands between the believer
and the non-believer, the one that is to be judged. He who
believes will not be judged. Now he who believes does not
sin; he who believes according to truth does not sin; he who
has true faith does not sin. Actually, when we commit sin,
it is because our mind is wavering in faith. When we are giving
way to anger, when we are detracting from the reputation of
another, when we are committing murder, when we are yielding to fornication, just where is our faith? Hence, the words:
'He who believes in me will not be judged'; there is no need
to judge him, he is already blessed. Further, he who does not
believe is already judged; he has already been judged unto
punishment. Who, therefore, is to be judged? The one who
indeed believes and yet yields to sin; he who has goodness,
but has evil too; he who performs good acts at the time when
he believes, but commits sin when his faith is weak.

---

31 Cf. John 3.18.

Let us at this point consider the meaning of the words: 'Therefore in judgment the wicked shall not stand.' They shall not rise to be judged because they have already been judged, for 'he who does not believe in Me is already judged.' 'Nor shall sinners in the assembly of the just.'[32] It does not say that sinners shall not rise again; but that they shall not stand in the assembly of the just; they do not deserve to stand with those who are not to be judged. If they believed in Me, says the Lord, they would rise up with those who do not have to be judged.

'For the Lord knows the way of the just, but the way of the wicked vanishes.'[33] 'For the Lord knows the way of the just.' Why is it so extraordinary that the Lord knows the way of the just? The Scriptures also say that God knows those whom He deigns to know.[34] In regard to the wicked, it says: 'I never knew you. Depart from me, you workers of iniquity.'[35] Moreover, the Apostle says: 'If anyone acknowledges the Lord, the Lord will acknowledge him.'[36] 'For the Lord knows the way of the just.' The Lord does not know the sinner, but the just man He does know.

We read in Genesis that when Adam transgressed, when he paid heed to the serpent rather than to God, when he hid himself from the face of God, God came into the Garden and was walking about in the cool of day.[37] Now listen to what the Scripture says. God sought out Adam, not at midday but in the evening. Adam had already lost the sunlight, for his highnoon was over. It was toward evening—deilinón[38]—and God was walking about, for as far as the sinner is concerned, God is not standing, but is walking.[39] He knew that Adam was

---

32 Cf. *Against the Pelagians* 1.28, PL 23.545 (725).
33 Cf. Ps. 1.6.
34 Cf. John 9.31; 10.14; 13.18.
35 Matt. 7.23; Luke 13.27.
36 Cf. 1 Cor. 14.38; Matt. 10.32; Mark 8.38; Luke 12.8; Apoc. 3.5.
37 Cf. Gen. 3.8-10.
38 Cf. *Hebrew Questions on Genesis* 3.8, PL 23.991 (309).
39 A favorite allegory of St. Jerome; cf. Homily 14 on Ps. 81, p. 102; 26 on Ps. 98, p. 204; 44 on Ps. 131, p. 329.

in the Garden and He was well aware of what had happened,
but because Adam had sinned, God knew him not. And God
said: 'Adam, where are you?'

We have heard enough on how God does not know the
sinner, so we ought to consider now how the just man is known
by Him. God said to Abraham: 'Leave your country, your
kinsfolk.'[40] Abraham accordingly came into Palestine; he was
in Abramiri; he sojourned a long time in Gerara. When his
son Isaac was born, he had received the promise: 'In your
descendants all the nations of the earth shall be blessed.'[41]
He took Isaac and offered him to God, and a voice from
heaven was heard to say: Spare thy son. Straightway, at the
very moment that he offered his son, what does God say to
Abraham? 'I know now that you fear the Lord, your God.'[42]
Have you just now known Abraham, Lord, with whom You
have communicated for such a long time? Because Abraham
had such great faith in sacrificing his own son, on that account
God first began to know him. Why have we said all this?
Because it is written: 'For the Lord knows the way of the just.'
Let us put it another way: The way, the life, and the truth
is Christ;[43] let us walk, therefore, in Christ and then God the
Father will know our way.

'But the way of the wicked vanishes.' That does not mean
that the wicked will perish. If they repent and do penance,
they too will be saved. When the Apostle Paul was persecuting
Christ and His Church, he was wicked. If the wicked perish,
there is no chance for their repentance. It does not say that
the wicked shall perish, but that the way of the wicked vanishes, that is, wickedness shall perish. Not the wicked, but
wickedness itself; not the man who was wicked will perish,
but while he is repenting, wickedness vanishes.

God vouchsafes to instruct us that there are three things we

40 Gen. 12.1.
41 Gen. 22.18.
42 Cf. Gen. 22.12.
43 Cf. John 14.6.

must not do, and two things that we must do. Let us be the just man compared to the tree of life; let us not be the wicked who are compared to dust; let us not be sinners, for sinners shall not stand in the assembly of the just. Let us take heed that the path of evil may vanish; and let us bless God to whom be glory forever and ever. Amen.

HOMILY 2

ON PSALM 5

THE FIFTH PSALM has for its title: 'Unto the end, for her that obtains the inheritance. A psalm of David.'[1] There are many who insist that the titles do not belong to the psalms but who really do not know why they hold such a view. If the titles were not found in all the manuscripts —Hebrew, Greek, and Latin—their position would be tenable. Since, however, there are titles in the Hebrew books, and this one in particular marks the fifth psalm, I am amazed at the implication that there can be anything in Scripture without reason. If it be true that 'not one jot or one tittle shall be lost from the Law,'[2] how much more shall not a word or a syllable be lost?

'Unto the end for her that obtains the inheritance. A psalm of David.' Our inheritance is not promised at the beginning, but at the end of the world. The Jews thought that they had obtained theirs at the beginning; we obtain ours at the end. That is precisely why the Apostle John says: 'Dear children, it is the last hour.'[3] The end means the last hour; the inheritance is at the end.

'Unto the end, for her that obtains the inheritance.' Who is she who is to obtain the inheritance? I believe it is the Church, for it is the Church who receives the inheritance. 'A psalm of David.' David sings at the beginning that the Church wins the inheritance at the end. The fifth psalm, therefore, sings

---

1 Cf. Ps. 5.1.
2 Matt. 5.18.
3 1 John 2.18.

in the name of the Church. There are, however, several other interpretations. Many say that the psalm accords with the history of the people of Israel who long to return to Judea from Babylon, but they have failed to interpret 'Unto the end' and 'for her that obtains the inheritance.' We, then, by 'combining spiritual with spiritual'[4] shall endeavor with the help of your prayers to consider this psalm as applying to the Church.

'Hearken to my words, O Lord.' No one has confidence like this except the Church. The sinner does not dare to say: 'Hearken to my words, O Lord.' The man who has cursed in his rage does not dare to say: 'Hearken to my words, O Lord,' but rather hopes that God wills not to hear him. 'Attend to my cry.'[5] The word 'cry' in Scripture does not refer to the cry of the voice, but to the cry of the heart.[6] In fact, the Lord says to Moses: 'Why are you crying out to me?'[7] when Moses had not uttered any cry at all. Again, the Apostle says: 'into our hearts, crying, "Abba, Father,"'[8] But you would say: one who cries out does not cry out with his heart but with his tongue. With what meaning then does the Apostle say: 'into our hearts, crying'? When our lamentation and our conscience entreat the Lord, this is the cry that God heeds. Likewise, the words of Jeremia: 'Let there be no repose for my eyes.'[9] Notice what he says: 'Let not even the pupil of my eye be silent.' Sometimes, the very pupil of our eye cries out to God. But does one not cry out with his tongue, and not with his eye? No, just as we cry in our hearts when we beseech God with our groaning, so, too, when we pour forth our tears to God, the pupil of our eye is crying out to the Lord.

'My King and my God!' In truth, only he has dared to say, 'My King and my God,' in whose mortal body sin does not

---

4 1 Cor. 2.13.
5 Cf. Ps. 5.2.
6 Cf. *Commentarioli in ps.* 65.
7 Exod. 14.15.
8 Gal. 4.6.
9 Lam. 2.18.

reign.[10] 'My King and my God.' Because You reign in me and
sin does not, that is why You are my God. You are my God
because my stomach is not my God, gold is not my God, lust
is not my God. Since You are virtue and I desire to possess
virtue, You are my God, You are my virtue.

'At dawn you hear my voice.' Some exegetes explain these
words quite simply in this way: I rise at dawn to pray and
make supplication to You. Certainly, this interpretation is
allowable. But what does the verse really mean? God hears our
voice in the morning; will He not hear us in the evening? Nor
in the middle of the night? Listen to what the words really
mean: As long as I am wandering in the darkness of error,
You do not hear me, but after the sun of justice has come into
my heart, then You will. 'At dawn you hear my voice.' The
psalm does not say, at the third hour, nor at the sixth hour,
nor in the full daylight, but 'at dawn'; just as soon as the
shades of night have begun to scatter, You hear my voice; just
as soon as I begin a good work, You hear my voice; You do
not wait for the end. It is mine to will; Yours to accomplish.[11]

'At dawn I will stand before you, and will see.'[12] Notice the
order: at dawn, not in the evening; not in the darkness, but
at dawn. 'At dawn I will stand before you.' I shall stand steadfast; I shall imitate Moses. 'At dawn I will stand before you':
I will stand before You and before no other. Moreover, when
morning comes I shall continue to be standing, standing before You. Then I will deserve to see You.

'And will see.' It is understood, of course, I will see You.
Many make a poor reading of these words and say, καὶ ἐπόψῃ με,
but we know that this reading is incorrect and should be,
καὶ ἐπόψομαι, that is, 'I will see.' Hence, that order which we
mentioned before: while the light of virtue is beginning to
penetrate my soul and I stand before You—not sit down, not

---

10 Cf. Rom. 6.12.
11 Cf. *Against the Pelagians* 3.1, PL 23.596 (781); 1.5, PL 23.523 (700);
   Letter 130.12, PL 22.1117 (989).
12 Cf. Ps. 5.4.

lie down, but stand—and You fix my steps firmly upon a rock,[13] then, by degrees, I shall deserve to see You.

'For you, O God, delight not in wickedness.' You will not hear me in the broad daylight, but early in the morning, because, my God, You do not will iniquity. The very moment that I begin to withdraw from iniquity, that very moment do I merit Your attention to my prayers.

'No evil man remains with you.' Whenever an evil man leaves us, we ought to rejoice. It shall be with us as with the Lord, that an evil man does not live with us any more than he dwells with the Lord. Hear what the Holy Spirit says: 'No evil man remains with you'; the wicked will not remain with you. For 'what fellowship has light with darkness? What harmony is there between Christ and Belial?'[14] Thus, when any of the wicked part from our company, we, too, shall say: 'They have gone forth from us, but they were not of us. For if they had been of us, they would surely have continued with us.'[15] The words: 'No evil man remains with you,' are addressed to God, for if God is fire and a consuming fire,[16] everyone who is stubble, everyone who is wood, runs away from the fire lest he be consumed.

'The arrogant may not stand in your sight.' Since the Scripture says they may not stand, it is obvious that at some time they were in the presence of God. God permitted them to remain in His sight while He was waiting for them to repent, but because they held out in their wickedness, they could not remain before Him.

'You hate all evildoers.' Unhappy the man whom God hates! Whom does God hate? The evildoer. But if we are all sinners and every sinner is hated by God, it would naturally follow that we are all hated by God. If, however, we are all hated by God, how is it that we have been saved by grace?[17] 'You

---

13 Cf. Ps. 39.3.
14 2 Cor. 6.14, 15.
15 1 John 2.19.
16 Cf. Deut. 4.24.
17 Cf. Eph. 2.5, 8.

hate all evildoers.' The psalmist did not say, those who have
been guilty of wrongdoing, but those who are wrongdoers.
Those who persevere in sin are those who are held in ab-
horrence by God, but those who abandon the ways of sin are
loved by the Lord. 'You hate all evildoers.' These words are
intended for sinners who are persisting in sin. Let us look
at the next verse.

'You destroy all who speak falsehood.' I find a new thought
in these words.[18] The worker of evil is hated by God; the liar
perishes. Let us see now which is the worse state, to be hated
by God or to perish. The man whom God hates is unhappy
indeed, for he exists in the enmity of God; nevertheless, he is
still alive, but the liar who is destroyed has ceased to exist.
The man who lies is more unfortunate, therefore, than the
one who does evil. Though the evildoer is subject to the hatred
of God, the liar perishes altogether. 'A lying mouth slays
the soul.'[19]

What meaning is there, further, to the words: 'For God is
true, and every man is a liar'?[20] If everyone who utters a lie
has already destroyed his soul, and all of us are liars, are we
all going to perish? What Scripture says in the words: 'You
destroy all who speak falsehood,' we should interpret as referring to heretics, both from the forward movement of the
psalm and from the order within the movement itself. The
doer of evil has, indeed, killed his own soul; but the heretic
—the liar—has killed as many souls as he has seduced.

'You destroy all who speak falsehood.' But who are these
people who speak falsehood? 'The bloodthirsty and the deceitful the Lord abhors.' Every heretic is bloodthirsty, for every
day he spills the blood of souls. 'The bloodthirsty and the
deceitful.' Deceitful is the right word. He is both a murderer
and a practitioner of deceit. How is he deceitful? His words

---

18 Cf. Letter 55.4, PL 22.563 (299); Letter 69.3, PL 22.656 (415); *Against
the Pelagians* 1.14a, PL 23.530 (708); *Against the Luciferians* 12, PL
23.175 (184).
19 Wisd. 1.11.
20 Rom. 3.4.

deliberately misrepresent the words of the Lord. 'The blood-thirsty and the deceitful the Lord abhors.' Just think of the condition of the heretic: the Lord abhors him! The psalm says of sinners: 'You hate all evildoers'; of false teachers, 'the Lord abhors them.'

'But I, because of your abundant kindness, will enter your house.' The wicked in their iniquity depart from Your house; I, by Your mercy, shall enter Your house. 'I will enter your house,' which is the Church. 'I will worship at your holy temple in fear of you.' The Church is Your house; also Your temple.

'O Lord; because of my enemies, guide me in your justice.' Indeed, do I long to enter Your house, and I desire to enter it by Your way of justice. Because my enemies are continually besetting my path with snares and setting traps for me all along the way—while my one longing is to enter Your house —I am beseeching You to keep my feet firm in Your path to the very end. It is mine to set my feet in Your way; it is Yours to direct my steps.

'Because of my enemies, make straight your way before me.'[21] Make straight Your way before me on account of the enemies who seek to ensnare me. What is this way of Yours? The reading of Holy Scripture. Direct my steps, therefore, lest I stumble in the reading of Your Word through which I desire to enter Your Church, for everyone whose understanding of Holy Writ is faulty falls down in the path of God.

'For in their mouth there is no sincerity.' This is a description of heretics. The heretic is the bloodthirsty and deceitful man whom the Lord abhors. 'In their mouth there is no sincerity.' Heretics do not have Christ, the Truth, on their lips because they do not have Him in their heart. 'Their heart is vain.'[22] The Hebrew text is better here, their heart ἐπίβουλον [is treacherous], for truly the heart of the heretic lies in wait

---

21 Cf. *Against the Pelagians* 3.8, PL 23.605 (791); Letter 106.4, PL 22.839 (644).
22 Cf. Ps. 5.10.

for all whom he may ensnare. 'Their throat is an open grave.'
Heretics are unhappy men; they are whited sepulchres, full
of dead men's bones.[23] 'Their throat is an open grave.' Arius,
Eunomius, and other heretics have tongues like arrows, jaws
like empty tombs. 'Their throat is an open grave.' 'Open' is
well said, for whenever anyone has been deceived enough to
enter that tomb, the heretic is ready and draws him right in.
The mouths of heretics are forever gaping. 'Their throat
is an open grave; they flatter with their tongue.' They mean
one thing in their heart; they promise another with their
lips. They speak with piety and conceal impiety. They speak
Christ and hide the Antichrist, for they know that they will
never succeed with their seduction if they disclose the Antichrist. They present light only to conceal darkness, through
light they lead to darkness. 'They flatter with their tongue.'
   'Punish them, O God.' Let them know that You are Judge
and that You are mindful of human affairs. You are going to
judge in the end; judge now also in the present. You are going
to judge in general; judge now in particular. Those who refuse
to know the Father, let them experience the Judge. 'Punish
them, O God.' And how? The answer follows: 'Let them fall
by their own devices.' If you repay them now in the present
as they deserve, they will begin to withdraw from their evil
schemes. As long as they do not experience You as Judge
they are without fear. 'Let them fall by their own devices.'
Excellently said, 'by their own devices,' for heretics change
or alter their doctrine from day to day. In fact, if a theologian
learned in the Scriptures contends with them, overwhelming
them with proof from the Sacred Books, what do they do but
straightway look around in search of a new doctrine. They do
not seek knowledge for the sake of salvation, but look around
for new doctrine to vanquish the opponent; hence, the psalmist
said: 'Let them fall by their own devices.' Let them fall by
their own countless contrivances and let them have but one
recourse, You, my God.

---

23 Cf. Matt. 23.27.

'For their many sins, cast them out.' Now, it does not say from which place God should cast out the wicked, whether He should cast them out of heaven or from the face of the earth. Scripture is not clear in this point because of the transposed word order of this verse, hyperbatón and hysteró-proteron. We have to read, therefore: 'For their many sins, cast them out'; but the meaning is, because of Your mercy, cast them off from their many wickednesses; do not let them go on living in their many sins. There is, however, another interpretation. Because the wicked have been so thoroughly wicked, they have not wanted to give up their evil schemes, but have gone on adding sin to sin and heaping up their sins daily; their wickedness grows increasingly and for that reason, they are to be cast out.

But 'cast them out' from where? From her who obtains the inheritance, that is, from the Church who obtains Your inheritance. Cast them out, for they may not abide in the Church, since they do not have faith in her. 'Because they have rebelled against you.' You are, O Lord, sweet by nature, but sinners and heretics change the sweetness of Your nature into bitterness because of their evil devices.

'But let all who take refuge in you be glad.' Let sinners and heretics perish; let Your churchmen be glad. 'And exult forever.' Here, we ought to say something about eternity, not about the present but the future world. As a matter of fact, Scripture did not say they rejoice in the present world, as 'let them exult' implies the future world. Here, sorrow; then, there will be true joy. In the present world, heretics laugh; in the future, they will lament; we, indeed, lament in the present that we may rejoice in the future. 'And exult forever.'

What will this joy of holy men be like? 'And you will dwell in them.'[24] They will be blessed and happy who deserve to possess Christ as their guest. 'And you will dwell in them.' Happy are they who will become the tabernacles of Christ! 'That you may be the joy of those who love your name.'

24 Cf. Ps. 5.12.

Everyone who loves the Lord will exult in the Lord. See what it says: 'That you may be the joy of those who love your name'; they who love; not they who fear, but they who love. Wherever there is fear, love is absent, for 'perfect love casts out fear.'[25] Whoever love the name of the Lord, they will rejoice.

'That you may be the joy'; our beatitude is of the future, to which alone the promise refers. Let some rule with power; others possess wealth; still others receive honors and recognition. We, on the other hand, are miserable in this life in order to be happy in the next. Let us follow Christ our Lord. He who says he believes in Christ 'ought himself also to walk, just as he walked.'[26] Christ, the Son of God, 'has not come to be served but to serve';[27] He did not come to command, but to obey; He did not come to have His own feet washed, but to wash the feet of His disciples; He did not come to strike others, but to be struck; He did not give blows, but He received them; He did not crucify, but was crucified; He did not destroy, but Himself suffered destruction; He was poor to make us rich; He was scourged for our sake that we might escape scourging. As often as we are struck, let us offer our cheek to the blows; let us lay bare our back to receive the stripes; let us imitate Christ. He who is struck with blows imitates Christ; he who strikes imitates the Antichrist.

Now why do I say all this? To glorify the name of Christ in whatsoever we suffer in this life. While we are talking, while we are walking, suddenly we are carried off. I myself who speak to you today, know not what tomorrow holds for me. If a slight fever should come upon me, where is that voice of mine? Where is my pride? Suddenly turned into ashes. 'Why are dust and ashes proud?'[28] We are nothing but dust and ashes. 'For dust you are, and unto dust you shall return.'[29] And dust vaunts itself against its maker! The next words of

25 1 John 4.18.
26 1 John 2.6.
27 Mark 10.45.
28 Sirach (Ecclus.) 10.9.
29 Gen. 3.19.

the psalm are: 'For you will bless the just man.'[30] You will bless the just in the future life; so beatitude is postponed.

'O Lord, you crown[31] him with the shield of your good will.' In the world, a shield is one thing and a crown another, but with God, He Himself is our shield, He Himself is our crown. He protects us as if He were a shield; as God He crowns us. He is our shield; He is our crown.[32] So says Scripture: 'O Lord, you crown him with the shield of your good will.' You surround us with Your shield, and Your protection is our crown; Your shield is our crown; it is our triumph, for the crown is the symbol of victory.

Let us give thanks to God, and let us beseech Him in His good will to be our shield and crown that we may never depart from Him and that we may follow Him and declare with Jeremia: 'I was not weary of following you.'[33] To Him be glory forever and ever. Amen.

---

30 Cf. Ps. 5.13.
31 *Ibid.*
32 Cf. *Against the Pelagians* 3.1, PL 23.596 (781).
33 Cf. Jer. 17.16, LXX.

HOMILY 3

ON PSALM 7

NAMES ARE GIVEN to individual things that we may be
able to identify them, and psalms have titles for the
same reason. The fifth psalm bears the title, 'Unto
the end, for her that obtains the inheritance';[1] the sixth, 'Unto
the end, in verses, a psalm of David, for the octave.'[2] In the
fifth are the words, 'for her that obtains the inheritance'; in
the sixth, 'for the octave.' Last Sunday, we read the sixth psalm,
but because of my illness, we could not interpret it; today,
however, we have read the seventh, which, likewise, is sung
after the Alleluia.[3] In contrast, this psalm has for its superscription: 'A plaintive song of David which he sang to the
Lord because of Chusi the son of Jemini.'[4] How fraught with
mystery are these words! Is there no reason for their place
here? In the fifth psalm: 'For her that obtains the inheritance';
in the sixth: 'for the octave'; in the seventh: 'because of Chusi
the son of Jemini.' How much mystery has been interwoven
in the text!

'For her that obtains the inheritance.' We interpreted the
fifth psalm as having been sung in the person of the Church
which had won the inheritance of Christ. The sixth refers most

---

1 Cf. Ps. 5.1.
2 Cf. Ps. 6.1.
3 Cf. Gregory the Great, Letter 12 to John of Syracuse: 'our custom here
of saying the Alleluia follows, it is said, the Church of Jerusalem from
the tradition of the blessed Jerome in the time of Pope Damasus of
happy memory.' Cf. *Against Vigilantius* 1, PL 23.355 (387); *Commentarioli in ps.* 104.1 Cf. Homily 32 on Ps. 105, p. 234; 58 on Ps. 148,
p. 416; 56 on Ps. 146, p. 400.
4 Cf. Ps. 7.1.

appropriately to the Lord's Resurrection, which is the eighth day. But, we have both a first and an eighth day; we receive the kingdom of heaven on the eighth; the eighth day after the sabbath is again the first day from the beginning. It would take a long time if we delayed to expand upon the number eight: how in Matthew there are eight beatitudes; how the separate divisions of Psalm 118, designated by the letters of the alphabet, consist each of eight verses; how fifteen psalms are songs of ascent;[5] how they divide into seven and eight; how Ecclesiastes says: 'Make seven or eight portions';[6] how the east gate in Ezechiel has seven steps and eight steps.[7] There is no time either to digress on how David[8] who received the kingdom was the eighth son of Isai. And here in the sixth psalm, it says: 'for the octave,' for on the eighth day we receive the kingdom of heaven, whence the words: 'O Lord, reprove me not in your anger, nor chastise me in your wrath.'[9] Since, however, we cannot divide our time equally between Psalms 6 and 7, let us be content with this comment on the title of the sixth.

Now let us return to the exordium of Psalm 7 which begins: 'A plaintive song of David which he sang to the Lord because of Chusi the son of Jemini.' I know many, and certainly very learned, men who have interpreted this title as referring to the time when Absalom rose in revolt againt his father David. Listen very attentively, for we want to interpret Holy Writ, not merely exercise our oratory.

At the time that Absalom rose up against David, one of David's friends, Chusi by name, wanted to go with David, but David sent him back to Absalom to counteract the counsel of Achitophel. Achitophel had advised Absalom to pursue

---

5 Cf. Psalms 119-133; Letter 53.8, PL 22.548 (280); *Against Jovinian* 2.34, PL 23.346 (378).
6 Eccles. 11.2.
7 Cf. Ezech. 40.22, 31; cf. *Dialogue Against the Luciferians* 1.22, PL 23.185 (195).
8 Cf. 1 Kings 17.12-14.
9 Ps. 6.2.

David at once, take him by surprise and kill him. Chusi advised him, successfully, to the contrary and, further, sent a messenger to David with word, Absalom is preparing this and this. David, therefore, immediately began to prepare himself for flight. It was when Chusi sent word to David that David sang this song to the Lord because the counsel of Achitophel had been defeated.[10] This, then, is the interpretation they give and surely it sounds reasonable. But let us read the Scripture carefully, for there it is written that this Chusi is the son of Arachi. In the second place, the Chusi in the Book of Kings[11] is spelled with a different letter. There, it is written with the letter SAMECH; here, with the letter SIN. Furthermore, that Chusi was the son of Arachi. It is because they do not know this fact that many of the Greeks read: 'Chusi, David's friend.'[12] That is not the way it appears in the Hebrew text, for in the Hebrew, it is written thus: 'Chusi, son of Arachi, friend of David.' So you see now that the Greeks have made an error in their reading.

It is quite clear from the Scriptures that Chusi is the son of Arachi, but this Chusi is called the son of Jemini. Since we have said that that Chusi was the son of Arachi, who is this son of Jemini? By combining spiritual with spiritual,[13] we ought to find the principle of the name. Where in Scripture do we find the name Jemini? Now, everyone knows that one of the twelve tribes was by name the tribe of Benjamin. Benjamin, moreover, is translated, son of the right hand. At the time when Rachel died in Ephratha (we see her tomb from here with our own eyes; we are not looking for representations of it), at the time that Rachel was dying, she gave birth, it says, to a child, and the midwife—or else she while she was dying—called him Benoni, that is, son of my affliction. But Jacob, his father, turns the grief of the mother into joy and does

---

10 Cf. 2 Kings 15, 16, 17.
11 Cf. *Commentarioli in ps.* 7.8.
12 2 Kings 15.32, 37; 16.16 (cf. 16, LXX); 17.5.
13 Cf. 1 Cor. 2.13.

not call him Benoni, the son of my affliction, but Benjamin, the son of the right hand, the son of my strength.[14] The name Benjamin is a combination, then, of two words, son and right hand: BEN means son and JAMIN means right hand.

Let us remember once and for all that the tribe of Benjamin was called Jemini. We read in the Book of Kings, where it speaks of Saul, the words: 'Now there was a man of Benjamin whose name was Saul, the son of Cis, the son of Abiel, son of Jethra, son of Jether, son of Gera, son of Jemini,'[15] and immediately following, it says, a man of Jemini, that is, from the tribe of Jemini, or Benjamin. To give further testimony—lest any doubt remain, Semei was the man on Mount Olivet where David fled from his son Absalom. Of him Scripture says: 'Behold Semei, a man of the kindred of the house of Saul from the tribe of Benjamin. And he threw stones at David and cried: Come out, come out, thou man of blood.'[16] When one of David's leaders named Abisai says: 'I will go and kill him,'[17] what does David answer? 'What have I to do with you, ye sons of Sarvia? Behold, my son who came forth from my bowels, seeketh my life: how much more now a son of Jemini—that is, from the tribe of Benjamin, from the tribe of Saul who was my enemy?'[18] Now why have I said all this? To show that the tribe of Jemini was the tribe of Benjamin.

We have identified Benjamin, we have mentioned the name of his father; let us consider who Chusi, the son of Jemini, is. Chus in Hebrew means Ethiopian, that is, black and dark, one who has a soul as black as his body, of whom Jeremia says: 'Can the Ethiopian change his skin? the leopard his spots?'[19] In the psalm, then, Chusi signifies Saul as David's black and dark enemy. This, then, is what David is saying:

14 Cf. Gen. 35.17-20; cf. *Hebrew Questions on Genesis* 35.18, PL 23.1042-(361); Letter 108.10, PL 22.884 (698).
15 Cf. 1 Kings 9.1, 2; 2 Kings 19.16; 3 Kings 2.8; 2.5, 32; *Commentarioli in ps. 7.*
16 Cf. 2 Kings 16.5-7.
17 Cf. 2 Kings 16.9.
18 Cf. 2 Kings 16.10, 11.
19 Jer. 13.23.

Just as the Ethiopian cannot change his skin, Saul cannot change his character. Twice he has come into my hands;[20] I could have killed him; I could have spilled his blood; I wanted to conquer him with kindness, but his ill-will remains unconquered. Just as the Ethiopian cannot change his skin, Saul cannot change his malice. Finally, what does David say? 'O Lord, my God, if I am at fault in this,' that is, if I have done Saul any evil; 'If there is guilt on my hands, if I have repaid my friend with evil.'[21] Notice what he says, I have repaid good for evil, Saul has rendered evil for good. It is evident, therefore, that this psalm is against Saul, and David thanks God and implores His help lest he fall into the hands of Saul.

'O Lord, my God, in you I take refuge.' I have not put my trust in my sword, nor have I put my trust in my strength; but in Your help I have taken refuge. 'Lest I become like the lion's prey.' These words befit Saul; they do not become Absalom. How could David call Absalom a lion, of whom he says: 'Save me the boy Absalom'?[22] If in that passage of Scripture he calls him a boy and, as it were, a little boy without knowledge, how here in the psalm, does he proclaim him a lion? This interpretation, by the way, accords with history. There is much that could be said, and the entire psalm, as a matter of fact, can be interpreted historically with reference to Saul. Be that as it may, because it is our concern to interpret Scripture, not according to history, but with spiritual understanding, we are interpreting Chusi, this Ethiopian, to be no other than the devil. The question now is, how is this Chusi the son of Jemini; how is this Ethiopian devil the son of the right hand? He is Ethiopian by reason of his vice; he is the son of the right hand because he was created by God. Rightly does it say of the devil: 'Lest I become like the lion's prey.'

---

20 1 Kings 24; 26.
21 Ps. 7.4.
22 2 Kings 18.12.

'Our adversary the devil, as a roaring lion, goes about seeking someone to devour.'[23]

'O Lord, my God, if I am at fault in this': 'For the prince of the world is coming, and in me he has nothing.'[24] 'If there is guilt on my hands': 'Who did no sin, neither was deceit found in his mouth.'[25] 'If I have repaid my friend with evil': they say: 'Crucify, crucify a man like that';[26] I say: 'Father forgive them, for they do not know what they are doing.'[27] 'Let the enemy pursue and overtake me': 'And the last enemy to be destroyed will be death.'[28] 'Let him trample my life to the ground': life cannot be trampled down to the ground. 'And lay my glory in the dust.' If, it says, I render evil to my enemies for evil, I shall not rise again. 'Rise up, O Lord, in your anger'; since they did not recognize You in Your kindness, let them experience You through Your wrath.[29] 'And be exalted in the borders of my enemies':[30] the psalmist pleads for his enemies, that God be glorified in the land of his enemies. When they will have ceased to be enemies, then You, O Lord, will be exalted among them.

'Wake, O Lord my God, to the judgment you have decreed. Let the assembly of the peoples surround you.' We say this; we, the faithful, are uttering these words, for the psalms are constantly changing person.[31] If we cared to, there is much we could say on the frequency of this change in person. 'Wake, O Lord my God, to the judgment you have decreed.' Actually, this is what we are saying: You suffered for us; You were crucified for us; arise and save us. We seem to be doing violence to the Scripture, but the following words free us from

---

23 Cf. 1 Peter 5.8.
24 John 14.30.
25 1 Peter 2.22.
26 Cf. John 19.6; *Commentarioli in ps.* 68; *Against John of Jerusalem* 34, PL 23.403 (443).
27 Luke 23.34.
28 1 Cor. 15.26.
29 Cf. *Commentary on Ezechiel* 7.27, PL 25.76 (80).
30 Cf. Ps. 7.7.
31 Cf. *Commentary on Isaia* 3.14, PL 24.67 (58); 21.3-5, PL 24.191 (214); on *Jeremia* 8.15, PL 24.739 (902).

such suspicion. What words follow? 'Let the assembly of the peoples surround you.' Arise, in order that a vast multitude may believe in You, for after You have risen, what else would we pray for? Return to the Father. 'Above them on high be enthroned.' For whose sake? For the assembly of the peoples. In that You suffered, You suffered for us; in that You rose again, You rose for us; in that You ascended to the Father, ascend for us. 'Above them on high be enthroned.' 'And no one has ascended into heaven except him who has descended from heaven: the Son of Man who is in heaven.'[32]

'Do me justice, O Lord, because I am just, and because of the innocence that is mine.' David could not say this; these words properly belong to the Savior who has not sinned. 'Let the malice of the wicked come to an end, but sustain the just.' My justice cannot be sustained unless their iniquity has been satisfied—the iniquity, of course, of the Jews.

'Unless you be converted, he will brandish his sword.'[33] This verse admits of two interpretations. Many think that it refers to God and is intended as a warning to sinners. And what does it mean? 'Unless you be converted, he will brandish his sword.' That means unless you repent and do penance, the Lord will brandish His sword against you, but let us consider if the following words really apply to the person of the Lord. 'He will bend and aim his bow.' That can be said of God. He will 'prepare his deadly weapons against him.'[34] This, however, is difficult, for the Lord does not have the weapons of death, but the instruments of life. These words, nevertheless, are not completely devoid of meaning with reference to the person of the Savior. The next verses, on the other hand, in no way can apply to God. 'He who conceived iniquity and was pregnant with mischief, brings forth failure, He has opened a hole, he has dug it deep.' The very context, therefore, compels us to reject any reference to God in words

---

32 John 3.13.
33 Cf. Ps. 7.13.
34 Cf. Ps. 7.14.

so impertinent and expressive of pride as: 'Unless you be
converted, he will brandish his sword.'

That is why many maintain that these words of the psalm
refer to the devil; they mean, unless you will have been
converted, unless you will have repented, you will be in the
power of the devil. 'He will bend and aim his bow.' The devil
always has his bow ready and he is ever alert to shoot his
arrows and strike us down. 'He will prepare his deadly weapons
against him.' These words are certainly applicable to the devil.
'And use darts for arrows for those who burn.'[35] Well said, 'for
those who burn.' They whose hearts are burning with lust
and passion are the very ones whom the devil conquers. 'And
use darts for arrows for those who burn.' Excellently said,
'for those who burn.' The psalm did not say for those who
are about to burn[36]—that is, about to burn from his arrows.
The hearts of those he sees already burning, no matter whose
they are, are his target. The Apostle also says the devil has
fiery darts.[37] 'He who conceived iniquity and was pregnant
with mischief, brings forth failure.' That is the kind of mother
the devil is, that is the kind of father; thus does he conceive;
thus does he bring forth; thus he nurtures; thus he rears. 'He
has opened a hole, he has dug it deep, but he falls into the
pit which he has made.' The hole itself—which is also the
pit—belongs to the devil. 'He has opened a hole,' for since,
according to Jeremia, his cistern cannot hold water, it has
become a hole. 'He has opened a hole, he has dug it deep.'
All the miserable assemblies of heretics[38] are pits of the devil.

'His mischief shall recoil upon his own head; upon the
crown of his head violence shall rebound.' Just as anyone who
tosses a stone straight up into the air, and is foolish enough
not to move out of its way, is struck on the head and wounded
by his own stone; in the same way, the devil downs himself
by his own arrogance; the pride that exalts him is the same

---

35 *Ibid.*
36 Cf. *Commentarioli in ps.* 7.14.
37 Cf. Eph. 6.16; cf. Letter 130.10, PL 22.1116 (987).
38 Cf. *Commentary on Ezechiel* 32.17, 18, PL 25.315 (391).

pride that defeats him. 'His mischief shall recoil upon his own head.' All the devil wants is to hold his head up high, but he cannot. Why can he not? Because his 'mischief shall recoil upon his own head' and crush him down.

The devil— (understand, spiritual reader, according to the principle of the Scriptures)—we have read in Genesis[39] that the devil is a snake, that he is the serpent in the Garden of Eden, the very serpent who spoke to Eve, who has power on earth. He is called a snake because the whole of his body moves on the ground. Other animals may walk on the ground, but their entire bodies do not cleave to it; certainly, their feet touch it, but the rest of their bodies they lift off it. Not so the devil, that is, the serpent and that old snake. According to Isaia,[40] every part of him is completely on the ground; his head and the rest of his body are all on the same level. Why am I saying all this? Because the other animals (understand, prudent reader) may rest on the ground but long to rise up from it, but the devil cleaves to it with head, tail, and the middle part of him.

'His mischief shall recoil upon his own head; upon the crown of his head his violence shall rebound.' See what it says; both upon his own head and upon his crown. Because violence presses down upon his head and upon the crown of his head, where is the devil's repentance?[41] This is the devil's end: 'His mischief shall recoil upon his own head; upon the crown of his head his violence shall rebound.' Excellently has Scripture said, 'shall rebound,' for his punishment shall rebound everlastingly from heaven.

This is the way that the devil will be damned. We in truth are they who believed in Christ, who in the fifth psalm have received the inheritance, who on the eighth day, I mean the day of resurrection, say: 'O Lord, reprove me not in your anger,

---

39 Cf. Gen. 3.
40 Cf. Isa. 27.1.
41 Cf. *Commentary on Isaia* 14.20, PL 24.224 (257); 17.12-14, PL 24.245 (284); 25.9-11, PL 24.292 (343); 27.1, PL 24.507 (361); *on Jona* 3.6, PL 25.1141-1142 (418).

nor chastise me in your wrath.'[42] Because Chus, that is, our Ethiopian, is himself the lion of whom it is said: Lest I become like the lion's prey; who has bent and aimed his bow, and has prepared his deadly weapons to destroy us; because he is pregnant with iniquity, and has brought forth failure; because he has opened a hole and has dug it deep, and has fallen into the pit that he has made, he has been sent into hell, and so 'his mischief shall recoil upon his own head; upon the crown of his head his violence shall rebound.' Because the devil has been so punished according to his own desert, let us say: 'I will give thanks to the Lord for his justice, and sing praise to the name of the Lord Most High.' Beautifully said, Most High, for the Lord has been exalted as far as the devil has been humiliated.

---

42 Ps. 6.2.

HOMILY 4

ON PSALM 9 (9A, 9B)

ESUS, SON OF NAVE, was fighting in the desert and as long as Moses kept on praying, he was victorious.[1] One was fighting; another was really conquering by prayer. And so, with the words of Scripture, I say: 'Open wide your mouth, and I will fill it,'[2] for I certainly seem to be the one speaking, but it is while others are praying that I speak. The ninth psalm, which you have sung to the Lord, is grand in its poetry and noble in its mysteries, but since we cannot discuss the entire psalm, it will be enough for the time being to say a few words about the title. Since we cannot enter the palace of the king (for it is boundless, nor is it possible for us to know all the king's mysteries),[3] we shall pause in the vestibule—in the title, as it were—and see whose mansion this is.

'Unto the end, for the hidden things of the Son.[4] A psalm of David.' The words, 'Unto the end,' do not refer to the Jews, but to us who in the end have believed. The Jews are the first son; we are the last sons. We, who are the last, ought to heed this psalm because it concerns those who are at the end. 'For the hidden things of the Son.' What are these hidden things of the Son? They are the mystery[5] hidden to all ages in the past, but revealed to us who are at the end. 'For the hidden things of the Son.' There is a difference here in the

---

1 Cf. Exod. 17.11, 12.
2 Ps. 80.11.
3 Cf. Letter 120.8.2, PL 22.992 (832).
4 Cf. Ps. 9A.1.
5 Cf. Letter 53.4, PL 22.543 (274); *Commentarioli in ps.* 9.1.

Hebrew text. The Hebrew reading is ALAMOTH, which means, 'for the death.' AL is the equivalent of 'for' and MOTH equals 'death'; hence, the correct reading is 'for the death': for the death, therefore, of the Son as the Hebrew text has it. Because the translators of the Septuagint were doing their work under the Gentile king, Ptolemy,[6] it was difficult, you see, for them to say the 'death of the Son,' so they translated the word 'death' as 'hidden things.' They did not write, 'for the death of the Son,' but they knew that the Scripture was speaking about the Son of God. They saw what was written, but were afraid to say that the Son of God would die.

So much for the title. We really need to understand the whole psalm in its relation to the death of the Savior. In order that you may know that the psalm refers to the Savior, the following words are said of the Jews: 'In the snare they set, their foot is caught.'[7] In the next place, in reference to the calling of the Gentiles, are the words: 'All the nations that forget God.'[8] Finally, against the devil[9] it says: 'There is no God in his sight. He lurks in ambush with the rich.'[10] Unhappy the rich with whom the devil lurks! Notice what the psalm says about the devil, he lurks in ambush with the rich. It is almost impossible for the rich man to be rich without robbing the poor.[11] That is the meaning behind the words: 'He lurks in ambush with the rich.' Whenever the rich persecute the Christians, we may say that the devil is lurking in ambush with them. 'He lies in wait to catch the poor; he catches the poor and drops them off in his net. With his noose he brings them down.'[12] This is the ungodly one; this is the

---

6 Cf. Preface to *The Book of Hebrew Questions on Genesis* PL 23.985 (303-304).
7 Ps. 9A.16.
8 Ps. 9A.18.
9 Cf. *Commentary on Isaia* 14.16, PL 24.162 (178).
10 Cf. Ps. 9B (10).4, 8; cf. Letter 14.4, PL 22.349 (31).
11 Cf. *Commentary on Michea* PL 25.1213 (509); *on Isaia* 33.13, PL 24.366 (436); Letter 120.1, PL 22.982 (820).
12 Cf. Ps. 9B (10).9.

devil. 'The poor,' not only in riches, but also in spirit: 'Blessed are the poor in spirit.'[13] 'With his noose he brings them down.' Whom? The poor, of course. Observe what the Scripture says: 'He brings them down.' It does not say he kills them. When the devil has humbled the poor, their humiliation is his own downfall. For what follows? 'He stoops and lies prone till by his violence fall the unfortunate.'[14] Does it not seem evident to you that during the persecution when the devil was destroying Christians, when he was slaying martyrs, he was himself struck down in his very act of slaying? 'He stoops and lies prone till by his violence fall the unfortunate.' The martyr who has been slain goes straight to heaven; the slayer, thus humiliated, falls himself in the very act of slaying.

This has been, indeed, a very brief explanation of the psalm entitled: 'For the hidden things of the Son.' These are the words of the Old Testament, for the Old Testament speaks of the Son in a hidden manner. In the Gospel let us read openly of the manifestations of the Son.

---

13 Matt. 5.3.
14 Ps. 9B (10).10.

HOMILY 5

ON PSALM 14 (15)

Lent: To those preparing for baptism

OST OPPORTUNELY do we read the fourteenth psalm; so timely is its place in the proper course of the liturgy that it seems to fall there almost by plan. The psalm is read, moreover, in its regular sequence. This has happened, I think, by the dispensation of God, so that what would be of special profit to you might be read aloud today in the normal process of exegesis. You have heard the fourteenth psalm, and its title is 'A psalm of David.' David is our Christ, as we have said so many times. Besides, we read in Exodus[1] that on the fourteenth day a lamb is sacrificed; on the fourteenth day when the moon is a full moon, when its light is at its brightest. You see Christ is not immolated except in perfect and full light. Because, therefore, on the fourteenth day, the lamb is to be sacrificed by you, the prophet is now wondering, and asks:

'O Lord, who shall sojourn in your tent?' You are they who desire to make your house in the tent of the Lord. 'Who shall dwell on your holy mountain?' Notice what it says: 'Who shall sojourn in your tent? Who shall dwell on your holy mountain?' Not first on the mountain and, then, afterwards in the tent; but first in the tent and thereby on the mountain. A tent is not a fixed abode; a tent does not have a foundation, but is moved hither and thither with the nomad. That is why it says

---

1 Exod. 12.6.

38

'paroikía'—sojourn—and not 'habitatio'—dwelling.[2] 'O Lord, who shall sojourn in your tent?' Because it is a tent, that is why 'paroikía' is used. Let us see, therefore, what is this tent that is a mountain. We said that a tent does not have a foundation, but is a temporary dwelling place; a house, however, has a fixed foundation. The tent seems to me to be the church of this world. Now the churches that you see are tabernacles, for we are not here as permanent dwellers, but rather as those about to migrate to another place. If 'this world as we see it is passing away,'[3] and it says elsewhere that 'heaven and earth will pass away';[4] if, then, heaven and earth will pass away, how much more will the stones of the churches that we see also pass away? Now that is why churches are tabernacles, because we are going to migrate from them to the holy mountain of God. What is this holy mountain of God? It says in Ezechiel against the prince of Tyre: 'Thou hast been cut off as one slain from the mountain of God.'[5] 'Who shall dwell on your holy mountain?'

Since, then, we are going to migrate from the tabernacles to the mountain, we ought to get acquainted with those who are going to migrate to God's holy mountain. The words: 'Who shall sojourn in your tent? Who shall dwell on your holy mountain?' are the words of one seeking an answer. As the prophet has asked the question, the Holy Spirit responds. And what does He say to the prophet? 'Do you wish to know, O prophet, who will sojourn in My tent, or who will dwell on My holy mountain? Listen to what follows, and if you heed, you will dwell on My holy mountain.' You, therefore, who wish to sojourn in the tent and ascend the mountain of God, need not my words. Hear what the Lord has answered the prophet; obey His commands and you will ascend into the holy mountain of God: 'He who walks blamelessly and does justice.' Likewise in Psalm 118, it says: 'Happy are they

2 Cf. Letter 106.3, PL 22.839 (643).
3 1 Cor. 7.31.
4 Matt. 24.35.
5 Cf. Ezech. 28.16, LXX.

whose way is blameless.'⁶ Right there in the very beginning
it says: 'Happy are they whose way is blameless.' Just as in
that psalm it says: 'whose way is blameless,' so here in our
psalm it says: 'He who walks blamelessly.' Moreover, he who
walks is on the way. 'He who walks blamelessly.' Understand
what is being commanded. The Holy Spirit did not say, he who
arrives at the end without stain; but he who is still on the
road and is without spot.

Someone may say: 'I am without fault, I have done no evil.'
It is not enough for us to restrain from doing evil, unless we
shall also do good. In fact, the very next words are: 'And does
justice.' Note exactly what the psalmist is saying: 'And does
justice.' Now, the Holy Spirit did not say, he that practices
chastity, that applies wisdom, that exercises fortitude. Yet
these are excellent virtues indeed. Wisdom, for example, is
of great advantage to us; fortitude is valuable in resisting
persecution; finally, temperance and chastity are indispensable
in preventing us from losing our souls. Justice alone is the
great virtue and the mother of them all. Someone may ask:
'How is justice greater than all the other virtues?' The other
virtues gratify the one who possesses them; justice does not
give pleasure to the one possessing it, but instead pleases
others. If I am wise, wisdom delights me; if I am brave, my
fortitude comforts me; if I have been chaste, my chastity is
my joy. On the contrary, justice does not benefit the one who
has it, but all the wretched who do not have it. Suppose that
some poor man has a quarrel with my brother; suppose that
my brother is powerful and with his power crushes the other
one, I mean, the stranger to me, the poor and wretched man.
Of what avail is my wisdom to the poor man? Of what avail
my courage? My chastity, how does it help the poor man?
Justice is the virtue that benefits him for I do not regard the
person of my brother but judge according to truth. Justice
knows no brother; it knows no father, it knows no mother;
it knows truth; it is not a respecter of persons; it imitates God.

---

6 Ps. 118.1.

For that reason He said: 'And does justice,' lest He seem to have excluded all the other virtues.[7] He who is indignant in the interests of another, who takes no satisfaction in the troubles of others, he is a just man.

Let us say a few words, too, on the rest of the psalm. 'He who thinks the truth in his heart.' There are many who speak with truth on their lips, but not with truth in their heart; they seem to be speaking truth, but their heart is not in accord with their lips. 'And slanders not with his tongue': he who brings forth in speech what he has conceived in his heart. 'Who harms not his fellow man.' There are some who think that their neighbor is their brother, or their kindred, or their relative, or their kinsman. But our Lord teaches who he is in the Gospel parable where a certain man was going down from Jerusalem to Jericho:[8] a priest passed by, a Levite passed by, neither one was moved to compassion; a Samaritan passed by and he was moved to compassion. And the Lord, after He had finished the parable, asks: 'Which of these was the neighbor?' Without a moment of hesitation comes the answer: 'He who did well.' And the Lord says: 'Go and do thou also in like manner.' All men are our neighbor, and we should not harm anyone. If, on the contrary, we understand our fellow man to be only our brother and relatives, is it then permitted us to do evil to strangers? God forbid such belief! We are neighbors, all men to all men, for we have one father.

'Nor takes up a reproach against his neighbor.' This is a noble thing to say.[9] Never, says the psalmist, has a neighbor murmured against him; never, he says, has he found occasion for his disparagement. This virtue is beyond man's human power; it exists by the grace of God. 'By whom the reprobate is despised.' Mark what it says: 'By whom the reprobate is despised.' Even if he is an emperor, even if he is a governor,

---

7 Cf. *Commentary on Isaia* 56.1, PL 24.538 (654).

8 Luke 10.30-37; cf. *Commentary on Ezechiel* 18.5-10, PL 25.173 (206); on *Zacharia* 7.8, PL 25.1462 (835); 8.16, PL 25.1173 (850); on *Ephesians* 4.25, PL 26.542 (627).

9 Cf. *Letter* 127.3, PL 22.1088 (952).

if he is a bishop, if he is a priest (for these are dignitaries in the Church), whoever he is, if he is evil, he is nothing in the sight of the saint. Immediately there follow the words: 'While he honors those who fear the Lord.' This holy man of yours, who walks blamelessly, who despises the powerful that are wicked, if he sees one who fears God, even though he be a pauper, nevertheless, he honors him. 'Who, though it be to his loss, changes not his pledged word to his neighbor';[10] and here in this verse we ought to understand 'neighbor' in the same sense as above.

'He who lends not his money at usury.' There are many things that could be said, but time prevents us. Three days ago, moreover, we discussed the principle of κατηχήσεως—the science of instruction—and how with the mercy of God you went out from Chaldaea with Abraham, and you remember what we said: that as surely as you went forth from Chaldaea and came into the land of promise, that surely the land of promise is guaranteed to you. And, briefly, how, after Abraham came into the land of promise, from then on he met with adversaries; enemies were in possession of the land. The Lord came and led him up and placed him on a high mountain and showed him the whole land about and said: 'All this I will give to you and to your posterity.'[11] To Abraham He made the promise; to us He will render it.

10 Cf. Ps. 14 (15).4.
11 Cf. Gen. 13.15; 12.7.

HOMILY 6

ON PSALM 66 (67)

AY GOD HAVE PITY on us, and bless us.' May He not be our Judge, but may He be merciful to us. 'May God have pity on us.' It is the voice of the apostles speaking to the assembly of the nations: You have believed in our words, behold you are the Church that has been assembled in the name of God; for this reason do we say, may God have pity on us and bless us, so that with His blessing He may absolve the first malediction against man in Adam.[1] 'May he let his face shine upon us.' May we not look upon Him as sorrowful, but as rejoicing. May we not behold Him sorrowful because of our sins, but rejoicing in our virtues; may we not experience Him as Judge, but know Him as Father. 'May he let his face shine upon us.' The face of God, what is it like? As His image, certainly, for as the Apostle[2] says, the image of the Father is the Son. With His image, therefore, may He shine upon us, that is, may He shine His image, the Son, upon us in order that He Himself may shine upon us, for the light of the Father is the light of the Son. He who sees the Father, sees also the Son; and he who sees the Son sees also the Father.[3] Where there is no diversity between glory and glory, there glory is one and the same.

'So may your way be known upon earth.' This, indeed, is our petition, that the light of Your countenance, that is, Your image, may shine upon us, Your image which has always been

---

1 Gen. 3.17; cf. Homily 1 on Ps. 1, p. 3.
2 Cf. 2 Cor. 4.4; Col. 1.15.
3 John 14.9.

43

hidden in You, and is one of Your secret mysteries cloaked in darkness, as it were, in conformity with the Scripture: 'And he made darkness the cloak about him.'[4] This is our prayer, that You may shine upon us, that the mystery which has been hidden for ages and generations according to the Apostle,[5] may now be clearly shown in us. Why is this our urgent prayer? Why is this our one desire? Unless You cause the light of Your image to shine upon us, we cannot know Your way and know as You know. That is the reason behind the following words: 'So may your way be known upon earth,' that Your majesty which is known in heaven, may be known also by us on earth. 'So may your way be known upon earth.' 'I am the way,' He says, 'and the truth, and the life.'[6] 'So may your way be known upon earth,' that we on earth may know it. May 'thy will be done on earth, as it is in heaven';[7] in order that Him whom the angels adore in heaven, men also may adore upon earth. Someone may object and say that the way of God was known, for 'God is renowned in Juda; in Israel great is his name.'[8] God was known, but the way of God was not known in Judea. The way of God the Father was not known among the Judeans; hence, that is why Scripture now says 'Among all nations, your salvation'; not in one people only but in all nations without exception. 'Among all nations your salvation.' Where we have in Latin 'salutare'—salvation —in the Hebrew it says 'Jesus.' As a matter of fact, this is what the angel says: 'And thou shalt call his name Jesus: for he shall save his people.'[9] 'Among all nations your salvation.' See how the apostles' prayer has been fulfilled? His salvation is known among all nations. Wherever human speech is able to penetrate, there resounds the name of Jesus.

'May the peoples confess to you, O God; may all the people

---

4 Ps. 17.12.
5 Col. 1.26.
6 John 14.6.
7 Matt. 6.10.
8 Ps. 75.2.
9 Matt. 1.21.

praise you!'[10] The Hebrew people? No, 'all the peoples'; just
as all nations, so all the peoples. 'May the peoples confess
to you, O God.' Confess what? Their sins by all means; or
else may they admit without any doubt that Your image is
in You. May they confess You in the Son; may they see You
in Him; may they adore You in Him. 'May the nations be
glad and exult,' because they have been set free from the
captivity of the devil; because they who formerly were bent
over in the adoration of idols, wood and stone, now gaze upon
the heavens, erect with uplifted faces. 'Because you rule the
peoples in equity.' Wherever there is equity and judgment,
there is no joy, but the fear of sinners. How, then, did the
psalmist first say: 'May God have pity on us and bless us,'
and now say: 'May the nations be glad and exult because you
rule the peoples in equity'? This seems to be a contradiction.
If the peoples are in need of mercy, how are they to be glad
and exult, since You rule them in equity? Now, wherever
there is mercy, there is not judgment; on the other hand, where
there is judgment and the justice of the judge, mercy is far
from there. Yet the words are clear: 'May the nations be
glad and exult.' Why be glad? 'Because you rule the peoples
in equity,' for never is Your concern reserved only for the
people of one nation; You are the God of all. It is not the
Jews only who please You; the whole world is Yours.

Someone may say: 'You are forcing the Scripture, that is
not what it means.' Let Holy Writ be its own interpreter
where it says: 'Because you rule the peoples in equity.' What
peoples? 'The nations on the earth you guide.' The nations
that formerly were not walking with the right foot, the nations
that formerly were not walking on the right path, You have
caused to walk in Your way, that they might know Your way
upon earth, that they might walk in the one path and not
in many paths, that by the one way they might come to You
from whom that one way is begotten. We do not go to the
Father except through the Son.

---

10 Cf. Ps. 66 (67).4.

Someone may charge: 'That is the dogma of the Arians. Does one come to the Father through the Son?' I say this because through the image, we go to the face, and in the light, we see the light,[11] in the Son, we see the Father. This is a mystery and a divine dispensation. Be that as it may, if anyone thinks it blasphemy because we said that the way is the Son, and through the way we go, as it were, to God, let us see what this way itself says: 'No one can come to me, unless my Father draw him to me.'[12] In the same way that the Son leads to the Father, in that same way the Father also leads to the Son. These are human words. Notwithstanding, the Son leads to the Father, and the Father leads to the Son; and they are one nature, one substance.

'May the peoples confess to you, O God.' The psalmist has already said this. He repeats these two versicles once again in this tiny psalm. Above he had said: 'May the peoples confess to you, O God; may all the peoples praise you! May the nations be glad and exult,' and so on; and now again he repeats the versicles. Like apostles they sing to all the nations: 'Much have they oppressed me from my youth, let Israel say, much have they oppressed me from my youth.'[13] Notice how they sing first and the multitude of all the nations sings back. So it is now the same with those saying at the beginning of the psalm: 'May all the peoples praise you,' and directing the peoples and chanting: 'May the peoples confess to you, O God; may all the peoples praise you'; for they see that they are not responding and for this reason they repeat reproachfully: 'May the peoples confess to you, O God; may all the peoples give praise to you.' We have said this once already; you did not hear; let us sing it again that you may take up the song. Why have we urged not once but twice, that the peoples praise God? Why is this our bidding? Why our exhortation?

---

11 Cf. Ps. 35.10.
12 Cf. John 6.44.
13 Ps. 128.1, 2.

'The earth has yielded her fruit,'[14] earth, holy Mary who is from our earth, from our seed, from this clay, from this slime, from Adam. 'Dust you are and unto dust you shall return.'[15] This earth has yielded its fruit; what it lost in the Garden of Eden, it has found in the Son. 'The earth has yielded her fruit.' First, it brought forth a flower. It says in the Canticle of Canticles: 'I am the flower of the field, and the lily of the valleys.'[16] This flower has become fruit that we might eat it, that we might consume its flesh. Would you like to know what this fruit is? A Virgin from a virgin, the Lord from the handmaid, God from man, Son from mother, fruit from earth. Listen to what the fruit itself says: 'Unless the grain of wheat fall into the ground and die, it cannot bring forth much fruit.'[17] 'The earth has yielded her fruit'; it has yielded a grain of wheat. Because the grain of wheat has fallen into the ground and died, it produces many fruits. The fruit is multiplied in the head of grain. Because one had fallen, it rose again with many; one grain of wheat has fallen into the ground and a fruitful harvest came of it.

'The earth has yielded her fruit.' For that reason: 'May the peoples confess to you, O God; may all the peoples praise you! The earth has yielded her fruit.' What is this fruit? 'God, our God, has blessed us, may God bless us.' God, the Father; God, the Son, for He is our God. 'And they shall call,' the prophet says, 'his name Emmanuel,'[18] that is, God with us. 'May God bless us,' our God, the Holy Spirit. Behold the mystery of the Trinity embraced in one tiny verse. 'The earth has yielded her fruit' with many fruits; in this fruit is contained the mystery of the Trinity. 'God, our God, has blessed us.' The God of all through nature has become our God personally. 'May God bless us'; may He banish the ancient curse. A male-

---

14 Cf. Ps. 66 (67).7.
15 Gen. 3.19.
16 Cant. 2.1; cf. Letter 22.19, PL 22.406 (102); 75.1, PL 22.686 (452); 130.8, PL 22.1114 (985).
17 Cf. John 12.24, 25.
18 Cf. Isa. 7.14; Matt. 1.23.

diction drove us out of Paradise; may a benediction lead us
back. 'God, our God has blessed us. May God bless us.'

'And may all the ends of the earth fear him!' The prophet
did not say, may all the ends of the earth love Him; 'but
perfect love casts out fear.'[19] Fear is the mark of beginners;
love, the sign of the perfect. He who still fears is still a novice;
he does not have full and perfect faith; moreover, for him
who loves God, all things work together unto good.[20] This
seems a brief and simple maxim, but we shall sift and examine
it, and in these simple words we shall find a mighty mystery.
We shall discover on the inside that which was hidden from
the outside.

'For those who love God all things work together unto
good.'[21] Job, a holy man, was tempted; he lost his sons and his
daughters; his home fell into ruins; he lost everything he had;
suddenly everything was gone. He was neither father nor
lord; nothing remained sound in his body save his tongue with
which he could blaspheme. See the temptor, the devil. 'From
the sole of the foot,' Scripture says, 'even to the top of his
head he struck him with a very grievous ulcer,'[22] that is, with
leprosy. From the ulcer, vermin spread over his entire body
and disease and putrefaction. Only his tongue the devil left
untouched that he might be able to blaspheme his God. 'In
all these things Job sinned not by his lips.'[23] Just realize the
magnitude of the temptation; reflect upon the magnitude of
the virtue. Ponder well and comprehend how the saying of
the Apostle has been fulfilled: 'For those who love God all
things work together unto good.' When Job lost all his
wealth, when he lost his sons, everything seemed to militate
against him, but since he loved the Lord, the evils that befell
him worked together for his good. The vermin of his body
were preparing for him the crown of heaven. Before the time

---

19 1 John 4.18.
20 Cf. Rom. 8.28.
21 Rom. 8.28.
22 Job 2.7.
23 Job 1.22.

he was tempted, God had never spoken to him; after he had been tempted, however, God comes to him and speaks familiarly with him, as a friend with his friend. Let calamity strike, let every kind of disaster fall, as long as after the catastrophe, Christ comes.

We have digressed from the psalm, but not needlessly, for we read the words of Scripture: 'And may all the ends of the earth fear him!' and remarked that fear is the sign of little souls, while love the mark of the perfect. To prove our point, we quoted from the Apostle: 'For those who love God all things work together unto good.' 'And may all the ends of the earth fear him,' by no means only Judea, but all the ends of the earth. In accordance with tropologian—allegory—moreover, the psalmist means all lands far and wide, not only the mediate lands, not those that are in the center of earth, but those at the ends of the earth, that are leaving earth and hastening to heaven. Let us, therefore, say at the close of our psalm what the apostles said at the beginning: 'May God have pity on us, and bless us; may he let his face shine upon us, and may he have mercy on us.'

HOMILY 7

ON PSALM 67 (68)

OD ARISES; his enemies are scattered.' This psalm may be interpreted both in particular and in general. In particular, it refers to the Lord Himself, how He rose from the dead and scattered all His enemies, I mean the devil and his army or the Jews. In general, it applies to us when, in straits and distress, we cry out: 'Awake! why are you asleep, O Lord? Help us!'[1] just as the apostles in the boat roused the Lord from sleep with the cry: 'Lord, save us, we are perishing!'[2] 'And those who hate him flee before him.' Now the psalmist did not say, they perish, but they flee, for sinners cannot stand in the presence of God. 'As smoke is driven away, so are they driven.' Not that they vanish into nothingness, but that they cease from their sinning. 'As wax melts before the fire.' In the same way that wax melts and does not lose its nature but softens, so may the enemies of God not perish, but lay aside their hardness and be converted unto repentance and be saved. 'So the wicked perish before God'; the wicked do not deserve to see God. 'But the just rejoice.' Those who guard their innocence, who have no vices, delight in the Lord.

'And exult before God; they are glad and rejoice.' It is a sign of great confidence to rejoice before the Lord. The steward[3] who has managed his lord's affairs badly and lost his property fears to face his lord; on the contrary, the steward who has managed well always meets his lord with pleasure.

---

1 Ps. 43.24, 27.
2 Matt. 8.25; cf. Letter 108.27, PL 22.903 (721).
3 Cf. Luke 16.1-3; cf. Letter 121.6, PL 22.1018 (864).

'Sing to God, chant praise to his name.' 'Cantate' in Scripture invariably denotes consideration: sing meditatively, that is, think about the mystery and the sense of divine Scripture. 'Psallere,' on the other hand, implies the chanting of praise to God through a good work: for example, that the sense of hearing offer its service, and likewise the mouth, and the eyes, and the hands, and all the members of the body harmonize, as it were, and thereby pluck the chords of the psaltery in noble acts. 'Prepare a way for him who advances towards the west, whose name is the Lord.'[4] If the sun of iniquity does not set for us, our Sun of justice cannot rise, whose health is in his wings.[5]

'God in his holy dwelling.' God always dwells among His saints; wherever there is sanctity, there is the dwelling place of God—'God gives a home to men of one way,'[6] to them who choose one way of life and persevere in it. Indeed, the just man is constant because he has resolved once and for all to live a just life. The sinner, on the other hand, is fickle: 'the godless man, like the moon, is inconstant.'[7] The Hebrew text, however, has: 'God gives a home to monks,'[8] that is, to monks among whom sin finds no lodging. 'He leads forth prisoners to prosperity.' God Himself with His own power releases those who have been bound in sin by the devil, just as He released that woman in the Gospel who had been bound by the devil for eighteen years.[9] 'Only rebels remain in graves.'[10] God is sweet by nature; they who move Him to bitterness are sinners, and they make God bitter for themselves. God does not change His nature, but sinners themselves make God their bitterness. 'Remain in graves': 'Woe to you, Scribes and Pharisees! be-

---

4 Cf. Ps. 67 (68).5.
5 Cf. Mal. 4.2.
6 Cf. Ps. 67 (68).7.
7 Sirach (Ecclus.) 27.11.
8 Cf. Symmachus and Theodotion.
9 Luke 13.11-13.
10 Cf. Ps. 67 (68).7.

cause you are like whited sepulchres.'[11] As the saint is a temple
of God, so the sinner makes of himself a tomb.

'O God, when you went forth at the head of your people.'
This accords with history, when God preceded His people as
they marched out of Egypt.[12] 'When you marched through
the wilderness.' God did not delay in the desert, but passed
through it. 'The earth quaked; it rained from heaven at the
presence of the God of Sinai.'[13] 'It rained from heaven': that
is, it rained[14] manna. Sinai signifies temptation.[15] God dwells,
therefore, in those who are tempted and overcome temptation;
in the voluptuous, however, He does not dwell. 'A bountiful
rain you showered down, O God, upon your inheritance.' This
refers to the law which was given through Moses. 'You restored the land when it languished.' The law languished because no one was able to fulfill it except the Lord who said:
'I have not come to destroy the Law but to fulfill.'[16] Likewise,
the Apostle said: 'For what was impossible to the Law, in that
it was weak, God sent his Son.'[17] 'Your flock settled in it,' in
His inheritance. By 'flock' the psalmist meant those who live
for God, the saints. 'In your goodness, O God, you provided
it for the needy.' 'Blessed are the poor in spirit.'[18] You have
provided rain, which means the law. 'The Lord gives the word
to those who hear the glad tidings with great power.'[19] The
Hebrew text reads: 'women who were to publish the good
tidings,' that is, to the women to whom was announced the
glad news for the apostles when the Lord says: 'Go take word
to my brethren.'[20] Or the Hebrew may signify souls that believed in Christ. According to the Septuagint translators, how-

---

11 Cf. Matt. 23.27.
12 Exod. 13.21.
13 Cf. Ps. 67 (68).9.
14 Cf. *Commentarioli in ps.* 67.10.
15 Cf. Letter 78.8, PL 22.705 (475); 12, PL 22.707 (479).
16 Cf. Matt. 5.17.
17 Cf. Rom. 8.3.
18 Matt. 5.3.
19 Cf. Ps. 67 (68).12.
20 Matt. 28.10.

ever, the psalmist refers to the apostles because the Lord gave them great powers to preach the Gospel.[21]

'The king of the hosts of the beloved.'[22] King, or Father, of the hosts, that is, of the saints, of the beloved, of the Son. 'This is my beloved Son; hear him.'[23] 'Of the beloved.' When one loves, he is forever speaking of the beloved. The Holy Spirit is ever mindful of the Son because of His love in Him. 'And the household shall divide the spoils.' The apostles themselves distribute among the churches the spoils [nations] that they have taken from idols.

'Though you rested amid your portions,'[24] or, though you rested amid the New and Old Testament. The portions are also the individual books of Scripture, as Genesis, Exodus, The Gospels, The Apostles. 'The wings of the dove shone with silver.' You will find the grace of the Holy Spirit in the two Testaments. 'Shone with silver' symbolizes the clear word of divine Scripture; 'And her pinions with a golden hue,' the mysteries contained in Scripture understood spiritually.[25]

'While the Almighty appointed the kings there.'[26] The kings are the saints who rule over their own passions; hence, such holy men are assigned among the churches, for example, Paul among the Gentiles, Peter in the church of the circumcised. 'They were like snow on Salmon.'[27] That is what it says: they may be saints, but, nevertheless, in this world they are as a shadow, knowing only in part.[28] Salmon stands for shadow.

'The mountain of God is rich in blessings.'[29] This is the mountain that in Ezechiel[30] had punished the king of Tyre. They say, moreover, that the mountain is the Lord Himself.

21 Cf. *Commentarioli in ps.* 67.12.
22 Cf. Ps. 67 (68).13.
23 Matt. 17.5.
24 Cf. Ps. 67 (68).14.
25 Cf. *Commentary on Ecclesiastes* 2.8, PL 23.1080 (400).
26 Cf. Ps. 67 (68).15.
27 *Ibid.*; cf. *Commentarioli in ps.* 67.15.
28 Cf. 1 Cor. 13.9, 12; *Against the Pelagians* 3.12, PL 23.609 (795).
29 Cf. Ps. 67 (68).16.
30 Cf. Ezech. 28.16.

'Why look you jealously, you rugged mountains?' This means the Jews who think that Moses and the prophets rank with the Savior. 'At the mountain in which it has pleased God to dwell'[31] indicates the presence of the Savior made flesh, for Divine Nature inhabited a body. In no other, indeed, has the Holy Spirit taken up His abode immediately and perpetually save in the Savior. As John says: 'He upon whom thou wilt see the spirit descending, and abiding upon him, he it is.'[32] 'Where the Lord himself will dwell forever' in the body which He received from blessed Mary.

'The chariots of God are myriad, thousands on thousands.' This is hyperbole in reference to the countless ministering powers and spirits, just as Daniel said: 'Thousands upon thousands were ministering.'[33] Ezechiel,[34] in fact, describes the Cherubim as creatures with four wings on four sides and with four faces, of which God is the charioteer.[35] The Cherubim are also a symbol of the store of knowledge.[36] Again, the Cherubim symbolize the nature of the lion, the sovereign nature reigning over its passions; the nature of man as rational; the nature of the bullcalf in work; the nature of the eagle in contemplation—in speculation that elevates us among the Virtues. At the same time, however, that we may say the throne of God is in His saints, the psalmist says: 'The Lord is among them on Sinai, in the sanctuary.'[37] That means that God is in His saints when they are being tempted, and that sanctity is consequent upon temptation. It is impossible for anyone, even though he be a saint, to pass through this world without temptation. As Job says: 'The life of man upon earth is a warfare.'[38]

'You have ascended on high, taken captives.' You have ascended into heaven; You have redeemed us who were being

---

31 Cf. Ps. 67 (68).17.
32 John 1.33.
33 Dan. 7.10.
34 Ezech. 1.6-12; cf. 1.26-28.
35 Cf. Sirach (Ecclus.) 49.8; *Commentary on Ezechiel* 1.7, PL 25.22 (11).
36 Cf. Letter 53.8, PL 22.548 (280).
37 Cf. Ps. 67 (68).18.
38 Job 7.1; cf. *Against the Pelagians* 2.4, PL 23.563 (745).

held captives by the devil. 'Received men as gifts.' Well said, 'You received.' He received from the Father; He received as man; He gives as God; and that which He received, He received for men to give to men. He Himself is perfect and is not in need of anything. 'Even rebels; the Lord God enters his dwelling.' You have saved even those who did not believe that it is possible for God to dwell in man, for the Savior to assume a body. 'Blessed be the Lord God.'[39] Those who formerly refused to believe that it is possible for God to dwell in man, now believe and say: 'Blessed be the Lord God.'

'Blessed day by day be the Lord.' The man who makes progress can bless God every day. What does it profit me if yesterday I blessed God and today I cannot bless Him? 'Who bears our burdens; who is to us a God of salvations.'[40] Be assured, sinner; do not doubt that you can bless God day by day, for God will bear our burdens for us. God helps us and works with us. 'Of salvations.' The plural is good here, for we have been saved as many times as we have sinned. 'Diapsalma':[41] in the Hebrew text the word is SELA which means always and instantly; hence, God is always bringing us aid.

'God is a saving God for us; the Lord, my Lord, controls the passageways of death.' Since God rose from the dead, He has caused us to rise with Him. By another interpretation, the devil is the entrance of death, the Lord in truth, the exit. 'Surely God crushes the heads of his enemies,' the devil and all his hosts. 'You smashed the heads of the dragons in the waters.'[42] The devil has as many heads as there are sins. 'The hairy crowns of those who stalk about in their guilt.' God smashes the devil's head so completely that all his strength to goad sinners is gone. His hair is the top of his head, a hairy crown; hence, the meaning here is that every bit of the devil's power is shattered.

---

39 Cf. Ps. 67 (68).20.
40 *Ibid.*
41 Pause or interval in the singing of the psalm.
42 Ps. 73.13.

'The Lord said: "I will fetch them back from Basan," ' I will turn mankind away from the confusion of this world. Through My passion and cross, which they look upon as foolishness and confusion,[43] I will bring back My people. Basan, of course, stands for confusion. 'I will fetch them back from the depths of the sea' is another way of saying, I will turn back My people from the deep-seated vices and sins of this world, from the violence of its waves. 'So that you will bathe your feet in blood.' His foot has been stained in His own blood. 'The wine press, I have trodden alone, and of my people there was no one with me.'[44] And again: 'Who is this that comes from Edom, in crimson garments from Bosra?'[45] Edom translates as blood; Bosra, flesh, a figure of our crucified Lord Himself. 'The tongues of your dogs will have their share of your enemies.' The dogs are the very Jews who cried out: 'Crucify him! Crucify him! We have no king but Caesar.'[46] 'Of your enemies' refers, on the other hand, to those who in submission to demons deny and blaspheme the Savior. In another sense the words could mean: Of Your own will You have come and suffered and of Your own will the Jews have crucified You.

'They view your progress, O God,'[47] for You ascended into heaven before the eyes of five hundred men, all the apostles, the Cherubim, and the choirs of angels. 'The progress of my God, my King into the sanctuary.' You who are the God of all, and the Lord of dominions, and the King of kings, You are especially my God,[48] just as You are the God of Abraham and the God of Isaac and the God of Jacob and the God of the Hebrews.

'The singers lead, the minstrels follow.' The apostles[49] led the way followed by those who have believed through them—

---

43 Cf. *Commentarioli in ps.* 67.23, 24.
44 Isa. 63.3.
45 Isa. 63.1; cf. *Against John of Jerusalem*, 34, PL 23.403 (443).
46 John 19.6, 15.
47 Cf. Letter 106.41, PL 22.851 (657).
48 *Ibid.*
49 Cf. *Commentarioli in ps.* 67.26.

or, undoubtedly, by the churches. Moreover, 'the maidens play on timbrels,' because their body is dead to sin. In the Book of Exodus, Mariam, the sister of Moses and Aaron, took a tambourine in her hand and led the singers with the refrain: 'Sing to the Lord, for he is gloriously triumphant.'[50]

'In the churches[51] bless God.' O you who glory in abstinence, glory in your gatherings and do not defend heresies to your own satisfaction. These words can well be addressed to Tatian, the chief of the Encratites.[52] 'The Lord, you of Israel's well-spring!' Manichaeus cannot bless the Lord because he does not bless from the wellspring of Israel; he does not accept the Old Testament. 'You of Israel's wellspring,' not of Jacob's. Jacob means supplanter, one who is still wrestling; Israel has finished the struggle triumphantly, seeing God[53] with his understanding.

'There is Benjamin, the youngest, in ecstasy.'[54] This means St. Paul,[55] in the Church, the youngest, the least of all the apostles, from the tribe of Benjamin.[56]

'The princes of Juda are their leaders.'[57] The apostles are the princes of Juda, that is, of the Lord, just as Jacob says: 'Juda, your brothers shall praise you.'[58] 'The princes of Zabulon, the princes of Nephthali.' Zabulon suggests the pollution of the night;[59] Nephthali, latitude. When we have been liberated from the passion of lust, that is, from its effects, then we begin to acquire the virtues.

'Confirm, O God, what you have wrought in us.'[60] Confirm

50 Exod. 15.20, 21.
51 Cf. Ps. 67 (68).27.
52 Cf. Letter 48.2, PL 22.494 (213); 9, PL 22.500 (220). *Commentary on Amos* 2.12, PL 25.1010 (247); *on Joel* 1.14, PL 25.959 (180).
53 Cf. *Hebrew Question on Genesis* 32.28, 29, PL 23.1039 (357).
54 Cf. Ps. 67 (68).28.
55 Cf. *Commentary on Isaia* 9.1, PL 24.124 (129).
56 Cf. Rom. 11.1; Phil. 3.5; 1 Cor. 15.8, 9; Eph. 3.8; cf. Letter 38.1, PL 22.463 (174).
57 Cf. Ps. 67 (68).28.
58 Gen. 49.8.
59 Cf. *Hebrew Questions on Genesis* 30.19, 20, PL 23.1034 (352).
60 Cf. Ps. 67 (68).29.

the salvation You have brought us through Your passion, and help us, for we are men and unable to advance in virtue without Your aid. 'Let the kings bring you gifts.' Kings are those who rule over themselves, as it is written: 'The king's heart in the hand of God.'[61] They are bringing gifts to God. The virtues of the saints are gifts to God.

'Rebuke the wild beast of the reeds.' This points to the heretics who preach and write against You in order to ensnare us.[62] 'For there must be factions among us.'[63] They are called the wild beast because they attack souls and slay them. The wild beast can also be the devil and his angels. 'The herd of strong bulls and the bullocks, the nations.' This again refers to heretics, because they deceive only the weak and guileless, that is the bullocks; they cannot trap the bulls, for they are the wary and strong. 'Who seek to exclude those who have been tried like silver.'[64] Their whole purpose in misleading the unguarded, in other words the crowd, is to overtake the saints and keep them from the kingdom of heaven.

'Scatter the peoples who delight in war,' scatter the heretics who are attacking the Church. 'Let nobles come from Egypt.' Egypt represents darkness, the darkness of this world. 'Let Ethiopia extend its hands to God.' Whereas we were black from sin and passion, we have outstripped the Israelites and believe in the Savior, like the woman with the hemorrhage who prevented the daughter of the ruler of the synagogue and was healed.[65]

'Who rides on the heights of the ancient heavens towards the East.'[66] Earlier in the psalm it said, 'Who advances towards the west'; here it says, 'towards the east.' When our passions subside and the sun of our iniquity sets, the sun of justice rises for us; the Lord reigns over us and in us takes up His

---

61 Cf. Prov. 21.1.
62 Cf. Letter 108.22, PL 22.900 (716); 121.2, PL 22.1012 (856).
63 Cf. 1 Cor. 11.19.
64 Cf. Ps. 67 (68).31.
65 Matt. 9.20-22.
66 Cf. Ps. 67 (68).34.

abode. 'Behold his voice resounds, the voice of power.' 'Lazarus, come forth!'[67] 'Behold his voice resounds, the voice of power. . . . Over Israel is his majesty': the majesty of God in Israel who sees God. 'His power is in the clouds,'[68] in the prophets and in the apostles. 'I will command the clouds not to send rain upon Israel.'[69] 'Awesome in his saints is God.'[70] God is awesome because He so loves the human race that He performs miracles through His saints. He is more awesome in His saints than in the rest of His creatures.

---

67 John 11.43.
68 Cf. Ps. 67 (68).35.
69 Cf. Isa. 5.6.
70 Cf. Ps. 67 (68).36.

HOMILY 8

ON PSALM 74 (75)

NTO THE END.[1] (Do not destroy!) A psalm of Asaph; a song.' The Hebrew text does not have 'unto the end,' but has instead, 'for the victor.' The translators of the Septuagint have not erred very seriously, however, inasmuch as victory certainly implies the end. Well said: 'Unto the end,' ('ne corrumpas' Do not destroy!). The word destroy—'corrumpas'—has many shades of meaning. David uses it in speaking to someone about his friends: 'Ne corrumpas eum'—'Kill him not,'[2] that is, Saul. The sense here is obvious. In another place,[3] we learn that David blessed the Lord because his hands were held back from killing Saul. With us, too, when we do not commit murder, it is because our hands are held in check. Some say that this psalm was composed by David and sung by Asaph; others, however, that Asaph both composed and sang it. As I was saying, however, according to the Septuagint it means this: O Lord, who has stayed my hand from Your anointed Saul, restrain me unto the end.[4]

'We give you thanks, O God.' Here, the expression 'confitebimur'—we will confess—does not signify repentance, but rather, give praise or thanks. 'And we invoke your name.' The name of God is Father.[5] This name was not known in times

---

1 Cf. Ps. 74 (75).1.
2 1 Kings 26.9.
3 Cf. 1 Kings 26.11, 23, 24; 25.32-34; 24.11, 13.
4 1 Kings 26.11; 24.11.
5 Cf. *Commentary on Jeremia* 32.16-20, PL 24.893 (1084).

past, for the Lord says: 'Father, I have manifested thy name to the men.'[6] Every son in truth bears the name of his father.[7] 'We declare your wondrous deeds.' The Church is speaking, the hosts of the faithful. 'We declare your wondrous deeds.' This verse is joined to the preceding verses, but the next verse speaks in the person of the Lord, for so the ancients have interpreted it.

'When I seize the appointed time, I will judge with equity.' The Lord is not judge now, but will be later. If He were judge now, sinners would not be arrogant and gain the wealth of the world. Is it a scandal to you that the just are in exile and sinners persecute them? Does it scandalize you that wickedness reigns in the world? Hear the Lord saying: 'When I seize the appointed time, I will judge with equity.' The time for judgment has been set aside. The present world is not the time of judgment, but of contest. 'For neither does the Father judge any man, but all judgment he has given to the Son.'[8] As you listen to this, do not be scandalized and say that it is the inferior who receives from the giver. See what the Gospel says: 'For neither does the Father judge any man, but all judgment he has given to the Son, because he is the Son of Man.'[9] He renders judgment for the simple reason that He received judgment, for He is the Son of Man. Do you hear the Son of Man, and do you doubt wherefore He received the power of judgment?

6 John 17.5, 6; cf. Commentary on Habacuc 3, PL 25.1310 (635).
7 Cf. Commentary on Matthew 24.36, PL 26.181 (200); 26.29, PL 26.196 (217).
8 John 5.22.
9 John 5.22, 27; cf. Commentary on Ecclesiastes, PL 23.1111 (432); on Isaia 2.7, PL 24.47 (35); 21.6-10, PL 24.191 (215); 26.10, PL 24.297 (349).

HOMILY 9

ON PSALM 75 (76)

EFORE THE CROSS brought light to the world, before the Lord was seen on earth, 'God' was 'renowned in Juda, in Israel,' moreover, 'great was his name';[1] but when the Savior came, 'through all the earth his voice re sounded, and to the ends of the world, His message.'[2]

'In peace is his abode':[3] for which the Hebrew has 'in Salem.' You see, therefore, the literal translation is Jerusalem— that is Salem[4]—which first was called Salem, later Jebus, and finally Jerusalem. This is that Salem in which Melchisedec was king. We read: 'You are a priest forever, according to the order of Melchisedec.'[5] The psalmist did not say according to the order of Aaron, but Melchisedec.

What is the meaning of, 'You are a priest according to the order of Melchisedec'? Obviously, the reference is to Christ But why does it say, according to the order of Melchisedec Aaron offered victims; he poured out the blood of sacrificia animals. Melchisedec did neither of these; he merely offered bread and wine; that is why it says, according to the order o Melchisedec.

The Hebrew has, 'And there was set up in Salem his tent. Understand what that means: figuratively speaking, there i no tent of the Lord except where there is peace. Where there

---

1 Cf. Ps. 75 (76).2.
2 Cf. Ps. 18.5; cf. Letter 60.4, PL 22.591-592 (334).
3 Cf. Ps. 75 (76).3.
4 Cf. Letter 73.7, PL 22.680 (445); 46.3, PL 22.485 (201); *Hebrew Ques tion on Genesis* 14.18, PL 23.1010-1011 (329); 33.18, PL 23.1040 (358).
5 Ps. 109.4.

is strife and discord, God is not there as Protector. Let us, too, follow the interpretation of the Septuagint. The abode of God is only in a peaceful soul; therefore, let the soul that is without peace know that it is not the dwelling place of God. 'Peace I leave with you, my peace I give to you.'[6] Peace is our legacy from the Savior.

'His dwelling is in Sion.' A literal interpretation permits us to say of Jerusalem and Sion, that the temple was there, but in a tropological and anagogical sense, we mean that the dwelling of God is in Sion. Now Sion means stronghold or watchtower;[7] hence, where there is in the soul the knowledge of Scripture and its doctrine, that soul is the dwelling place of God.

'There he shattered the flashing shafts of the bow.' There. Where? In Jerusalem and Sion. Jerusalem stands for peace, and Sion, watchtower. Let us consider, then, the nature of this peace and watchtower. We may explain them in two ways: first, as the human soul in which there is the peace of God and contemplation; second, either as certainly the Church or surely Holy Scripture. There truly is peace, and there, too, the dwelling place and citadel of God. 'There he shattered the flashing shafts of the bow': the fiery darts that the devil shoots. 'Shield and sword, and weapons of war.' Of war: that war mentioned in another psalm: 'Scatter the peoples who delight in war.'[8] And now, what follows? 'Sela' which the Septuagint translates as 'diapsalma,'[9] and which in Hebrew means 'always.' See, the Lord always shatters the shield, the sword, and the weapons of war.

'Resplendent you come, O powerful One, from the everlasting mountains.' We interpret mountains in two ways: in the Old Testament as prophets; in the New, as apostles. Of these mountains Scripture says: 'I lift up my eyes toward the moun-

---

6 John 14.27; cf. Letter 13, PL 22.347 (28).
7 Cf. Letter 75.1, PL 22.686 (452); 108.9, PL 22.884 (697).
8 Ps. 67.31.
9 Cf. *Commentary on Habacuc* 3.3, PL 25.1312 (637-638); Letter 28, PL 22.433-435 (135-139).

tains, whence shall help come to me?'[10] Upon these mountains, too, rested the city of God. 'A city set on a mountain cannot be hidden.'[11] We were all sitting in darkness and in the shadow of death, and the Lord shone upon us from His eternal mountains, that is, from the prophets and the apostles. 'Despoiled are the stout-hearted.' This we may say of infidels.

'They sleep their sleep; the hands of all the mighty ones have failed.' Truly, this life is a dream, a dream of riches; for when we seem to have them within our grasp, immediately they slip away. Isaia expresses this same thought: 'As when a thirsty man dreams he is drinking and awakens faint and dry,'[12] so, indeed, are the riches of this world; while we are reaching out for them they are gone.

'Chariots and steeds lay stilled.' Let us examine this verse in its tropological significance. At last Pharao mounted his steeds, sank into sleep, and perished. The Egyptians, too, had steeds, but they perished. That is the reason for the prescription found in the Law[13] that no Hebrew should possess a horse. Solomon, you recall, had no horse from Jerusalem or Judea, but bought some from Egypt.[14] Horses are always for sale in Egypt. 'Some are strong in chariots; some, in horses; but we are strong in the name of the Lord, our God.'[15] They, in truth, who mounted horses slumbered and perished. Our Lord has horses, too, and He has shining mountains besides, whereas the devil's mountains are full of darkness.

Now just as there are bright mountains and dark mountains, there are good horses and again bad horses. We have made a few remarks about bad horses; let us say something about good horses. When horsemen came to Eliseus[16] to arrest him, and the servant boy went out and saw an army of Assyrians round about the city, Eliseus said: 'Fear not: for there are more

---

10 Ps. 120.1.
11 Matt. 5.14.
12 Isa. 29.8.
13 Cf. Deut. 17.16.
14 3 Kings 10.28.
15 Ps. 19.8.
16 4 Kings 6.13-17.

with us than with them.' A little further on in Kings it says:
'Lord, open the eyes of your servant that he may see.' And
when his eyes had been opened, he saw chariots and horses.
These were helpmates. You notice what it says, chariots and
horses. There were no men on the horses, only chariots and
horses, in other words, a multitude of angels. They were the
chariots and they were the horses; the charioteer was the Lord.
That is why the prophet Habacuc sings: 'Thy chariots are
salvation.'[17] This is said to God. O, if only we, too, were God's
horses, and God deigned to ride us! But those other horses
slept their long sleep and their charioteers with them.

'The fury of your anger.' When was this anger of God?
When the people cried out to Aaron in the desert saying:
'Come, make us a god who will be our leader; as for the man
Moses, who brought us out of the land of Egypt, we know not
what has happened to him.'[18] You brought them out of the
land of Egypt, and right after that they denied You. 'From
heaven you made your intervention heard.' You spoke from
heaven; all the people heard and trembled and still they did
not believe in You. 'The earth feared and was silent.' Israel,
however, was neither afraid nor silent.

'For the thought of man shall confess to you.'[19] This same
idea occurs in another psalm: 'Cleanse me from my unknown
faults! From wanton sin especially, restrain your servant,'[20]
from thoughts that estrange You and that are sent secretly by
the devil. What follows? 'Let it not rule over me. Then shall
I be blameless.'[21] If I do not yield to sinful thoughts, I shall be
clean in Your sight. And the next words? 'And I shall be innocent of serious sin.'[22] Understand what the psalmist says. If
an evil thought does not become deliberate and lead to sinful
action, I have been delivered from a serious sin. 'For the

---

17 Hab. 3.8; cf. *Commentary on Habacuc* 3.8 PL 25.1317 (644); cf. Letter
    66.2, PL 22.639-640 (394).
18 Exod. 32.1.
19 Cf. Ps. 75 (76).11.
20 Ps. 18.13, 14.
21 Ps. 18.14.
22 *Ibid.*; cf. Letter 130.8, PL 22.1114 (985).

thought of man shall confess to you.' 'No one can be found clean of defilement in the sight of God, no one, however short his days.'[23] 'The heavens are not clean in the sight of God,'[24] and 'with his angels he can find fault.'[25] Why do I say all this? If the heavens are not pure and even angels are not flawless, how much more is there evil in the thoughts of men? Where are they who say: 'Depart from me because I am clean'?[26] We know what we suffer day by day, what is in our thoughts, and we blush with shame to reveal them. There are many who have never committed a serious wrong, there are others who have never sinned with their tongue; but on the other hand, there is no one among men who has not sinned in thought. That is why the psalmist says: 'For the thought of man shall confess to you.'

'To the terrible Lord.' To whom? To God. 'Who checks the spirit of princes.'[27] When we see persons of power, like emperors, governors, and the potentates of this world, we also may say to God: 'Who checks the spirit of princes.' We can take the spirit here in two ways: either the spirit of the soul or the spirit of pride. Let us, however, explain this verse in a different way altogether. 'Who checks the spirit of princes.' Let us consider the saints as princes. Solomon, for example, was a prince, and the other saints were princes— even the Apostle Judas was a prince—and because they sinned, God checked their spirit. Let no one, therefore, say: I am a bishop; I am a priest, or a deacon or a monk; I am a prince in this world. God is powerful enough to destroy the spirit of princes. Again, that you may be sure that God curbs the spirit of pride, recall how the good spirit of God departed from Saul and an evil spirit troubled him. Holy Writ says: 'And an evil spirit of God troubled him,'[28] a spirit from God. Does

---

23 Cf. Job 14.4, 5.
24 Cf. Job 15.15.
25 Job 4.18.
26 Cf. Isa. 65.5, LXX; cf. Luke 5.8.
27 Cf. Ps. 75 (76).13.
28 Cf. 1 Kings 16.14, 15.

God, then, have an evil spirit? Not at all. God had withdrawn so that afterwards an evil spirit might trouble Saul. In that sense, the spirit of God is called evil. Finally, holy David, knowing that God could take away the spirit of princes, entreats Him: 'And your holy spirit take not from me.'[29]

'Who is terrible to the kings of the earth.' This is in the strict sense. On the other hand, God may permit us also to be kings of the earth, 'kings of earth' in order to rule over our own flesh. In this connection the Apostle says: 'Therefore do not let sin reign in your mortal body.'[30] In another part of Scripture it is written: 'The king's heart in the hand of God.'[31] Was the heart of Julian, the persecutor, in the hand of God? The heart of Saul, was it in the hand of God? Was the heart of Manasse in the hand of God? The heart of Achab? Were the hearts of all the impious kings of Juda in the hand of God? Do you see that this verse does not admit of a literal interpretation? The kings, therefore, are the saints and their hearts are in the hand of the Lord. Let us beg God to make us kings that we may rule over our flesh that it be subject to us. The following words of the Apostle are appropriate here: 'But I chastise my body and bring it into subjection, lest perhaps after preaching to others, I myself should be rejected.'[32] May our soul be in command, our body in subjection; then Christ will come at once to make His abode with us. What does He Himself say in the New Testament? 'Behold, I stand at the door and knock. If any man listens to my voice and opens the door to me, I will come in to him and will sup with him.'[33] Every day Christ stands at the door of our hearts; He longs to enter. Let us open wide our hearts to Him; then He will come in and be our host and guest;[34] He will dwell in us and sup with us.

---

29 Ps. 50.13.
30 Rom. 6.12.
31 Prov. 21.1.
32 1 Cor. 9.27.
33 Apoc. 3.20.
34 Cf. *Commentary on Osee* 11.3, 4, PL 25.917 (125).

HOMILY 10

ON PSALM 76 (77)

LOUD TO THE Lord I cry; aloud to God, and he hears me; on the day of my distress I seek my God.'[1] See how troubled he is, for he cries in loud appeal to God, God, God; yet there is but one God. 'Aloud to the Lord I cry.' A loud cry is all the more necessary when the troubled heart is far away. This is what he is saying: because of my sins I am far away from You, and so I must cry out loud that in Your gracious mercy You may hear me. 'Aloud to God, and he hears me.' Another psalm echoes this same appeal: 'In my distress I called to the Lord, and he answered me.'[2]

'On the day of my distress I seek my God.' It is not always easy to do that. When we are in trouble we are dejected and think of nothing but our trouble; yet the best recourse in time of affliction is to pray earnestly to God. For example, I have lost a son, my house has burned down, I am reduced to beggary. I do not go around looking for what I have lost; I look for God. If I find Him, in Him I shall regain everything. 'Seek first the kingdom of God, and all these things shall be given you besides.'[3]

'By night my hands stretched out, and I am not deceived.'[4] There is a variation here in the Hebrew: 'By night my hand is stretched out without flagging.' 'By night my hands stretched out': I cry aloud is understood. Notice that our good works cry out to the Lord even when we are silent. On that account,

---

1 Cf. Ps. 76 (77).2, 3.
2 Ps. 119.1.
3 Cf. Matt. 6.33.
4 Cf. Ps. 76 (77).3.

it says in Holy Writ: 'the Lord came by the hand of Aggai the prophet.'[5] The word did not come by his mouth—his speech—but by his hand through his deeds. 'For the kingdom of God is not in word'[6] but in the hand—in works. 'By night my hands stretched out': I cried out, I cried out with my hands. Under similar circumstances the Lord said to Moses: 'Why are you crying out to me?'[7] Certainly, it is not written that Moses cried to God; but just as the heart of the Apostle cried, 'Abba, Father,'[8] so did Moses' heart cry out. For that reason God says, Why do you cry out to Me? It is in this same spirit that Jeremia says: 'Let there be no repose for my eyes.'[9] See, not even the pupil of our eye is silent; actually, we cry to God with our hands as many times as we cry to Him with our tears. 'By night stretched out.'

Again in another psalm, it says: 'During the hours of night lift up your hands toward the sanctuary, and bless the Lord.'[10] In the night of this world and in its darkness, while others were hurrying to their vices, I was offering up my deeds to You alone. 'And I am not deceived.'[11] Because it is thus that I have cried, with my works, I am not deceived. Two explanations are possible here: either my prayer has been answered, or I am not at all being deceived by the snares into which the devil tries to lure me. The Hebrew text says moreover: 'By night my hand is stretched out without flagging.' My hand is always stretched out to virtuous deeds; never is it drawn backward to sins.

'My soul refuses comfort.' My soul is so immersed in sin; I cannot console myself with any hope. 'When I remember God, my spirits rise.'[12] So deep is my soul in sin, I have not been able to find any comfort; but I turn my thoughts back

---

5 Cf. Ag. 1.1.
6 1 Cor. 4.20.
7 Exod. 14.15.
8 Gal. 4.7.
9 Cf. Lam. 2.18.
10 Ps. 133.1, 2.
11 Cf. Ps. 76 (77).3.
12 Cf. Ps. 76 (77).4.

to God, and take heart again in His compassionate kindness. The Hebrew reverses this phrase, saying: 'When I remember God, I moan.' I have reflected upon the merciful compassion of God; I have meditated on His faithfulness, His loving kindness; I have considered His purity; and seeing myself so impure, I am exceedingly grieved. 'And I am exercised, and my spirit grows faint.'[13] The Hebrew is better: 'When I ponder, my spirit grows faint,' either with despair or with longing for God.

'My eyes prevent the watches.'[14] The Hebrew again is different: 'I keep my eyes cast down; I am as one paralysed and cannot speak.' This is what it means: when I ponder over my sins, I do not dare raise my eyes to heaven, for: 'to the wicked man God says: "Why do you recite my statutes?"'[15] That is why I am paralyzed, why I am afraid, why I cannot utter a word. This, then, is in conformity with the Hebrew. 'My eyes prevent the watches'; before anyone else wakes up, I am awake. We read also in Daniel:[16] 'And behold,' he says, 'ir,' that is, 'a sentinel.' 'Indeed he neither slumbers nor sleeps, the guardian of Israel.'[17] And so the monk who is not watchful cannot say that verse. 'I am troubled and cannot speak.' This is the teaching of the Apostle: 'Do not let the sun go down upon your anger.'[18] I am upset because I am human; I control my tongue because I am a Christian. Anger surges up in my heart, but I do not give vent to it.

'I consider the days of old; the years long past I remember.' As far as my sins are concerned, I despair and my soul refuses to be comforted. I begin to muse over the beginning of the world, when God made man, and all the way down to my years, from Adam down to my time.

---

13 *Ibid.*
14 Cf. Ps. 76 (77).5.
15 Ps. 49.16.
16 Cf. Dan. 4.10; cf. *Commentary on Daniel* 4.10, PL 25.515 (647); Letter 75.5, PL 22.688-89 (455); 109.3, PL 22.909 (728).
17 Ps. 120.4.
18 Eph. 4.26; cf. Letter 79.9, PL 22.731 (506); 130.13, PL 22.1118 (989).

'In the night I meditate in my heart; I ponder, and my spirit broods.' I am not brooding over my anger, nor over my enemy; all my musing is of God. The night that is wont to be a time for rest, or for lust, is for me a time of pondering deeply upon virtue. 'I meditate in my heart, I ponder, and my spirit broods'; I am like one digging a field[19] to plant in it the seed of the Lord's teachings.

'Will God reject forever?'[20] This is the whole burden of my meditation. God made man from clay and promised him eternal life. How, then, is he cast off from Paradise? From the kingdom of God? 'And nevermore be favorable? Will his kindness utterly cease, his promise fail for all generations?' Will he reject both generations, the chosen people and their successors? Granted that He rejected the Jews; will He also reject the Gentiles? 'Does he in anger withhold his compassion?' This could not be better expressed. No matter how long He restrains His compassionate mercy, nevertheless, His kindness will always triumph.

'And I say, "Now I have begun." '[21] The Hebrew says by contrast: 'And I say, "This is my weakness." ' In other words, my suffering is not from the cruelty of God, but from my own sins. 'The right hand of the Most High is changed.'[22] That the Lord is merciful and grants His grace to the whole universe and does not in anger withhold His clemency, that is the change of the right hand of the Most High. Unless His right hand, that is, His Son, has changed and taken upon Himself the human body of man, we cannot receive His mercy. 'And I say, "Now I have begun. The right hand of the Most High is changed." ' 'Who though he was by nature God, did not consider being equal to God a thing to be clung to, but emptied himself, taking the nature of a slave.'[23]

'I remember the deeds of the Lord': His wonderful deeds

---

19 Cf. Letter 106.49, PL 22.854 (661).
20 Cf. Ps. 76 (77).8.
21 Cf. Ps. 76 (77).11.
22 *Ibid.*
23 Phil. 2.6, 7.

for Moses, the deeds He had performed for His saints. 'Yes, I remember your wonders of old. And I meditate on your works; your exploits I ponder.' I occupy all my thoughts with Your wondrous deeds. Meditating upon the compassionate kindness You have shown toward Your saints, I am no longer without hope.

'O God, your way is in holiness.'[24] If you are not holy, the way of God is not in you. What is the way of God? 'I am the way, and the truth and the life.'[25] It is the Savior who says this. The way, therefore, is the Son of God. The way of God, moreover, is only in the saintly man. If we want Christ to dwell in us, let us be saints, for the way of God is holiness. 'What great god is there like our God?' Just as 'there are many gods and many lords,'[26] the saints are called gods. (This is from the Apostle. 'God arises in the divine assembly';[27] and 'I said, You are gods: all of you sons of the Most High';[28] and God said to Moses, 'I have made you as God to Pharao.'[29]) They are gods by grace, but You are God by nature. 'You are the God who works wonders.' The psalmist did not say, who 'worked,' but who 'works.' Every day God works wonders; He works,[30] and the Son, and the Holy Spirit. 'You are the God who works wonders.' Yesterday a thief, today a Christian; yesterday a fornicator, today continent; yesterday you were plundering the goods of others; today you are offering your own.

'Among the peoples you have made known your power.' 'Christ, the power of God and the wisdom of God';[31] 'the mystery which has been hidden for ages';[32] now You have made Your power known among the peoples. 'With your strong

---

24 Cf. Ps. 76 (77).14.
25 John 14.6.
26 1 Cor. 8.5.
27 Ps. 81.6.
28 *Ibid.*
29 Exod. 7.1.
30 Cf. John 5.17.
31 1 Cor. 1.24; cf. Letter 53.4, PL 22.543 (274).
32 Col. 1.26.

arm you redeemed your people,' 'Lord, who hath believed our report? and to whom is the arm of the Lord revealed?'[33] 'With your strong arm you redeemed your people,' in Christ, of course. 'The sons of Jacob and Joseph': of both peoples, of Jews and of Christians; the sons of Jacob in the Jews, of Joseph in the Gentiles. Joseph, furthermore, means 'increase,' in Hebrew.[34] The Jews came first and we have followed; hence, the saying 'the sons of Jacob and Joseph.'

'The waters saw you, O God; the waters saw you and shuddered.' First, let us consider the literal meaning; let us stay close to earth for the sake of the less experienced. When the people crossed the Red Sea and the River Jordan, the waters recognized their creator, but the people did not. 'The very depths were troubled'; 'The sea beheld and fled; Jordan turned back.'[35] 'Mighty was the roar of the waters';[36] 'the clouds poured down their waters,' as the Hebrew has it. 'The clouds gave forth their voice.'[37] They say this refers to God when He was seen in Mount Sinai. 'Your arrows also sped abroad. Your thunder resounded in a wheel.'[38] This they interpret as thunder and lightning: 'When God thunders, He rolls His voice along like a wheel.' You notice how, up to this point, I am hugging the ground and speak in the manner of the literal West.

'Your lightning illumined the world.' What do you gather from this, my Jew? 'Through the sea was your way, and your path through the deep waters.' Grant that this refers either to the sea or to the Jordan. 'Though your footsteps were not seen.' What does this mean literally? For the benefit of the unsophisticated, we have been giving you a literal interpretation; let us go back now for the spiritual message.

'The waters saw you, O God.' Let us quote from John's

---

33 Cf. Isa. 53.1.
34 Cf. *On Hebrew Names* PL 23.825 (12).
35 Ps. 113.3.
36 Cf. Ps. 76 (77).18.
37 *Ibid.*
38 Cf. Ps. 76 (77).19.

Revelation. 'The many waters,' he says, 'are many peoples.'[39] 'The waters saw you, O God.' What waters? 'And you waters above the heavens. Let them praise the name of the Lord.'[40] 'The waters saw you, O God?' What waters? Pure minds and hearts. 'The waters saw you and shuddered.' They feared, not from hatred, but from faith. 'The very depths were troubled.' Let us digress a bit for the sake of the spiritual implications. In the beginning of Genesis, it is written: 'And the spirit was stirring above the waters.'[41] It says also that 'darkness covered the abyss.'[42] You see, then, what it says in the beginning of Genesis; now for its mystical meaning. 'The spirit was stirring above the waters'; already at that time baptism was being foreshadowed. It could not be true baptism, to be sure, without the Spirit.[43] Over the abyss there certainly was darkness. This is the abyss[44] into which the devils implored Jesus not to send them. Over the abyss there was darkness. In the waters there was cleanliness; in the unfathomable depths, darkness. You know what the abysses are without my telling you— seeing that the demons were in dread of them.

'The clouds gave forth their voice.' The clouds, or prophets; they who were silent to the Jews spoke to us. 'The clouds gave forth their voice; your arrows also sped abroad': the preaching of the word of Christ has sped throughout the world. 'Your thunder resounded in a wheel.'[45] Thunder is the proper word for a mighty voice; in fact, at the time that God said: 'This is my beloved Son, in whom I am well pleased,'[46] His voice sounded like a peal of thunder. It is written, furthermore: 'Deep calls unto deep in the roar of our cataracts,'[47] this signifying the two Testaments, the New and the Old. 'Your

39 Cf. Apoc. 17.15.
40 Ps. 148.4, 5.
41 Cf. Gen. 1.2.
42 Gen. 1.2.
43 Cf. Letter 69.6, PL 22.660 (420); *Against the Luciferians* 6-7, PL 23.169 (177).
44 Cf. Luke 8.31.
45 Cf. Ps. 76 (77).19.
46 Matt. 3.17; 17.5; cf. John 12.28, 29; cf. Letter 78, PL 22.701 (470).
47 Ps. 41.8.

thunder resounded in a wheel.' Your teaching resounded in a wheel; the voice is majestic, for the teaching is sublime. 'Your thunder resounded in a wheel': throughout the world it rolls along in an orbit. Not only is it heard in Judea, but You speak and Your voice resounds throughout the world.

We have been speaking in a general way; let us now speak in particular about the interior man. A wheel, as you know, rests upon the ground with a very slight base. Nor does it merely rest; it rolls along; it does not stand still but barely touches the ground and passes on. Further, when it rolls onward, it always mounts higher. So the saintly man, because he has a human body, has to give some thought to earthly matters; and when it comes to food and clothing and other such things, he is content[48] with what he has, and merely touching the ground with them, hastens on to higher things. He who runs in haste to higher things carries within himself Your word. We read in the prophet: 'Holy stones roll over the land.'[49] Notice what he said: 'Holy stones roll over the land.' Because they are wheels, they roll over the land and speed on to higher places. Do you want to hear about more wheels? We read: 'And one wheel within another';[50] and again in Ezechiel: 'The wheels move one within the other.' The two wheels are the New and the Old Testament; the Old moves within the New and the New within the Old. And Ezechiel goes on: 'Wherever the spirit wished to go, there the wheels went.'[51] Ecclesiastes, moreover, says of the end of the world: 'And the broken wheel falls into the well.'[52] Much more could be said about wheels;[53] but our sermon speeds on to the rest of the psalm.

'Your lightning illumined the world' refers to apostolic preaching. 'The earth quivered and quaked.' If our earth had

---

48 Cf. 1 Tim. 6.8; cf. *Commentarioli on ps.* 76.19.
49 Cf. Zach. 9.16, LXX; cf. Letter 22.19, PL 22.406 (102).
50 Ezech. 1,16, 17; cf. Letter 53.9, PL 22.548 (280).
51 Ezech. 1.20.
52 Cf. Eccles. 12.6; cf. *Commentary on Ecclesiastes* 12.6, PL 23.1168 (492).
53 Cf. *Commentary on Ezechiel* 1.15-19, PL 25.27 (17).

not been thoroughly shaken and troubled, we would not be Christians. 'The earth quivered and quaked.' The Spirit of the Lord rests only upon the lowly, the peaceful, and those who tremble at His words.[54]

'Through the sea was your way,' through waves, through bitter waters, where the dragon dwells, where tiny fish cling. 'Through the sea was your way.' You who were in heaven descended upon earth. Following the literal sense we may say: At the time when Moses led forth, You were the one who led the way. 'Through the seas was your way.' Then again, and also in agreement with history, we may say: The seas were Your way. But that is history past and gone; on the other hand, He says to the sea every day: 'Peace, be still!'[55] The Lord calms you, O sea, to give us passage through this world. 'Through the sea was your way.' He came as the fountain of life to sweeten the sea, the bitter sea, the Dead Sea. That is why, according to Ezechiel,[56] a spring of living water issues out from the temple of the Lord and flows to the Dead Sea that contained in it no living creature. Not even tiny fish could live in it; nothing with life. From the temple of the Lord, that is, from His bosom, the Savior came forth and sweetened the Dead Sea and the bitter waters. 'Through the sea was your way, and your path through the deep waters.' Your way was through the sea, so that You might lead the way and Your apostles follow You. 'And your path through the deep waters.'

'Though your footsteps were not seen. You led your people like a flock.' The Good Shepherd led His people like a flock, 'under the care of Moses and Aaron.' This He did in actual fact and He does it also for us every day. 'Under the care of Moses,' that is, under the law, under the spiritual law. (We know, moreover, that the law is spiritual.[57]) 'And Aaron':

---

54 Cf. Isa. 66.2; cf. Letter 14.9, PL 22.353 (36).
55 Mark 4.39.
56 Cf. Ezech. 47.1-12.
57 Rom. 7.14.

that is, under the priesthood.[58] Under Your spiritual law
and under Your spiritual priesthood, You have guided us,
Your people. We may understand this historically of Moses
and Aaron. Moses—and Aaron, also—was conducted, but not
inducted, into the promised land. Jesus took Moses' place.
Be sure that you grasp the significance of what is written.
Moses died in the desert; Aaron died; Mary died; and hear
now what is written in the prophet: 'In a single month I did
away with three shepherds.'[59] They died, for they could not
enter the promised land. They merely looked over toward the
land of promise, but enter it they could not. The Jews beheld
the promised land but could not enter it. They died in the
desert and their dead bodies lie in the wilderness, the corpses
of those who died in the desert.[60] We, their children, under
the leadership of Jesus, have come to the Jordan and have
entered the promised land; we have come to Galgala and have
been circumcised with a spiritual circumcision, and have been
cleansed of the reproach of Egypt. Even now Jesus Himself,
our leader, holds the sword and always goes before us and
fights for us and conquers our adversaries; and for seven days,
we march around the city of Jericho, in other words, this
world. We sound the priestly trumpets and march around
Jericho, this world, and the walls fall and we enter, and consider ourselves victors. Next, we conquer the city Gai; then
go to Jebus, to Azor, to other cities; we conquer the enemies
that we were unable to vanquish under Moses.

Let us, therefore, thank our leader, Jesus, for with Him as
leader, with Him fighting for us, we are victorious. Josue it
was who commanded the sun to stand still and it obeyed, and
he was a great type of the Lord; he gave the commands, but
the Lord brought them to pass. He is outstanding as a conqueror; he, as I have said so many times, killed five kings in
the cave; he led us into the land of promise. Let us thank

---

58 Cf. Letter 78.2, PL 22.700 (469).
59 Zach. 11.8; cf. *Commentary on Zacharia* 11.8, PL 25.1503 (888).
60 Cf. Heb. 3.17.

him; he is the son of Nun (we read Nave); he is the one who was called Osee (we read Ause).[61] According to the Hebrew truth, he is not called Ause, but Osee, that is, savior, truly a savior, for he saved us and led us out of the desert into the land of promise.

---

61 Cf. Num. 13.8, 16; cf. *Against Jovinian* 1.21, PL 23.250 (270).

HOMILY 11

ON PSALM 77 (78)

OLY WRIT WARNS us to partake of the feast prudently when we have been invited to dine at the table of a rich man.[1] I might say that a rich man's table of Scripture has been laid before us. We enter a meadow filled with flowers; here the rose blushes; there the lilies glisten white; everywhere flowers abound in all varieties.[2] Our soul is drawn hither and thither to pluck the most beautiful. If we gather the rose, we leave the lily behind; if we pluck the lily, the violets remain. Likewise, in the seventy-seventh psalm, mystically fruitful in divine secrets, wherever you look the words are flowers of different kinds, and it is not possible to gather them all. We shall pick, however, as many as we can; from the few, we may contemplate the grandeur of the many.

'Understanding for Asaph.'[3] This title identifies the psalm and is a challenge to our understanding. Asaph was one of the choirmasters, like the sons of Chore, and Idithun, and the others. Consequently, this choirmaster is also a prophet. Because the theme is simple enough in its narration of history, necessity compels us to expound what is written in its historical character. 'In the land of Egypt, in the plain of Tanis, he cleft the sea and brought them through, and he made the waters stand as in a vessel. He led them with a cloud by day, and all night with a glow of fire,'[4] and so on. Obviously, this is plain historical fact. If, however, we accept a literal explana-

---

1 Cf. Prov. 23.1.
2 Cf. *Commentary on Zacharia* 14.20, PL 25.1540 (936).
3 Cf. Ps. 77 (78).1.
4 Cf. Ps. 77 (78).12-14.

tion, there is no reason for the title, 'Understanding for Asaph.' If, on the other hand, we direct our attention as the title demands, we have to look for one meaning in the letter and another in the spirit.

'Hearken, my people, to my law; incline your ears to the words of my mouth. I will open my mouth in a parable, I will utter mysteries from of old.'[5] Now you see how appropriate is the title, 'Understanding for Asaph'! In the next place, the prophecy itself begins with the words: Hearken My people to My law: not to the Law of Moses, but to My law. 'Incline your ears to the words of my mouth.' This same thought recurs in the Gospel verse: 'He who has ears to hear, let him hear!'[6] 'I will open my mouth in a parable': I will open to you that which was closed to the Jews; I will speak to you in parables. 'And without parables he did not speak to them,'[7] but to His disciples, however, He explained the parables in private. 'I will open my mouth in a parable': what I speak to them openly in parables, I shall make known to you in private. 'I will utter mysteries from of old.' For the word 'mysteries,' the Hebrew text has 'enigmas.' Everything is said enigmatically; the riddle, however, does not lie in the words themselves but in their import.[8]

Somebody may say to me: You are forcing Holy Writ, for whenever the title of a psalm is 'Understanding for Asaph,' you interpret that phrase in reference to the person of Christ. If we are Christians (we, who have received the baptism of Christ are, indeed, Christians and not only confess but profess that we are), because we are Christians, we must believe the evangelists. Now where it is written in the Gospel according to Matthew:[9] 'when our Lord and Savior had spoken in parables and the crowd did not understand him,' and so on with the rest of the Gospel, what is the evangelist's conclu-

---

5 Cf. Ps. 77 (78).1, 2.
6 Luke 8.8; cf. Letter 58.9, PL 22.585 (325).
7 Matt. 13.35; Mark 4.34.
8 Cf. *Commentary on Ezechiel* 17.1-7, PL 25.161 (190).
9 Cf. Matt. 13.

sion? 'All these things,' he says, 'were brought to pass that the
Scripture might be fulfilled: "I will open my mouth in parables, I will utter mysteries from of old." '[10] You see, therefore,
that the evangelist Matthew accepts that verse in the name of
Christ. When he had introduced the Lord as speaking in
parables beyond the comprehension of the people, he says:
This happened in fulfillment of the Scripture: 'I will open
my mouth in a parable, I will utter mysteries from of old.'

It seems that our question has been answered and that there
is no room for doubt, but pay close attention, for it is not
my desire to declaim rhetoric, but to penetrate the meaning
of Holy Writ. Besides, what has the Lord and Savior Himself
said? 'You search the Scriptures, and you will discover how
they bear witness to me.'[11] And to the Jews He said: 'You err
because you know neither the Scriptures nor the power of
God.'[12] Notice just what He says: 'You err.' In what way? By
not knowing the Scriptures. Moreover, because you do not
know the Scriptures, you do not know Christ who is the power
of God and the wisdom of God.[13] Consequently, Matthew
says: 'All these things were done in fulfillment of what was
spoken through the prophet Asaph.'[14] This is the reading
found in all the ancient scrolls, but men in their ignorance
changed it. As a result, to this day many versions of the Gospel
read: 'In fulfillment of what was spoken through the prophet
Isaia, "I will open my mouth in a parable, I will utter mysteries
from of old." ' This is not the utterance of Isaia, but of Asaph.

Indeed, Porphyry, that unbeliever, exploits this very point
in his attack upon us and says: 'Your evangelist, Matthew, was
so ignorant that he said: "What is written in Isaia the prophet:
I will open my mouth in parables, I will utter mysteries from
of old." ' Let us answer frankly: there is a similar problem

---

10 Cf. Matt. 13.34, 35.
11 Cf. John 5.39, 40.
12 Matt. 22.29.
13 1 Cor. 1.24; cf. Prolog. *Commentary on Isaia*, PL 24.17 (1-2).
14 Cf. Matt. 13.35; *Commentary on Matthew* 13.35, PL 26.95 (94-95).

in Matthew[15] and in John[16] where it is written that our Lord was crucified at the sixth hour, whereas in Mark[17] it is written that He was crucified the third hour. There seems to be a discrepancy here, but really there is none. The error was on the part of the scribes, for originally in Mark the sixth hour, likewise, was written, but many thought there was a gamma instead of an ἐπισήμῳ, the Greek number sign. Now, just as this was the scribes' error, it was, likewise, their error to write Isaia instead of Asaph. Hence, when the inexperienced (because the early Church was a congregation of ignorant peoples) were reading in the Gospel: 'In fulfillment of what was written in Asaph the prophet,' the one who first transcribed the Gospel began to ask: Who is this Asaph the prophet? He was not known to the people. And what did the scribe do? While amending an error, he made an error.

Let us take another example from Matthew's[18] Gospel. When Judas brought back the thirty pieces of silver and the chief priests would neither accept the money nor put it into the treasury because it was the price of blood, they bought with the money a potter's field as the burial place for strangers. The price of Christ is our burial place and the field is called Haceldama, that is, the Field of Blood—the field of the blood of the Jews, but our burial place, for we were strangers and foreigners,[19] and had no place to rest. He was crucified and died, and we were buried together with Him. Now Matthew says that this was done in fulfillment of the prophecy of Jeremia,[20] namely, that Judas brought back the thirty pieces of silver, the price that is written, and so on. Just as it is written, Matthew says, in Jeremia the prophet. That is what is written in Matthew and we have searched through Jeremia again and again and cannot find this reference at all. We

---

15 Matt. 27.45.
16 John 19.14.
17 Mark 15.25.
18 Matt. 27.6-11.
19 Cf. *Commentary on Zacharia* 11.12, 13, PL 25.1506 (891-92).
20 Matt. 27.9; cf. Letter 57.7, PL 22.572-3 (310); Zach. 11.12, 13.

have, however, located it in Zacharia.[21] You see, therefore, that this was an error similar to the one described above.

'What we have heard and know.' The verses, 'Hearken my people, to my law' as far as 'I will utter mysteries from of old,' are said in the person of Christ—the Savior Himself is speaking, but the remaining verses to the end of the psalm are to be understood in the name of the apostles. Hence, when the Lord says: 'Incline your ears to the words of my mouth,' He is saying: O Apostles, what you hear whispered, preach it on the housetops.[22] How do the apostles answer? 'What we have heard and know, and what our fathers have declared to us'; the things, Lord, that you are telling us, our fathers, patriarchs and prophets, have declared to us. 'What our fathers have declared to us, we will not hide from their sons; we will declare to the generations to come.' Their whole purpose in speaking was that we, their sons, might know. 'He established it as a law in Israel, that what he commanded our fathers they should make known to their sons,' that is, to us. (He spoke according to the flesh, but we understand according to the spirit); He spoke to them that they might hand down His word to us.

'Their sons yet to be born, that they too may rise and declare to their sons.' 'The place of your fathers your sons shall have.'[23] We are their sons. They have taught His message to us—we are their sons—and we have taught it to our own sons.

'That they should put their hope in God': that they may no longer believe in idols, but believe in God. 'And not forget the deeds of God': that they might recognize the order of creation and from the creature come to know the Creator. 'But keep his commands': not despise them as the Jews did, but diligently seek to obey them as Christians.

'And not be like their fathers': nor murmur, as some of them did in the desert and perished.[24] They should not murmur

21 Cf. *Commentary on Matthew* 27.9, PL 26.213 (228).
22 Matt. 10.27.
23 Ps. 44.17.
24 Cf. 1 Cor. 10.10.

as the Jews did and perish in the desert. 'A generation wayward
and rebellious.' I am not the one saying this; it is your prophet
who is saying this about you. 'A generation wayward and rebellious'; 'an evil and adulterous generation demands a sign,
and no sign shall be given it but the sign of Jonas.'[25] Why
did the prophet say 'wayward'? Because that generation became a bow with a false aim, for a bow is never aimed against
the one who shoots the arrow, but against foes. Although
this generation had been created straight by God and He held
it in His hand as a bow to shoot His arrows, nevertheless, it
'recoiled like a treacherous bow,'[26] and blasphemed against
its Creator.

'A generation that kept not its heart steadfast.' To this very
day Israel is perverse. 'Nor its spirit faithful toward God.'
Because Israel did not accept this Son, Israel did not receive
the Holy Spirit.

When the Holy Spirit descended in the form of a dove,
moreover, He did not descend upon the crowds of Jews, but
only upon Jesus. If, O Jew, you wish to receive the Holy
Spirit, believe in Jesus, for the Holy Spirit abides upon Jesus.[27]

'The sons of Ephraim, ordered ranks of bowmen.' O how
many mysteries, how many flowers! I do not say a day, but
a whole month would not suffice for the understanding of this
psalm. Every word is packed with meaning. We have a treasure
in such vessels of clay.[28] There are many who construe this
last expression in reference to the body and to the Holy Spirit,
meaning, of course, that we possess a treasure in earthen
vessels. There is certainly that interpretation, but I think the
better treasury-concept is that we have a most precious treasure
in vessels of clay symbolizing the homely words of the Scriptures.

'The sons of Ephraim, ordered ranks of bowmen, retreated
in the day of battle. They kept not the covenant with God;

25 Matt. 16.4.
26 Ps. 77 (78).57; cf. Letter 125.19, PL 22.1083 (946).
27 Cf. Luke 3.21; John 1.32-34.
28 2 Cor. 4.7.

according to his law they would not walk; and they forgot his deeds, the wonders he had shown them.' We have learned in the books of Kings[29] that under Roboam, the son of Solomon, Jeroboam, the son of Nabat, made a division among the people, and led ten tribes into Samaria. The tribes of Juda and Benjamin, however, remained under the rule of Roboam; and many likewise from the tribe of Levi who were dwelling in Jerusalem as priests and Levites—as it is written in Paralipomenon[30]—returned to the temple of God, that is, to Jerusalem. Thus, there were three tribes in Judea: Juda itself the royal tribe, and Benjamin, and later the Levites from the various tribes, when they had come to the temple.

They who were in Samaria had a king from the tribe of Ephraim. Just as they who held sway in Judea had a king from the tribe of Juda and from the family of David, so they who prevailed in Samaria had a king from the tribe of Ephraim, and their kings were called Ephraim. Let us study the prophet Osee and we shall discover that his whole prophecy is against Ephraim. He says in it: 'Ephraim is like a dove, silly and senseless.'[31] Notice that he compares him to a foolish dove. He left the temple and went to dwell in the woods. Now, doves always live in dovecots. Ephraim, in truth my dove, has abandoned the temple; he has deserted the house and lives in the woods; he dwells in the wilderness.

All this, incidentally, has been a literal interpretation, for it is necessary to take history into account. After this strict interpretation, however, we ought to mount by degrees, as it were by steps, to a higher plane. Then, we may say that the sons of Ephraim are all the heretics. They are the ones who have withdrawn from the house of God; they have deserted David and the kingdom of David and are living in the wilderness. They are called doves to be sure, because, although they read the Scriptures, nevertheless, their reading is folly.

---

29 Cf. 3 Kings 12; 2 Par. 10-13.
30 Cf. 2 Par. 11-13, 16.
31 Osee 7.11.

There is much to be said about this. 'The sons of Ephraim,
ordered ranks of bowmen.' Recognize all the heretics, for who
deserted Jerusalem? Who deserted the temple? Who live in
Samaria where they made the golden calves? 'One in Bethel
and the other in Dan.'[32] And see what it says: they made golden
calves in Bethel, in the house of God. In the house of God
they became idol worshipers. They did it also in Dan—unto
their own judgment and condemnation. They have abandoned
completely the house of the Lord and think of nothing but
gold. Somebody may ask: Why did they make calves of gold?
Our treasure has been preserved in vessels of clay.[33] Church
men are truly rustic and simple men, but all the heretics
are Aristotelian and Platonic. Briefly, that you may know that
gold is the usual simile for worldly eloquence, that the
heretic's tongue, for example, is as brilliant as gold, hear the
words of the prophet: 'Babylon was a golden cup in the hand
of the Lord.'[34] Note how he describes the Babylon of confusion
This world, therefore, is that golden cup. All nations drink
from that cup of gold.

'The sons of Ephraim, ordered ranks of bowmen.' No mat
ter who the heretics are, they all have their superstitions
They 'retreated in the day of battle.' They do not know Him
who said: 'Peace I leave with you, my peace I give to you,'[35]
but they do know how to speak with eloquence. They are
facile with words, but let them heed these words: 'Scatter
the peoples who delight in war.'[36] Somebody may object that
this is our way of thinking. Let us examine the words that
follow.

'They kept not the covenant with God; according to his
law they would not walk; and they forgot his deeds.' They rose
up against Him who regenerated them in baptism. 'The
wonders he had shown them; before their fathers he did

32 3 Kings 12.29.
33 2 Cor. 4.7.
34 Jer. 51.7; cf. *Commentary on Jona* 3.6-10, PL 25.1143 (420).
35 John 14.27.
36 Ps. 67.31.

wondrous things.' Take note that just as the meaning of
Scripture in respect to the sons of Ephraim rested upon history that is past and gone, the verse: 'I will open my mouth
in a parable, I will utter mysteries from of old' reveals that
the story is a parable.

'Before their fathers he did wondrous things, in the land of
Egypt, in the plain of Tanis. He cleft the sea and brought
them through; and he made the waters stand as in a vessel.
And he led them with a cloud by day.'[37] Somebody may say:
You are forcing Holy Writ for clearly it speaks about the
Israelites and their departure from Egypt. It is history. Besides,
we have read how the ten tribes abandoned God and became
idolatrous and adored calves of gold. Let us look into the times
of Asaph the prophet. He certainly lived at the time of David,
but under David the ten tribes had not yet separated. David
reigned forty years and Solomon another forty years. Eighty
years after, under Roboam, the ten tribes were divided. Obviously, what is said, therefore, does not aim at the ten tribes,
but rather is prophetical of the heretics.

'Before their fathers he did wondrous things.' The heretics
have forgotten their Father and His wonderful deeds in the
land of Egypt; in the darkness of this world, have forgotten
how by His deliverance they were reborn in the Church. And
after they have been reborn, the Church does not satisfy them.
'In the land of Egypt, in the plain of Tanis': where there was
idolatry, where the king of Egypt was, where Egyptian horsemen were, where Jamnes and Mambres resisted Moses,[38] where
the worship of idols flourished. We were all in Egypt and we
have all been delivered by the Lord.

'He cleft the sea and brought them through.' The Lord
walked on the sea, calmed the waves, and led us through. 'He
cleft the sea and brought them through.' To this very day,
O faithful monk, when you are being led forth from Egypt,
the sea is cleft, and that is how you are brought through. 'And

37 Cf. Ps. 77 (78).12-14.
38 Cf. 2 Tim. 3.8.

he made the waters stand as in a vessel.' (Instead of 'vessel,' the Hebrew text has 'mound.')

'He led them with a cloud by day.' 'See, the Lord is riding on a swift cloud on his way to Egypt.'[39] We must think of that swift cloud as befitting either the body of the Savior, because His body was light, not weighted down by any sin; or certainly holy Mary who was heavy with child by no human seed. Behold the Lord has entered the Egypt of this world on a swift cloud, the Virgin.

'He led them with a cloud by day.' Beautifully said, by day, for the cloud was never in darkness, but always in light. 'And all night with a glow of fire.' 'For you darkness itself is not dark, and night shines as the day.'[40] 'And all night with a glow of fire.' 'The Lord, our God, is a consuming fire.'[41] A consuming fire. The psalmist did not say what the fire is consuming; he left that to our intelligence. They who have built wood, hay, straw, on the foundation of Christ,[42] for them the Lord is a consuming fire. Fire has a two-fold nature: it gives light and it burns. If we are sinners, it burns; if we are just, it gives us light.

'He cleft the rocks in the desert.' The rock was struck for us in the desert. The rock was struck and from it water gushed forth, that Rock which says: 'If anyone thirst, let him come to me and drink';[43] and from within Him there flowed rivers. 'And gave them water in copious floods.' In the desert where there was no water, water has been made to flow in abundance for us.

There are so many things that could be said, and the psalm is endless, and time is prohibitive. Let us pray our Lord, however, that He cleave the sea for us, that for us the rock flow water in abundance, lest our bodies, likewise, perish and lie

---

39 Isa. 19.1; cf. *Commentary on Isaia* 19.1, PL 24.250 (290).
40 Ps. 138.12.
41 Cf. Deut 4.24; Heb. 12.29.
42 Cf. 1 Cor. 3.12; cf. *Against Jovinian* 2.22, PL 23.331 (360); Letter 48.2, PL 22.494-95 (213).
43 John 7.37, 38.

buried with the people in the desert. You know, of course, that the bodies of our fathers to this very day are lying in the wilderness. Believe me, whenever I see a synagogue, the thought of the Apostle[44] always comes to me: that we should not boast against the olive whose branches have been broken off, but rather fear; for if the natural branches have been cut off, how much more we who have been grafted on the wild olive should fear lest we become as our fathers, 'a generation wayward and rebellious, a generation that kept not its heart steadfast nor its spirit faithful toward God.' Because they do not possess the Spirit of God, they are dead and their bodies lie in the wilderness. I think of their synagogues as nothing but sepulchres in the desert. Read the ancient books for yourself. Let us pray the Lord that even these graves may rise again. If the sons of Abraham have become stones, it is possible for the dead sons of Adam to rise again if Jesus so wills. Even if they are dead and lie in graves, even if they have been there for four days, even if they are decaying, Jesus has the power to say: 'Lazarus, come forth!'[45]

---

44 Cf. Rom. 11.17, 18.
45 John 11.43; cf. Letter 4, PL 22.336 (14); 7.3, PL 22.340 (19).

HOMILY 12

ON PSALM 78 (79)

OR WE ARE brought very low.'[1] Because for our sake You became lowly and as one in sore need, we, too, are brought very low. This is 'The prayer of an afflicted one when he is faint and pours out his anguish before the Lord.'[2] Because You became poor, although You were rich,[3] we, too, have become poor and wretched.

'Help us, O God, our Savior.' In Hebrew the psalm has: 'Help us, O Jesus, our God.' Wherever, in fact, our text has 'Savior,' the Hebrew text has 'Jesus.' We know that when Gabriel[4] came to Mary, he said: 'Thou shalt call his name Jesus; for he shall save his people.' 'Help us, Jesus, our God.' Mark you that it says 'help.' Now, one who cries 'help,' is himself making an effort to be saved, for it is not while we are sleeping that God helps us, but while we are exerting ourselves. 'Because of the glory of your name, O Lord, deliver us';[5] because Your new name which is blessed among the Gentiles has been invoked upon us. 'And pardon our sins for your name's sake.' You the Savior, You the Christ, and we the Christians: have mercy upon us for Your name's sake.

'Let the prisoners' sighing come before you.' The followers of the teachings of Origen[6] are wont to maintain that the sighing of prisoners refers to the sighing of angels that are im-

---

1 Ps. 78 (79).8.
2 Ps. 101.1.
3 Cf. 2 Cor. 8.9.
4 Cf. Matt. 1.21; cf. Luke 1.31.
5 Cf. Ps. 78 (79).9.
6 Cf. *Against John of Jersualem* 17, PL 23.385 (423).

prisoned in bodies, for in the same way that shackles weigh down the body and prevent it from running, our bodies imprison souls—or angels—and hold them down to earth. What proof for this do they adduce from Scripture? 'Unhappy man that I am! Who will deliver me from the body of this death?'[7] And again from the Apostle: 'I desire to be released and to be with Christ,'[8] to return and to be with Christ. Be sure, they say, that you understand what the Apostle means; anyone who says, I desire to return, certainly means to that place where he had been before. 'Let the prisoners' sighing come before you.' I shall answer you very candidly, indeed, with the rustic simplicity of the churchman, for that is how the apostles gave their answers, that is how they spoke; they did not speak in diabolical rhetoric. 'It is better to return and to be with Christ.' That is the way it is rendered in Greek. The Greek does not have 'to be released' but 'to return';[9] to return and to be with Christ. Where Adam my father was, there is where I also long to be; I desire to return to that place whence he was banished. In Adam we have all been cast out of Paradise. 'Let the prisoners' sighing come before you.' What, in fact, prevents me from interpreting this simply as a reference to the martyrs who are confined in prisons? How many, in truth, have been sent to the mines! Most sincerely do I pray, may God graciously hear the cry of those captives.

'With your great power take possession of the children of those doomed to death.'[10] All of us, if only we deserve to be, are the sons of martyrs. When the Apostle was in prison, he was shackled; all the apostles were in chains when they were in prison; all the martyrs who have been killed in prisons were in chains. That is why Scripture says: Set free the sons of those who are doomed to death. 'And repay our neighbors sevenfold into their bosoms.' This does not seem to me a

---

7 Rom. 7.24.
8 Phil. 1.23.
9 Cf. *Commentary on Ephesians* 1.4, PL 26.476 (548-49); *Against Rufinus* 1.25, PL 23.437 (481).
10 Cf. Ps. 78 (79).11.

petition against our neighbor, but in his behalf and means
accordingly: Grant them Your sabbath. Sabbath, moreover, is
a synonym for rest. The real meaning is: Grant that they halt
in their malice; or else, surely, punish them now in this world
and not in the future.

'Then we, your people and the sheep of your pasture.' When
Holy Writ says sheep, it is a figure for the innocent. Sheep
have nothing save a shepherd. 'Will confess to you forever.'[11]
We will confess: either we will repent, or better still, we shall
give glory to You forever. 'Unto generation and generation':[12]
in the first people and in the second people. Ezechiel may have
spoken in the literal sense, but we shall interpret him spiritually and say that there are two nations implied where he says,
two sticks are united and made one kingdom.[13] 'Unto generation and generation we will declare your praise.' This is the
voice of the apostles, of Peter among the people of the circumcision; of Paul and Barnabas among the Gentiles.

11 Cf. Ps. 78 (79).13.
12 *Ibid.*
13 Cf. Ezech. 37.16-22; cf. Letter 74.3, PL 22.683 (448); *Commentary on Ezechiel* 37.15, PL 25.353 (440); *on Isaia* 54.4, 5, PL 24.518 (630).

NTO THE END, for the wine presses, a psalm of Asaph.'[1] It is written in the law that there are three solemn festivals: the Passover, Pentecost, and Tabernacles. The tenth day [of the month][2] before the feast of Tabernacles, was a fast day, and the fast lasted until evening. On this occasion they blew the trumpet, that is to say, they fasted and during the fast blew the trumpet, and ten days later came the feast of the Booths. Mark this attentively: three solemn festivals are described in the law: first the Passover, second Pentecost, third Tabernacles. Before Tabernacles a fast; during this fast, moreover, trumpets sounded. Consider the full impact of Holy Writ. Remove the veil that was placed over the eyes of Moses,[3] and see that we cannot become Tabernacles unless we have fasted beforehand. Unless that same fast, moreover, is the banner of victory to keep off our adversaries, Amalec is not conquered.[4] Because there are three solemn celebrations, Passover, Pentecost, Tabernacles, there are, likewise, three psalms bearing the title 'for the wine presses': the eighth, the eightieth, and the eighty-third. You see, then, why in the psalter three psalms have 'for the wine presses' in their title. Notice that they are the eighth, eightieth, the eighty-third.

Before we discuss the symbolism of number, let us examine the significance of the phrase 'for the wine presses.' 'For the

---

1 Cf. Ps. 80 (81).1.
2 Day of Atonement? Cf. Num. 9; 10; 28; 29; Lev. 23; 25.9.
3 Cf. Exod. 34.34.
4 Cf. Exod. 17.11-13.

wine presses.' There are no wine presses except where there
is a vineyard and a plentiful harvest of grapes. 'For the wine
presses.' The Lord and Savior says: 'The wine press I have
trodden alone, and of my people there was no one with me.'[5]
That is why He brought the vine out from Egypt and trans-
planted it.[6] Further, by Jeremia, He says: 'I had planted you
a choice vine of fully tested stock; how could you turn out
obnoxious to me, a spurious vine?'[7] Noe drank wine and became inebriated. Then, too, Solomon says, and it is said with
mystery: 'Drink my friends and be inebriated.'[8] Again in
another place, we read about Joseph, that holy man who was
a type of our Lord the Savior[9] who was sold by his brothers
—by his own brothers—and who ruled in Egypt, just as our
Lord and Savior was sold by the Jews and reigned in the
Egypt of this world. Joseph, as I was saying, was a holy man,
an especially holy man who conquered cruelty with true piety;
who was sold into Egypt, not by chance, but that he might
supply Egypt with food and his own brothers, too, who had
sold him. That Joseph invited his brothers to dine. But just
listen to what happened: 'And he drank, and became merry
at noon.'[10] Is that true, and is it literally possible that a holy
man became drunk? Noe also was inebriated, but had been
really inebriated. Joseph had been intoxicated; Noe also was
intoxicated, and he was intoxicated in his own house. See
there is a mystery. First, let us review the mystery itself, and
when we have done that, let us fathom its meaning. After
the deluge, Noe drank and became drunk in his own house
and his thighs were uncovered and he was exposed in his
nakedness. The elder brother came along and laughed; the
younger, however, covered him up.[11] All this is said in type of

---

5 Isa. 63.3.
6 Cf. Ps. 79 (80).9.
7 Jer. 2.21.
8 Cf. Cant. 5.1; cf. *Against Jovinian* 1.30, PL 23.265 (286).
9 Cf. Letter 109.2, PL 22.908 (727).
10 Cf. Gen. 43.25, 34.
11 Cf. Gen. 9.20-24.

the Savior, for on the cross He had drunk of the passion: 'Father, if it is possible, let this cup pass away from me.'[12] He drank and was inebriated, and His thighs were laid bare —the dishonor of the cross. The older brothers, the Jews, came along and laughed; the younger, the Gentiles, covered up His ignominy.[13] Hence, the imprecation: 'Cursed be Chanaan; meanest of slaves shall he be to his brethren.'[14]

Behold, that condemnation continues down to this day. We, the younger people, give orders to the older people, the Jews. As the Lord is inebriated in His passion, His saints are inebriated every day in the ardor of their faith, inebriated in the Holy Spirit. You, who yesterday were heaping together gold, today, you are throwing it away. Are you not a madman to those who do not know what it is all about? Finally, when the Holy Spirit descended upon the apostles and filled them and they spoke many different languages, they were accused of being full of new wine.[15]

There is a great deal more that could be said on the mystery of wine and inebriation. 'Unto the end, for the wine presses, a psalm of Asaph': the eighth psalm, the eightieth, and the eighty-third. No other number could have wine presses except the eighth, eightieth, eighty-third. The eighth day, symbol of the day of Resurrection, is in the singular number. On the other hand, the eightieth in eight decades is a different and greater number. You note that these wine presses are superscribed only on the day of Resurrection, the eighth day and the eightieth. Someone may ask: Why does it say wine presses later on in the eighty-third psalm? These wine presses belong to the mystery of the Trinity. That is why there are also three choirmasters. In the eighth it says, a psalm of David; in the eightieth, a psalm of Asaph; in the eighty-third, a psalm of the sons of Core. The eighth is of David, and David means brave

---

12 Matt. 26.39.
13 Cf. *Against the Luciferians* 22, PL 23.185 (195).
14 Gen. 9.25.
15 Acts 2.13.

in battle. Because our first victory is full of wrestling and warfare, it is symbolized by David, brave in battle. Our second
victory, in the eightieth psalm, is truly typified by Asaph. The
meaning of Asaph is assembly.[16] In the eighth psalm, we are
victorious, and in the eightieth, we gather together with the
Lord. The eighty-third, however, is of the sons of Core, and
Core signifies Calvary. 'Go up, thou bald head; go up, thou
bald head';[17] that is what the boys shouted at Eliseus, for
he had suffered in the place called the Skull [Calvary]. Much
could be said on how Eliseus was laughed at in Bethel by
forty-two boys. These are the wine presses about which the
Savior says: 'Make friends for yourselves with the mammon
of wickedness, so that when you fail they may receive you
into the everlasting dwellings.'[18]

'For it is a statute in Israel, an ordinance of the God of
Jacob.' What ordinance is this of the Lord? In victory to
acclaim God; not presume it our own, but to acknowledge it
as the Lord's.

'When he came forth from the land of Egypt. An unfamiliar
speech he heard.'[19] When we came out of the land of Egypt,
we, too, heard a language unknown to us. Who of us knew
the Gospel? Who the apostles? Who the prophets? We came
forth from Egypt, and we heard an unfamiliar speech and we
learned a language that we had never known of before.

The next verse continues right along with: 'He relieved his
shoulders of the burden.'[20] When we were in Egypt, in slave
labor we built the cities of Pharao; we carried clay and brick
and wore ourselves out in search of straw. We had no grain;
we had no divine bread that came down from heaven. Not
yet were we given heavenly manna; not yet had the bronze
serpent been mounted on the pole for us; not yet had the rock
yielded its water; not yet were we extending our arms and

---

16 Cf. *Commentarioli in ps.* 80.1.
17 4 Kings 2.23; cf. Luke 23.33; Matt. 27.33; Letter 46.3, PL 22.485 (201).
18 Luke 16.9.
19 Cf. Ps. 80 (81).6.
20 Cf. Ps. 80 (81).7.

Amalec was losing in battle. We were sitting in mud and we were slaving for Egypt; we were building the cities of Pharao.

'He relieved his shoulders of the burden.' What heavy burdens we endured in those days! That is why our Moses says: 'Come to me, all you who are burdened with sins, and I will give you rest.'[21] 'His hands were enslaved in a basket.'[22] Whose hands? Israel's. Some are Egypt's baskets; others are Jesus'. Jesus has His own baskets. He filled twelve of them with fragments, our Savior did. O wondrous deed communicating sublime secrets! Five thousand people were in the desert not counting women and children. Only five loaves were found in that place for it was barren. I am going to ask you a question, you who admit only a literal meaning. There are only five loaves of bread to be found in the desert and yet how do you account for twelve baskets? Certainly, if the place was barren, there could not be twelve baskets of fragments! Now listen to the whole explanation. The Lord led His people forth from Egypt into the desert of this world. He fed them with His bread and whatever was left over He stored away in twelve baskets, that is, in the twelve apostles; so that what had been lost in the twelve tribes[23] might be saved in the twelve apostles.

'In distress you called, and I rescued you.' The prophets and the psalms are perplexing because suddenly without any warning there is a change in person. Up to this verse the prophet has been speaking; now, all of a sudden, it is God who speaks to the people.[24] 'In distress you called, and I rescued you.' Whenever you are in trouble, do not be disturbed; call upon Me and in My mercy I shall give you a gracious hearing. 'Unseen, I answered you in thunder': I was in the midst of that storm, the storm that was crushing you and tossing you about like waves hither and thither. 'I tested you at the Waters

---

21 Cf. Matt. 11.28.
22 Cf. Ps. 80 (81).7.
23 Cf. Letter 108.13, PL 22.889 (704).
24 Cf. *Commentarioli in ps.* 80.8.

of Rebellion.'[25] Strictly, this verse speaks of Moses and Aaron, for they offended God at the waters of contention;[26] that is precisely the reason why they did not enter the promised land. It is to us, moreover, that God says: I tested you in the midst of waters of rebellion. Simon was tested at the waters of rebellion because he received baptism hypocritically. Anyone, therefore, who is not sincere in the reception of baptism proves it at the waters of strife and discord.

'Hear, my people, and I will admonish you.' God is speaking to us. Whatever He said to His people, He speaks also to us. 'O Israel, will you not hear me?' What is it you ask me to heed? Let us see what He commands. 'There shall be no strange god among you.' The man whose god is his stomach has a strange god. We have as many alien gods as we have vices and sins. I give way to anger; anger is my god. I look upon a woman covetously; lust is my god. The thing that each one covets and worships, that is his god. The miser has a god of gold. 'Nor shall you worship any alien god.' Our God is virtue; the god of others is vice and sin.

'I, the Lord, am your God who led you forth from the land of Egypt.' We are the ones who have been rescued from the land of Egypt, if, indeed, we have left Egypt; if we are in the desert; if we long to see the promised land. If we have abandoned Sodom, let us not look back at Sodom. We have been rescued on the mountain. Let us not sigh for the flesh pots of Egypt, let us not complain: How well off we were in Egypt when we were eating meat with vegetables and so on, and cucumbers.[27] Do you want to receive food from the Lord? Do you want to feed upon the Lord Himself, your Lord and Savior? Hear what He has to say: 'Open wide your mouth, and I will fill it.' Open wide your mouths; He is both Lord and Bread. He exhorts us to eat and He is Himself our food. However wide you open your mouth, that much you will

---

25 Cf. Ps. 80 (81).8.
26 Cf. Num. 20.7-13; Exod. 17.7.
27 Cf. Num. 11.5.

receive, for that is in your power, not in Mine. If it is your desire, you shall receive all of Me; if you do not want all, you shall receive at least a part.

'But my people heard not my voice.' I am standing at the door and am knocking.[28] I want you to open, and I shall enter; but you do not want to open. 'And Israel obeyed me not; so I gave them up to the hardness of their hearts; they walked according to their own counsels.' Unhappy the man whom the Lord does not chastise. Anyone whom the Lord does not punish while he is sinning is most unfortunate. For that reason the Lord says: I gave them up to the hardness of their hearts. I gave them up because I have punished them many times and they have refused to submit to My authority; I have called and they have not listened; I have struck them and they have not even felt the blow. I am giving them up to their own desires that either they may be surfeited with their own vices or else be driven to repentance.

'If only my people would hear me.' O most clement Father,[29] O merciful God! He pleaded with His people and they did not listen. Like an angry father, He sends His wanton son away. Once more He sees him on the road to perdition, and grieves because he is destroying himself. And what does He say? 'If only my people would hear me; and Israel walk in my ways, quickly would I humble their enemies.' Was it a mighty thing for Me to deliver you from tribulation? Was I not able to exercise My sovereign power and snatch you away from danger?[30] But because I have given you up to your own free will, and have set before you a race course, and I am giving the crown only to the winner, I am leaving the victory to your own efforts.

'The enemies of the Lord have lied to him.'[31] The Hebrew text is better: 'the enemies of the Lord will deny him,' which means, His enemies, the Jews, will deny Him. But these

---

28 Cf. Apoc. 3.20.
29 Cf. *Commentary on Isaia* 1.24, PL 24.40 (27).
30 Cf. *Commentarioli in ps.* 80.14, 15.
31 Cf. Ps. 80 (81).16.

enemies who are going to deny Him, will they, therefore, perish? Will there not be remnants? How, then, did You swear to Abraham, and Isaac, and Jacob that their seed would be as the stars in the sky and as the sands of the sea? Why did You make a promise to the fathers and then not render it to their sons? 'The enemies of the Lord will deny him.' What does that mean? 'But their fate would endure forever.' 'When the full number of the Gentiles shall enter, then all Israel shall be saved.'[32] In the future, they will believe; up to the present, they have not believed. I shall now address the Jews, for they are always bragging and boasting: their time will be forever. Let this be our answer: It is true, for of the Jews there are going to be some who believe. In fact, we read in the Apocalypse[33] of John that twelve thousand from each tribe, that is, 144,000 are going to believe; and this is the number of virgins.[34] When, moreover, will there be as great a number of virgins as of non-virgins? So let us say to the Jews: Your time will be unto eternity, that is, in the future world. But what is the message for you who today do not believe? 'But their fate would endure forever.' Your fate will be the same as that of the enemies of God.

'And he fed them with the fat of wheat.'[35] He led them into the land of promise. He fed them, not with manna as in the desert, but with the wheat that had fallen, that had risen again. 'And he fed them with the fat of wheat.' Be sure you penetrate the mystery in the scriptural words: 'With the fat of wheat.' Does wheat have fat? Does it also have intestines? The prophet wanted to show the abundance and richness of spiritual grace, hence, called it fat. 'And with honey from the rock he would fill them.'[36] He is the wheat; He also is the rock[37] who slaked the thirst of the Israelites in the desert. He

---

32 Cf. Rom. 11.25, 26; cf. *Commentarioli in ps.* 80.16.
33 Apoc. 7.4-8.
34 Cf. Apoc. 14.14; cf. *Against Jovinian* 1.40, PL 23.281 (305).
35 Cf. Ps. 80 (81).17.
36 *Ibid.*
37 Cf. 1 Cor. 10.4.

satisfied their thirst spiritually with honey, and not with water, so that they who believe and receive the food taste honey in their mouth. 'How sweet to my palate are your promises, sweeter than honey to my mouth!'[38] Lastly, that is why our Lord ate honeycomb after the Resurrection, and was satisfied with honey from the rock. I am going to tell you something new. The Rock Himself ate honey in order to give us honey and sweetness, so that they who in the law had drunk myrrh, or bitterness, might afterwards eat the honey of the Gospel.

---

38 Ps. 118.103.

HOMILY 14

ON PSALM 81 (82)

OD ARISES in the divine assembly.' There are many different postures that one adopts. Frequently we are sitting down; sometimes we are standing; other times we are lying down; at times we are running; then again we are walking. In the same way, God is described in terms of human individual differences, and His attitude is represented in a variety of ways. If we are saints, then, we are like Moses, and God says to us: 'You wait here near me,'[1] for that is what He said to Moses. Now Moses at that time was standing on a rock; hence, for him, God also was standing. If, however, from saints we have afterwards become sinners, for us God no longer is standing, but is walking about; He who before had been standing for us moves from His place. As soon as we change, God changes at the same time with us. I may even say, as long as Adam was in Paradise and observed the law, God for him was standing. After Adam sinned, however, he heard the voice of God who was now walking about in the Garden of Eden. Would you like proof that as far as Adam was concerned God was walking? What did God say to him? 'Adam, where are you?'[2] He who had not avoided God while He was standing, fled from Him walking.

We have talked about standing; we have talked about walking; let us talk about sitting. Whenever God is represented as seated, the portraiture takes one of two forms: either He appears as the ruler or as the judge. If He is like a king,

1 Deut. 5.31.
2 Cf. Gen. 3.9.

102

one sees Him as Isaia does: 'I saw the Lord seated on a high and lofty throne.'[3] There He is presented as the sovereign king. When He is portrayed as judge: 'Thrones were set up, and the books were opened.'[4] This description comes from the Book of Daniel. What does it mean? 'Thrones were set up, and the books were opened': the Lord shall be seated upon a throne as judge and He shall rehearse everyone's deeds. The books that up to that time had been closed will then be opened. We shall give an account of everything we do, every word we utter, every thought, even the most idle word;[5] everything is recorded in God's books. Some think that there are actually books in heaven in which our sins are inscribed. I think these books are our consciences[6] which will be revealed on that day, and each one will see for himself just what he has done. 'There is nothing concealed that will not be disclosed.'[7] So thrones were placed, and the books were opened. How much is written in my book, I dare not confess even to my brother, nor to my friend! The angels know what I have done; the thrones know; the seraphim know; the Father and the Son and the Holy Spirit knows.

We have mentioned how for some God is standing; for others He is walking; for still others, indeed, He is seated either in the role of king or of judge; but for another some in truth He sleeps. If at any time He abandons us to temptation—granted we are saints, nevertheless, we are abandoned to temptations in order to prove ourselves—at that time, for us God is asleep. In fact, what does the psalmist say? 'Awake! Why are you asleep, O Lord?'[8] For the apostles, too, when they were in the boat and the waves were beating in upon them, the Lord was asleep and that is why their boat was

---

3 Isa. 6.1; cf. *Commentary on Isaia* 6.1, PL 24.91 (88).
4 Cf. Dan. 7.9, 10; cf. *Commentary on Isaia* 3.13, PL 24.67 (58).
5 Cf. Matt. 12.36.
6 Cf. *Commentary on Daniel* 7.10, PL 25.532 (699).
7 Matt. 10.26; Luke 12.2.
8 Ps. 43.24.

being tossed about. At length they rouse Him, He awakes, and immediately the storm subsides and the sea is calm.

We have discussed four of God's postures; for some He stands; for some He walks; for some He sits; for some He seems to sleep, but for others He awakes and arises. 'God arises in the divine assembly.' Because they were gods, for them God was standing. In all our assemblies, God takes different positions: He is standing for some; for others He is seated; for some He is walking; for others He is sleeping. Although God is in Himself immutable, He adapts Himself to our human individuality. Just appreciate the dignity of man! 'God arises in the divine assembly.' He bestows a title of that kind upon us that He may also bestow its merit. 'He judges in the midst of the gods.' As a commander in the midst of His army He judges gods. 'He judges gods'—a fearful thought, full of terror. If He judges gods, what does He do about the sinner?

The psalmist uttered the last two verses as a prophet. In the next short verse, however, God Himself is speaking to the judges, that is, to the rulers of the people: 'How long will you judge unjustly?' The following versicles are addressed especially to judges. If they are secular judges, the sense is obvious; but if they are judges of the Church, we must understand them to be bishops and priests. 'How long will you judge unjustly?' He who perverts justice is the judge of injustice; he is that unjust judge of whom the Gospel says he neither feared God nor respected man.[9] 'How long will you judge unjustly?' I gave you power over My flock and over the people of God; you must be judges, not wolves.

'And favor the cause of the wicked? Defend the lowly and the fatherless; render justice to the afflicted and the destitute,' and so on. When jurisdiction falls to you, it is not the case that you espouse, it is not the legal process, but the persons who have the lawsuits. If, for example, a poor man comes with

---

9 Luke 18.2.

just grounds for redress and a rich man with a criminal claim, you respect the persons and not the case. This, by the way, is just one manner of interpretation. There is also another more hallowed explanation. It is frequently a practice in the theatre for one actor to have many different masks[10] and thereby to play many different roles. At one time he steps into the mask of a woman, at another time that of a man, now that of a king; and the one who had just appeared as a king, comes out again in the character of a slave. I have given this example that from the carnal we may arrive at the spiritual. We ourselves assume different characters. When I am angry, I put on the mask of a lion; when I grasp at other peoples' property, I play the part of the wolf; when, indeed, I am cruel and a murderer, I am wearing the mask of a brutal man. In the same way that sinners wear different masks in their sins, saints also have different masks but in their good deeds. When I give alms, I have, as it were, the mask of a kind person; when truly I do right in judging, I have the mask of a good judge; when I suffer an injury with humility, then, mine is the mask of a humble man. Unhappy the man who has many masks for evil; happy the man who has a variety of masks for good.

'They know not, neither do they understand; they go about in darkness.' Who? Evil judges. Those whom I was calling gods, are called wicked judges because of their vice. 'They know not' Me; 'neither do they understand' My judgment; 'they go about in darkness.' They grope in darkness because they have forsaken the light. I have said: 'You are the light of the world,'[11] but you have turned away from the light, and have become darkness. Because that is what they have done, let us see what follows.

'All the foundations of the earth are shaken.' You see the kind of punishment meted out to evil rulers; because of evil judges the foundations of the earth are shaken. Thus far we have been giving the literal sense, namely, that the convulsion

---

10 Cf. Letter 43.2, PL 22.479 (193).
11 Matt. 5.14; cf. Letter 15.1, PL 22.355 (38).

of the whole world is due to wicked judges. Let us now, however, look into a different meaning. 'All the foundations of the world are shaken.' I shall overthrow wicked judges that have laid their foundations on earth and not in heaven; they who should have for their foundation Christ, upon whom the architect Paul[12] built, rejected Him and laid their foundations upon earth.

'I said: You are gods, all of you sons of the Most High.' Let Eunomius hear this, let Arius, who say that the Son of God is son in the same way that we are. That we are gods is not so by nature, but by grace. 'But to as many as received him he gave power of becoming sons of God.'[13] I made man for that purpose, that from men they may become gods. 'I said: You are gods, all of you sons of the Most High.' Imagine the grandeur of our dignity; we are called gods and sons! I have made you gods just as I made Moses a god to Pharao,[14] so that after you are gods, you may be made worthy to be sons of God. Reflect upon the divine words: 'With God there is no respect of persons.'[15] God did not say: 'I said, You are gods,' you kings and princes; but 'all' to whom I have given equally a body, a soul, and a spirit, I have given equally divinity and adoption. We are all born equal, emperors and paupers; and we die as equals. Our humanity is of one quality.

'Yet like men you shall die.' You see, therefore, that man will die. God does not die. Adam, too, as long as he obeyed the precept and was a god, did not die. After he tasted of the forbidden tree, however, he died immediately. In fact, God says to him: 'The day you eat of it, you must die.'[16] The Hebrew has a better way of expressing this: 'But you like Adam shall die.' Just as Adam was cast out of the Garden of Eden, so, likewise, were we. 'And shall fall like one of the princes.'[17]

---

12 Cf. 1 Cor. 3.10; cf. Letter 48.2, PL 22.494-495 (213).
13 John 1.12.
14 Cf. Exod. 7.1.
15 Rom. 2.11.
16 Gen. 2.17.
17 Cf. Ps. 81 (82).7.

Since the Lord had said: 'all of you sons of the Most High,'
it is not possible to be the son of the Most High, unless He
himself is the Most High. I said that all of you would be
exalted as I am exalted. But, you 'shall fall like one of the
princes.' It is precisely because we had been so elevated that
we are said to have fallen.

Where are they who say that the devil was created the devil?
Where are they who say that an evil nature had been created
by God? The Hebrew text admits of two alternatives.[18] You,
indeed, like Adam shall die; just as your father refused to
obey the command of the Lord and thereby fell, even so you
shall die. That, to be sure, was said of Adam. But in the words
that follow: 'you shall fall like one of the princes,' who is this
prince who fell? If you mean Adam, he has already been taken
care of in the earlier versicle: yet like Adam you shall die. At
the same time, grasp the import of the words: Yet like Adam
you shall die. Adam died; we, too, are subject to death, but
the devil who was a prince and fell did not die. It is not
possible for the angelic order to submit to death, but only to
damnation; hence, He said you shall fall like one of the
princes. 'How has the morning star fallen, the son of the
dawn?'[19] Behold, here he fell, and there he fell. He fell, for
his dwelling place was always in heaven. He is the one to
whom the words of Ezechiel are addressed: 'You were stamped
with the seal of perfection.'[20] Notice exactly what the prophet
says: 'the seal of perfection.' He did not say to the devil, you
are the sign of perfection, but the seal of perfection. God had
set His impression upon you and made you like unto Himself;
but you afterwards destroyed the resemblance. You were created in the image and likeness of God.

In that same prophecy[21] it says, moreover: 'With the Cherub
I placed you; you were in the Garden of God among precious

---

18 Cf. *Commentarioli in ps.* 81.7.
19 Cf. Isa. 14.12; cf. Letter 22.4, PL 22.396 (90).
20 Ezech. 28.12; cf. *Commentary on Ezechiel* 28:11-20, PL 25.269 (331).
21 Cf. Ezech. 28.13, 14, 16; cf. *Against Jovinian* 2.4, PL 23.302 (328).

stones, the beryl and the garnet. And you fell,' Ezechiel says
'and were banned from the mountain of the Lord.' This princ
is the king of Tyre, the king of Tyre from the time he fell—
inasmuch as Tyre in Hebrew means SOR, that is tribulation.[2]
That prince, therefore, who at first was in heaven, has no
become the king of Tyre, the king of the tribulation of thi
world. 'You shall fall like one of the princes.' Since it say
'like one,' it shows that there are others also. Read the Apoc
lypse[23] of John: when the dragon fell from heaven, he dre
down with him a third part of the stars.

Up to this point, God has been speaking to man; once mor
the prophet speaks. 'Rise, O God; judge the earth.' Rise, fc
our boat is being tossed about by the waves. 'Rise, O Goc
judge the earth'; for evil judges are not rendering judgmen
but perverting Your law and slaughtering Your flocks. Ris
O You, who are the true Judge. Because the wicked judges ai
dead like Adam, and have fallen like one of the princes, Yoι
rise; You, judge; You, save Your creature. 'But the hirelin
sees the wolf coming and leaves the sheep and flees';[24] he ca
not suffer for a stranger as he suffers for a father and a mothe

Let us express this otherwise. Arise, You who have suffere
for us and have died for us; arise and save us. Let us say th
in still another way. You who have come in humility and lo
liness, come as a judge and set us free. 'Rise, O God; judge tl
earth.' Note the proper meaning and the exact choice of worc
He did not say, judge heaven, but judge the earth; henc
earth is judged, not heaven. If, therefore, earth is to be judge
and not heaven, sins are not committed in heaven. If, ho
ever, sins were committed in heaven, he would say: Ris
O God; judge earth and heaven. Notice the clemency of tl
prophet. He did not say, destroy earth; but judge, judge ai
save. He did not say, judge through Your angels, judge throuς
Your ministers, for if they judged, they could not be mercifι

---

22 Cf. *Commentary on Ezechiel* 26.1-6, PL 25.240 (294).
23 Apoc. 8.12.
24 John 10.12.

they are the executors of Your judgment. But if You judge, You Yourself can be merciful. 'Rise, O God; judge the earth.' The emperor is able to change his sentence; the governor, on the other hand, cannot. That is why we are imploring You to be Judge, not in a spirit of defiance, but with entreaty. Men and angels are cruel, indeed, when compared to You; You alone are the most kind Judge. Do you want me to prove that God is compassionate, whereas every man is cruel? While the householder was asleep, his enemy came and sowed weeds among the wheat. The servants want to root up the weeds, but the householder says: 'No, let them grow, lest in gathering the weeds you root up the wheat along with them.'[25]

'For you shall inherit all the nations.'[26] We pray that You be Judge because You have compassion on all nations. What was the prophet's intention in saying: 'You shall inherit all the nations,' instead of, You shall have all the nations? Whenever an inheritance has been bestowed, death has preceded; hence, we are called heirs and co-heirs. Heirs, the Apostle said, of Christ because Christ died for us; co-heirs because Christ will reign with us.

'You shall inherit.' You sent Your servants (we revert again to the apostles), one among the circumcised, another among the Gentiles. As long as You had sent Moses, as long as You had sent Isaia, as long as Jeremia, as long as all the other prophets, God was renowned in Juda, in Israel great was His name.[27] Knowledge of God's name was heralded to a moderate part of the earth. You sent Peter, Peter the fisherman who had let down his nets, who had calloused his hands with hard work. You did not send an orator, You did not send a philosopher; You sent a rustic, a fisherman. That fisherman, that rustic from Jerusalem, ruled throughout Rome; a rustic captured the Rome that the eloquent could not. Next, Paul the Apostle went forth from Jerusalem and preached the word of God all

---

25 Cf. Matt. 13.29.
26 Cf. Ps. 81 (82).8.
27 Cf. Ps. 75.2; cf. Letter 60.4, PL 22.591 (333).

the way to Illyricum. He preached where the Gospel had not been preached before, lest he build[28] on another man's foundation. After that, he says, from Rome he intended to set out for Spain.[29] See, Paul the persecutor, who had been a persecutor in Judea, preaches among the Gentiles! Where are they who proclaim Alexander, the great Macedonian Commander, because in such brief time he conquered so many nations? He had an army, he had vast multitudes; yet he was not able to accomplish anything really stupendous but rather something comparatively slight. But this Paul, a one time persecutor, who used to say: 'Even though I be rude in speech, yet I am not so in knowledge,'[30] who commits so many solecisms in speaking, carries the Cross of Christ and as a victor captures all. He conquered the whole world from the ocean all the way to the Red Sea.[31]

Somebody may say: But they did all that for the sake of money. Porphyry says: Rustic men and paupers, because they had nothing, worked certain wonders with magic arts. There is nothing to boast about in performing wonders. The magi worked wonders in Egypt in contradiction to Moses. Apollonius worked wonders, Apuleius, too; in fact, they performed any number of marvels. I grant you, Porphyry, that the men you mention, worked signs by the arts of magic in order to obtain riches from wealthy common women whom they had seduced; for that is what you say. Why did they die? Why were they crucified? Some did work miracles with magic arts, but they did not give their lives for a man who had died, for a man who had been crucified. They know that man has died for Him, yet they do not die for a worthy cause. Happy, indeed, is our victory consecrated in the blood of the apostles. By their blood alone our faith is confirmed. Let us, therefore, bless God to whom is glory forever and ever. Amen.

---

28 Cf. Rom. 15.20.
29 Cf. Rom. 15, 24, 28; cf. Letter 71.1, PL 22.669 (431).
30 2 Cor. 11.6.
31 Cf. *Commentary on Amos* 5.8, 9, PL 25.1043 (290-291).

HOMILY 15

ON PSALM 82 (83)

GOD, WHO IS like to you?'[1] Because there is no one like You, we look for no other Creator except You. 'Be not silent, O God, and be not still!' We are silent; do You intercede in our behalf. This is the voice of the just man, for he who says: 'Be not silent, O God,' is at peace with his conscience.

'For behold, your enemies raise a tumult.' By following the tropological method of interpretation, we are able to apply this verse to the Church and to heretics. Then again, in accordance with its literal character, we can take it as a reference to the Jews and the rest of the nations that on all sides were assailing Judea. 'For behold, your enemies raise a tumult.' The psalmist purposely called the garrulousness and detraction of adversaries a tumult. 'For behold, your enemies raise a tumult.' See what he says: they made a noisy commotion; they made a clinking sound in my ears like tinkling cymbals. 'Tumult' is the word, for one hears only an uproar and does not distinguish a voice; hence, the meaning: They were uttering words, to be sure, as if they were determined to denounce me, but what I heard was not at all a voice, only a noise. 'And they who hate you lift up their heads.' Notice that the man who holds his head high in arrogance hates God. 'God resists the proud, but gives grace to the humble.'[2]

'They who hate you lift up their heads.' If you ever have anything against another, if a brother disparages you, and

---

1 Cf. Ps. 82 (83).2.
2 James 4.6; Peter 5.5; Prov. 3.34; 18.12; cf. Letter 76.1, PL 22.689 (456).

you are humble for the sake of Christ while your opponent is haughty for the sake of the devil, you are imitating Him who says: 'Learn from me, for I am meek and humble of heart.'[3] But the proud man who glorifies himself follows the example of him who says: 'I will scale the heavens, above the stars I will set up my throne; I will be like the Most High!'[4] 'And they who hate you lift up their heads.'

'Against your people they plot craftily.' All that is necessary is to be God's people. 'They conspire against those whom you protect.' No need here for interpretation; the implication is obvious enough. 'They say, "Come, let us destroy their nation." ' Let them be wiped out as a nation because they are the people of God. 'Let the name of Israel be remembered no more!' Blotted out be his name who knows God by experience!

'Yes, they consult together with one mind.' Unfortunate creatures that we are, unhappy people of God; it is not possible for us to be as united in good as wrong-doers are allied in evil. 'And against you they are allied: The tents of Edom and the Ismaelites.' Perceive that there is mystical meaning concealed in these names. 'The tents of Edom and the Ismaelites, Moab and Agarenes, Gebal and Ammon and Amalec, the strangers with the inhabitants of Tyre; the Assyrians, too, are leagued with them; they are the forces of the sons of Lot.'[5] There are eleven nations fighting against the saints. Because they fought against saints, they could not reach the perfect number, twelve. 'The tents of Edom.' Edomites do not live in stable houses with firm foundations, but in tents that they easily move about from place to place. The name Edom has a twofold connotation, sanguinary or terrene.[6] Distinguish, therefore, the enemies of the saints; the tents of Edom are the worldly. 'And the Ismaelites.' The Ismaelites represent those who are a law unto themselves, who yield to

---

3 Matt. 11.29.
4 Cf. Isa. 14.13, 14.
5 Cf. Ps. 82 (83).7-9.
6 Cf. *Commentarioli in ps.* 107.

their own capricious hearts and evil desires. Ezechiel expresses the same thought: 'Son of man, prophesy against the
prophets that prophesy their own thought, and do whatever
their spirit impels.'[7] We, however, must not follow our own
inclinations and be labeled Ismaelites, 'obedient to themselves,' but rather be called Ismael, 'obedient to God.'[8] 'Moab'
means 'from the father'; therefore, those who withdraw from
God the Father.[9] 'Agarenes'[10] are proselytes. They who were
to be the blest dwellers of God have become proselytes.
'Gebal' connotes a 'fruitless valley'; GE is the equivalent of
valley and BAL surely implies empty. These enemies of
God's people are not, therefore, from the mountain, but from
the fruitless valley. 'And Ammon' indicates a confused people
who place their trust in the mob and not in true childlike
faith. 'Amalec' means 'licking the ground,'[11] for the adversaries of the people of God do not eat of heavenly bread,
but lick the ground like snakes. 'Strangers': wherever our
text has the word 'alienigenae,' the Hebrew has 'Philistines.'[12]
As 'Philistines' means 'dying from a poisonous draught,'[13] the
interpretation is that they who have been inebriated from
the cup of the devil fall headlong in their drunkenness. 'With
the inhabitants of Tyre.' The Hebrew for Tyre is SOR,
which means 'anguish and tribulation.'[14] They who should
have been only pilgrims in this world have become attached
to it, thus the assailants of God's people live in SOR, that is,
in the anguish and tribulation of their soul.

Now let us see whom such great foes of the saints have for
their leader, whether it be the Savior or the devil? What does
it say in the next verse? 'The Assyrians, too, are leagued with

7 Cf. Ezech. 13.2, 3.
8 Cf. *Hebrew Questions on Genesis* 16.11, PL 23.1012 (330).
9 Cf. *Commentary on Isaia* 15.1, PL 24.167 (184); *Hebrew Questions on Genesis* 19.36, PL 23.1017 (335).
10 Cf. *On Hebrew Names*, PL 23.819.
11 *Ibid.*
12 Cf. *Commentary on Isaia* 2.8, PL 24.48 (36).
13 Cf. *On Hebrew Names*, Lagarde 6.12; Letter 65.4, PL 22.625 (376).
14 Cf. Letter 65.18, PL 22.635 (388); *Commentary on Isaia* 23.1, PL 24.275 (320).

them.' The Assyrian is Nabuchodonosor, the enemy of God who led His people into captivity. Although they seem to have a great number of nations fighting on their side, nevertheless, their leader is the Assyrian, or the devil, for the Assyrians 'are the forces of the sons of Lot.' The name 'Lot' designates 'one who turns aside.'[15] Evil spirits formerly were angels who fell with the devil and became his satellites, just as it is written in John's Book of Apocalypse that the dragon fell from the heavens and drew down with him a third part of the stars.[16] What, then, does the prophet mean? This: they who have come with so many nations to attack Your people and have with them the Assyrians, and the devil for their leader, are the forces of the sons of Lot—the fallen angels—who have turned aside from You and are doing just what evil spirits do.

You see that these are very difficult passages; you appreciate their obscurity, how practically every word is packed with divine secrets, and that we are forced from necessity to pause over a Hebrew vocabulary so loaded with mystery. We certainly are not engaged in airing a point of rhetoric, but are endeavoring to understand and explain what the Holy Spirit said. Unless we interpret this passage as we have done, what benefit is it to the churches of Christ to read of the tents of Edom, and the Ismaelites, and so on, with all the other names?

Because these nations have come as enemies against Your people, let us hear what judgment the psalmist calls down upon them. 'Deal with them as with Madian; as with Sisara.' You have read the Book of Judges; this is that Madian[17] whom Gedeon defeated. 'As with Sisara and Jabin.' Jabin and Sisara are the foes whom Debora and Barac[18] conquered. 'At the torrent Cison, who perished at Endor.' Debora and Barac destroyed Sisara, the general of

---

15 Cf. Letter 66.11, PL 22.645 (401); *Commentary on Ezechiel* 25.1, PL 25.234 (286).
16 Apoc. 8.12.
17 Judges 7, 8.
18 Judges 4.

the army. So much for what Scripture says; learn now what
it means. Lord, because they are so arrogant, because they
have come with a mighty army, because their prince is
Nabuchodonosor the king of the Assyrians,[19] because they are
the forces of the sons of Lot, because they follow the example
of the fallen angels, because in their pride they have claimed
equality with You; for all these reasons, I beg of You to
overpower them, not by a man, but to their shame by a
woman.

'They became dung on the ground.' Who? Madian,
Sisara, and Jabin, these three became putrid on the ground
like dung. The name 'Madian' means 'one who is negligent
of judgment.' The warriors against Your people are heedless
of the judgment that is to come. 'Sisara' is understood as
'the vision of a horse.' Your people's enemies are not of Your
flock or of Your herd, but are stallions that rage with madness
over the fillies.[20] Stallions are always ready for battle. 'And
Jabin.' 'Jabin' means 'discernment.' They who trust in their
own wisdom and not in the glory of God rot on the ground
like dung. They who were glorying in their army, whose
king was the Assyrian, and who used to boast 'I will scale
the heavens,'[21] not only fell down to earth, but on the ground
became dung.

'Make their nobles.' What nobles? Those who fight against
Your people. 'Like Oreb and Zeb; all their chiefs like Zebee
and Salmana.' I suppose you have read in the Book of Judges
the story of Gedeon, who is also called Jerobbaal, how he out-
witted those four kings while fighting for the people of God
and put an end to them. And notice the kind of nobles
these Madians are who abandoned the judgment of God:
'Oreb and Zeb; all their chiefs like Zebee and Salmana.'
Who would dream that such words contain mysteries of the
Savior? The philosophers read them and smile; the rhetori-

---

19 Cf. Letter 123.16, PL 22.1057 (914).
20 Cf. Commentary on Jeremia 5.7, 8, PL 24.715 (875).
21 Isa. 14.13.

cians read them and sneer. Not only the rhetoricians, however, but the Jews, too; they have not the key to their treasures, for a veil covers their eyes.[22] 'Oreb' means a 'hole in which a snake lurks'; 'Zeb' equals 'wolf.' Mark, now, the names of the chiefs of Christ's opponents: 'Zebee,' 'victim or spoil that the wolf will strangle'; and 'Salmana,' 'masters of malice.' See, then, the divine secrets hidden away in names? 'Who said, "Let us take for ourselves the dwelling place of God." ' They bragged, but they did not accomplish their boast for God was fighting in behalf of the people He had set apart for Himself.

'O my God, make them like a wheel.'[23] Notice the mercy of the phophet; he does not pray against them, but for them. See what he says: My God, who art the God of all, my very own God, O my God, make them like a wheel. They who lay their foundation in malice, let them have no foundation at all, but let them roll back and forth and never remain fixed in their malice. 'Like chaff before the wind. As a fire raging in a forest.' 'Like chaff': not as the wheat, but as chaff; if there is anyone among them who is nothing but stubble and chaff, let him perish. 'As fire raging in a forest.' The psalmist did not say 'fruit-bearing trees' but a woodland that bears no fruit. If, therefore, anyone is like stubble, non-productive of grain, if anyone is like a forest of trees without fruit, let him perish. 'As a flame setting the mountains ablaze,' let the pride that is in them burn up.

'So pursue them with your tempest and . . . with your storm.' Do what? Will You strike them down? No, 'rout them' in order to save them. 'Darken their faces with disgrace' in order to dismay them. Why do that? 'That men may seek your name, O Lord.' You see how he is pleading, not against them, but for their salvation. Besides, note what he says in the following verse: 'Let them be shamed and put to rout forever, let them be confounded and perish'; let them cease

---

22 2 Cor. 3.15; cf. Letter 58.9, PL 22.585 (325).
23 Cf. Ps. 82 (83).14; cf. *Commentarioli in ps.* 82.14.

to exist as far as their evil is concerned, but let the good in
them be saved. Notice that this perdition does not signify
annihilation but salvation. What comes next? 'Knowing that
you alone are the Lord, the Most High over all the earth.'
Let him who will, exalt himself and be exalted; but let us say:
'You alone are the Most High over all the earth.' No matter
how high anyone may exalt himself, we have God who is
Lord over all.

HOMILY 16

ON PSALM 83 (84)

NTO THE END, for the wine presses. A psalm of the sons of Core.'[1] There are three psalms with the phrase, 'for the wine presses,'[2] as part of their title: the eighth, the eightieth, and the eighty-third. The eighth is superscribed with David's name, the eightieth with the name of Asaph, and the eighty-third with the sons of Core. I am going to give you a rule whereby you may know what to look for in Scripture. Any psalm that has the sons of Core in its title will always be joyful without any note of sadness. Whereas Core, and Dathan, and Abiram were punished by the Lord for their revolt against Moses,[3] the sons of Core, who did not rebel with their father, were blessed with eternal joy. Further, since the name of Core means Calvary [or skull][4] and obviously symbolizes the place of the Resurrection, whoever is a son of Core is a son of the Resurrection. A son of the Resurrection, moreover, can never be sorrowful.

'How lovely are your tabernacles, O Lord of hosts! My soul yearns and pines for the courts of the Lord.'[5] Shortly after this verse, the psalmist cries: 'Happy they who dwell in your house!' Note that there is a triad of dwelling places: tents, courts, and last of all, houses. 'How lovely are your tabernacles, O Lord of hosts!' What are these tabernacles? Let us turn to the Gospel and see if it offers a clue to their

1 Cf. Ps. 83 (84).1.
2 Cf. *Commentarioli in ps.* 8.1.
3 Cf. Num. 16.
4 Cf. Letter 65.4, PL 22.625 (376).
5 Cf. Ps. 83 (84).2, 3.

118

identification. The Lord is speaking and says: 'Make for yourselves friends with the mammon of wickedness, so that when it fails they may receive you into the everlasting dwellings.'[6] When what fails? The mammon of wickedness. Then those friends will welcome you into everlasting dwellings. Mark well that the mammon of wickedness fails in this world; nevertheless, be aware that this mammon of iniquity provides a man with alms and prepares beforehand reward or penalty. In the Hebrew language,[7] 'mammon' is the term for wealth, not gold, as some people think. 'With the mammon of wickedness.' Much truth there is, indeed, in a certain saying of a philosopher: 'Every rich man is either wicked or the heir of wickedness.'[8] That is why the Lord and Savior says that it is difficult for the rich to enter the kingdom of heaven.[9] Someone may raise the objection: 'How, then, did the wealthy Zachaeus enter the kingdom of heaven?' He gave away his wealth and replaced it at once with the riches of the heavenly kingdom. The Lord and Savior did not say that the rich will not enter the kingdom of heaven, but that they will enter with difficulty.

'How lovely are your tabernacles, O Lord of hosts!' The sole ambition of some people is to possess property; others long to be enriched with the wealth of the world; still others wish to hold prominent places at conventions and be esteemed among men. But for me, there is only one longing: to see Your eternal dwelling places. To me, those are the lovely dwelling places where the virtuous and not the vicious congregate. 'My soul yearns and pines for the courts of the Lord.' This is my one desire, this my only love, that I may see

---

6 Cf. Luke 16.9; cf. Letter 54.12, PL 22.556 (289); 71.4, PL 22.671 (433); 77.11, PL 22.697 (466); 79.4, PL 22.726-27 (501); 108.16, PL 22.892 (707); 118.4, PL 22.963 (795); 123.6, PL 22.1050 (904); 130.7, PL 22.1111 (981); *Against Vigilantius* 14. PL 23.366 (399).
7 Cf. Letter 121.6, PL 22.1019 (865); 22.31, PL 22.417 (116); *Commentary on Matthew* 6.24, PL 26.46 (36); cf. Acts 21.40.
8 Cf. Letter 120.1, PL 22.984 (821).
9 Matt. 19.23; cf. *Commentary on Matthew* 19.23, PL 26.143 (149); Letter 79.4, PL 22.727 (501); 145, PL 22.1192 (1080).

Your courts. Notice the order. First, he longs for the tabernacles, tents without a foundation and easily portable. A
tent, moreover, is always on the move, folded up and carried
hither and thither. Courts, on the other hand, although
certainly not houses, do have a kind of foundation, and from
the court we enter the house. Our psalmist, therefore, at
first longs for a tabernacle, and then afterwards pines and
yearns with love to see Your courts; and when he is in Your
court, then he cries out: 'Happy they who dwell in your
house!'

'My heart and my flesh cry out for the living God.' It is
difficult for anyone's body and soul to be in perfect harmony.[10]
If it is true, as the Apostle says, that the spirit struggles against
the flesh and the flesh against the spirit,[11] what mean the
words: 'My heart and my flesh cry out'? This prayer can be
his alone whose whole soul is fixed in the love of God. 'My
heart and my flesh'; that is the same thought that another
psalm expresses: 'For you my flesh pines and my soul thirsts.'[12]
'My flesh.' This is the flesh that longs for the Lord, of which
it is written in another place: 'And all mankind shall see the
salvation of God.'[13] But that flesh of which Scripture says:
'All mankind is grass,'[14] does not desire the Lord. 'My heart
and my flesh.' Meditate with me upon any chaste man who
deems the death of his flesh gain for his soul. Fasts and harsh
treatment are the mortification of his flesh. What is the
Apostle's judgment? 'To deliver such a one over to Satan for
the destruction of the flesh, that his spirit may be saved.'[15]
Unless the flesh die, the spirit cannot be enlivened; therefore,
the Apostle also says: 'For when I am weak, then I am
strong.'[16] Let each one reflect for himself on how true it is
that when he has become weak and faint from fasting, his soul

10 Cf. *Commentarioli in ps.* 83.3.
11 Cf. Gal. 5.17.
12 Ps. 62.2.
13 Luke 3.6.
14 Isa. 40.6.
15 1 Cor. 5.5.
16 2 Cor. 12.10.

is vigorous, his thoughts are wholly preoccupied with God, and he repeats over and over again: 'How lovely are your tabernacles, O Lord of hosts!'

'Even the sparrow finds a home, and the turtle-dove a nest in which she puts her young.'[17] For the present, let us be satisfied with a simple interpretation. Notice all that the verse implies: I long, O Lord, for Your eternal dwelling places; my soul yearns and pines for the courts of the Lord; I long for some place to dwell, a nest for my soul and my body. The birds that fly about to and fro with no restraint, nevertheless, after their flight, have a place and a nest in which to rest. How much more ought not my body and soul procure for itself a resting place?

Now let us mount to something higher. 'In the Lord I take refuge; how can you say to me, "Flee to the mountain like a sparrow"?'[18] Take heed that it is only the sparrow that migrates to the mountains. 'And the turtle-dove a nest.' This is the turtle-dove of which the Canticle of Canticles says: 'The voice of the dove is heard in our land.'[19] 'The turtle-dove a nest.' The dove is a chaste bird.[20] It never makes its abode in low places, but always builds its nest high up in lofty treetops. As the birds of purity, the sparrow and the dove, make their nests in the higher places, so the tabernacles, courts, and houses are not on this lowly earth, but on high in the kingdom of heaven. Note further what the psalm says: 'Happy they who dwell in your house!' We do not stay in tabernacles, we sojourn; in the courts, no matter how long we are there, we do not remain as dwellers, but as pilgrims, for from the courts we move on into the house. When we have come into the house, however, what does the psalmist say? 'Happy they who dwell in your house,' the house that has a foundation, for from that house we shall never depart, though from the courts we may.

17 Cf. Ps. 83 (84).4.
18 Cf. Ps. 10.2.
19 Cant. 2.12.
20 Cf. *Against Jovinian* 1.30, PL 23.263 (285).

'Happy the man whose strength you are!' Truly, do we long for Your tabernacles, and Your courts, and Your house, but to attain our hearts' desire is not within our power; it does not depend upon our strength, but upon Your help. 'Their hearts are set upon the pilgrimage.' Who have set their hearts upon pilgrimage? The blessed who find their strength in the Lord; they are the ones who determine to ascend step by step. Day by day, the saint reaches out for the better things before him, unmindful of what is past. That is, in fact, why in the Psalter there are fifteen gradual canticles, and the first song of ascent begins with the words: 'In my distress I call to the Lord, and he answered me';[21] the second with: 'I lift up my eyes toward the mountains; whence shall help come to me?';[22] the third: 'I rejoiced because they said to me.'[23] The saint is always moving forward, advancing steadily and ascending to heights ever more sublime; that is the meaning of 'their hearts are set upon the pilgrimage.' Happy the man who makes progress daily, who does not weigh what he did yesterday, but makes his resolution for today and keeps it. The holy man sets his heart on ascending; the sinner, on descending. Just as the saintly man progresses day by day, the sinner regresses day by day. Happy the man who wholeheartedly ascends the highways.

Consider now the logical sequence of Holy Writ. 'Through the vale of tears, in the place that he has set.'[24] Where it says, 'through the vale,' we immediately picture a mountain. Where, then, is the man who has set his heart on mounting upwards step by step? In the valley of tears.[25] Let us reflect for a moment that we are in this valley: we are not on the mountain; we are not in the Garden of Eden; we are not on the heights of Paradise; but in the lowliness of earth, of an

---

21 Ps. 119.1; cf. Letter 7.3, PL 22.340 (19); 53.8, PL 22.546 (277).
22 Ps. 120.1.
23 Ps. 121.1.
24 Cf. Ps. 83 (84).7.
25 Cf. *Commentarioli in ps.* 83.7; Letter 22.10, PL 22.400 (95); 130.16, PL 22.1120 (993).

earth, furthermore, over which hangs a curse which brings forth for us thistles and thorns, the food of serpents, and of which it is said to Adam: 'For dust you are, and unto dust you shall return.'[26] As long as we are in the vale of tears, we must not laugh but weep, for the Lord says: 'Blessed are you who weep now, for you shall laugh.'[27] For the time being, we are in the valley of tears, and this world is the place for weeping, not for rejoicing. We must not laugh, for this is the world and this is the time for tears; the future world is the world of joy. 'Through the vale of tears, in the place that he has set.' What does the psalmist mean by 'in the place that he has set'? He means in the valley of tears. 'In the place that he has set': God has entered us as contestants in a race course where it is our lot to be always striving.[28] This place, then, a valley of tears, is not a condition of peace, not a state of security, but an arena of struggle and of endurance.

'For the lawgiver will give a blessing.'[29] Somebody may ask: 'Why in the valley of tears, in the place that God has set for the contest—or for the conflict—why has He placed us as athletes? Why has He willed us to fight?' The psalmist himself gives the answer: He has willed that this place be set for us as an arena that He may reward our victory with a crown. 'For the lawgiver will give a blessing.' This Lawgiver, our President of the contest,[30] has willed us to contend only that He may bless us. Just consider what the victory means! What are the blessings of this Master of the Games? 'They go from strength to strength'; they win the victory here that they may receive the crown there. If a man of courage gives evidence of strength here, there he becomes stronger. 'They go from strength to strength'; hence, unless we are strong here, we cannot have greater strength there. The psalmist did not say, they shall go from weakness to strength, but from strength

---

26 Gen. 3.19.
27 Luke 6.21.
28 Cf. Heb. 12.1-3; Letter 22.3, PL 22.395 (89).
29 Cf. Ps. 83 (84).7.
30 Cf. Letter 71.2, PL 22.670 (432); *Against Jovinian* 1.12, PL 23.238 (257).

to strength. Do you want to be a man of fortitude there?
Then be one here first. Do you want to be crowned there?
Fight here.

'They go from strength to strength.' We can say this in
another way: 'Christ the power of God and the wisdom of
God.'[31] He who has power here, there will possess Power
Himself. 'They go from strength to strength.' What gain
will they have when they go from strength to strength?
What will be their reward? 'They shall see the God of gods
in Sion.' 'Blessed are the pure of heart, for they shall see
God.'[32] Reward enough for the victors is the face of Christ,
reward enough for those who have fought! To see God is
an infinite crown. 'They shall see the God of gods in Sion.'
What joy, what happiness to go from strength to strength
and win the sight of Christ as due reward!

'Behold, O God, our Protector, and look upon the face of
your Christ.'[33] Mark what he says: 'And look upon the face
of your Christ.' Mind, it is man who is earnestly praying that
the Father look upon the face of the Son. Realize what he
means. The Apostle asked: 'Do you seek proof of the Christ
who speaks in me?'[34] and the Savior Himself answered: 'He
who receives you, receives me';[35] therefore, what the psalmist
is saying is: Look upon us, for in us You behold Your own
Son who dwells in us.

'I had rather one day in your courts than a thousand elsewhere.' Notice that he says 'one day.' A certain commentator
thinks that this verse must be understood to mean: I had
rather have little in the kingdom of heaven than possess
everything here that this world offers. That is a true and very
good interpretation. Let us say, however: If it were possible
for anyone to be in the kingdom of heaven for a single day and
after that be cast out, rightly would he say, I had rather one

---

31 1 Cor. 1.24.
32 Matt. 5.8.
33 Cf. Ps. 83 (84).10.
34 2 Cor. 13.3.
35 Matt. 10.40.

day in Your courts. Actually, this is the meaning of 'one day':
the kingdom of heaven is one day; there is no night, nor
darkness, but always light. Whoever is in the kingdom of
heaven for one day is there forever.

'I had rather lie at the threshold of the house of my God,
than dwell in the tents of the wicked.' This thought is akin
to what the Savior says about John: 'Amen I say to you,
among those born of women, there has not risen a greater
than John the Baptist.'[36] Besides this, He even calls John
an angel.[37] Then He adds: 'Yet the least in the kingdom of
heaven is greater than he.' Now His meaning is: John is
greater than all men, and if you want to know, he is even
an angel; nevertheless, he who is an angel [messenger] on
earth is the very least in the kingdom of heaven, that is, he
is of a lesser rank than the angels. Moreover, he who is a
minor in the kingdom of heaven, that is, an angel,[38] is greater
than he who is greater than all men on earth. What the
prophet means, therefore, by his words: 'I had rather lie at
the threshold of the house of my God,' is: I have chosen to be
the least in heaven rather than the first in this world. 'I had
rather lie at the threshold of the house of my God, than dwell
in the tents of the wicked.' Attend carefully to what he says:
'than dwell in the tents of the wicked.' Tents are without
foundations and perishable; the sinner, for all that, is never
one who dwells near earth but who dwells in it and holds
on to it.

'For God loves mercy and faithfulness.'[39] God's love embraces both mercy and fidelity. If He were only merciful, He
would be inviting us all to sin; if He loved only faithfulness,
no one would have any hope of repentance. God, therefore,
has recourse to both and tempers one with the other. If you
are a sinner, heed the mercy of God and do not despair, but
do penance. If, on the other hand, you are just, do not grow

---

36 Matt. 11.11.
37 Cf. Matt. 11.10.
38 Cf. *Commentary on Matthew* 11.11, PL 26.74 (70); *Against the Luciferians* 7, PL 23.170 (178); *Against Jovinian* 2.27, PL 23.338 (367).

careless because God is clement, for God is just and loves faithfulness.

'Grace and glory he bestows.' The prophet did not say the Lord gives glory and grace, but what did he say? 'Grace and glory he bestows.' First, He grants pardon to the sinner; then, He bestows a crown.

'The Lord withholds no good thing from those who walk in sincerity.' The Hebrew wording, 'in perfection,' is better, for sincerity is not complete virtue. Unless the guileless have wisdom besides, their virtue is incomplete and imperfect; hence, the Lord says in the Gospel: 'Be wise as serpents, and guileless as doves.'[40] 'O Lord of hosts.' Grasp the full import of 'Lord of hosts.' Whenever we are guilty of any sin, God who is the Lord of hosts, is not our Lord, for He is not the Lord of sinners but of the just. 'Happy the men who trust in you!' The man who trusts in the Lord is the man whose conscience is free from sin, who lifts his eyes to heaven with assurance. The trustful man is he who knows that he has committed no offense against his Lord.

39 Cf. Ps. 83 (84).12.
40 Matt. 10.16.

ON PSALM 84 (85)

NTO THE END. A psalm of the son of Core'[1] is the title of the eighty-fourth psalm. As I have said frequently before, you will always find joy and never sadness in a psalm that has 'for the sons of Core' in its title. This is so because the sons' joy is to console the father's sorrow. Reread the psalms with that in mind and you will discover that wherever you come upon the title, 'of the sons of Core,' you will find no sadness. I have remarked likewise many times that the name Core signifies the place of Calvary [or the skull] and must, therefore, connote joy.

Now, then, who is this Core? He is the man who was making his way up from Jericho to Bethel. Bethel means the 'House of God.' Note this carefully: anyone in Jericho who wants to go to the House of God has to climb upward along the road; hence, our Core, that is, Eliseus, is making his way upward from Jericho to Bethel, the House of God. As he approaches the city, forty-two young boys come out from Bethel—from the House of God, from the synagogue where first had been the House of God—and mock Eliseus, our Core, crying out: 'Go up, thou bald head; go up, thou bald head.'[2] He is on his way to his own house and he is made sport of by urchins from Bethel. Eliseus, truly that most patient of men who had come to Bethel in order to save the city, at length turned and looked back; looked back and commanded two bears to come forth from the forest, and the

---

1 Cf. Ps. 84 (85).1.
2 4 Kings 2.23.

bears came and they tore the forty-two boys to pieces. Even
so our Lord, that is, our Core, when He had come into
Bethel ready for His Ascension and was mocked by young
boys, command two bears, Vespasian and Titus, to come forth,
and they destroyed the forty-two boys. Who are these forty-
two boys? From the Ascension of Christ to the destruction
of Jerusalem, there are forty-two years. Ponder this diligently
and you will find that it is so. Thus, for forty-two years after
His Resurrection and Ascension to Bethel, the Lord gave His
people the opportunity to repent, but because they cried
out in derision: 'Go up, thou bald head; go up, thou bald
head,' two bears came out and killed them.[3]

'You have favored, O Lord, your land.' This refers to the
coming of the Savior and is properly historical; later, after
we have considered its history, we shall discuss its tropological
significance. 'You have favored, O Lord, your land.' We have
said that this verse speaks of the coming of the Redeemer.
The land which had offended You and had been defiled by
idolatrous worship has been redeemed at Your advent. 'You
have favored, O Lord, your land.' Let this be the prayer of
the sinner, in view of the fact that he has obtained pardon:
Lord, You have blessed this clay of Yours. Even though it
has brought forth thistles and thorns,[4] it is, nevertheless,
Your creature and for that reason has been restored. 'You
have restored the well-being of Jacob,' of those who have
believed in Christ. 'You have restored the well-being of
Jacob': every sinner is held captive. 'You have forgiven the
guilt of your people'; not on account of their works, but
because of Your mercy, You have delivered Your people; 'you
have covered all their sins.' Down to the very last word, this
psalm, as I have indicated, tells of the coming of the Savior.

'Kindness and truth shall meet. Near indeed is his salvation
to those who fear him, glory dwelling in our land.'[5] Veritably

---

3 Cf. Letter 120.8, PL 22.993 (833).
4 Cf. Gen. 3.18.
5 Cf. Ps. 84 (85).10, 11.

has the glory of God dwelt in our land, and furthermore: 'justice has looked down from heaven; the Lord himself will give his benefits.'[6] What benefits? 'Our land shall yield its increase': Mary, our clay, our flesh, has yielded her fruit. 'Justice shall walk before him': the virgin earth has brought forth the fruit of justice.

Thus far, we have given the historical character of the psalm; now let us turn to the tropological method of interpretation. 'You have forgiven the guilt of your people.' Remission presupposes a debt. 'You have covered all their sins': You have covered them with virtues, so their sins do not appear; You have, for example, covered injustice with justice, impurity with purity, blackness with whiteness. 'You have withdrawn all your wrath; you have revoked your burning anger.' 'Restore us, O God of our salvations.'[7] Note the meaning: Because it was Your will to do so, You have mercifully revoked Your burning anger. 'Restore us, O God': You have turned away from wrath; You have turned us away from sin.

'Restore us, O God of our salvations.' Why did not the psalmist say 'our salvation' instead of 'our salvations'? If we were sinning just once, we would need but one salvation; but we have sinned many times, hence, are in need of many salvations. 'Will you not instead, O God, give us life?'[8] Until the Lord restores us to life, we are dead. 'Show us, O Lord, your kindness, and grant us your salvation.' The Savior's descent is the work of God's mercy. He would not have come as a Physician if most men were not sick. Because so many were sick, He came as Physician; because we were in need of compassion, He came as Savior.

'I will hear what the Lord God proclaims within me.'[9] Many there are who think that when Moses and Isaia, and the others, say: 'Thus saith the Lord'; and that when the

6 Cf. Ps. 84 (85).12, 13.
7 Cf. Ps. 84 (85).5.
8 Cf. Ps. 84 (85).7.
9 Cf. Ps. 84 (85).9.

Scripture says: 'The word of the Lord came to Isaia'—or to Ezechiel—'the prophet,' that the communication comes from God externally and that the prophet hears actually with his ears the word of the Lord. This is not so. What does our Lord Himself say to the Pharisees and the Jews? 'He who has ears to hear, let him hear.'[10] And Isaia says: 'The Lord has given me an ear.'[11] Comprehend what he means: 'The Lord has given me an ear.' Because I did not possess that ear which is of the heart, He gave me one that I might hear God's message. Whatever the prophet hears, therefore, he hears in his heart, for just as we cry in our hearts, 'Abba, Father,' and the cry is a silent one and the silence is heard by the Lord, in that same way the Lord speaks to our heart that cries, 'Abba, Father.' So it is that the prophet now says: 'I will hear what the Lord God proclaims within me.'[12] Such is the meaning also of the prophet Habacuc in: 'I will stand at my guard post, and keep watch to see what answer the Lord will give me and what answer I will give Him,'[13] and I will hear what the Lord God proclaims within me. The words: 'I will hear what the Lord God proclaims within me,' refer, therefore, to what the Lord speaks in the heart—in the understanding.

Would you like to know what this cry of the heart is? Would you like to know that the cry that rises to God is not that of the voice but that of tears? Listen to the Lamentations of Jeremia: 'Let there be no repose for your eyes.'[14] 'For he proclaims peace to his people.' This is appropriate for the Jews who were to believe in Christ, for it speaks of the Advent of Christ and of the faith of the Jews, that is, the faith of the apostles and all those who believed them. 'For he proclaims peace to his people.' Peace implies that there is war.

'And to his faithful ones, and to those who put in him

---

10 Matt. 11.15; Luke 8.8.
11 Cf. Isa. 50.5; cf. *Commentary on Isaia* 50.5, PL 24.477 (579).
12 Cf. *Commentarioli in ps.* 84.9.
13 Cf. Hab. 2.1; cf. *Commentary on Habacuc* 2.1, PL 25.1289 (608).
14 Cf. Lam. 2.18.

their hope': this points to those who first obeyed the flesh, but afterwards came back to Him with all their heart. That you may be sure that this versicle is about the Jews—those of them who believed in the Savior—think over the examples we have considered. Suppose with me that a Jew is reading Leviticus,[15] about all the rites described there: under what conditions the leper enters the synagogue, how a hen is bled by having its neck wrenched, what it says about the sprinkling of blood, and about water and hyssop; how the leper's garments are torn away from him, and how, then, he enters the synagogue. If we were to take all of this literally, what benefits would we derive from such reading? If, however, our conversion has been genuinely wholehearted, if we have a spiritual hold on what we have read, we shall discern that it is not possible for the leper to go before the people of God without first having his garments rent, without first revealing what had been concealed.

In the second place, perceive that this leper does not gain entrance to the synagogue except through blood and water and hyssop; hence, you, too, who up to this very day have been a leper, were not conscious of your leprosy until you had come to the priest. But since you came to the priest, he tore open your garments, and what seemed to be sound while it was covered up, proved to be leprous when exposed. The priest made you see your sins and your leprosy, and led you back into God's assembly through blood and water: through blood, the Passion of Christ; through water, by baptism. After you have contracted the leprosy of corruption, you cannot be healed save through the Blood of Christ and through baptism. When you have been healed, then the following words are in order: 'Cleanse me of sin with hyssop, that I may be purified; wash me, and I shall be whiter than snow.'[16]

You are still in Egypt to this day; as long as you do not come to blood and water, you cannot be saved. Do you want

---

15 Cf. Lev. 13, 14.
16 Ps. 50.9.

to be spared the destroying angel of Egypt? Take some hyssop, dip it in blood, sprinkle your door posts, and when the destroyer sees the blood on your forehead, he will leave you untouched. Why have I dwelled so long on all this? Because it is written: 'And to those who put in Him their hope.' God cannot speak peace to His people except to those who hope in Him with all their heart.

'Near indeed is his salvation to those who fear him': I have shown you the way of salvation; I am merciful to you. Although your conversion is not yet complete, nevertheless, I am waiting; I am giving you time for repentance. And all this, indeed, 'that glory may dwell in our land.'[17] He calls you to repentance in order that you, who were a leper, may have Christ for your Guest.

'Kindness and truth shall meet; justice and peace shall kiss.' O what wonderful friendship! 'Kindness and truth shall meet.' Are you a sinner? Heed that it says 'Kindness.' Are you a faithful servant? Hear that it says, 'and truth.' If you are a sinner, do not despair; if you are just, do not yield to complacency.

Let us state this in a different way. There are two peoples that believe: the Gentiles and the Jews. To the Jews was given the promise that the Savior would come, but the promise was not made to us who were outside the law of God. Kindness, therefore, is symbolic of the Gentiles; truth, of the Jews, for the promise has been fulfilled; the promise made to the fathers is fulfilled in the sons. 'Justice and peace shall kiss'; mark: 'Justice and peace shall kiss.' This is equivalent to what was said above: kindness and truth shall meet, kindness equates to peace, truth to justice. Whatever pertains to peace belongs, likewise, to kindness; whatever refers to truth applies also to justice. Realize to the full what the psalm says: 'Justice and peace shall kiss,' kindness and truth have embraced in friendship. In other words, the Gentiles and the Jews are under one Shepherd, Christ.

---

17 Cf. Ps. 84 (85).10.

'Truth shall spring out of the earth.'[18] 'I am the way, and the truth, and the life.'[19] He who said: 'I am the truth,' has sprung out of the earth. What is this truth that has risen up out of the earth? 'But a shoot shall sprout from the stump of Jesse, and from his roots a bud shall blossom';[20] and in another place: 'O God, you doer of saving deeds on earth.'[21] What have you to say, Manichaeus, who deny that the Savior assumed a body? Behold Truth, the Savior, is born of earth, that is, of Mary. 'And justice shall look down from heaven,' for it was just that the Savior have mercy on His people. Think what this means:—O, the just judgments of God, and how unsearchable his ways![22]—'Truth shall spring out of the earth': that means the Savior. Again, 'justice shall look down from heaven': justice is the Savior. How has He sprung out of the earth? How has He looked down from heaven? He grew up out of the earth since He was born as man; He has looked down from heaven since God is always in heaven. Assuredly, He is born of earth, but He who was born of earth is always in heaven, for God is everywhere. His appearance on earth was such that He never left heaven. He looked down; as long as we were given to sinning, He turned His eyes away from us.

Now listen to what that means. It is right for the Potter to feel pity for His works, for the Shepherd to be compassionate of His flock. We are His people, we are His creatures. He sprang out of the earth and looked down from heaven to fulfill His justice and take pity on the work that He wrought. That you may know, moreover, that justice bespeaks not cruelty, but mercy, the psalmist says: 'The Lord himself will give his benefits.' To be compassionately kind to all His works, He looked down from heaven. 'Our land shall yield its increase.' Truth has sprung out of the earth, indeed; that

---

18 Cf. *Commentarioli in ps.* 84.12.
19 John 14.6.
20 Isa. 11.1.
21 Cf. Ps. 73.12.
22 Cf. Rom. 11.33.

refers to the past. Now the psalmist turns to the future: our land shall yield its harvest. Do not give up hope because He was born once of Mary; every day He is born in us. 'Our land shall yield its increase.' We, too, have the power to bring forth Christ if we so desire. 'Our land shall yield its increase.' These words refer to Him who became the Bread of Heaven, to Him who says: 'I am the bread that has come down from heaven.'[23]

We have stressed the mercy of the Lord because His whole purpose in coming was to redeem mankind. We ought, nevertheless, to know that He Himself is going to sit in judgment over the living and the dead; that He Himself will come to judge us. 'Justice shall walk before him.' Do not be heedless: justice will lead Him. 'And salvation, along the way of his steps.' Note the exact words: 'his steps'—where there are no rocks, where there are no thorns nor thistles, where the path is even, where He may walk, where He cannot stumble. Let us, therefore, make way for the Lord in our heart, that way for which John was giving his life's effort, and for which he was crying in the desert that we should make ready the way of the Lord.[24] That is why the psalmist says now: 'And salvation, along the way of his steps'; where He finds the way, there He will walk. Although formerly we had obstacles of thorns and thistles, although we had stones, He declares to us in Isaia: 'clear the highway of stones.'[25] He proclaims this, furthermore, lest He stumble upon them when He is ready to walk in the way of our heart. Now the stones that He bids us throw out from our way are our sins. Christ does not walk in our heart if there is any sin there. He stumbles at once against these stones. 'And salvation, along the way of his steps.' Let us make ready the way, and Jesus will set His steps in it.

---

23 John 6.41.
24 Matt. 3.3.
25 Cf. Isa. 62.10.

HOMILY 18

ON PSALM 86 (87)

PSALM OF the sons of Core. A song.' I have called your attention frequently to the difference between the psalm and the song. The psalm is named from the psalter, but a song comes forth from the voice. The psalm, a work of art, relates to the practical; the song, to meditation and is speculative.[1]

'His foundation upon the holy mountains.' The psalmist did not predicate whose foundation, but merely stated: 'His foundation upon the holy mountains.' These are the utterances of a prophet; the sons are Core's sons. The meaning of the name Core, as I have indicated before, is 'Calvary'; hence, his sons are 'sons of the Resurrection.'

'His foundation': either God's, or surely, the Church's. What, in truth, is the foundation, if not the Father and the Son and the Holy Spirit? This foundation is not, therefore, in valleys, but upon mountains; and not upon any mountains, but upon holy mountains. Paul declares: 'As a wise builder, I laid the foundation,'[2] namely, faith in the Trinity. Then, in another place he says: 'For he was looking for the city that has foundations, of which city the architect and builder is God.'[3] 'His foundation upon the holy mountains.' The psalmist specified holy mountains simply because there are other mountains that are not holy. Besides, Isaia says: 'Upon the dark mountains set up a signal.'[4] In another passage of

---

1 Cf. *Commentary on Ephesians* 5.19, PL 26.561 (651).
2 1 Cor. 3.10.
3 Heb. 11.10.
4 Cf. Isa. 13.2.

Holy Writ we find: 'What are you, O perverse mountain?'[5]
·and Jeremia says: 'Give glory to the Lord, your God, before
it grows dark. Before your feet stumble on darkening mountains.'[6] You see, then, there are dark mountains, and Jeremia
warns us that we should give glory to God before our feet
begin to stumble on them, for if our feet should be bruised
in stumbling upon these mountainways, we cannot give glory
to the Lord. 'His foundation upon the holy mountains.'
Whom can we name as foundations? The apostles. Upon
them the foundations were laid; where the faith of the Church
was first established, there, too, the foundations were laid.

Because everyone builds upon a foundation, one gold, another silver, another precious stones,[7] 'The Lord loves the
gates of Sion, more than any dwelling of Jacob.' Does He
love the gates that we see fallen in ruins?[8] Does He love these
gates, and this Sion that has become a plowed field?[9] But
just consider what it says: the gates of Sion are dearer to the
Lord than any dwelling of Jacob. Mark: more than all the
cities of Jacob—of Judea—so much does He love this city!
How does it happen, then, that we see other cities preserved
in part, but this one completely in ruins? Let us read the
Apocalypse of John; let us read Isaia,[10] too, where the city
of Jerusalem is being built and its twelve gates are said to be
wrought of precious stones, and the city itself is coming down
from heaven with its walls of gold and its broad streets
covered with jasper and each gate made from a single precious
stone. These are altogether the riches of the Lord, and
how does the Lord love them and mankind also? Does He
restrain us from avarice and He Himself build a city because
of avarice? But the Lord loves the gates of Sion, those twelve
gates of Sion. Obviously, then, the psalmist wrote of the

5 Cf. Zach. 4.7; cf. *Commentary on Matthew* 21.22, PL 26.160 (168).
6 Jer. 13.16.
7 Cf. 1 Cor. 3.12.
8 Cf. Letter 108.9, PL 22.884 (697); 129.2, PL 22.1101 (968).
9 Cf. Jer. 26.18.
10 Cf. Apoc. 21; Isa. 62; Ezech. 40-42; cf. Letter 108.16, PL 22.892 (707).

apostles. 'More than any dwelling of Jacob,' more than all the saints of old.

Thus far in our interpretation, we have confined ourselves to one figurative meaning. Let us now consider another trope. 'The Lord loves the gates of Sion.' It seems to me that the gates of Sion are the virtues. Just as vice and sin are the gates of death, I think the gates of Sion are the virtues.[11] Furthermore, there is another passage in the psalms that says: 'You have raised me up from the gates of death.'[12] If the gates of death are sins, surely the gates of Jerusalem are virtues. 'More than any dwelling of Jacob.' Note that the people of old—Jacob—do not have a foundation nor a house built upon foundations, but instead they dwell in tents that they readily carry from place to place.

'Glorious things are said of you, O city of God!' As we have suggested, we may refer the verse: 'His foundation upon the holy mountains,' to God Himself. Moreover, we may also refer to God the words: 'Glorious things are said of you, O city of God!' What city is this? Where shall we find these glorious sayings? All the prophets speak of this city.[13] Isaia says: 'Awake, awake! put on your strength, O Jerusalem,'[14] and again: 'I am a strong city, the city that is being brought down.'[15] David says in one psalm: 'There is a stream whose runlets gladden the city of God';[16] in another: 'O Lord, in your city you will set at nought their phantoms.'[17] Also the Savior Himself has spoken gloriously of this city: 'A city set on a mountain cannot be hidden.'[18]

'I will be mindful of Rahab and Babylon among those that

---

11 Cf. *Commentary on Isaia* 26.2-4, PL 24.293 (344); *on Amos* 5.10, PL 25.1045 (292).
12 Ps. 9A.14.
13 Cf. *Commentarioli in ps.* 86.3.
14 Cf. Isa. 52.1.
15 Cf. Isa. 27.10; 26.1, 5; 25.2, 12; 27.3 LXX; *Commentary on Isaia* 27.3, PL 24.307 (362); Letter 30.14, PL 22.444 (150); *Commentary on Ecclesiastes* 10.15, PL 23.1153 (475).
16 Ps. 45.5.
17 Cf. Ps. 72.20.
18 Matt. 5.14; cf. Letter 58.2, PL 22.580 (320).

know me.'[19] Since the psalmist said: 'Glorious things are said of you, O city of God,' and we understand this city to be the Church gathered together from the nations, the psalm now speaks of the calling of the Gentiles: 'I will be mindful of Rahab and Babylon among those that know me.' Let the sinner be at peace; the Lord was mindful of Rahab. I mean, at peace, if the sinner returns to the Lord; otherwise, there is no healing peace in a tearless security. 'I will be mindful of Rahab,' of Rahab, that harlot[20] who lodged Jesus' secret agents, who lived in Jericho whither Jesus had come and had dispatched the two spies. Jericho, that collapsed in seven days, is a type of this world,[21] and as such is determined to kill the secret agents. Because, therefore, Jericho is bent upon killing the spies, Rahab, the harlot, alone received them, lodged them not on the ground floor, but in the upper story of the roof—or, in other words, in the sublimity of her faith. She hid them under her stalks of flax.

We have been following so far the historical interpretation and you perceive how from the history itself we are ascending upward gradually to a mystical understanding. Jesus, the leader, who had led the people out of Egypt; Jesus, whose name means Savior, after the death and burial of Moses in the land of Moab in the land of Arabia—that is, after the law was dead—Jesus desires to lead His people into the Gospel and sends out two men on secret mission to Jericho. Two messengers He sends: one to the circumcised; the other to the Gentiles, Peter and Paul. Jericho seeks to kill them; the harlot takes them in, meaning, of course, the Church gathered together of the Gentiles. She believes in Jesus; and those whom Jericho is determined to destroy, she protects in safety on her own roof. She harbors them on the roof—in the loftiness of her faith—and hides them under the stems of flax. Even though she is a harlot, she covers them with flax.

---

19 Cf. Ps. 86 (87).4.
20 Jos. 2; cf. *Commentarioli in ps.* 86.4.
21 Cf. *Against Jovinian* 1.21, PL 23.251 (271).

Flax with much labor and care becomes of dazzling white-ness. You yourselves know that flax grows from the soil and that when it has come forth from the ground, it is black; it has no beauty; it has no use. First, it is pulled up from the ground, broken, then twisted, afterwards washed. Next, it is pounded; finally, combed, and after so much care and hard work, it finally becomes white. Here, then, is the meaning: this harlot took the messengers in and covered them with her flax so that these agents might turn her flax into dazzling whiteness. And then what? She counsels them and says: 'Wait here for three days.'[22] Not one day does she specify, nor two days, but definitely three days. Notice what she says: 'Wait three days.' She does not designate three nights, but three days, for hers was an enlightened heart. Then she says, and after three days—but what does she say? 'Do not go through the open plains,' she warns, 'but go up the mountain way.'[23] The faith of the Church is not laid in the valleys, but is established on the mountains. Later, indeed, Jericho is overthrown, but this harlot alone is preserved untouched; hence, the Lord says: 'I will be mindful of Rahab'; that is, on the day of judgment, I will be mindful of her who welcomes My messengers.

'I will be mindful of Rahab.' Rahab; what is the force of her name? We have been following the historical sense; let us now reflect upon the anagogic significance of the name. Rahab thus admits of two interpretations:[24] the name may imply either a 'broad space' or, better, 'pride.' Consider, therefore, its impact. She who formerly walked the broad, spacious road to death,[25] she whose pride was driving her to destruction, was later converted unto humility. 'I will be mindful of Rahab and Babylon.' The meaning of Babylon is 'confusion.' See what the Lord says: Not only of Rahab will I be mindful, but even of Babylon, and of any soul that

---

22 Cf. Jos. 2.16.
23 Ibid.
24 Cf. Commentarioli in ps. 86.4.
25 Cf. Matt. 7.13.

is troubled over its faults and sins. 'And of Babylon among those that know me.' Realize what this actually means. Even though anyone has been a Rahab, even though anyone has been a Babylon, nevertheless, I will be mindful of him who knows Me. So if we have been Rahabs and Babylons, even we ought to be at peace and say: The Lord said, I will be mindful of Rahab and Babylon. But now see what follows: 'among those that know me.' They have been Rahab and they have been Babylon, but later they turned to Me in hope. 'I will be mindful of Rahab and Babylon among those that know me.' She who was at one time on the broad road to perdition, afterwards mounted upward into the memory of God.

So far, the psalmist has been speaking almost enigmatically, but now he speaks more plainly of the calling of the Gentiles, for notice what he says: 'Of Philistia, Tyre, Ethiopia: "These were born there." '[26] He designates Philistines to distinguish them from the Jews, for we are the Philistines. 'Tyre.' Tyre connotes tribulation, or SOR. 'Ethiopia': black and cloaked in the filth of sin. 'Ethiopia.' We find the same typology in the versicle: 'Let Ethiopia extend its hands to God.'[27] 'Of Philistia, Tyre, Ethiopia.' Now for the meaning: they who before were strangers, they who previously were in tribulation, who had dwelt in the midst of the sea (for it is said of Tyre: 'Tyre that is situated in the heart of the sea'),[28] they, therefore, who at first were in the sea and beaten about by waves, are found later in the Church. 'Ethiopia.' At one time we were Ethiopians in our vices and sins. How so? Because our sins had blackened us. But afterwards we heard the words: 'Wash yourselves clean!'[29] And we said: 'Wash me, and I shall be whiter than snow.'[30] We are Ethiopians, therefore, who have been transformed from blackness into whiteness. 'Of Philistia,

---

26 Cf. Ps. 86 (87).4.
27 Ps. 67.32.
28 Cf. Ezech. 27.3.
29 Isa. 1.16.
30 Ps. 50.9.

Tyre, Ethiopia: "These were born there." ' Where were they born? 'Glorious things are said of you, O city of God!' 'These were born there': in the city of God.

'Shall not Sion say a man, a man is born in her?'[31] The rendition of the translators of the Septuagint is: 'Shall not Sion say a man?' Many, therefore, have surmised, but have not understood, the meaning of μήτι Σιών and have added the letter 'r' to make the reading μήτηρ Σιών ἐρεῖ ἄνθρωπος.[32] They base their emendation on the words that immediately follow: 'and a man is born in her.' It is, likewise, their supposition that this verse should read: 'Mother Sion shall say a man.' Since there is the implication that a son has been born, they go astray on a word for 'mother.' Let us consider this interpretation first (for we cannot afford to overlook it) and also translate: Mother Sion shall say a man, and a man is born in her. These, then, are they who had been begotten in the Church: Philistia, Tyre, and Ethiopia; these are they who are born in the Church. They believe in the Church and begin life in the Church, for unless they have been baptized, they are not sons of the Church. They, indeed, who have been baptized in the Church call the Church 'Mother.'

Now let us turn to the Hebrew truth. 'Shall not Sion say a man, and a man is born in her?' The true sense of the Hebrew is this: Who will be able to announce to Sion, who of men will be able to announce to her, that a man shall be born in her and shall be her Savior? In other words, no mere man has the power to announce to Sion that she will be saved in the man who will be born in her. 'And a man is born in her.' Who is this man? 'And he who has established her is the Most High Lord.' Let the Arians answer, for they say that the Father alone is the Highest. Behold, here it speaks of the Son and says: 'And he who has established her is the Most High Lord.' The psalmist did not say, the Son of God who was in the beginning with the Father,

---

31 Cf. Ps. 86 (87).5.
32 Cf. *Commentarioli in ps.* 86.5.

but what did he say? 'A man is born in her, and he who has
established her is the Most High Lord.' If, moreover, He is
said to be the Most High Lord, how much the more is He
the Word of God?[33]

'In his record of the peoples and princes the Lord shall tell
of these who have been born in her.'[34] Now the psalm did
not say, those who are born in her, but who have been born
in her. 'The Lord shall tell.' How shall He tell? Not by word
of mouth, but in His writings. In His writings of whom?
Of the peoples. That is not enough, for it also speaks of the
princes. And which princes? Those who are born in her?
No, it did not say that; but, those who have been born in her.
Just see how full of mystical meaning Sacred Scripture is!
We have read the Apostle Paul; we have read Peter; and
we have read Paul's words: 'Do you seek a proof of the Christ
who speaks in me?'[35] What Paul speaks, Christ speaks, for:
'He who receives you, receives me.'[36] Our Lord and Savior,
therefore, speaks to us in the writings of His princes.

'In his record of the peoples the Lord shall tell': in the
sacred writings, in His Scripture that is read to all peoples
in order that all may know. Thus the apostles have written;
thus the Lord Himself has spoken, not merely for a few, but
that all might know and understand. Plato wrote books,
but he did not write for all people but only for a few, for there
are not many more than two or three men who know him.
But the princes of the Church and the princes of Christ did not
write only for the few, but for everyone without exception.[37]
'And princes': the apostles and the evangelists. 'Of those who
have been born in her.' Note: 'who have been' and not 'who
are.' That is to make sure that, with the exception of the
apostles, whatever else is said afterwards should be removed
and not, later on, hold the force of authority. No matter how

---

33 Cf. *Commentarioli in ps.* 86.1.20.
34 Cf. Ps. 86 (87).6.
35 2 Cor. 13.3.
36 Matt. 10.40.
37 Cf. *Commentary on Galatians* 5.6, PL 26.428 (487-488).

holy anyone may be after the time of the apostles, no matter
how eloquent, he does not have authority, for 'in his record
of the peoples and princes the Lord shall tell of those who
have been born in her.'

'The home as it were of all rejoicing is within you.'[38] The
prophet is speaking to the Church and tells her that all who
dwell in her are, as it were, full of joy and gladness. Why
did he not say, 'The home of all rejoicing is within you,'
rather than 'as it were of all rejoicing'? Another psalm says:
'When the Lord brought back the captives of Sion, we were
like men dreaming,'[39] not 'we were men dreaming'; hence,
this verse: 'The home as it were of all rejoicing is within you.'
Why have I made such a point of all this? For the reason
that in the present world no matter how faithful one may
be, no matter to what degree he renounces the world, his is
not a perfect victory.[40] In fact, the Gospel says: 'Blessed are
they who mourn, for they shall be comforted.'[41] If, moreover,
it has been said: 'Blessed are you who weep now, for you
shall laugh,'[42] it is evident that in the present world there
is no lasting joy; our joy is only ephemeral. 'The home is
within you.' Grasp what that means: no one may ever withdraw from the Church.

We ought to know that what we have interpreted in reference to the Church can be understood also as applying to
our soul. If Sion is taken to mean a watchtower, our soul
ascends to a contemplation ever more sublime. The true
Church, the true temple of Christ, is no other than the human
soul. The Church of Christ is nothing other than the souls
of those who believe in Christ. 'Do you not know that you
are the temple of God and that the spirit of God dwells in
you?'[43] 'His foundation upon the holy mountains': there

---

38 Cf. Ps. 86 (87).7.
39 Ps. 125.1.
40 Cf. Letter 22.4, PL 22.396 (90); *Against the Pelagians* 2.5, PL 23.565
(748); *Commentary on Jeremia* 31.38, PL 24.887 (1077).
41 Matt. 5.5.
42 Luke 6.21.
43 1 Cor. 3.16.

are no foundations of God except upon the holy mountains, upon the doctrine in the soul of the one who believes in Christ.[44] 'The Lord loves the gates of Sion.' Our Sion has any number of gates, and if we open them wide to our Spouse, He will enter and will rest with us. Indeed, He Himself says: 'Behold, I stand at the door and knock. If anyone listens to my voice and opens the door to me, I will come into him and will sup with him.'[45]

'Glorious things are said of you, O city of God!' A city is not just one building, but many. Even so the Church, and also our Sion, unless it has many virtues, will not be the city of God. 'I will be mindful of Rahab and Babylon among those that know me.' She who of old walked the broad road of sinners climbed up afterwards into the remembrance of God. 'Shall not Sion say a man, and a man is born in her?' Shall I tell you something marvelous but true? Our Sion, in which at times there are Philistines, and Tyre, and Ethiopia; that watchtower, that meretrix, that harlot, that Rahab, that Babylon, that one who, according to Ezechiel, has prostituted herself to everyone on the crossroads;[46] that meretrix, if she wills it, suddenly becomes a virgin. A virgin she becomes, conceives the Son of God, and brings Him forth. 'From your fear, O Lord, we conceived, and suffered the pangs of childbirth, bringing forth the spirit of your salvation upon the earth.'[47] Understand, therefore, that she who was a prostitute conceives of God and is in labor and brings forth the Savior. We have brought forth upon earth the spirit of Your salvation. Thus, our soul, that Rahab, that meretrix, has the power to conceive and bring forth the Savior.

'And a man is born in her.' If it is our desire, every day Christ is born; through each virtue Christ is born. If 'Christ is the power [virtue] of God, and the wisdom of God,'[48]

---

44 Cf. Letter 75.1, PL 22.686 (452).
45 Apoc. 3.20.
46 Cf. Ezech. 16.25.
47 Cf. Isa. 26.18.
48 1 Cor. 1.24.

whoever performs virtuous acts, engenders virtue. 'And he who has established her is the Most High Lord.' The very one who is born in you has Himself established your Sion. 'In his record of the peoples the Lord shall tell.' It is clear that what the Lord speaks in Scripture, He speaks to no one as he speaks to Sion. Yet, although all these things are so, although Christ has been born in her, nevertheless, victory is not complete nor secure, for we are always in peril. 'The home as it were of all rejoicing is within you.' He who is joyful is fearless from joy itself; but he who is fearless is soon deceived.[49] The man, however, who is wary of snares through fear can readily escape them, with the help of the Lord to whom be glory forever and ever. Amen.

---

49 Cf. *Commentary on Isaia* 26.15 PL 24.501 (354).

PRAYER OF Moses, the man of God.' There are four psalms characterized as a prayer:[1] the sixteenth and the following psalm, the eighty-ninth, and Psalm 101. The one-hundred-and-first psalm is: 'The prayer of an afflicted one when he is faint and pours out his anguish before the Lord.'[2] The one we are considering is entitled: 'A prayer of Moses, the man of God.' We have read the Song of Moses in Exodus,[3] the song that Mary and Moses sang after the Israelites had crossed the Red Sea, and Pharao and his army had been drowned to a man. Then again, in Deuteronomy,[4] we have read a song that Moses composed. If, therefore, these psalms are also songs of Moses, why are they not included in his own books?[5] As I have indicated, the title of the one-hundred-and-first psalm is: 'The prayer of an afflicted one.' Now he who wrote about the afflicted one is not the afflicted man; that afflicted one who prays for us is the Lord, who 'being rich, became poor for our sakes,'[6] and so on. We have a parallel situation here with Moses, for he wrote a history on the origin of the human race. He wrote on how heaven and earth were made, how man was made, and on the creation of mankind; and this psalm

---

1 Cf. Letter 140.3; this Letter is a commentary on Ps. 89; PL 22.1167 (1050).
2 Ps. 101.1.
3 Cf. Exod. 15.
4 Cf. Deut. 32.
5 Cf. Letter 140.3-4, PL 22.1167-1169; cf. Augustine, *Enarr. in ps.* 89.2.
6 Cf. 2 Cor. 8.9.

speaks of the creation of man, his nature, and his end. Consequently, he who wrote in Genesis on the creation of mankind, is now instructed by the Holy Spirit to discourse on what man is.

'O Lord, you have been our refuge through all generations.' One who seeks refuge is looking for protection, either from the rage of fire and burning heat, or from some beast's attack, or from enemies who seek to kill him. We, too, are in the scorching fire of this world; we, too, are the prey of beasts; hence, we cry: 'Give not to the wild beasts the souls that confess to you';[7] enemies are pressing upon us; therefore, we seek refuge under Your wings. 'Through all generations': in the past, in the present, and in the future; or, 'Through all generations': in the ancient people of the Jews, and in our people, the Christians.

'Before the mountains were begotten and the earth and the world were brought forth.' This is the passage in which heresy steals in like a thief[8] and declares: If the Lord was our refuge before the mountains were made, or the earth and the world were formed, there were souls before the world was made. What else does Scripture say? 'O Lord, you have been our refuge through all generations,' from the beginning of the world, before the beginning of the world. That is what the heretics maintain. 'And lest you imagine that this is simply my claim,' says heresy, 'listen: "Before the mountains were begotten, or the earth and the world were brought forth, You,"' quotes heresy, '"have been our refuge." If, moreover, the Lord was our refuge before the world was made, then there have been souls before the world was made.' You are making a very poor division of the verses, heresy. Why do you calumniate the Holy Spirit? Quote Holy Writ correctly, just as the Holy Spirit has uttered it. The verse should be read thus: 'O Lord, you have been our refuge through all generations.' And right here at this point is the division.

---

7 Cf. Ps. 73.19.
8 Cf. Letter 140.6. PL 22.1169 (1053).

Another verse begins in turn: 'Before the mountains were begotten and the earth and the world were brought forth, from everlasting to everlasting you are God.' You are God before the mountains were begotten; You are God before the earth and the world were brought forth; from everlasting to everlasting, You are God, You are always, You are eternal.

'Turn not man back to dust, saying, "Return, O children of men." '[9] O Lord, that we may dare to utter this plea, that we may implore, 'Turn not man back to dust,' You have made us bold by saying: 'Return, rebellious children, and I will cure you of your rebelling.'[10] 'Saying, "Return, O children of men." For a thousand years in your sight are as yesterday, now that it is past':[11] turn not man back to dust. 'Or as a watch of the night.' What did the psalmist intend to convey with the expression, 'or as a watch of the night'? Here we have to be cognizant of the historical fact that the night is divided into four watches. Recall, too, that the Gospel says: 'In the fourth watch of the night.'[12] Three hours constitute one watch; hence, the night is divided into four watches. Furthermore, the soldiers have four stations when they take turns in the night watch.

Understand, then, what the psalm means. Our whole existence: Adam, our first parent, lived 930 years; Mathusala, too, lived 965 years. Supposing that they had lived even a thousand years, compared to Your eternity, our mighty age is but a little while.[13] In truth, how can anything be very great that has an end? Our long life of a thousand years, before we began to commit sin, was as one day in Your sight. Did I say, one day? I mean one watch of the night. 'Turn not man back to dust.' Listen to what this means: You deigned to descend for our salvation; You poured out Your blood for

---

9 Cf. Ps. 89 (90).3.
10 Cf. Jer. 3.22.
11 Cf. 2 Peter 3.8.
12 Matt. 14.25.
13 Cf. *Commentary on Letter to Philemon* 16, PL 26.650 (758); on *Ezechiel* 30.1-20, PL 25.290 (359); Letter 140.8, PL 22.1172 (1056).

us; do not suffer us to perish and die in our dust. You
Yourself have said: 'When I shall be lifted up from the earth,
I will draw all to myself.'[14] You have been lifted up, and
You have lifted us up. Do not forsake us that we may be
drawn to You.

'The next morning they are like the changing grass, which
at dawn springs up anew, but by evening wilts and fades.'
O the mysteries of the Scripture! 'The next morning they are
like the changing grass.' In the Gospel, Our Lord and Savior
speaks of the grass of the field which today is alive and tomorrow fades and dies.[15] Even as the grass that is green and
in flower and in the morning seems as fresh as a blossom,
after the sun comes out and covers it with its rays, all but
withers and dies toward evening, so, too, our whole life
seems like a flower when it is fresh and vigorous and again
when it wilts and dies. You have seen a young boy not ten
years old; nothing was more beautiful than he as he ran
hither and thither. If you should behold him now, he seems
like an old man, almost dead. Even though he is still alive
in his old age, nevertheless, his youth has vanished.[16] 'The
next morning they are like the changing grass,' that is, our
youth, for it is the morning of our life. 'Like the changing
grass, which at dawn springs up anew.' We blossom in youth;
we wither in old age. 'But by evening wilts and fades. Truly
we are consumed by your anger, and by your wrath we are
put to rout.' We used to live for nine hundred and thirty
years; we even reached the thousand mark; behold how brief
the span of our shortened life!

'You have kept our iniquities before you.' Nothing eludes
You; night does not conceal our sins, nor does the darkness
cover them; all things are clear before You: 'Our life in light
of your scrutiny.'[17] This is expressed much better in He-

---

14 Cf. John 12.32.
15 Cf. Matt. 6.30.
16 Cf. Letter 140.9, PL 22.1173 (1057-1058).
17 Cf. Ps. 89 (90).8.

brew:[18] 'our hidden sins in the light of your scrutiny.' Whatever we do, whatever we think we are doing in secret, lies
open before Your eyes. 'All our days have passed away.' Our
life hurries on at a great pace, and when we least expect it,
it slips away, and we die. These very words we speak are
of death and we do not take thought. 'We have spent our
years like a spider.'[19] Meditate on these words of the psalmist.
In the same way that the spider produces, as it were, a thread
and runs to and fro, back and forth, and weaves the whole
day long, and his labor, indeed, is great but the result is nil;
so, too, the life of man runs about hither and thither. We
search for possessions and we accumulate wealth; we procreate children; we labor and toil; we rise in power and
authority; we do everything; and do not realize that we are
spiders weaving a web.

'Seventy is the sum of our years.' Where are the thousand
years for our lives? Our span is shortened to seventy years;
if we live much longer, we reach eighty. If, moreover, we
live beyond eighty, our existence is no longer life, but death.
'Or eighty, if we are strong.' Whom will you find strong and
healthy as an octogenarian? There is a Greek saying: 'Old
age itself is a disease.' 'And most of them are fruitless toil.'
Whatever more there is of life is not life, but toil and sorrow.

So far we have been considering the direct meaning of the
psalm. It is time now to interpret it anagogically. Indeed, the
entire psalm admits of tropology; I could run through the
verses one by one, and draw forth from each its symbolism,
but time prohibits. All I can do is to sample one versicle
with you, merely give you a taste of its mysticism. Whatever
I pass over in silence, therefore, you may consider as having
been said.

'Seventy is the sum of our years.' Three score and ten
years make seven decades, and fourscore years are eight dec-

---

18 Cf. Letter 140.11, PL 22.1174 (1058).
19 Cf. Ps. 89 (90).9.

ades.[20] Take note how the numbers seven and eight are emphasized. In the same sense that we said: 'You have been our refuge through all generations,' meaning both in the Old Testament and in the New Testament, the psalmist now employs the numbers seven and eight. Ecclesiastes, moreover, says this: 'Give a portion to seven and also to eight.'[21] That is why, too, there are fifteen gradual psalms, seven and eight, that lead us up step by step to the kingdom of heaven. Further, after the seventh step has been mounted, what is the title of the next psalm? 'A song of ascents, of Solomon'[22] who had built the ancient house. And what does Solomon say? 'Unless the Lord build the house, they labor in vain who build it.' What, then, does he mean whose name is inscribed in the title itself? I have built a temple; but unless it is the eighth number that has built it, that house has been built in vain. We have read, too, in the Gospel according to Matthew:[23] Blessed are the poor; blessed are the meek; blessed the hungry and thirsty; and so on, through eight beatitudes. Our Lord, therefore, concluded His teachings with the number eight. I may say that nowhere do we find eight beatitudes all at the same time except in the Gospel— with the number eight, that is, on the day of Resurrection.

'Seventy is the sum of our years.' Would you have me digress a bit and show you the many mystical meanings hidden in the numbers seven and eight?[24] Let us read Ezechiel in reference to a gate: 'And he shall enter by the east gate into the temple which is being built,'[25] and later: 'And the priest goes up first by seven steps and then by eight steps.'[26] Could it be possible that in that entrance there were both seven steps and eight? But just notice what he says: the east gate,

20 Cf. Letter 140.13, PL 22.1175 (1059).
21 Eccles. 11.2; cf. *Against the Luciferians* 22, PL 23.185 (195).
22 Ps. 126.1.
23 Cf. Matt. 5.3-12.
24 *Against Jovinian* 2.34, PL 23.346 (377).
25 Cf. Ezech. 44.1; 46.8; 43.1, 2, 4; cf. *Commentary on Michea* 5.6, PL 25.1201 (494).
26 Cf. Ezech. 40.

the gate from which the light enters—Our Lord and Savior. There is, indeed, a gate, and no one enters it except the high priest. And what does Holy Writ say about it? 'This gate is to remain closed';[27] it is not opened, moreover, except to the priest. Even so the Testament, both Old and New, has always been closed; it has not been opened except to the Savior. He it is who has the key; 'he who opens and no one shuts; who shuts and no one opens.'[28] One gate, then, has both seven steps and eight. In the Old Testament, for example, the divine mysteries point to the Gospels, and in the New Testament back to the law.

Listen to even greater mysteries. At the time when Solomon built the temple, it was our Peacemaker who says: 'Peace I leave with you, my peace I give to you,'[29] 'for he himself is our peace,'[30] 'the peace of God which surpasses all understanding,'[31] who Himself built the temple for God. Observe what Scripture says about the building of the temple by Solomon: 'And there were seventy thousand quarrymen and eighty thousand carriers.'[32] Mark the number. The masons who were cutting stones, who were preparing, as it were, the foundations of the buildings, who were taking up stones from the ground to build the temple of God, are reckoned in the number seven, in the prophets, in the patriarchs, for while they seemingly were driving the human race from off the earth, they were making preparations for the temple of the Lord. The latter, the eighty thousand, symbolize the apostolic preaching and the Gospels; these are they who with the Lord Savior, and Solomon himself, were carrying the heavy burden of the nations. This surely is the height of mystery, but hear of even deeper mysteries! 'And the overseers over the works and the temple, were three thou-

---

27 Cf. Ezech. 44.2; cf. Letter 48.21, PL 22.510 (233).
28 Cf. Apoc. 3.7; cf. Letter 53.5, PL 22.543 (274).
29 John 14.27.
30 Eph. 2.14.
31 Phil. 4.7.
32 Cf. 3 Kings 5.15.

sand.'[33] They cannot be greater, not even the overseers in charge of the work, except that they proclaim the Trinity. 'Seventy is the sum of our years.' There is so much more to say, but time prevents.

'So make your right hand known that fettered we may gain wisdom of heart.'[34] Some codices say 'trained'; others 'fettered.' 'Trained' implies one thing; 'fettered,' another. What, then, is the meaning of 'make your right hand know'? Why have You restrained Your right hand so long, God? 'Why draw back your hand and keep it idle beneath your garment?'[35] says another psalm. Here is its meaning: we are lying prostrate in sickness; we are powerless in our sins; send forth Your right hand and raise us up. Why do you keep Your right hand so long idle beneath Your cloak? Your heart overflows with a goodly theme;[36] send forth Your right hand and set us free. Make known to us the mystery which has been hidden from generation to generation. 'Make your right hand known.' What are you pilfering, Arius? The psalmist did not say: 'Make Your right hand,' for God was never without His right hand. But what did he say? Your right hand, that You have always had and that has been in Your bosom, make it known to us. Because we are not able to know Him abiding in His Godhead, He assumes our humanity, and in that way we know Him.

'So make your right hand known that fettered we may gain wisdom of heart': those who are bound by the chains of wisdom, those whose hearts are shackled by Your wisdom. Do not let the obscurity of the passage disturb you. The prophets were in possession of wisdom, but Wisdom itself, as it were, fettered them; they could not fly without Christ. See, then, what it means: Send forth Your right hand, that is, Your Son, and make Him known to us; the prophets who have been

---

33 *Ibid.*
34 Cf. Ps. 89 (90).12; cf. *Commentarioli in ps.* 89.11.
35 Cf. Ps. 73.11.
36 Cf. Ps. 44.2.

prophesying in shadow, let them begin to herald the Lord in plain sight.

'Return, O Lord! How long?' We have sinned exceedingly; You are turning away Your face from us; it is not proper for Your eyes to look upon our sins; that is why we plead: 'Return, O Lord! How long?' Behold how many ages have already come and gone! The prophets have never ceased to proclaim Your coming to the nations, yet up to this time You have not come. 'And direct the children of men.'[37] We who have been deflected by evil, may we be led back by You. 'And direct the children of men.' Well said, direct the children of men. For that very reason be their guide, because they are the children of men, for if they were Your children, they would have stayed straight. You have said Yourself: 'I said: "You are gods: all of you sons of the Most High; yet like men you shall die, and fall like any prince." '[38] And in another place: 'Sons of men, how long will you be dull of heart?'[39] Again: 'My spirit shall not remain in man forever, since he is flesh.'[40] Because they are men, they are flesh. Consequently, because we are the sons of man and have lost the right to be the sons of God and have been perverted; on that account guide us that once again we may become Your children.

'And may the brightness of the Lord our God be upon us.'[41] The Apostle, likewise, tells the Hebrews[42] that the Lord and Savior is the brightness of the glory of the Father. 'And may the brightness of the Lord our God be upon us.' Parallel to this, is another passage: 'O Lord, the light of your countenance is signed upon us!'[43] The sign of the cross is our banner.

We have been discussing the psalter for some time now, and I think that we have delayed longer than we should.

---

37 Cf. Ps. 89 (90).16.
38 Ps. 81.6, 7.
39 Cf. Ps. 4.3.
40 Gen. 6.3.
41 Cf. Ps. 89 (90).17.
42 Heb. 1.3.
43 Cf. Ps. 4.7.

We realize that we have said much more than we ought, but we cannot keep secret the words of our Lord; we cannot leave the psalm half begun. Whatever is of profit to the soul is never too much; the good is never enough, if, indeed, it is good. Let us pray the Lord our Savior that His brightness illumine our hearts, that it banish all our darkness, that it ward off from our hearts all black and sinful thoughts, that it enlighten our darkness; that the shadows may scatter and brightness dwell within. The temple of the Lord, and the tabernacle, and the shrines of the saints always had a glowing lamp; the lamp in the temple of the Lord was always aglow. If the lamp should ever be extinguished, the Lord will not make His abode in darkness. Let us pray, therefore, with the psalmist: 'A lamp to my feet is your word, a light to my path.'[44]

---

44 Ps. 118.105.

ON PSALM 90 (91)

OU WHO DWELL in the shelter [*adiutorio*] of the Most High.' Now, it is the name, Ezra, that is translated 'adiutorium' and means 'help.' In fact, the prophet Esdra is called Boēthós, helper.[1] He is the one who led back the Jews from the Babylonian Captivity, back into the land of promise. He, therefore, who dwells in Ezra, who dwells in Jesus (in accordance with tropology), who, as the Apostle says,[2] built His house without human hands—that house that the Lord had also built for the midwives in Egypt[3]—'shall abide under the protection of the God of heaven.'[4]

'Say to the Lord, "My refuge and my fortress, my God." ' I am hemmed in by enemies, You, therefore, are my refuge. ' "In whom I will trust." For he will rescue you from the snare of the hunters.'[5] Note carefully that the psalmist did not say 'I trust,' but 'I will trust.' As long as we continue in a life of sin, we certainly are not trusting; if we put an end to sin, then our hope is confident. 'For he will rescue you from the snare of the hunters.' There are many hunters in this world that go about setting traps for our soul. Nemrod[6] the giant was a 'mighty hunter before the Lord.'[7] Esau, too, was a hunter, for he was a sinner. In all of Holy Writ,

---

1 Cf. Letter 45.6, PL 22.482 (198); 53.8, PL 22.548 (279).
2 Cf. 2 Cor. 5.1.
3 Cf. Exod. 1.21.
4 Cf. Ps. 90 (91).1; cf. *Commentarioli in ps.* 90.1.
5 Cf. Ps. 90 (91).3.
6 Jerome, 'Nembroth.'
7 Gen. 10.8, 9.

never do we find a hunter that is a faithful servant;[8] we do find faithful fishermen.

'For he will rescue you from the snare of the hunters.' 'We were rescued like a bird from the fowler's snare; broken was the snare, and we were freed.'[9] What snare is this that has been broken? 'The Lord,' says the Apostle, 'will speedily crush Satan under our feet';[10] 'that you may recover yourselves from the snare of the devil.'[11] You see, then, that the devil is the hunter, eager to lure our souls unto perdition. The devil is master of many snares, deceptions of all kinds. Avarice is one of his pitfalls, detraction is his noose, fornication is his bait. 'And from the destroying word.'[12] As long as we are in the state of grace, our soul is at peace; but once we begin to play with sin, then our soul is in trouble and is like a boat tossed about by the waves.

'With his pinions he will cover you.' We find this same thought in Deuteronomy:[13] As an eagle, the Lord spreads His wings over us, His nestlings. There the Lord is compared to the eagle guarding its young. The simile, therefore, is appropriate that God protects us as a Father, and as a hen guarding her chicks lest they be snatched away by a hawk; nevertheless, a different interpretation is also permissible. 'With his pinions he will cover you': He will be lifted up on the cross; He will stretch forth His hands to shelter us. 'And under his wings you shall take refuge.' You will look upon His crucified Hands, the prophet says, and if the serpent bite you, you will be healed. Even though you are wandering about in the desert of this world, if a scorpion should sting you, if a viper, if an asp, if any other venomous creature, be assured that you will recover; the serpent has been lifted up in the desert.[14]

---

8 Cf. *Commentary on Michea* 5.6, PL 25.1209 (494).
9 Ps. 123.7; cf. Letter 22.3, PL 22.396 (90).
10 Cf. Rom 16.20.
11 Cf. 2 Tim. 2.26.
12 Cf. Ps. 90 (91).3.
13 Cf. Deut. 32.11.
14 Cf. Num. 21.8, 9.

158 SAINT JEROME

'His truth will surround you with a shield.'[15] Our shield is spherical; that is to say, it protects us on all sides. It is not only a shield, it is also a bulwark. 'O Lord, you crown us with the shield of your good will.'[16] Does anyone really crown with a shield? Notice that it says: 'O Lord, you crown us with the shield of your good will.' What does that mean? You will guard us, and You will make us victorious, and after the victory, You will give us a crown. 'His truth will surround you with a shield.' Since the psalmist had said that the Lord will rescue us 'from the destroying word,' we may comprehend this word of destruction to be the teaching of heretics, of philosophers, of Jews; this word seemingly sharp is not truth, but a lie. Moreover, because it is a lie, it is turbid; it is full of turbulence because it is false and troubles our soul. So the Lord who is Truth and says: 'I am the truth,'[17] surrounds us with His truth like a shield to protect us against the stinging darts of the devil. Christ who is Truth, holds up His shield that the shield of truth may vanquish falsehood and deceit. 'You shall not fear the terror of the night.' The devil always lurks in darkness, 'shooting from ambush,' Scripture says, 'at the innocent man.'[18] Notice it is the guileless and the innocent that are his secret target. 'You shall not fear the terror of the night.' That means: even though you are in the terror of the dark night, nevertheless, you will not be afraid because you are armed with the shield of truth.[19]

'Nor the arrow that flies by day.' It seems like a contradiction here to say 'nor the arrow that flies by day.' The flying arrow of the devil, if you ask me, is the disputation of heretics and philosophers,[20] for they promise the light of knowledge and claim that they have the light of day. They cannot de-

---

15 Cf. Ps. 90 (91).4.
16 Cf. Ps. 5.13.
17 John 14.6.
18 Ps. 63.5.
19 Cf. Letter 3.5. PL 22.334 (12).
20 Cf. *Against the Pelagians* 2.20, PL 23.583 (766).

ceive us, however, except by promising light. The real light
they promise, however, is the fire of flaming arrows. So it
says: 'Nor the arrow that flies by day.' 'Not the pestilence
that roams in darkness.' To be sure, the arrow seems to fly
in daylight, but it is the pestilence that roams in darkness.

'Nor the attack of the noonday demon.'[21] This is better
expressed by the Greek ἀπὸ συμπτώματος. Symptosis implies
a chance occurrence when something strange happens unexpectedly; or symptoma may denote a disaster in which many
perish at the same time. Grasp, then, what it means. Even
though many have been seduced, nevertheless, you who are
in the state of grace may escape seduction. I shall give you
an example so that even the more simple among you may
understand what I mean. If you should go to the city, a
monk all by yourself, and while you are strolling about you
hear a shout in the circus and someone says to you: 'Come
and see, it is the circus,' and you hold back remonstrating, 'I
have no permission, I cannot go'; if he should call your attention to the thousands of men there and say to you: 'Two
hundred thousand men are there, are they all going to be
lost, and you alone be saved?'[22] You have to be aware that
symptoma is the devil's own doing. What I am trying to say
is that you have to know that many do perish and are lost.

'Of the noonday demon.' There are, indeed, many who
claim that at midday demons possess a special power, and
this is a common saying. Be that as it may, I shall maintain
candidly that the devil has power over us at any time that
we commit sin. If we sin in the morning, the devil enters into
us; in the evening, at night, at whatever time we commit sin,
the devil is there in us. On the other hand, if at noon we are
not committing sin, he does not enter into us. You see, then,
that this common expression is rather silly. What, then, does
'of the noonday demon' mean? Listen to this: Abraham
entertained angels at noon, and Joseph invited his brothers

---

21 Cf. Ps. 90 (91).6.
22 Cf. Letter 125.17, PL 22.1082 (944).

to lunch at noon. Both Abraham and Joseph were faithful servants; therefore, they dined with their guest in the clear light of the sun at its brightest; hence, their feasting is at midday.[23] So if I am filled with the knowledge of Holy Writ, even though it is the third hour, nevertheless, I am feasting you in the noonday. The Spouse in the Canticle of Canticles asks moreover: 'Where do you pasture your flock, where do you give them rest at midday?'[24] You see that it is not in the third hour that the Spouse dines or reclines, but at midday. Where do you dine, where do you rest, where shall I find you, where do you enjoy delights, where can I find you, O my Spouse? Do you want to find Me? At noon, in perfect knowledge, in good works, in the bright light. Because we have the noonday, that is why the devil disguises himself as an angel of light[25] and pretends that he has the light, that he has the noonday. When heretics promise any pseudo mysteries, when they promise the kingdom of heaven, when they promise continence, fasts, sanctity, the renunciation of the world, they promise the noonday. But since their midday is not the light of Christ, it is not the noonday, but the noonday demon.

'Though two thousand fall at your side, ten thousand at your right hand.'[26] Every word of scripture is a symbol all its own. These rustic words that men of every age ponder over are packed full of mystical meaning. 'But we carry this treasure in vessels of clay';[27] we have a divine treasury of meaning in the most ordinary words. 'Though two thousand fall at your side, ten thousand at your right hand.' At whose side? At his side to whom the psalmist had said: 'His truth will surround you with a shield; you shall not fear the terror of the night.' Who is this man? The same one of whom it was said: he 'who dwells in the shelter of the Most High, shall

---

23 Cf. Jerome's translation of Origen, *On Canticle of Canticles* 1.7, PL 23.1183 (511-13).
24 Cf. Cant. 1.7; cf. Letter 108.12, PL 22.887 (701); 122.1, PL 22.1039 (890).
25 2 Cor. 11.14.
26 Cf. Ps. 90 (91).7.
27 2 Cor. 4.7.

abide under the protection of the God of heaven.' At the side of him, therefore, who dwells in the shelter of the Lord, a thousand fall, and ten thousand fall at his right hand. The right hand of the just man is specified; his left hand is not mentioned, but his left side is. See for yourselves that it says: ten thousand at your right hand.

What did you mean by saying, two thousand fall at the side? Naturally, when the right hand is designated and the left is not, the side is named in place of the left hand. It would not be right, certainly, for the just man to have a left hand: 'If someone strike thee on the right cheek,' counsels the Lord, 'turn to him the other also.'[28] Notice that He did not say, 'the left also,' for it is not the left cheek that is offered, but another right cheek.[29] I shall express this very plainly, therefore, by saying that the just man has two right cheeks. The man, Aod, for example, who is written of in the Book of Judges, is said to have two right hands because he was a just man and killed that fat stupid king.[30] 'Though two thousand fall at your side, ten thousand at your right hand.' There are very many who lie in wait at our right hand, not so many who plot against our left; hence, a thousand fall at our side and ten thousand at our right hand. Where there is greater combat, there is, of course, greater victory. Few lie in ambush at our side, but many at our right hand.

'For to his angels he has given command about you, that they guard you in all your ways.' The devil has deliberately interpreted this passage as referring directly to the Lord, for when the devil tempted the Lord, he said: 'If thou art the Son of God, throw thyself down; for it is written of thee, "He will give his angels charge concerning thee; to keep thee in all thy ways. And upon their hands they shall bear thee up, lest thou dash thy foot against a stone." '[31] But the devil

---

28 Matt. 5.39.
29 Cf. *Commentary on Matthew* 5.39, PL 26.41 (31); *on Ezechiel* 41.23-26, PL 25.406 (506); *on Ecclesiastes* 10, PL 23.1146B (469).
30 Cf. Judges 3.15-20.
31 Matt. 4.6; cf. *Commentary on Matthew* 4.6, PL 26.32 (21).

did not quote the sacred text in full; he said no more than:
'For he has given his angels charge concerning thee, and
upon their hands they shall bear thee up, lest thou dash thy
foot against a stone.' Craftily, he left out the middle verse:
'To keep thee in all thy ways' because he knew that it was
aimed against him. The Lord could have replied to him: If
the Lord guards Me in all My ways, He guards Me against
you. But the devil was silent over what he knew was directed
against himself and cited the words only that were of profit
to him. Truly a devil, just like a devil he interprets as referring to the Savior that which has no reference to Him at
all.

If the entire psalm applies to the Savior, just as you are interpreting it, O devil, then the words: 'I will protect him because he acknowledges my name'[32] also apply to the Savior
and mean, I, the Father, will protect My Son. I am interpreting the psalm, O devil, in the way that you choose to
take it. Let us see if it makes sense. 'I will protect him because he acknowledges my name'; I, the Father, will protect
My Son. 'He shall call upon me, and I will answer him';
that is, on the day of His crucifixion. 'I will be with him in
distress, I will deliver him and glorify him'; I shall cause
Him to rise from the dead. 'With length of days I will gratify
him'; He shall live for all eternity. We may understand of
the Son of God the words: 'With length of days I will gratify
him,' but how do the words that follow: 'And will show him
my salvation,' apply to the Savior? The salvation of God
is the Son of God. If this is said of the Son, how can it make
sense, for the salvation of God is the Son of God? So you
see that your exegesis is very poor, O devil. But let us suppose that your interpretation is legitimate. You said: 'For
he has given his angels charge concerning thee; and upon
their hands they shall bear thee up, lest thou dash thy foot
against a stone.'[33] Do not stop there; continue with what

---

32 Cf. Ps. 90 (91).14.
33 Matt. 4.6.

follows. Why are you silent? 'You shall tread upon the asp and the viper; you shall trample down the lion and the dragon': Christ our Lord, who lives and reigns forever and ever. Amen.

HOMILY 21

ON PSALM 91 (92)

HE NINETY-FIRST PSALM is inscribed with the title: 'A psalm; a song for the Sabbath day.' There could be no sabbath day without six preceding days. We work for six days, on the seventh day we rest. We cannot sing to the Lord, therefore, save on the day of the sabbath. As long as we are engaged in the works of the world, that is, for the six days, we cannot sing to the Lord. Leviticus says: 'On the sabbath day you shall do no servile work.'[1] No one, therefore, on the day of the sabbath and on the day of the Lord's rest may do servile work—work pertaining to this world; but he ought to do the work that belongs to the sabbath. Would you know that on the sabbath the priests work in the temple of the Lord? It is not permitted anyone to cut wood on the sabbath; in fact, the man who was discovered gathering wood in the wilderness was stoned to death.[2] Neither may one even kindle a fire nor do any kind of work.

You will observe, however, that all the things that the layman is not allowed to do on the sabbath, the priests alone are permitted to do, for they cut wood, enkindle a fire, and perform other services, and immolate victims. Why am I making such a point of this? To show you that it is written in the law that we must withdraw from all worldly pursuits on the sabbath and perform only those works that pertain to God. A psalm, therefore, is a song on the sabbath day when we do not work for the world, but for God. Let us see now

1 Cf. Lev. 23.3.
2 Cf. Num. 15.32-36.

164

what we must sing on the sabbath when we are abstaining from the works of the world.

'It is good to confess to the Lord, to sing praise to your name, Most High.'[3] The psalmist did not say that it is good to sing and after that confess; but note the order; it is good to confess, and it is good to sing. First repent and wash away sin with your tears; then sing to the Lord. 'It is good to confess to the Lord': not to men, but to God; confess your sins to Him who is able to heal you. 'And to sing praise to your name, Most High.'

'To proclaim your kindness at dawn, and your truth throughout the night.'[4] Attend closely: To proclaim Your kindness at dawn and Your truth throughout the night. Each of these versicles refers in turn to a different versicle. 'It is good to confess to the Lord, to proclaim your kindness at dawn.' If you confess to the Lord, you are proclaiming His kindness at dawn. 'And to sing praise to your name, Most High.' This versicle is related to the following one: 'and truth throughout the night.' When we confess to the Lord, we are trusting in His mercy; when we sing, we are performing a good work.

'To proclaim your kindness at dawn.' Where are they who take the Scriptures literally? Are we not able to proclaim the kindness of God at noon? Certainly, too, it is the duty of Christians, and monks especially, to confess their sins at night. What, then, does 'to proclaim your kindness at dawn' mean? It means this. It is not possible for us to confess to the Lord and obtain His mercy unless a clear light has begun to enlighten our heart. Unless the shades of night have withdrawn and dawn has arrived, we cannot attain the compassionate mercy of God. Then, in truth, do you proclaim at dawn the kindness of God, when the sun of justice has risen in your heart.

'And your truth throughout the night.' The truth of the

---

3 Cf. Ps. 91 (92).2.
4 Cf. Ps. 91 (92).3.

Lord does not shine forth in its brilliance save at night. In the daytime it cannot be proclaimed because the weak are not able to sustain its sublimity nor endure its dazzling splendor. For this reason another psalm says of God: 'And he made darkness the cloak about him.'[5] In other words, the Lord shrouds Himself in darkness. That is how the truth of the Lord is proclaimed at night; it is shrouded, so to speak, in an obscurity of words. In parables, moreover, and enigmatically, the Lord says: 'Seeing they may not see, and hearing they may not understand.'[6]

We read in Osee that the prophet is bid: 'Go take a harlot wife.'[7] The Jews hear this and the heathens, too, and they laugh. Why do they laugh? Because truth is set forth in the darkness of night, not in the light of day. Do you want proof that the truth of God is in the night, and, as it were, cloaked in darkness and enclosed in parables? Moses went up into Mount Sinai; and he went up[8] in a cloud and in a mist and in darkness, and there he spoke with the Lord. The Israelites, however, could not see the mysteries of God because they had not entered the cloud that covered God.

'With ten-stringed instrument and lyre, with melody upon the harp.' I shall paraphrase this in simple language: Whenever we lift up pure hands in prayer, without deliberate distractions and contention,[9] we are playing to the Lord with a ten-stringed instrument. 'With ten-stringed instrument and lyre, with melody upon the harp.' Our body and soul and spirit—our harp—are all in harmony, all their strings in tune.

'For you make me glad, O Lord, by your deeds; at the works of your hands I rejoice.' No matter what the Christian looks upon, it becomes for him a source of edification. Nothing injures the monk save sin. Whatever you gaze upon holds a lesson for you. You look up at the sky; you see the sun; you

---

5 Ps. 17.12.
6 Luke 8.10; Matt. 13.13; Mark 4.12.
7 Osee 1.2.
8 Cf. Exod. 24.15, 16.
9 Cf. 1 Tim. 2.8.

behold the stars, the moon; these are all grist for your meditation. You ought to reflect upon them and say: 'If the sun,
and moon, and heaven, and the stars serve God, why do I not
serve Him?' You look down at the ground; you see the tiny
animals and everything that is there. Apply this to your
soul, learn from it, and say to your soul: 'Everything proceeds
at its appointed time, for example, spring and summer,
autumn and winter; why do they not change the order of
their course? Because all creatures serve God as He ordains.
Heaven obeys, and earth obeys, and I, unhappy man, do not
obey.'

Let us focus our attention now on tiny beings.[10] I am dis-
missing elephants, lions, all the various kinds of animals; I
come down to little insects. Consider the bee or the ant; see
its body and search into its wisdom—a wisdom far greater than
the magnitude of its body! Bees and ants plan ahead for the
winter that is to come, but the monk and the Christian give
no thought to the judgment that is on its way. The bee and
the ant know that they can be imperiled by hunger if they
do not labor in the summertime for their winter supply of
food; we do not reflect that without good works we shall be
tormented in hell. Why have I said all this? Because the
psalm says: 'For You make me glad, O Lord, by your deeds.'
Whatever I look upon fills me with gladness, for I recognize
the Creator and I bless God.

'At the works of your hands I rejoice.' I look at a tree and
I reflect upon the bark that clothes it like a garment; I notice
how the tree is ready to burst into flower just like a bud.
Then, I muse how like a flower it is, how the blossom fades,
and the flower itself becomes a fruit. I meditate on how
gradually, day by day, in every season, nature works for me
and becomes my food. I ponder over how God in all His
creatures labors for me that I may lack nothing; and then I
rejoice in You, O Lord.

10 Cf. Letter 60.12, PL 22.596 (340).

'How great are your works, O Lord!' This is the verse[11] in which Marcion and Manichaeus make their noisy entrance. What, pray, are they saying? If God has made all things, and has made them all for the needs of man, why did He have to make bugs and fleas? I shall make my answer to you brief and to the point: in order to expose your frailty, O man. You, who set your thoughts in heaven, look down; you are being bitten by a bug and you are trembling. Why do you hold your head on high and even transcend heaven with your thought? Look, you are being bitten by a bug![12] 'How great are your works, O Lord!' Tiny bodies, indeed, but mighty planning. They all have their own proper usefulness.

Just as I marvel at the Lord in the elephant, I wonder at the Lord in the ant. As I proclaim Him in the camel, even so I proclaim Him in the gnat. Look at the gnat, how it is practically a mere dot[13] with its tiny body. Yet in that tiny speck of a body all the parts, every member is distinct from the other. It has six feet, it has two eyes, it has a mouth and a paunch, it has also a trumpet for its voice, and it has wings. If you concentrate on each member by itself, you cannot find the rest of the body and you marvel at the work of God, for where there seems to be no body at all, not a single member is missing![14]

'How very deep are your thoughts!' However much I probe, I cannot fathom them. 'Your judgments, like the mighty deep.'[15] 'Oh, the depth of the riches of the wisdom and of the knowledge of God!'[16] With Ecclesiastes I, too, shall say: 'I said, "I will acquire wisdom"; but it was beyond me, much farther than before; it is deep, very deep: who can find it out?'[17] What Ecclesiastes is saying is this: Before I turned

---

11 Cf. *Against the Pelagians* 1.19, PL 23.536 (715).
12 Cf. *Commentary on Joel* 2.22-28, PL 25.973 (198).
13 Cf. *Against Rufinus* 3.28, PL 23.500 (557).
14 Cf. *Commentary on Osee* 13.3, PL 25.932 (146).
15 Ps. 35.7.
16 Rom. 11.33; cf. Letter 39.2, PL 22.467 (178); *Against the Pelagians* 1.33, PL 23.551 (731).
17 Cf. Eccles. 7.24, 25.

my thoughts to ponder over God's work, I was not aware of God's magnificence. I said, I must have wisdom; that is, I must inquire into the nature of every cause; and wisdom withdrew farther away from me than it ever was before. By that I mean, formerly I was not in quest of wisdom because I was unaware of it, and afterwards, when I began to seek it, I could not find it. 'A senseless man knows not, nor does a fool understand this.' Anyone who is not a Christian and does not recognize the Creator in His creatures is a fool.

'Though the wicked flourish like grass.' You have seen generals, you have seen governors, you have observed armies, you have witnessed victories and triumphs. Yesterday they were and today they are no more. 'And all evildoers thrive, they are destined for eternal destruction.' Yesterday, a flower was barely in blossom; today, the flower is not to be seen. Yesterday, a plant was fresh and green; today, it is dried up and withered. What has become of all that beauty?

Nothing is good save the eternal; nothing is good except the everlasting. Anything that is finite is not to be counted among the good. What good does it do me if yesterday I feasted and today I am dying with hunger? What good to me if in the days gone by I was king and today I am dying in prison? Whatever is passing and has an end is nothing. Each one of us has come from the world to embrace this state of life. One has left his mother; another, his children; one, his wife; another, his parents. Let us recall our childhood, our youth; let us recall the time when we had wealth and each one through his own efforts possessed whatever he could. Behold, we have crossed over to this life. Where are all those possessions of ours? Reminiscence brings more pain than pleasure. Nothing is good except that which lasts forever.

'While you, O Lord, are the Most High forever. For behold, your enemies, O Lord, for behold, your enemies shall perish; all evildoers shall be scattered.' If they shall perish, how shall they be scattered? He who has once perished cannot be scattered. It ought to say: Behold they shall be scattered, and shall vanish, for, what it means is: Your enemies, O Lord, shall perish; since every creature is subject to You, everyone who has been Your enemy is afterwards made a friend; that means, of course, that not man shall perish, but the enemy shall vanish. The one-time enemy will become a friend, so the enemy will perish. 'For behold your enemies shall perish; all the evildoers shall be scattered.' Just as when holy men live together, it is a great grace and blessing; so, likewise, that congregation is the worst kind when sinners live together. The more sinners there are at one time, the worse they are. Indeed, when the tower was being built up against God,[18] those who were building it were disbanded for their own welfare. The conspiracy was evil; the dispersion was of true benefit even to those who were dispersed.

'You have exalted my horn like the wild bull's.' A horn is always set up in a kingdom. 'Our foes through you we struck down with the horn.'[19] As a matter of fact, no animal is immolated to the Lord in the temple unless it is horned.[20] In the temple there are three animals sacrificed to the Lord: the bull, the ram, and the buck. Three are sacrificed and all three are horned. Unless one has a horn with which to rout his enemies, he is not worthy to be offered to God. That is why, too, the Lord is described as a horn[21] to those who believe in Him; and it was with the horns of the cross that He routed His enemies. On the cross He confounded the devil and his entire army. To be sure, Christ was crucified in His body, but on the cross, it was He who was crucifying there the devils. It was not a cross; it was a symbol of triumph, a banner of victory.[22] His whole purpose in mounting the cross was to lift us up from earth. I think the cross of the Savior was the ladder[23] that Jacob saw. On that ladder,

---

18 Cf. Gen. 11.1-9.
19 Cf. Ps. 43.6.
20 Cf. Commentary on Isaia 5.1, PL 24.74-5 (67); on Zacharia 1.18, 19, PL 25.1428 (790); on Habacuc 3.4, PL 25.1313 (639).
21 Cf. Ps. 17.3.
22 Cf. Commentary on Habacuc 3.4, PL 25.1312 (638).
23 Cf. Letter 58.2, PL 22.580 (319).

angels were descending and ascending; on that ladder, that
is, the cross, the Jews were descending and the Gentiles
ascending. 'You have exalted my horn like the wild bull's.'
Others may have many horns; I have only one. 'But as for
me, God forbid that I shall glory save in the cross of the Lord,
through whom the world is crucified to me, and I to the
world.'[24]

'And my old age with the rich oil of mercy.'[25] Our old age
needs the oil of God. Just as our bodies, when they are
wearied from toil (I am speaking very simply for the sake
of our guileless brethren who are unable to grasp a more
subtle analogy), just as our bodies, when they are tired from
manual labor, are refreshed by rubbing them with oil; just
as the light in a lamp burns out unless you feed it oil; so,
likewise, the light of my old age requires the oil of God's
mercy to keep it burning brightly. Then, too, the apostles
ascended Mount Olivet in order that they might be illuminated with the oil of the Lord because they were weary and
their lamps were in need of His oil. In line with this thought,
the just man says: 'But I, like a green olive tree in the house
of God.'[26] And in another place Holy Writ says: 'Your children like olive plants around your table.'[27]

Was there no other mountain, moreover, except Mount
Olivet from which the Lord might ascend into the kingdom
of heaven? Was there not a higher mountain in Galilee,
Thabor? Why was it necessary for the Lord to ascend into the
kingdom of heaven from Mount Olivet? But just realize
what Scripture is teaching you. Unless you oil yourselves
and your lamps, you shall not be able to ascend into the
kingdom of heaven. You have to be on Mount Olivet; not in
the Valley of the Olives, but on the Mount. Someone may
ask: What is this Valley of Olives? The devil, too, has his
own olives; he has the philosophers; he has the heretics; they

24 Gal. 6.14.
25 Cf. Ps. 91 (92).11.
26 Ps. 51.10.
27 Ps. 127.3.

also have oil; they also promise the light of knowledge. But those olive groves lead down into the valley: 'Let not the festive oil of sinners anoint my head.'[28] Let us pray, then, to the Lord, that our old age and all our labor and all our darkness be illuminated with oil of the Lord.

I am reviewing carefully the places in Scripture where I might find old age mentioned for the first time. Adam lived for 930 years, yet he is not called an old man. Mathusala's life was 969 years, and he is not called an old man. I am coming down all the way to the Flood, and after the Flood for almost three thousand years, and I find no one who has been called old. Abraham is the first one, and certainly he was much younger than Mathusala, but he is called an old man because his old age had been anointed with rich oil. In fine, it is written there in the Scripture: 'Abraham died at a good old age; full of days.'[29] His was a good old age because it was full of days, for the whole of his life was day and not night. This same attribute is given also to Isaac and to Jacob. They who had served the Lord in the same age, rightly should be called old men of the Lord at the same time.

'Like a cedar of Lebanon shall he grow,' a truly fragrant wood, the wood from which the roof of the temple had been constructed. 'Like a cedar of Lebanon shall he grow,' a wood that never decays.

'They that are planted in the house of the Lord shall flourish in the courts of our God.'[30] In one place we are planted; in another place we flourish; here we are planted; in the kingdom of God we shall flourish. 'I have planted,' says the Apostle, 'Apollos watered, but God has given the growth.'[31] I have been planted in the house of the Lord, I mean in the Church; not in the walls, but in its doctrines: 'For the kingdom of God,' the Lord says, 'is within you.'[32]

---

28 Cf. Ps. 140.5.
29 Cf. Gen. 25.8. Cf. *Commentary on Zacharia* 8.4, 5, PL 25.1465 (839).
30 Cf. *Against the Pelagians* 2.20, PL 23.583 (766).
31 1 Cor. 3.6.
32 Luke 17.21.

Everyone who has been planted in the house of the Lord, who has grown roots here, brings forth flowers there.

'They that are planted in the house of the Lord shall flourish in the courts of our God.' These are the eternal dwelling places. What are these courts? Different mansions in heaven. At the same time, note that: 'They that are planted in the house of the Lord shall flourish in the courts of our God.' Here is the house; there is the court. According to proper order, it should have said court first and then house. But just see what it means. Even though we seem to be in a house here, nevertheless, when we shall have migrated to the kingdom of heaven, in comparison with the angels and the other powers, we shall not be in the house at all but only in the court. We are at the beginning, not at the end of perfection. We shall not be angels, but like angels. Do not let that seem a slight thing to you, O man, if you shall be like an angel.[33]

'They shall bear fruit even in old age.' Happy the man who grows more vigorous from day to day; he who grows feeble in age grows feeble likewise in virtue.

We have been talking about the psalter, we have said a few words about the Gospel; we have also mentioned the Apostle. Let us beg the Lord that everything that we have said—both that which we have said and that which you have heard—we may fulfill in good works; that we may translate words into works;[34] that we, who have been planted here in the house of the Lord, may flourish there in the court of Christ. To Him be glory forever and ever. Amen.

---

33 Cf. Lettter 75.2, PL 22.687 (453); 108.22, PL 22.900 (717).
34 Cf. Letter 58.2, PL 22.580 (319).

HOMILY 22

ON PSALM 93 (94)

E HAVE ALWAYS maintained that from its title one may learn the theme of a psalm. 'A psalm for David himself on the fourth day of the week.'[1] The fourth day is midway to the sabbath; it is, as it were, the heart of the week, the middle day in seven. It is the fourth day, and the fourth day has an equal number of days on each side. On one, the first, second, and third; and on the other, the fifth, sixth, and seventh. You see, therefore, that the fourth day of the week is supported on both sides by a trinity. At the same time you must remember that the fourth number is the tenth in power. How is that? If you sum up one, two, three, four consecutively, the total is ten, so you see the fourth number produces the tenth. From this computation consider, too, that the four Gospels are summed up in the decalogue. Everything contained in the decalogue is fulfilled in the four Gospels; hence, the Old Law does not contradict the authority of the Gospels. So much for the title; now let us turn our attention to the psalm itself.

'God of vengeance, Lord, God of vengeance, show yourself.' He, who concealed Himself for a long time and did not appear among the people, at long last revealed Himself. He, who before was unknown, afterwards triumphed on the cross. 'God of vengeance, Lord.' If God is the Lord of vengeance ('Vengeance is mine; I will repay, says the Lord'[2]), why do you seek revenge, O man? You have the Lord as your

---

1 Cf. Ps. 93 (94).1, LXX.
2 Rom. 12.19; cf. Deut. 32.35; Heb. 10.30.

Avenger. That is in substance what the Apostle says: 'If thy enemy is hungry, give him food; if he is thirsty, give him drink: For by so doing thou wilt heap coals of fire upon his head.'[3] But that does not seem like an act of kindness; rather it seems like cruelty. If I do an enemy good only that God may do him evil, I am acting not from piety, but from a motive of cruelty. What, then, does the Apostle mean? 'If your enemy is hungry, give him food,' kind and pious words. 'If he thirsts, give him drink.' Thus far it sounds like compassion. The conclusion, however: 'for by doing this you will heap coals of fire upon his head,' does not seem kind but cruel. You seem, in fact, to be giving him bread to eat and water to drink only to torture him for all eternity. Does the Apostle really mean that; does the preacher of mercy teach cruelty? No, it is not to be taken that way but in another sense.[4] If your enemy strikes you, turn to him also your other cheek; if he does you wrong, you do him a good; for when you do that, you are heaping coals of fire upon his head. In other words, you will purify your enemy of sin, for your patience will conquer his cruelty. If you aim an arrow at a stone, and the stone is hard, not only will the arrow fail to penetrate, but it will even rebound. It is the same with your enemy; if he should strike you and you do not retaliate, he will be conquered by your patience and you will convert him.

'How long, O Lord, shall the wicked, how long shall the wicked glory?' Human impatience does not want God to have patience. Creatures truly pitiable are we who would have God patient with us but impatient with our enemies. When we commit sin, we beg God to be patient with us; yet when somebody wrongs us, we do not expect God to be patient with him. 'How long shall the wicked glory?' Not enough that they commit sin; they even glory in their sins.

---

3 Rom. 12.20.
4 Letter 120.1, PL 22.983 (821); *Against the Pelagians* 1.30, PL 23.548 (782).

Their first misfortune is to sin; their second degree of wretchedness—nay, rather their last—is impenitence. These sinners not only refuse to bend their necks in humility, but openly parade their wrongdoing.

'Mouthing insolent speeches.' These are the heretics without a doubt. 'Boasting, all the evildoers?' Watch for the signal: the man who is rebellious and insolent with his tongue must needs be evil in his deeds: 'for out of the abundance of the heart the mouth speaks.'[5] Wherever there is a damaged conscience, sins of the tongue abound.

'Your people, O Lord, they trample down.' God's people are always being crushed, ever being trampled down. 'Your people, O Lord, they trample down.' God's people are laid low in humility in imitation of God who was meek and humble of heart.[6]

'Widow and stranger they slay, the fatherless they murder, and they say, "The Lord sees not." ' Although this passage is obviously a record of history, for the unprotected are always the ready prey of tyranny, and the more humble the victim the more does the persecutor offend against God, nevertheless, we are going to follow tropology in our exegesis. I have already noted for you the appropriate application of this psalm to heretics: Widow and stranger, they have slain. The widow is the soul of the sinner who has lost God as his spouse; the stranger is a non-inhabitant, that is, one who is not a permanent dweller. He is the recent believer who quickly falls away the first time he meets with scandal. 'The fatherless they murder, and they say, "The Lord sees not." ' Are we wondering, since the fatherless are mentioned, where the widow is? By the same token that the widow is the soul of the sinner, the fatherless are they who have lost God their Father.[7] 'And they say.' What do they say? 'The Lord sees not; the God of Jacob perceives not.' This is the prating of one who

---

5 Luke 6.45.
6 Cf. Matt. 11.29.
7 Cf. *Commentary on Osee* 14.2-4, PL 25.942 (158).

treats the saints scornfully. Hear now the Holy Spirit's answer to those who mouth such insolence.

'Understand, you senseless ones among the people; and, you fools, when will you be wise? Shall he who shaped the ear not hear?' Does the potter not know his own pottery? He who makes another hear, will He Himself be deaf? He who gave me eyes, will He Himself be blind? He who is the author of my understanding, will He Himself be without intelligence?[8] This passage opposes especially the Anthropomorphites who say that God has the same human form and members that we have. They say, for example, that God has eyes: the eyes of the Lord behold all things; the hands of the Lord have made all things. 'And Adam heard the footsteps of the Lord walking in the garden,' says Holy Writ.[9] Naturally, they hear these words and collate human weaknesses with the magnificence of God. But I say that God is all eye; He is all hand; He is all foot. He is all eye because He sees everything; He is all hand because He is the maker of everything; He is all foot because He is everywhere. Consider again, therefore, the words: 'Shall he who shaped the ear not hear?' Scripture did not say, Shall He who shaped the ear not Himself have an ear? It did not say: Shall He not Himself, therefore, have eyes? But what did it say? He who fashioned the ear, shall He not have the power of hearing? He who implanted the eye with which to see, does He not survey all things? He produced the parts of the body; He gave them their efficient powers.[10]

'Shall he who instructs nations not chastise': shall the Teacher of others, Himself be ignorant? 'He who teaches men knowledge?' Is it to be understood, therefore, that He Himself is without knowledge? 'The Lord knows the thoughts of

---

8 Cf. *Commentarioli in ps.* 93.9.
9 Cf. Gen. 3.8.
10 Cf. *Commentary on Amos* 6.7-12, PL 25.1063 (316).

men, and that they are vain.' We read in the writing of a
profane poet:

O the conceit of mankind! How
great the vanity in human affairs![11]

Both the Gentiles and the philosophers praise this verse
excessively. And what do they say? This is positively the last
word in wisdom! Behold our rustic Hebrew has voiced this
same thought many ages before. And what did he say? 'The
Lord knows the thoughts of men, and that they are vain.'

Do you need proof that the thoughts of men are vain? A
father and mother rear a son; they look forward with great
promise to the fortune and happiness that he will bring them;
they send him to school, give him the best education; he
comes of age and they even arrange for his military service.
After thirty years of careful and matured planning, along
comes a slight fever and that is the end of all their schemes.
I have an enemy with whom I must go to court, and the
day of the trial is thirty days off; day and night I do nothing
but prepare my defense. When I am in bed, all I do is
frame answers to the charges of my enemy who is absent. My
enemy is not present but my words are answering him as if
he were. I rehearse in this way for days and nights. When
the day of judgment arrives, however, all my carefully planned
debate vanishes and I answer only what God inspires. That is
precisely why the Lord says in the Gospel: 'And when they
bring you before the magistrate, do not be anxious how or
wherewith you shall defend yourselves, or what you shall say,
for the Lord will teach you in that very hour what you
ought to say.'[12] 'The Lord knows the thoughts of men, and
that they are vain.' One preoccupation alone is worthwhile
and wholesome—thinking about the Lord.

'Happy the man whom you instruct, O Lord,' happy the
man who accepts God as his Teacher. 'Whom by your law
you teach, giving him rest from evil days.' Just think what

---

11 Perseus, *Satire* 1.1.
12 Luke 12.11, 12.

that means: Happy the man whom You school, O Lord, and instruct in Your law, in Your Scriptures. What profit, moreover, does he derive from instruction in Your law? 'Giving him rest from evil days.' So you see that the knowledge of Holy Writ, training in its lessons and performing its works, lightens for us our days of adversity. 'Till the pit be dug for the wicked.' When you have been schooled in the law of the Lord, it will benefit you twofold: it will give you a lift in days of trouble, and it will dig a pit for the sinner.

'Who will rise up for me against the wicked?' The psalms are involved and frequently change person;[13] for that reason they are obscure and it is often difficult to know in individual versicles just who the speaker is. 'Who will rise up for me against the wicked? Who will stand by me against the evildoers?' The Savior is speaking: 'I am the man of holiness; I have been raised up on the cross; I have died; I have risen from the dead; I have ascended into heaven in triumph. Who of the saints do you suppose will rise with Me?' This is what He means: I arose from the dead that others might rise up with Me.

'Who will rise up for me?' When He asks, 'Who,' He is inviting everyone to rise with Him, for just as we read in Isaia: 'Whom shall I send? Who will go for us?'[14] and Isaia offers himself, so, too, the Lord invites us with the words: 'Who will rise up for me against the wicked?' Whoever shall rise, shall rise up for Me; he is of My army. 'Against the wicked': against the devil and his army. 'Who will stand by me?' Mark the order. He did not say first, who will stand, and then, who will rise up; but who will rise up and then who will stand. First we arise, naturally; then we stand. 'Who will stand by me against the evildoers?'; like a commander may He stand and cry out: 'Who will join My army?' 'Were not the Lord my help, I would soon dwell in the silent grave.' That is why I rise again, Lord, because You have

13 Cf. Homily 3 on Ps. 7, p. 25; 13 on Ps. 80, p. 93.
14 Isa. 6.8.

been in the land of the dead and have risen from the dead. My soul would have been detained in hell, if Your soul had not arisen from the dead.

'When I say, "My foot is slipping." ' In view of my frailty and human infirmity, I did not see how my foothold could be firm and steady; with every step I feared to slip. But when I turned my thoughts back to You again and called upon Your name, my foothold became secure.

'When cares abound within me, your comfort gladdens my soul.' This is comparable to the saying of the Apostle that we shall receive a reward from God in heaven in proportion to our labor and sufferings on earth.[15] The magnitude of our tribulations determines the magnitude of our reward; as many wounds we endure, that many crowns do we merit. Now for the meaning of the verse: as many times as I have repented, that many times You have consoled me. I have shed one tear, I have earned one consolation; I have shed ten tears, I have merited ten consolations. The weight of my repentance equated the number of Your consolations.

'Who cause toil by your law.'[16] No one receives a crown while he is asleep; no one is secure in his possession of the kingdom of heaven; no one with a full stomach is fit to discourse on fasting.[17] You grasp now the force of the versicle: 'who cause toil by your law.' All the commandments of the Lord demand effort. Without labor and toil, we cannot possess the kingdom of heaven. Do you want to know why? 'If thou wilt be perfect, go, sell what thou hast, and give to the poor, and come, follow me.'[18] In other words, he who desires to attain the kingdom of heaven, let him pray night and day; let him keep watch; let him fast; let him make his bed on rushes, not on down and silk. Penitence has no fel-

---

15 Cf. 1 Cor. 3.8, 9.
16 Cf. Ps. 93 (94).20; cf. Letter 133.7, PL 22.1155 (1035).
17 Cf. Letter 52.7, PL 22.533 (262); 58.2, PL 22.580 (320).
18 Matt. 19.21.

lowship with soft luxuries. 'For I eat ashes like bread, and mingle my drink with tears.'[19]

'Who cause toil by your law. Though they attack the life of the just.' Notice that there is no apparent connection between these two versicles, for what relation is there between 'who cause toil by your law,' and 'though they attack the life of the just'? Now when the ear of the body does not understand, the ear of the spirit does. What is the meaning then? 'Who cause toil by your law': we are laboring day and night by the law of the Lord, in vigils, prayer, and fasts, for we have many adversaries who are setting traps for the soul of the just man. They attack the soul of the just, not of the unjust. They are out, not to harass those who have been trapped, but to ensnare the guiltless. That is why it says in Habacuc: 'His repast sumptuous.'[20]

'And condemn innocent blood.' There are always some who will assert that the slain would not have been slain if they had not been fornicators, or had not committed some other sin; disaster would not have overtaken this man, if he had not been a sinner; shipwreck would not have befallen that man, if he had not been a sinner. Perceive, therefore, the meaning of Holy Writ in: 'And condemn innocent blood.' As long as we are in this world, we endure all things together. The just man and the sinner equally suffer shipwreck; they are equals in flesh and equals in the condition of flesh. The just and the sinner perish equally; death comes to each alike; but there are different rewards that await the just and the sinner. One goes to hell, the other is conducted into the kingdom of heaven. 'And condemn innocent blood.' Your conscience is sufficient for you, O just man; if you are condemned, your blood is innocent, and it will cry out to the Lord.

'Yet the Lord has been made my stronghold.'[21] This text

---

19 Ps. 101.10.
20 Hab. 1.16; cf. Letter 22.4, PL 22.396 (90).
21 Cf. Ps. 93 (94).22.

provides refutation to the Arians. Since they deny the Lord
Savior because it says He has been made, behold we affirm:
the Lord has been made my stronghold! No one doubts but
that these words refer to the Father. If, moreover, it is said
of the Father: 'the Lord has been made my stronghold,' it
must be understood in this sense: the Lord who always was,
has become my stronghold; therefore, the Savior who always
was, has become my Redeemer.[22]

22 Cf. *Commentary on Isaia* 12.2, PL 24.152 (165).

HOMILY 23

ON PSALM 95 (96)

HE NINETY-FIFTH PSALM is distinguished by the title: 'A song of David when the house was being built after the captivity.'[1] A title such as this brims with mystery; it embodies the whole mystical meaning and plan of our salvation. 'A song of David, when the house was being built after the captivity.' The Jews interpret this title as follows: A song of David after the Babylonian Captivity when the temple was rebuilt under Esdra, Zorobabel, and Jesus, the son of Josedech, a song of David. According, then, to the Jews, David knew in his spirit five hundred years before that the temple would be rebuilt. So they assert. If the interpretation is as you say, O Jews, what is the meaning of the next verse: 'Sing to the Lord a new song'; and, then, the verse: 'Tell his glory among the nations'? What is this new song? What nations are these? You see, therefore, that your explanation, clinging to 'the letter that kills,'[2] is altogether impossible; the words: 'When the house was being built after the captivity,' must be understood mystically.

Would that my house were built after captivity! Many of us have been captured; many have been led into Babylon; many have borne the heavy yoke of Nabuchodonosor; many have been sent into the fiery furnace and have burned there; many have destroyed the temple of the Lord and have torn down the house of God within them. Unhappy Judas was the house of God when he was an apostle. The devil came

---

1 Cf. Ps. 95 (96).1, LXX.
2 Cf. 2 Cor. 3.6.

and Judas took the morsel; immediately Satan entered into him, his house was torn down, and was never rebuilt because he did not repent. If, after sinning, one sincerely repents, his house is rebuilt after captivity.

Let us, therefore, pray the Lord first of all, that our house may not be overthrown, that the Chaldaean and Assyrian may not come and destroy the temple of Christ within us. If, however, it should be overturned, we can be saved by the plank that is a second refuge in our shipwreck.[3] 'When the house was being built after the captivity.' Every day this house of Christ is being restored in the penitent. In fact, the psalmist did not say: 'When the house has been built,' lest it seem already to have happened and belong to the past, but he specified 'it was being built' in order to show that his rebuilding takes place every day. So far, we have been speaking of our souls, but it is possible to make another application, namely, when the Church of Christ was being prepared after the fall. Now let us review the verse that follows upon the title.

'Sing to the Lord a new song.' O happy repentance! Even though you fall, nevertheless, if you repent, you are pronounced a new house of Christ. 'Sing to the Lord a new song.' A new house is worthy of a new song. 'Sing to the Lord a new song.' Who is to sing? 'Sing to the Lord, all the earth.'[4] If this psalm refers to the temple of Jerusalem, O Jew, why is all the earth summoned to give praise to the Lord? 'Sing to the Lord, all the earth.' This versicle vanquishes at once both the Jew and Novatian. 'Sing to the Lord, all the earth'; not Jerusalem only, but the whole world. Here, the Jew falls. 'Sing to the Lord, all the earth.' Novatian is undone. How so? Because it is Novatian who says: There are some sins for which we must repent, for instance, lying, perjury, theft; but for the fornicator, for the murderer, there is no repentance possible. But listen, I beg, to what the psalm says: 'Sing to

---

3 Cf. Letter 122.4, PL 22.1046 (889); 130.9, PL 22.1115 (986).
4 Cf. Ps. 95 (96).1.

the Lord, all the earth.' 'All the earth,' includes the adulterer, the murderer; all sin is earthbound. If, moreover, every sin without exception bears the stamp of earth, no matter what sin you have committed, repent and in every respect you will be saved.

'Sing to the Lord; bless his name.' The Lord's name is Savior because of His work of salvation in us. 'Sing to the Lord; announce his salvation, day after day.' What is the meaning of 'announce his salvation day after day'? The guileless man understands it this way: Praise the Lord every day, that is, one day after another, or, praise Him today; praise Him again tomorrow. This interpretation certainly is obvious, but to me there is another deeper meaning beneath the words. 'Announce his salvation day after day.' The Savior cannot be praised except in daylight. The prophet should have said, praise the Lord day and night, if he were speaking of day in its usual sense, but if we take the words in their literal meaning, we are faced with the problem: Are we not able to praise the Lord again at night if we praise Him during the daytime? Learn, therefore, what it means. Whenever you praise the Lord, praise Him always in light, not in the darkness of sins, but in the light of virtues. May the sun of Christ rise in your soul always that always a new light may shine in you.

'Announce his salvation day after day.' Let us examine this versicle from another angle. There are two days, not three, nor four, nor five; there are two days, the Old Testament and the New. Christ shines forth in both. Do not praise Him in the Old Testament only, lest you be a Jew; do not praise Him only in the New Testament, lest you be a Manichaean. Praise Him day after day, in the Old and in the New Testament; these two days make one and the same light. That is why it is written in Leviticus: 'Any animal that is cloven-footed and chews the cud is clean.'[5] If, however, it has an uncleft hoof, it is not clean. The Jew is single-

---

5 Cf. Lev. 11.3.

hoofed and, therefore, is unclean. Manichaeus has an un-
divided hoof, hence, is unclean. Moreover, because he is
single-hoofed, he does not ruminate; once he has swallowed
his food, he does not regurgitate it and chew it over and
over again until it is very fine, in order that food, that had
been coarse, may be sent down again into his stomach refined. Truly does this saying pertain to divine mysteries:
'Any animal that is cloven-footed and chews the cud is clean.'
The Jew is single-hoofed, for he believes in only one Testament and does not ruminate. Indeed, he reads merely the
letter and does not reflect upon it; he looks for no deeper
meaning than the literal message of the word. The man of
the Church, however, is cloven-footed and ruminates; he believes in both Testaments and often ponders deeply over both,
and whatever lies buried in the letter, he brings forth in the
spirit.

Why have I insisted upon all this? Because it is written:
'announce his salvation, day after day.' That, by the way, is
the reason why the apostles are sent out two by two; that is
why we have not one eye but two eyes; that is why we have two
ears, two nostrils, two lips, two hands, two feet. We have
nothing in us that is single, except that which is unsightly;
and so the members of our body bear witness to the mystical
teachings in the two Testaments.

'Give to the Lord, you families of nations, give to the Lord
glory and praise.'[6] If this psalm refers to the temple of
Jerusalem, what is the meaning behind the words: 'Give to
the Lord, you families of nations, give to the Lord glory and
praise'? The multitude of nations, the calling of the Gentiles,
constitutes the Church. 'Give to the Lord glory and praise.'
When we honor the presence of the Lord in our body, then we
are giving Him praise and glory. 'Give to the Lord the glory
due his name!' The servant's glory is glory, likewise, for the

---

6 Cf. *Commentarioli in ps.* 95.7.

master. 'He who receives you, receives me.'[7] Happy that servant through whom the master receives honor and glory.

'Bring gifts, and enter his courts,' 'a sacrifice, living, holy, pleasing to God.'[8] 'Bring gifts.' Bring up your gifts. What kind of gifts? The gifts of yourselves. Virginity is a holocaust to Christ; all chastity, whether in virginity, widowhood, or continence, is a sacrificial offering to Christ.[9] I am going to mention a new thought here: chastity is the sacrificial gift that brings and gives itself.

'Bring gifts, and enter his courts; worship the Lord in his holy court.'[10] In this verse, I see many courts and again I see one court. Bring gifts, and come into His courts—many courts. On the other hand, worship the Lord in His holy court—one court. Notice that it is not possible from one court to enter many courts; but it is possible from many to enter into one. Would you like to hear this same mystery from another place in Holy Writ? There is that merchant who had many pearls and sold all that he had to buy one pearl.[11] Michea, too, says: 'Stand beside the roads of the Lord, ask the pathways of the Lord.'[12] Unless we stand in the crossroads, we cannot find the one road. What are we to understand by the many pearls, the many roads, the many courts, so that we may find the one pearl, the one road, the one court?[13] Abraham, Isaac, and Jacob; Moses, Jesus son of Nave; Isaia, Jeremia, Ezechiel, the twelve prophets; David, Solomon; all were courts. They are our courts; they are the courts we enter first; and from them we arrive later at the court of the Gospels and there we find Christ.

---

7 Matt. 10.40.
8 Rom. 12.1; cf. *Commentarioli in ps.* 95.8; Letter 66.12, PL 22.646 (401-402.); 118.5, PL 22.964 (796); 130.2, PL 22.1107 (976).
9 Cf. *Against Jovinian* 1.13, PL 23.240 (258).
10 Cf. Ps. 95 (96).8, 9.
11 Cf. Matt. 13.46; cf. Letter 54.11, PL 22.555 (289).
12 Cf. Jer. 6.16.
13 Cf. *Commentary on Isaia* 26.2-4, PL 24.294 (344); Letter 54.11, PL 22.555 (289); 107.5, PL 22.872 (683); *Commentary on Ep. to Titus* 1.2-4, PL 26.595 (693).

'Tremble before him, all the earth.' Attend to what the psalmist says! Heaven does not tremble in the presence of God, but earthly minded man regards the Lord anxiously, and is greatly disturbed, and trembles. 'Say among the nations: The Lord is king.' Unless the earth tremble and withdraw from its worldly pursuits, the Lord will not reign among the nations.

'He has made the world firm, not to be moved.' No need to restore order except where previous order has been disturbed.[14] Accordingly, therefore, we, and the whole human race, know God by nature.[15] There are no peoples, indeed, who do not naturally know their Creator. Granted that sticks and stones are worshiped; nevertheless, their worshipers grasp the fact that there is something greater than they, and in their very error reveal their discernment; there is no nation that does not naturally know there is a God. The Gentiles worship idols, adore sticks and stones, but if by chance they fall into dispute and if they swear any oath, they do not say: 'These stones see, these pieces of wood are witness,' but, 'God sees, and God hears.'

Understand, then, what the Scripture means: 'He has made the world firm, not to be moved.' In very truth, Christ came and made firm the human race that had been disturbed, so that it may not be moved for all eternity. His cross is the pillar of mankind; on this pillar He has built His house. When I say the cross, I am not thinking of the wood, but of the Passion. This cross, moreover, is in Britain, and in India, and in the whole habitable world. Furthermore, what is the warning in the Gospel? 'Unless you take up my cross, and daily follow me.'[16] Mark what it says: Unless your soul has been made as ready for the cross as Mine was for you, you cannot be My disciples.

---

14 Cf. *Commentary on Ecclesiastes* 1, PL 23.1074 (394); *Commentarioli in ps.* 17.36; 95.10.
15 Cf. *Commentarioli in ps.* 18.7.
16 Cf. Luke 9.23.

Happy the man who bears in his heart the cross and the Resurrection, the place of Christ's nativity, and the place of His Ascension! Happy the man who has Bethlehem in his heart, in whose heart Christ is born every day! In fact, what does Bethlehem mean? The house of bread. Let us be the house of Bread, of Him who came down from heaven. Every day Christ is crucified in us; we are crucified to the world; Christ is crucified in us. Happy the man in whose heart Christ rises daily,[17] and He will rise every day, if every day the sinner repents his sins, even slight ones. Happy the man who daily from Mount Olivet ascends to the kingdom of heaven, where the Lord keeps His green olive trees, where the light of Christ rises, where the Lord has His olive groves. 'But I, like a green olive tree in the house of the Lord.'[18]

Let us also light our lamp from the oil of this olive tree, and straightway with Christ we shall enter the kingdom of heaven. 'He has made the world firm, not to be moved': the οἰκουμένην, the whole inhabited world in which He Himself dwells. (The Greek oecumene has a clearer connotation[19] than the Latin 'habitatio.') Let us pray that our oecumene, too, be made firm for the indwelling of the Father and the Son and the Holy Spirit, for unless our oecumene is the dwelling place of the Trinity, it cannot be fixed and firm.

There is much more that we should say, especially because it is the Feast of the Dedication. The Dedication festal days always occur in bad weather; they fall in rainy weather; they come in the winter season. Then, too, it is written in the Gospel: 'At Jerusalem on the Feast of Dedication, the Lord was walking in the temple, in Solomon's porch, because it was winter and it was raining.'[20] Notice what it says. On the festal days of the Dedication, He was walking on the porch because it was stormy and raining. Whenever anyone desires

---

17 Cf. *Commentary on Ephesians* 1.18-20, PL 26.490 (564).
18 Ps. 51.10.
19 Cf. Letter 140.6, PL 22.1171 (1054); *Commentary on Isaia* 13.11, PL 24.157 (172); 26.18, PL 24.303 (356).
20 Cf. John 10.22-24.

to restore himself in Christ; when the house is built after the captivity; whenever anyone desires to rebuild his house and rebuild it for Christ; whenever anyone is ready to forsake the world and give himself entirely to Christ; at once a storm arises, winter comes, and the rains pour down. But Christ, nay rather the poor in Christ, comprehending that the days of Dedication are at hand, beholding the storm, seeing the floods, feeling the winter, brave the floods and seek refuge in the porch of Solomon; they find shelter in the peace of Christ. Peace-bearer is, indeed, the meaning of the name of the Solomon who said: 'Peace I leave with you, my peace I give to you.'[21] Let us, therefore, walk in the porch of Solomon; let us be sheltered by His majesty; let us hold fast to His assistance; let us sing with the Canticle of Canticles: 'winter is past, the rains are over and gone,'[22] in Christ Jesus.

---

21 John 14.27.
22 Cant. 2.11; cf. Letter 78.1, PL 22.700 (470); 121.4, PL 22.1015 (861); *Against Jovinian* 1.30, PL 23.263 (285).

HOMILY 24

ON PSALM 96 (97)

F DAVID, when his land was restored again to him.'[1]
We read in the Books of Kings and in Paralipomenon
that David was a valorous hero who subjugated to his
rule all the surrounding nations. This fact agrees with the
literal interpretation of the title, so that we understand its
meaning thus: The song of David that he sang to the Lord,
when he restored peace to his own land, Judea, after van-
quishing all his foes. That is history. On the contrary, if
David's name means 'strong of hand,'[2] then, the 'strong of
hand' is no other than the Conqueror of all nations, our
David at whom the demons cried out: 'Hast thou come here to
torment us before the time, Son of David?'[3] This song was
composed by Him when His land was restored. Excellently,
indeed, has our venerable priest compared the land that was
restored to our bodies. Certainly, when peace has returned to
our land is the time for us to sing to God.

Let us express this thought another way, however, for there
is no harm in putting the same thing two or three different
ways. It is written, in fact, in the Book of Solomon: 'Take
these words in three manner of ways on the tablet of your
heart.'[4] It does no harm to change the wording when the
spirit remains the same. 'When his land was restored to him.'
There was no peace in this land before our David did his

---

1 Cf. Ps. 96 (97).1, LXX.
2 Cf. *Commentary on Isaia,* bk. 17, PL 24.585 (715); *Osee* 3.4, 5, PL
25.845 (33).
3 Matt. 8.29.
4 Cf. Prov. 22.20; cf. Letter 120.12, PL 22.1005 (848).

conquering; everywhere there was confusion and discord. One nation was worshiping Jove; another, Mercury; another, Juno; every nation had its own particular god. The standard of the cross was lifted up, and with it every land was restored to order.

'The Lord is king; let the earth rejoice.' All the earth, and the whole world that had been under the sway of demons and idols, let it now rejoice under the Kingship of the Lord. 'The Lord is king.' The Lord Creator who made you is Himself King. O, you, who before had been subject to the dominion of the lord devil, are now subject to the rule of the Lord Creator. 'Let the many isles be glad.' The venerable priest applied this well to our own souls that are tossed hither and thither by distracting thoughts like so many waves beating and buffeting us.

Let us, however, speak also of the churches as islands. Moreover, Scripture says in another place: 'Many islands are converted to me.'[5] Would you know that churches are called islands? The prophet Isaia says in the name of the Lord: 'Speak to the inhabitants of this isle.'[6] 'Let the many isles be glad.' Even as islands have been set in the midst of the sea, churches have been established in the midst of this world, and they are beaten and buffeted by different waves of persecution.[7] Verily these islands are lashed by waves every day, but they are not submerged. They are in the midst of the sea, to be sure, but they have Christ as their foundation, Christ who cannot be moved.

'Clouds and darkness are round about him!' There are two things that surround the Lord, clouds and darkness. I think this is the same cloud mentioned in the Gospel: 'A bright cloud overshadowed them.'[8] That occurred when our Lord was transformed, and the apostles fell on their faces before

---

5 Cf. Eccles. 47.17; Isa. 42.10, 12; Soph. 2.11.
6 Cf. Isa. 20.6.
7 Cf. *Commentary on Isaia* 41.1-8, PL 24.412 (496); 42.1-5, PL 24.422 (508); 51.5, PL 24.484 (587).
8 Matt. 17.5.

Him and a bright cloud overshadowed them. I think, too, these are the clouds which the Lord commanded not to rain upon Israel.[9] I think, likewise, these are the clouds about which it says in another place: 'Your truth, to the clouds';[10] that Truth of the Lord that says in the Gospel: 'I am the way, and the truth, and the life.'[11] The Truth of God is Christ. The Truth of the Lord reaches even to the clouds. The clouds are the apostles and prophets; to them He gave the command not to rain upon Israel. This is in agreement with history as recorded in the Book of Judges[12] where it speaks of the fleece that was dry, while rain fell upon the rest of the world. It means that Israel is dry and the rain is pouring down over the whole world.

'Clouds and darkness are round about him.' 'The Lord is riding on a swift cloud on his way to Egypt.'[13] Appreciate what that means: the Lord comes, the Lord and Savior, into the Egypt in which we live; the Lord comes into the land of darkness where Pharao is. But He does not come save riding on a swift cloud. Now what is this swift cloud? I think it is holy Mary with child of no human seed.[14] This swift cloud has come into the world and brought with it the Creator of the world. What does Isaia say? 'The Lord will enter into Egypt upon a swift cloud; and the idols of Egypt shall be shattered.'[15] The Lord has come, and the false gods of Egypt tremble violently, crash together, and are destroyed. This is the cloud that in Alexandria destroyed Serapis;[16] no general did it, no mortal man, but this cloud that came into Alexandria.

'Clouds and darkness are round about him.' We have identified the cloud; now let us investigate the darkness. The

---

9 Cf. Isa. 5.6.
10 Cf. Ps. 35.6.
11 John 14.6.
12 Judges 6.37-40; cf. Letter 58.3, PL 22.581 (320); 108.10, PL 22.886 (700).
13 Isa. 19.1.
14 Cf. *Commentary on Ezechiel* 32.1-16, PL 25.308 (382).
15 Cf. Isa. 19.1.
16 Cf. Letter 107.2, PL 22.870 (679).

Lord is in the darkness. The Lord is either in light or He
is in darkness. He is in light for beginners, for He speaks
more plainly to them; but to the proficient He speaks mystically. He did not speak to the apostles in the same way
that He spoke to the multitudes; He spoke to the apostles
esoterically. What does He say? 'He who has ears to hear,
let him hear!'[17] That, then, is the meaning of the words,
'and darkness round about him' or, as we might say, 'and
mysteries round about him.' Consequently, Exodus says:
'And all the people were standing down below; Moses alone
went up into Mount Sinai in the darkness of a heavy cloud,'[18]
for all the people of God were not able to know the mysteries
that only Moses could understand. Holy Writ says of God:
'And he made darkness the cloak about Him.'[19]

'Justice and judgment are the support[20] of his throne.'
What is the sense of 'the support of His throne'? It ought to
have said 'the foundation of His throne.' The expression
'support of His throne' carries the implication that the throne
had been unsteady before it was given support. And, really,
God's judgment before the Last Judgment seems in a sense
to be unsteady. His judgment in this life seems unjust and
irregular, for when the wicked grow rich and the saints are
paupers, does not God's judgment seem out of order? When
He shall come to judge, however, to render unto each one
according to his works, then His throne will be set right, as
it were.

Would you know further, what the psalm says about the
Judge? 'Fire goes before him.' The man of holiness need not
be afraid of this fire; let the sinner fear it. This fire purifies
saints; it burns up sinners. 'Fire goes before him.' 'You make
your messengers spirits, and your ministers a flaming fire.'[21]

---

17 Luke 8.8; cf. Letter 58.9, PL 22.585 (325).
18 Cf. Exod. 19.
19 Ps. 17.12.
20 Cf. Ps. 96 (97).2.
21 Cf. Ps. 103.4; cf. *To Pammachius Against John of Jerusalem* 15, PL
23.384 (422).

I think His angel messengers are the fires. They, therefore, His fire, go before Him. Whom do these angels consume with fire? Whoever is of wood, hay, stubble. He who is gold, silver, and precious stone will be sent into the fire, assuredly, but he will come out with greater purity.[22]

'His lightnings illumine the world.' The philosophers[23] tell us that lightning generates from the collision of clouds, for one does not see lightning until there has been first the impact of thunder. They say the same of copper pyrites; unless such stones are rubbed together they do not produce sparks. This has all been according to the historical method of interpretation, and we shall continue to direct our remarks to the inexperienced. We have been discussing the nature of things, that from their nature, we may derive some spiritual gain. The stone commonly called copper pyrite is not able to yield fire by itself alone, but if it is rubbed against another stone, a spark is struck between them. Let us suppose that Jeremia is a cloud, that Isaia, Elia, that Paul and Peter, and the other apostles are clouds. Now, when these clouds are struck together, they send forth a fire from their midst, and that fire illumines the whole world. 'His lightnings illumine the world; the earth sees and trembles.' The lightning flashes of the apostles have lighted up the entire world, and the earth has trembled at the sight. They spoke and the whole world heard the thunder of their voice. Two powers they had in equal proportion: a mighty voice and brilliant lightning. These lightning flashes enlighten believers; they burn out non-believers.

'The mountains melt like wax.' To me, these mountains seem to be the powers of devils. Whether or not they are mountains, they are certainly proud men. This fire does not consume the lowly, but only the lofty. As a matter of fact,

---

22 Cf. *Commentary on Isaia* 66.24, PL 24.677 (830).
23 Cf. Jerome's translation of Origen, *Commentary on Jeremia*, PL 25.629 (797-798). Cf. Homily 5, p. 38.

lightning seldom strikes those who are in the valley, but never misses those who are up on the mountain.

'The heavens proclaim his justice.' These are the heavens of which Psalm 18 says: 'The heavens declare the glory of God.'[24] The heavens proclaim His justice; earth does not. A man who is in heaven does not fear the just God; the man from heaven does not fear to proclaim His justice. The man who is holy and of heaven does not fear the God of justice. The sinner, however, seeks the God of mercy.

---

24 Ps. 18.2.

HOMILY 25

ON PSALM 97 (98)

SING TO THE Lord a new song'; the story of the Son of God crucified is the new song that had never been heard of before. A new event should have a new song. 'Sing to the Lord a new song.' It was the man, indeed, who suffered; but, you, sing to the Lord. Suffer, certainly, He did as man; He redeemed as God. 'Sing to the Lord a new song.' A new name merits a new song. This thought is intrinsic to what Scripture says in another place: 'You shall be called by a new name.'[1] A new name is deserving of a new song. So in the Apocalypse: 'To him who overcomes I will give a white pebble, and upon the pebble a new name written.'[2] The new name is that of Christians.[3]

'Sing to the Lord.' Why? What has He done? Why is there a new song due Him? 'For he has done wondrous deeds.' He performed miracles among the Jews: He cured paralytics; He cleansed lepers; He raised the dead to life. But other prophets had done that too. He changed a few loaves into many and fed a countless multitude. But Eliseus did that. What new thing, then, did He do to merit a new song? Would you know what He did that was new? God died as man that men might live; the Son of God was crucified that He might lift us up to heaven. 'For he has done wondrous deeds.' Would you know what wondrous deeds He has done? The son of a widow was lying dead in an upper chamber;

---

1 Isa. 62.2.
2 Cf. Apoc. 2.17; 3.12; cf. Letter 69.7, PL 22.661 (421).
3 Cf. *Commentary on Isaia* 62.1-4, PL 24.605 (739).

197

Eliseus came and drew himself together over the child and
he put his mouth upon the mouth of the boy, and his hands
upon his hands, and his feet upon his feet.[4] If, instead of
contracting and decreasing himself, Eliseus had expanded and
increased himself, the widow's son would not have been restored to life; and so it was, in order to give life, that he
made himself less. Although He was in the form of God, He
received the form of man; thus did He decrease that through
Him we might increase.[5]

'His right hand has won victory for him.' This means He
redeemed mankind, His own workmanship, not the work of
another; or in other words, what He had made for Himself
He ransomed for Himself. He had made man for eternal
life, man who had perished through his own vice; He died
that with His own right hand He might preserve man for
Himself. 'Right hand' in this passage symbolizes 'power,' and
'arm' is the symbol of 'strength.' 'His holy arm.' Granted
that Christ is called both 'arm' and 'right hand'—'The right
hand of the Lord has struck with power.'[6] 'To whom has
the arm of the Lord been revealed?'[7] Because this psalm is
speaking of Christ, the right hand and arm of the Lord
represent His power.

'The Lord has made his salvation known.' The psalmist
did not say He 'has shown' but He 'has made known.' The
point is that the human race had known God, but by reason
of its vice had forgotten that it knew Him. God in coming
by His own will, therefore, manifested to man what he had
lost; hence, the verse says: He, whom Adam had known, whom
Seth had known, whom Enoch that had called upon the Lord
and had hoped in Him had known, and Noe had known,
but afterwards the human race had forgotten, came again into
the world in order that mankind, who had forgotten Him,
might come to know Him once more. 'The Lord has made

---

4 4 Kings 4.34.
5 Cf. John 3.30.
6 Ps. 117.16.
7 Isa. 53.1.

His salvation known': in the Hebrew: 'The Lord has made
His Jesus known.' Wherever, in fact, our word salvation appears, the Hebrew text has 'Jesus.'[8] 'In the sight of the
nations he has revealed his justice,' by no means in Judea
alone, but in the sight of the nations. It was just, surely, for
the Savior to redeem His creature. 'He has revealed his justice,' His justice that had been obscured by the incredulity of
mankind.

'He has remembered his kindness.' 'He has shut up all in
unbelief, that he may have mercy upon all.'[9] 'And his faithfulness toward the house of Israel': He remembers His promise of mercy; He keeps faith. 'He has remembered his kindness' towards the peoples of all nations; 'And his faithfulness
toward the house of Israel.' By this work, He fulfilled His
promise to the Patriarchs.

'All the ends of the earth have seen the salvation by our
God.' Not only Israel and Judea, but all lands have seen His
salvation. The phrase 'the ends of the earth' has, likewise,
a mystical implication. As long as we are in the midst of the
world, we cannot see God, but when we leave the world, as
it were, and reach the heights, then, we deserve to see God.
Do you want to know how all the ends of the earth see God?

We read in Ezechiel:[10] 'And the wheels, those which revolve,
to them he called, gelgel,' which means, 'revelation, revela-
tion.' GEL means revelation, GELGEL, revelation revela-
tion.[11] Those wheels, therefore, hear 'revelation revelation,'
for the wheel, with just a slight part of its base seemingly
touching the ground, the whole of it whirls up to heaven.
Whereupon another passage of Holy Writ says: 'holy stones
are rolled on his land.'[12] And what does Ezechiel say? 'Wher-

---

8 Cf. Homily 12 on Ps. 78, p. 90.
9 Cf. Rom. 11.32.
10 Cf. Ezech. 10.13, LXX.
11 Cf. *Against Jovinian* 1.21, PL 23.250 (270); *Commentary on Ezechiel*
10.8-14, PL 25.94 (103); *on Michea* 6.3, PL 25.1209 (504), where Jerome
gives 'volubilitas' as the meaning of Galgala instead of 'revelatio.'
12 Cf. Zach. 9.16, LXX; cf. *Commentary on Ezechiel* 1.15-19, PL 25.28 (18).

ever the spirit wished to go, there the wheels went.'[13] Let us, likewise, follow the Holy Spirit and be called wheels. What does Ezechiel say? 'There they went; they did not turn when they moved.'[14] At the same time, ponder carefully that it means they did not turn back, but always went forward. Forgetting what was behind, they strained forward to what was before.[15] 'They were full of eyes.'[16] All these wheels were full of the light of God. But this is not the time to discourse[17] on wheels, or the cherubim, or the creatures in Ezechiel.

'Sing joyfully to God, all you lands.'[18] Not Judea alone, but all the lands, sing joyfully to the Lord. Bring forth all the regalia of a victorious army. 'Break into song; sing praise.' Break into song with the praise of all your faculties: sing praise truly, sing with every part of your being. Let your hand sing in almsgiving; let your foot sing in haste to a good work.

'Sing praise to the Lord with the harp.' Let all your chords resound. If a single string is missing, there can be no harp.[19] What does it profit you to be chaste and at the same time greedy? What does it profit you if you are chaste, if you are generous in almsgiving, but at the same time you are envious? What benefit to you if you have six good strings and one that is broken? If there is even one string broken, a perfectly sounding harp is not possible.

'With trumpets and the sound of the horn.' We read in the Book of Numbers[20] that there are two kinds of trumpets: one, the long trumpet of silver; the other, the horn trumpet.

---

13 Ezech. 1.20, 12.
14 Ezech. 1.12, 17.
15 Cf. Phil. 3.13.
16 Cf. Ezech. 1.18.
17 Cf. Letter 21.3, PL 22.381 (71); 59.3, PL 22.588 (329); 65.3, PL 22.625 (375); 84.6, PL 22.748 (527); 133.13, PL 22.1160 (1041); *Against Jovinian* 1.31, PL 23.266 (287); *Hebrew Questions on Genesis* 10.6, PL 23.1001 (319).
18 Cf. Ps. 97 (98).4.
19 Cf. *Commentary on Isaia* 16.11-14, PL 24.238 (275).
20 Cf. Num. 10.

Both kinds are mentioned in this verse: 'With trumpets and the sound of the horn.' Hear what they symbolize. The long silver trumpet is the word of God. 'The promises of the Lord are sure; like tried silver, freed from dross, sevenfold refined.'[21] On the other hand, the sound of the horn represents the man of God in all His sovereignty. In Scripture, the horn properly signifies kingship and power just as it is written: 'He has raised up a horn of salvation for us';[22] and in another place: 'Our foes through you we struck down with a horn.'[23] See, then, what the psalmist means here? Have two trumpets, one of silver and one of horn: the silver for speech, and the horn for strength.

Would you have proof that the horn is used always in a favorable sense? We read in Leviticus:[24] No animal without horns may be offered in sacrifice. Three species of animals are immolated: the horned bull; the ram, a horned animal; and the buck which has horns. Do you think that there is no reason for specifying that a beast may not be presented for sacrifice unless it has horns? We, therefore, as long as we have a horn, are worthy to be dedicated holocausts of God, but if our horn has been broken, we are like feeble men and cannot enter the priesthood of God.

'Let the sea and what fills it resound.' Let the sea resound and the bitter waters be changed into sweet. In fact, Mara also was changed and rendered sweet tasting. Nothing made that bitter water sweet save the wood of the cross which had been let fall into it. It seems to me that the bitter sea is the Law of Moses. That is what Mara means—bitterness. This bitter water of the Old Law received the wood of the cross and was made sweet.[25]

'Let the rivers clap their hands.' Here, let us direct a question to the Jews who follow only a literal interpretation. Do

21 Ps. 11.7.
22 Cf. Luke 1.69.
23 Cf. Ps. 43.6; cf. Homily 21 on Ps. 91, p. 164.
24 Cf. Lev. 22.19-28; 4; 9; Num. 7; 28; 29.
25 Cf. Exod. 15.25; cf. Letter 69.6, PL 22.660 (419); 78.5, PL 22.703 (473).

rivers have hands? Do they have voices? Do rivers have feet?
Do they have a stomach? Someone may object: There is
nothing written about a stomach or about feet, but I answer:
When one member is mentioned, we take the others for
granted, for we cannot understand hands without feet, without
a belly, without the rest of the body.

'Let the rivers clap their hands.' Rivers that have drunk
from the fountain, Jesus. 'They have forsaken me, the source
of living waters.'[26] These are the rivers that flow from the
fountain of Christ. He is the fountain; we are the rivers;
if, indeed, we deserve to be rivers. Christ is the fountain, and
the saints are rivers; the less holy, however, are the rivulets.
Others, in truth, are torrents. Who are the torrents? They
who have water in quantity, but with the approach of temptation dry up.

'Let the rivers clap their hands.' There is not one river;
there are many rivers; there are as many rivers as there are
saints. But these rivers do not feud among themselves; because they are Christ's rivers, they are in perfect accord. 'Let
the rivers clap their hands.' Let them clap their hands: the
work of the saints is the praise of God. Christ is not praised
in word but in works; He does not heed the voice, but the
deed. 'Let the rivers clap their hands.' He Himself cries out
in the Gospel: 'If anyone thirst, let him come to me and
drink, and "From within him there shall flow rivers of living
water." '[27] Let 'the mountains shout with them for joy before the Lord.' What fellowship is there between rivers
and mountains? Because the prophet is speaking of proficients, he did not say let rivulets clap their hands, but let
rivers clap their hands. Notice the order. Let the sea resound, and the whole world; let the rivers clap their hands,
His holy ones, His mountains, who have arrived at supreme
justice.

Let us word this differently. Let the sea resound, the sea

---

26 Jer. 2.13.
27 John 7.37, 38.

that formerly had been still, let it resound at the coming of Christ. Let the sea resound; we have already mentioned that this refers to the Law of Moses. Let the rivers clap their hands, namely, the prophets. Let the mountains shout with them for joy in the presence of the Lord: the apostles. 'For he comes to rule the earth.' By no means does He come only humble in the flesh, but He comes glorious in His majesty. 'For he comes to rule the earth.' The prophet did not say, to destroy, but to rule. He comes to judge, to separate the cockle from the grain; He comes to separate the bad fish from the good.

'He will rule the world with justice and the peoples with equity.' Justice is placed first, then equity. If justice comes first, and equity afterwards, then εὐθύτης is the right word[28] to express the notion of rectitude: that the wrong has been corrected. He comes, therefore, to rule with His justice that through Him disorder may return to order. To Him be glory forever and ever. Amen.

---

28 Cf. *Commentary on Isaia* 26.7-9, PL 24.296 (347).

HOMILY 26

ON PSALM 98 (99)

'HE LORD IS KING; the peoples tremble.' There are three psalms that begin with the same versicle, the ninety-second, the ninety-sixth, and the ninety-eighth. Although the opening versicle is the same in each psalm, the verse ending is different. How, then, does the ninety-second psalm begin? 'The Lord is king, in splendor robed.'[1] The ninety-sixth, however, says: 'The Lord is king; let the earth rejoice';[2] the ninety-eighth: 'The Lord is king; the peoples tremble.'[3] You see that the order of these psalms seems almost in reverse. 'The Lord is king: the peoples tremble' logically should be first; 'The Lord is king; let the earth rejoice' should be second; and last, 'The Lord is king, in splendor robed.'

The reversed order, however, furnishes a clue for our exegesis. 'The Lord is king, in splendor robed.' The Lord is king, and He is robed in the splendor of patriarchs and prophets and a people that believes. He is robed in splendor: the patriarchs and prophets have been as the garment of Christ; they are the loincloth mentioned in Jeremia—the girdle that he wore about his loins. Would you know that the saints are like a girdle and the vestment of God? God Himself says to Jeremia: 'As close as the loincloth clings to a man's loins, so had I made my people cling to me';[4] God's people are as close to Him as man's clothing is to his body. But because

---

1 Ps. 92.1.
2 Ps. 96.1.
3 Ps. 98.1.
4 Cf. Jer. 13.11, 1; cf. *Commentary on Jeremia* 13.1-12, PL 24.764 (931).

this loincloth, this splendor in which the Lord had been robed, was cast off on the other side of the Pharat, and laid aside in the cleft of a rock and there rotted,[5] and was taken into captivity by the Assyrians, what does the Lord do? He is not naked; He cannot be without a loincloth; He cannot be without a covering. Because the first people had been lost, He makes Himself a garment of the Gentiles.

And what does the psalmist say? 'The Lord is king; let the earth rejoice.' Let the earth rejoice, the whole world, that is, of those who believe. Would you like proof that Scripture speaks of the Gentiles as a loincloth? 'The Lord,' it says, 'is king, let the earth rejoice; let the many isles be glad.' Not one isle, Judea, but the many islands, in other words, the whole world.

Someone may say to me: Give me an example from Holy Writ where Judea alone is spoken of as an island. Everything we say, we ought to confirm from Sacred Scripture. 'A judicial fact shall be established only on the testimony of two or three witnesses.'[6] The word of the witness does not have as much weight as the precept of God. We read in the prophet Ezechiel: 'And you, son of man, speak to the inhabitants of this isle,'[7] that is, of Judea.[8] Because, therefore, one island has been abandoned, Scripture now says: 'Let the many isles be glad.' So of the first people, the loincloth, the psalmist says: 'The Lord is king, in splendor robed'; of the second gathered from among the Gentiles: 'The Lord is king; let the earth rejoice; let the many islands be glad.' Now, of a third people, he says: 'The Lord is king; the peoples tremble.' Whether they be of the Jews, or of the Gentiles, if they do not believe, let them tremble. 'Why do the nations rage and the peoples utter folly?'[9]

'The Lord is king; the peoples tremble.' The Lord has

---

5 Cf. Jer. 13.4-12; cf. Letter 7.3, PL 22.340 (19).
6 Deut. 19.15.
7 Cf. Isa. 20.6; Ezech. 27.2, 3.
8 Cf. *Commentary on Isaia* 59.16, 17, PL 24.582 (711).
9 Ps. 2.1.

suffered; the Lord has been crucified; the Lord has died; the Lord has risen from the dead; the Lord has ascended triumphantly into heaven. 'The Lord is king, the peoples tremble.' Who are these people? Let us cite an example from the Gospel:[10] 'A certain nobleman went into a far country to obtain for himself a kingdom.' What is further away from earth than heaven? He left earth, he went to heaven to obtain for himself a kingdom. 'But his citizens hated him; and they sent a delegation after him to say, "We do not wish this man to be king over us." ' But he received the kingdom, and returned to his wicked citizens. He returned to them who did not want him for king. And now the Holy Spirit says to the wicked citizens: Whether you will or not: 'The Lord is king; the peoples tremble.' O the kindness of the Holy Spirit! He did not say, let them perish, but let them tremble. He wished to point out their fault, not their punishment. They tremble and the Lord intercedes for them. And what does He say? 'Come to me, all you who are burdened.'[11] I have received a kingdom from the Father—rather, not I, but the manhood that I have assumed has received it. I give as God; I receive as man.

'He is throned upon the cherubim; the earth quakes.' As long as earth is undisturbed, it cannot be healed. The psalmist is not speaking of the earthquake in which we see the earth violently shaken and every kind of living creature in terror, but of our own earthliness that cannot be healed as long as it is complacent. When it is disturbed and trembles, then, it will regain its health. 'On whom shall I rest,' says the Lord, 'but upon him that is the lowly and afflicted man who trembles at my word?'[12] Because the earthliness of the trembling man has been stirred up, that is why He who is throned upon the cherubim begins to make His throne upon trembling earth. Happy the man who is

---

10 Luke 19.12-16.
11 Matt. 11.28.
12 Cf. Isa. 66.2.

God's throne; happy the man in whom God always is enthroned!

There is a variety of attitudes and postures; either we are sitting or standing or walking or lying down. Unhappy the man for whom God is lying down, for God lies down with the man who is lying down. Just as He weeps with the tearful, and laughs with the joyous, He lies prostrate with the fallen. Just as He thirsts with the thirsty, and hungers with the hungry, and is naked with the naked, He lies prostrate with the prostrate. God, so to speak, lies prostrate with the man who has been prostrated from his wounds. But the man who is walking has God walking with him. He who is walking seems, indeed, to be better off than he who is reclining; but still he has not yet arrived at the happiness of the man who is standing. Even in the case of Adam when he was hiding from God, God for him was walking about in the afternoon.

Somebody may assert: If Adam had offended God and had been cast out of Paradise, any man for whom God is walking is utterly unhappy. But I say: If Adam had been struck down completely and given no opportunity for repentance, then, God would have been lying dormant for him; but because God is giving him an opportunity to repent, that is why for him God is walking.

Moses hears from God: 'Then you stand here near me.'[13] And Stephen the martyr, while he was fighting, saw Jesus standing at the right side of the Father. The concept of God as seated, however, bears a twofold connotation. If He is sitting among us, we are happy; but if He is sitting with others while we are walking, then, we are unhappy. To this effect, Daniel says:[14] 'The books were opened, and thrones were set up' and God is seated as the Judge. Although the one being judged is certainly unhappy, nevertheless, the one for whom God is sitting is happy.

---

13 Cf. Deut. 5.31.
14 Cf. Dan. 7.10, 9; cf. Homily 14 on Ps. 81, p. 102.

Likewise in our psalm, God is described as enthroned upon the cherubim. Now as cherubim means a 'treasury of knowledge,'[15] the man who possesses a treasury of knowledge is the throne of God. This treasury of knowledge is not, however, of mere knowledge; it also is a treasury of works, for that only is true knowledge which is confirmed by works. Otherwise, the promise of knowledge is sheer vanity, when the one who makes the promise deliberately sets out to destroy knowledge.

'The King in his might loves justice.' Every sinner fears the judgment of God; he does not want to know the judge, he wants to meet with mercy. The man of holiness, however, both heeds God and glorifies Him in his body; he does not fear the judge, he loves Him. For example, if a judge should come, very severe and even dubbed a blood-drinker in his reputation for cruelty, any murderer would dread a judge of that kind. The man, however, who has done no evil and hates it, not only does not fear the judge, but even loves him. For what does the good man say? It is a good thing that such a judge is coming; there have been so many robberies, so many vices are being practiced, there are so many murders; it is well that such a judge come. The faithful servant does not fear the judge but loves him. Then is the Scripture fulfilled: 'The King in his might loves justice.'

'You have established right ways.'[16] What this means is: You have made all men good, but by their own vice they have corrupted themselves. You created man in justice. Note what the psalmist said: 'right ways'; not one way, but many. Everything You have made has been made right.

'And worship his footstool for it is holy.'[17] What is this footstool of Jesus that is holy? We read in another place: 'The heavens are my throne, the earth is my footstool';[18] and here, 'worship his footstool.' If earth is Jesus' footstool, and the psalm says worship His footstool, then is earth to

15 Cf. Letter 53.8, PL 22.548 (280).
16 Cf. Ps. 98 (99).4.
17 Cf. Ps. 98 (99).5.
18 Isa. 66.1.

be adored? How, then, do we read in the Apostle,[19] that we must worship the Creator, not the creature. In Scripture, adoration conveys two different notions: worship as an act toward God, and worship in the sense of reverence. When we use the word 'worship' in relation to God, we mean the adoration that is proper to God. When, however, we use the term with reference to man, as for example Sara worshiped Abraham, and Elia, Achab a most ungodly king, it does not mean that Elia worshiped Achab as if he were God, but that this worship was more like a greeting.

Now, we are ready to examine the words: 'And worship his footstool,' and see in which way the word 'worship' is intended. Do we adore God's footstool just as we adore God, or in the same sense that we worship and pay respect to a man? We have read in the Lamentations of Jeremia and in another of the prophets: 'How has the Lord hallowed his footstool!'[20] In this passage, His footstool is Jerusalem, or the Temple; hence, the reference is historical.

We shall now consider the versicle: 'And worship his footstool' from another point of view. If feet rest upon a footstool, then the words: 'Let us worship in the place where his feet have stood,'[21] likewise refer to a footstool. In that event, we may hold to the letter and mean, for example, the place where He was born, where He was crucified, where He arose from the dead. This is the explanation for beginners. On the other hand, Jesus' footstool is the soul of the one who believes. Happy the man in whose heart Jesus sets His feet every day! If only He would set His feet in my heart! If only His footsteps would cling to my heart forever! If only I may say with the Spouse: 'I took hold of him and would not let him go.'[22] The Spouse is quick to take offense; He loves constant purity; whenever He sees defilement, He withdraws at once.

---

19 Cf. Rom. 1.25.
20 Cf. Lam. 2.1.
21 Cf. Ps. 131.7.
22 Cant. 3.4.

'And worship his footstool, for it is holy.' Not every footstool of His, but every holy one, as many as persevere in holiness. 'Worship his footstool'; worship, for example, Peter and Paul and the rest of the apostles, that is, venerate them. 'For it is holy.' Worship those who persevere in holiness, but do not worship those who have been footstools and are no longer faithful. Judas the betrayer, for instance, was God's footstool, but because he is not holy, do not worship him. I have read in the book of a certain author: 'The Incarnation, that is, the human nature which God deigned to assume from Mary, He calls His footstool.'[23] Granted assuredly that a human nature has been assumed, and in relation to God every creature is His footstool, nevertheless, this footstool of His human nature is united to God and to His throne.

Notice what a daring thing I am venturing to say: I adore the footstool that once was, just as I adore the throne. 'And even though we have known Christ according to the flesh, yet now we know him so no longer.'[24] Perhaps He had a footstool before His death, before His Resurrection, when He was eating, when He was drinking, when He was suffering our tokens of affections. After He arose, however, and ascended triumphantly into heaven, I do not distinguish the throne from the footstool. Do you question and ask: How is this, or why? How it is, I do not know, yet I believe that it is so. Do you wonder that I do not understand the mystery of divinity when I do not know my very own self? Do you ask me how the Incarnation and divinity are one, when I do not know how I myself have life? To have perceived there is a God is to have believed; to acknowledge God is to honor Him. Enough for me to know that it is written; enough for me to know that I believe; more than that, I neither want nor desire, for if I shall desire to know more, I shall begin to believe less. We are called the faithful, not the rationals.

---

23 Cf. *Commentarioli in ps.* 98.5; cf. Origen, *in Isaia,* Homily 5.1; Ambrose, *de Spiritu Sancto* 3.11.
24 2 Cor. 5.16; cf. *Commentary on Jeremia* 17.5, 6, PL 24.787 (958).

Then, too, the Lord asks: 'Do you believe that I can do this?'[25] And He says to the woman: 'Thy faith has saved thee,'[26] not reasoning, not searching, not weighing and examining, not why or how it was done. She believed because it was done, and it was done because she believed.

'Moses and Aaron were his priests; and Samuel, among those who called upon his name.' Many err in thinking that blessed Samuel was a priest. He was not a priest;[27] he was a Levite. Even his garment was not like that of a priest, but like that of a Levite, for it is written: 'And his mother made him a garment, a linen ephod.'[28] EPHOD means garment; BAD means linen, of course, but no one except the Levites wore a linen garment. The priests of God, moreover, had vestments of five different colors, namely, of gold, hyacinth, byssus, purple, scarlet.[29] All the members of the priestly class wore such garments, but the Levites wore an 'ephod bad,' a linen garment. Consequently, this is the distinction implied in the words: 'Moses and Aaron were among his priests, and Samuel, among those who called upon his name.' The former are priests; the latter, a Levite. Nevertheless, before God it is not a question of dignity, but of works.

As a matter of fact, the works Moses did, Samuel did too. Moses resisted God and prevented Him from destroying His people when God said to him: 'Let me alone, that I may strike this people.'[30] Just see the power of Moses! What does God say to him? Let Me alone; You are compelling Me, your prayers, as it were, restrain Me; your prayers hold back My hand. I shoot an arrow; I hurl a javelin; and your prayers are the shield of the people. Let Me alone that I might strike down this people. Along with this, consider the compassionate kindness of God. When He says: 'Let me alone,' He shows

---

25 Matt. 9.28.
26 Matt. 9.22.
27 Cf. *Against Jovinian* 1.23, PL 23.253 (274).
28 Cf. 1 Kings 2.18, 19, LXX; cf. Letter 29.5, PL 22.439 (144).
29 Cf. Letter 64.15, PL 22.615 (363); 14, PL 22.615 (362).
30 Cf. Exod. 32.10; cf. Letter 128.4, PL 22.1099 (965).

that if Moses will continue to importune Him, He will not strike. If you, too, will not let Me alone, I shall not strike; let Me alone, and I shall strike. In other words, what does He say? Do not cease your persistent entreaty, and I shall not strike.

Let us see if Samuel persistently importuned God in this way. We read in the Book of Kings[31] that he prevented God from venting His wrath against the people, and although it was harvest time, the Lord sent rain, thunder, and lightning. What does Scripture say in Kings? 'And there came hail stones and struck down the Philistines.'[32] See how wise the fire, how wise the hail! Where Samuel is, the thunderbolts do not dare to strike, for they see the prophet of God, they see the Levite. Samuel's hands were threatening the thunderbolts. He was praying and the lightning strokes were held back. Why have I said all this? Because Moses and Aaron and Samuel with different titles performed the same mighty deeds. Let us bless the Lord to whom be glory forever and ever. Amen.

---

31 1 Kings 12.17-19.
32 Cf. 1 Kings 7.10; cf. Jos. 10.11.

ON PSALM 100 (101)

F KINDNESS and judgment I will sing; to you, O Lord.'
Let sinners who are despairing of their salvation,
who are humble and broken down over their sins,
hear the song of mercy; let the arrogant who say: 'The Lord
is merciful, let us sin, He will pardon us,' hear the song of
justice.

'I will sing praise. I will persevere in the way of integrity,'
that I may understand what I am singing and meditate upon
the meaning of the psalm; that my mind may not wander off
on distraction; my body seem to be praying, but my soul be
without fruition. 'In the way of integrity': that while I am a
sojourner in this world, I may live justly with a stainless
heart. 'When will you come to me?' When I shall have
gained the power of discernment and lead a just life, then,
with unshaken confidence, I shall ask the Lord: When will
You come to me? 'Will you come' is to be taken, of course,
in the sense of His second coming.

'I will walk in the integrity of my heart, within my house.'
Nothing so pleases God as simplicity and purity of heart.
The Holy Spirit, in fact, takes great pleasure in no other
bird than the dove because of its simplicity, and no other
quadruped than the sheep because of its gentleness.

'I will not set before my eyes any base thing.' Nothing will
I ever choose in preference to the Lord, nor will I consent to
evil, but with my whole being I shall belong to God. 'I hate
him who does perversely.' Whether it be my father, my
mother, brother, sister, or my friend, if anyone withdraws

from the fear of the Lord, I will, nevertheless, hate him and have nothing to do with him. I will not set kinship nor friendship before my love and loyalty to God.

'A crooked heart shall be far from me.' There will be no obstinacy, no perversity in my dealings, only equity and justice. 'Evil I will not know.' No matter if it be my friend or relative, bishop or priest, no matter what position of dignity a man may have, if he corrupts himself in any way, I will shun him so completely that I will preserve no least remembrance of him.

'Whoever slanders his neighbor in secret, him will I destroy.' By no means are we to agree with a slanderer, but rather, insofar as it is possible, we are to persecute the maligner, fully cognizant of the double benefit we are bestowing upon him by deliberately not listening and by not permitting him to sin. The only difference between a fornicator and detractor is, moreover, that the fornicator slays only himself, but the slanderer ruins both himself and the one who listens to him.

'With the man of haughty eyes and puffed-up heart I will not dine.'[1] With a man who is proud or covetous, decidedly will I have no fellowship.

'My eyes are upon the faithful of the land, that they may dwell with me.' The psalmist did not say upon the rich, or upon emperors, or bishops, or priests, or deacons, but upon the faithful; with them I will abide. A bishop who is a holy man has a right to these words for he can say: 'I do not ordain him priest who is obsequious to me, or who is my relative; I ordain him whom I know to be faithful.' Again, the same good bishop may be saying: 'for all my clergy and laity are faithful.' And he may say as well in the name of the Lord the following versicle: 'He who walks in the way of integrity shall be in my service';[2] I am His loyal servant, for

---

1 Cf. Ps. 100 (101).5.
2 Cf. *Against the Pelagians* 1.22, PL 23.539 (718).

I do not ordain those who are related to me, but the just and the faithful.

'He who speaks falsehood shall not stand before my eyes.' So carefully do I avoid the company of anyone who disparages his neighbor that I neither believe nor ever listen to a person of that kind.

'Each morning I will destroy all the wicked of the land.' Well said: 'The wicked of the land,' for sinners are certainly earthy. This means that the enslavements which the devil suggests to me, I thrust from my heart and do not surrender to his bondage. As soon as evil thoughts are driven out, the demons are undone. The Jews, hearing this verse and following the letter that kills,[3] in their zeal to spill blood, killed anyone who transgressed the law. Indeed, not satisfied with the murder of the prophets, they crucified the Lord Himself. 'And uproot from the city of the Lord all evildoers.' If only we, too, could root out all evildoers from the city of the Lord! The city of the Lord is the Church of the saints, the assembly of the just. 'And I will uproot'; I shall rebuke and reprove the sinner that he may repent and purge all evil from his heart, for the prophet has not said that the guilty man is to be expelled.[4]

---

3 Cf. 2 Cor. 3.6.
4 Cf. *Commentarioli in ps.* 100.8.

HOMILY 28

ON PSALM 101 (102)

HE PRAYER OF a poor man, when he is faint and pours out his anguish before the Lord.'[1] The psalm is speaking of the poor man, not the pauper of this world, but him of whom it is written: 'Blessed are the poor in spirit.'[2] 'When he is faint'; when he remembers his sins, past and present. 'Pours out' with his whole heart, not with his lips. Who, indeed, is the man who is able to pour out his anguish in the presence of the Lord? Who is there who does not feel the prick of conscience?

'Hide not your face from me.' The man who prays with a pure heart and has a conscience free from blame, he it is who is able to utter this prayer. The sinner, on the other hand, does not dare to say: 'Do not hide Your face from me,' but says with more reason: 'Turn away Your face from my sins.'[3]

'For my days vanish like smoke.' I was a babe and before I knew it, I grew into childhood; then I reached the perfect age, and soon, almost imperceptibly, I became an old man; and my days have vanished like smoke. Some men there are, however, who imagine that their life is everlasting, and cling, therefore, stubbornly to sin. 'And my bones burn like fire.' Bones are the very symbol of strength. If the part of me that is strong becomes parched and feeble, how much more so will my flesh languish that is weak by nature?

---

1 Cf. Ps. 101 (102).1.
2 Matt. 5.3.
3 Ps. 50.11.

'Withered and dried up like grass is my heart.' In similar
strain it is written in another place of Holy Writ: 'Man's
days are like those of grass.'[4] Such is the life of man; today
he is fresh and vigorous, and tomorrow he withers away.
'I forget to eat my bread.' The psalmist did not say, I had no
desire to eat, or I disdained to eat. No, so great was the
memory of sin that rushed upon me, and so broken was I
in contrition, that I even forgot to eat; my sole longing was
for God; I was carried away completely in contemplation of
Him.

'Because of my insistent sighing I am reduced to flesh and
bone.' Let the penitent learn how they ought to repent.
So emaciated did I become from longing and sighing that I
was all skin and bones—the psalmist used the word 'flesh'
for skin.

'I am like a pelican of the wilderness.'[5] They say there
are two species of this kind of bird.[6] One is acquatic and its
food is fish; the other in lonely places feeds upon venomous
creatures—serpents, crocodiles, and lizards. In Latin, these
birds are called 'onocrotali.' Well, then, I have become like
the bird that is in the wilderness, that feeds upon living
things that are poisonous, so my food is like poison to me.
'I have become like a night raven among the ruins.'[7] We
know that the raven is black all over without a speck of
white. Hyperbolically, then, I have become like a night
raven. If the raven is black in the daylight, how much blacker
is it at night? That is what I have become in my own sight
because of my many sins.

'For I eat ashes like bread.' I dipped my bread in ashes
and ate it that way. If this is what the prophet says, what
are we to do? 'And mingle my drink with tears.' Nothing

---

4 Ps. 102.15.
5 Cf. Ps. 101 (102).7.
6 Cf. *Commentary on Sophonia* 2.12-15, PL 25.1368 (709-710). Pelicanus
    onocrotalus and nycticorax—Night Heron?
7 Cf. Ps. 101 (102).7.

was sweet to my taste, neither bread nor drink; only for heavenly bread was I longing, that is, for Christ.

'Because of your fury and your wrath.' This was the anguish of my heart as I meditated upon Your coming and the future judgment. 'For you lifted me up only to cast me down.' Let this be the cry of those who were once saints and then fell away from holiness, for after having been exalted in virtues, they failed in fidelity. But the prayer of the tried soul is: Lifting me up, You held me fast.

'My days are like a lengthening shadow.' If days are like a shadow, how much more are nights? If light, how much more darkness? 'And I wither like grass.' Just like the grass, so man comes and goes and withers away.

'You will arise and have mercy on Sion.' From this versicle, it is evident that the psalmist has been speaking in the name of Sion and not as the prophet. Sion is she who has been set up in a watchtower and beholds from afar approaching events; hence, it is this Sion that has been lifted up on the heights and from thence has fallen. Consequently, 'let him who thinks he stands take heed lest he fall.'[8] 'For it is time to pity her, for the appointed time has come.' Either because of repentance, it is time of mercy, or this versicle prefigures the second coming of the Savior. Let the man who repents have confidence, therefore, because the time of salvation is at hand; merciful and compassionate is the Lord.

'For her stones are dear to your servants.' The stones are the saints; but earth, in other words, sinners, are in need of the compassionate mercy of the Lord.

---

8 1 Cor. 10.12.

HOMILY 29

ON PSALM 102 (103)

BLESS THE Lord, O my soul; and all my being, bless his holy name.' Another of the psalms says: 'Know that the Lord is God';[1] this one: 'And all my being, bless His holy name.' If we say: 'Bless the Lord, O my soul,' and the Lord is 'Lord,' what name of the Lord is the psalmist thinking of here? If the Lord is called by name Lord, what does 'and all my being, bless His holy name' mean? Simply this, the advent of the Son implies the name of Father. Before the coming of Christ, God was known, but the Father unknown. Furthermore, He says Himself in the Gospel: 'Father, I have manifested thy name to men.'[2] We cannot pause over every versicle for the psalm is long; but we ought to select individual versicles for a brief comment, and in doing so bring out their meaning rather than display rhetoric.

'Bless the Lord, O my soul, and forget not all his benefits.' Many benefits has the Lord bestowed upon us. He has granted us great favors: He has made heaven; He has made earth; He has made all the elements for us. The sun itself and the moon and the stars and all the elements occur and recur for our sake. O sorry creatures that we are! The elements minister to us and we do not serve the Lord. Grand it is, indeed, that God made for us everything that we behold. One does not build a house except for the sake of its occupant. If we are the inhabitants of the world, then the world is the

---

1 Ps. 99.3.
2 Cf. John 17.6; cf. Homily 8 on Ps. 74, p. 60.

house of mankind; the house has been made, moreover, for the benefit of its occupant.

Magnificent it is, I say, that all that we see, God made for us; that He fashioned us to be born, to live, to be capable of motion, to know our Creator; that He distinguished us from beasts of burden; that He made them bent over to look upon the ground, but us He made erect to gaze into the heavens. Great, indeed, is all of this; but greater still that He was born for us! 'Who though he was by nature God, did not consider being equal to God a thing to be clung to, but emptied himself, taking the nature of a slave . . . becoming obedient to death, even to death on a cross.'[3] Because we were mortals subject to death on account of our sin, He deigned to die for mortals, that we might regain life through Him.

'He heals all your ills.' Our soul has many ills. There are as many diseases of the soul as there are sins. There is for our instruction that woman in the Gospel: 'who for eighteen years had had a sickness caused by a spirit; and she was bent over and utterly unable to look upwards. . . .'[4] Grasp the significance of what the Gospel says. When anyone has a sickness caused by a spirit, he is bent over, he looks downward, he gazes at the ground, he is unable to look up at the sky.

'He redeems your life from destruction.' 'You have been bought with a price; do not become the slaves of men.'[5] What greater price is there than that the Creator shed His blood for the creature?

'He crowns you with kindness and compassion.' 'He crowns you'; inasmuch as He has redeemed you, even so He crowns you. He bestows a crown, moreover, not on account of your merits, but because of His compassionate kindness. 'O Lord,

---

3 Phil. 2.6-8.
4 Luke 13.11; cf. Letter 147.9, PL 22.1202 (1092).
5 1 Cor. 7.23.

you have crowned us with the shield of your good will.'[6]
Mark what it says: Lord, You have crowned us as with the
shield of Your good will. Does anyone really crown with a
shield, you ask? Surely, he who crowns, crowns with flowers,
or with gold, or with other crowns. Now how does one
crown with a shield? But the Lord's shield is a crown, for
He surrounds us with His protection and defends us and so
crowns us. Compassion and kindness denote, therefore, in
this psalm, what shield designates in the other psalm; and
the shield as it surrounds and protects us is His loving
kindness.

6 Cf. Ps. 5.13; cf. Homily 2 on Ps. 5, p. 15; 20 on Ps. 90, p. 156; cf
Against the Pelagians 3.1, PL 23.596 (781).

HIS PSALM is the worship of the creature praising and blessing his Creator through the prophet and is similar in theme to the eighteenth psalm that says: 'The heavens declare the glory of God, and the firmament declares his handiwork.'[1]

'Bless the Lord, O my soul!' The prophet bestirs himself to praise God. To bless the Lord, that is, to praise the Lord, brings, moreover, a blessing upon oneself. 'O Lord, my God, you are great indeed!' You, who are God of all, are especially my God, for I am not the slave of sin; I have merited to be called Your servant. 'You are great indeed!' When I behold the sky, the earth, birds, quadrupeds, serpents, and all of Your creation, I marvel, and I magnify the Creator.

'You are clothed with praise and glory.'[2] The word 'confessio' may be understood in two ways. It may be used in praise of God—for example, You are clothed with glory— just as the Savior Himself says in the Gospel: 'I confess to thee, O Father,'[3] that is, I praise thee; or 'confessio' may indicate the confession of our sins to the Lord, for we give God praise and glory when we acknowledge our sins before Him. 'You are clothed with glory.' Notice the order: first, one makes his confession and receives thereby beauty and grace, and after that he receives light, for the next words of the psalm are: 'Robed in light as with a cloak.' This versicle,

---

1 Ps. 18.2.
2 Cf. Ps. 103 (104).1.
3 Cf. Matt. 11.25.

however, is directed especially to the Lord because His entire universe is robed in light, as, for instance, in Ezechiel the cherubim were 'full of eyes.'[4] I behold the sky, the earth, for example, and I discern the Creator. I see the trees sending forth leaves in their proper season, budding into blossom, bearing fruit, and I perceive the Creator. I see an ant, and any tiny creature, and I apprehend the Creator. All creatures, therefore, reveal God and are full of knowledge.

'You have spread out the heavens like a tent-cloth.' The prophet means to say that from the beginning God spread out the heavens, just as if He were unfolding a scroll and rolling it back again, as it is written in Holy Writ: 'And the heavens shall be rolled up like a scroll.'[5] 'You have constructed your palace upon the waters,' as similarly in Genesis,[6] there were waters above the firmament and, likewise, below the firmament. 'You travel on the wings of the wind.' This typifies the presence of God everywhere.

'You make your angels spirits.'[7] What God passed over in Genesis, He has made known in this versicle, for when God created all things, nowhere did He mention the angels. The prophet said, moreover: 'You make your angels spirits' because angels do not have bodies, but are all light. 'And flaming fire your ministers.' This refers to their purity and the fact that they are not subject to sin. There is another explanation, however. If a man is faithful, for example, a good angel is sent to him, an angel of light; if he is a sinner, an angel of wrath is sent to set him ablaze and torment him.

'You fixed the earth upon its foundation.' It is truly wonderful how the great weight of the earth rests upon the power of God. 'Not to be moved forever.' By the providence of God, it remains undisturbed.

'The deep like a cloak is its garment.'[8] In another psalm,

---

4 Ezech. 1.18.
5 Isa. 34.4.
6 Cf. Gen. 1.7.
7 Cf. Ps. 103 (104).4; cf. *Against John of Jerusalem* 15, PL 23.384 (422).
8 Cf. Ps. 103 (104).6.

we find this thought paralleled: 'he made darkness the cloak about him';[9] and again: 'The judgments of the Lord are like the mighty deep.'[10] This versicle suggests the ineffable dispensation of God and our inability to comprehend His wisdom. As with these eyes of ours we cannot look into an unfathomable depth, neither are we able to contemplate the majesty nor the wisdom of God. According to the Hebrew, moreover, we must understand 'its garment' to be earth's garment,[11] so that the meaning is that the deep they call ocean surrounds the whole earth; that is to say, waters encircle all the earth, and the earth is like an island.

'Above the mountains the waters stood'; not as some think that waters from storms and rains stand high above the mountains, but that the mountains were covered by the waters and dry land did not appear. Allegorically,[12] however, the waters stand for doctrine and the mountains for the saints.

'At your rebuke, they fled.' In truth did the waters recede at the command of God and the dry land appear, as it is written in Genesis: 'God gathered together the waters into one place.'[13] 'At the sound of your thunder they took to flight.' Thunder is the voice of the Lord; He gave the command and the waters obeyed and withdrew into one place.

'As the mountains rose, they went down the valleys': an indication of the force of the waters, for they rise high as mountains and sink down again into valleys.

'You set a limit they may not pass.' Cause for wonder it is, indeed, to hear the roar of the sea and its raging fury and the howl of the waves lashed as high as the sky, and see them rush in as if to submerge the entire world, hurl their full force as far as the shore, and then recede and not transgress the frontiers appointed by God—yet men do not keep the

---

9 Ps. 17.12.
10 Cf. Ps. 35.7.
11 Cf. *Commentarioli in ps.* 103.6.
12 Cf. *Commentarioli in ps.* 103.6, 7.
13 Cf. Gen. 1.9, 10.

commandments of God. 'Nor shall they cover the earth again' as happened at the time of Noe's flood.

'You send forth springs into the watercourses.' Perhaps someone is saying: If everything was made to serve mankind, what advantage is there for water to flow in the desert? That, too, was ordained for our welfare and provision that quadrupeds might have their nourishment to serve us. Or we may say: God made all things by His divine providence, all creatures are His, and He supplies even brute animals with their sustenance. 'That wind among the mountains.' God sent the waters because His creatures in the mountains also had need of the Lord's rain in order to grow. Allegorically, however, the allusion is to the holy works of the just.

'Beside them the birds of heaven dwell.' Recall the parable of the mustard seed[14] and the birds that dwelt in its branches. 'From among the rocks they send forth their song.'[15] Each one of them praises the Lord with its own song. The Hebrew text has 'from among the trees.'

'The earth is replete with the fruit of your works.' In one sense, the earth is replete with Your blessings; in another, from Your works, that is, from Your apostles, many have been filled.

'You raise grass for the cattle.' Note carefully that cattle eat grass. 'And vegetation for men's use.' God created everything for His glory. 'Producing bread from the earth.' This refers to the Lord who deigned to become man, as it is written: 'I am the bread that has come down from heaven.'[16] 'And wine to gladden men's hearts.' This is the wine which the Lord promised He would not drink until after the Resurrection.[17] 'So that their faces gleam with oil.' The face of God makes the just shine with joy, but 'it is not oil for the

---

14 Cf. Matt. 13.31, 32.
15 Cf. Ps. 103 (104).12.
16 John 6.41.
17 Cf. Matt. 26.29; Mark 14.22-25; Luke 22.18-20.

head'[18] of sinners. 'And bread fortifies the hearts of men': the bread which came down from heaven.

'Well watered are the trees of the Lord.' The Lord re-freshed the trees also, that they may give us their fruit. 'In them the sparrows[19] build their nests.' By sparrows we are to understand all birds, the genus from the species.

'Fir trees are the home of the heron.'[20] The heron is a mighty bird all right; they say, too, that it overpowers the eagle and feeds upon it. It is not like other birds that build their nests and fly to them in the evening; wherever darkness overtakes the heron, there it sleeps. Allegorically, on the other hand, the monk does not have a cell, but wherever he finds one, there, too, he stays. His battle is with the devil who reigns in this world; like the heron he prevails over the eagle, the king of the birds,[21] just as it is written: 'though you go as high as the eagle, from there I will bring you down, says the Lord,'[22] for, according to Ezechiel,[23] the eagle is the devil. 'The high mountains are for the stags.'[24] This animal kills serpents and eats them;[25] therefore, the mountains are the right habitat for the slayer of the wise serpent, the serpent that, in the Garden of Paradise, was wiser than all the beasts, the serpent that deceived Eve. 'The cliffs are a refuge for rock-badgers.' He who is fearful has a rock-fastness for his refuge; the rock, moreover, is Christ.[26]

'You made the moon to mark the seasons.' There is a saying that when the moon waxes, the yield of fruit increases; when it wanes, it decreases, hence: 'You made the moon to mark the seasons,' is well said. But let us interpret the moon in another way as the Church; for in propagating the Church,

18 Cf. Ps. 140.5.
19 Cf. Ps. 103 (104).17.
20 Ibid.
21 Cf. Commentary on Daniel 7.4, PL 25.528 (664); on Michea 1.16, PL 25.1164 (447).
22 Abd. 4; cf. Jer. 49.16.
23 Ezech. 17; cf. Commentary on Ezechiel 17, PL 25.164-165 (194-195).
24 Cf. Ps. 103 (104).18.
25 Cf. Letter 130.8, PL 22.1114 (985).
26 Cf. 1 Cor. 10.4.

we increase with her; when she suffers persecution and is decreased, we suffer persecution and decrease with her. 'The sun knows the hour of its setting.' If the sun sets, do we think that we are going to be everlasting? It is certainly amazing how so much light and such brightness, that the whole world is illuminated, in the flash of a moment is gone. Let us pray, however, that the sun of justice may not set for us.

'You bring darkness, and it is night; then all the beasts of the forest roam about.' Literally, this means that the nighttime was made for men to rest from their toil and for beasts to hunt for their food. Allegorically, when the sun of justice sets for us, we are in total darkness; then the beasts come after us, and the lion roars in its wild passion to snatch up and devour us.[27]

'Young lions roar for the prey and seek their food from God.' Well put, 'from God,' since, indeed, the devil is always laying traps for the saints, for example, Judas, David, Solomon, Peter, as it is written, 'his repast sumptuous.'[28]

'When the sun rises, they withdraw.' The man who has fallen into sin should not be downcast, but let him repent. The sun of justice will rise again, and all the beasts will be put to flight and his sins with them, and he will be restored to his state before his fall. Once more for him the sun of justice shall rise. 'Man goes forth to his work and to his tillage till the evening.' After the sun of justice has risen, moreover, we go back again to our work until evening, until death, of course. Very important it is, then, that we pursue the works of justice every minute of our lives.

'How magnificent are your works, O Lord!'[29] The prophet's heart overflows with gratitude. When he could not find sufficient words with which to praise the Lord, he cried: 'How magnificent are your works, O Lord!' Your works surpass all human understanding. 'In wisdom you have wrought them

---

27 Cf. *Commentarioli in ps.* 103.20.
28 Hab. 1.16; cf. *Commentary on Habacuc* 1.16, PL 25.1288 (606); cf. Letter 22.4, PL 22.396 (90).
29 Cf. Ps. 103 (104).24.

all'; in our Lord, Jesus Christ, for He is the wisdom of God, according to the saying of the Apostle, because through Him all things[30] have been created. 'The earth is full of your creatures.' True, indeed, it is that all the works of the Lord abound in wisdom. When we perceive that the ant knows when winter is coming and stores away its food; that the mosquito, such a tiny creature, has eyes, a belly, and all the other members just as we have, and the flea, too, and all other creatures; and when we see also that the elephant, such a huge beast, likewise has eyes, a nose, feet, a belly, just as we have and in the same places; similarly, too, the bee, and that it makes honey and wax: are not all these wonders worthy of admiration and are they not full of wisdom?

'The sea also, great and wide.' Is it not of wondrous wisdom that in the sea there are reptiles, countless in number, and fish of all sorts, great and small; that they exist in the deep and there renew their life, whereas if man should fall into it, he would die, but, on the other hand, if they come forth unto land, they die? 'And where ships move about.' Who of us is the strong ship that can escape shipwreck in this world and not be sunk or dashed against a rock, but has a conscience to steer him so that he may be safe?

'With the sea dragon, which you formed to make sport of it.'[31] The Jews say that God has made a mighty dragon called Leviathan which lives in the sea; and when the ocean recedes, they say it is because this dragon is turning over. But let us say that this is the dragon that was cast out of Paradise, that beguiled Eve, and is permitted in this world to make sport of us. How many monks and clerics has it dashed headlong! 'They all look to you to give them food in due time,' for all the creatures of God live at His bidding.

'If you take away their breath, they perish and return to their dust.' This prefigures the end of the world when, at the command of the Lord, all things will come to an end,

---

30 Cf. Col. 1.16.
31 Cf. Ps. 103 (104).26.

as it is written: 'Dust you are, and unto dust you shall return.'[32]

'When you send forth your spirit, they are created': on the day of creation. If the Spirit creates, He is, therefore, God;[33] that is to say, the Spirit creates even as the Father does.

'May the glory of the Lord endure forever.' If the glory of the Lord endures forever, we, too, who glorify Him will be everlasting. 'May the Lord be glad in his works!' Joy it is for the Lord when we, His creatures, greet Him on the day of resurrection. 'He who looks upon the earth, and it trembles.' Our earth will, indeed, tremble on the day of judgment. The reference here is, of course, to worldly sinners. 'Who touches the mountains, and they smoke!' If the mountains smoke, how much more will earth? The saints smoke because all of us shall be saved through fire. Naturally, there is no smoke without a fire. 'I will sing to the Lord all my life; I will give praise to my God while I live.' Another psalm says the same: 'Turn your gaze from me, that I may find respite ere I depart and be no more.'[34] Grant me a little time that I may repent for my sins, for in hell no one has the power to confess his sins.

'Pleasing to him be my theme.' May it be pleasing to Him that anyone justly be able to praise and bless God. The prophet said this in the optative mode, not in the imperative. 'I will be glad in the Lord.' Happy are they who utter these words after the judgment.

'May sinners cease from the earth.' The prophet did not pray that sinners might perish, but that sin itself might vanish. When sin no longer makes its appearance, no longer are there sinners, and all shall be found just. 'And may the wicked be no more';[35] may they not be wicked, but just.

---

32 Gen. 3.19.
33 Cf. *Hebrew Questions on Genesis* 1.2, PL 23.987 (306).
34 Ps. 38.14.
35 Cf. *Against the Pelagians* 1.28, PL 23.544 (724).

HOMILY 31

ON PSALM 104 (105)

IVE THANKS to the Lord, invoke his name'; give thanks to Him and say: we, indeed, are sinners but You are merciful, have pity on us. 'Invoke his name.' There will be no setting up of idols in our hearts, but we shall call upon the Lord and He Himself will be our redemption. 'Make known among the nations his deeds.' Shame on the Jews who say that His miracles and works were performed only in Israel.

'Sing to him, sing his praise.' He who understands the Sacred Scriptures, who meditates constantly on the law of the Lord, and contemplates the things of heaven, he is the one who sings to God. He, moreover, who possesses all virtue and is skilled in good works, fashions, as it were, a harp of virtues and sings praise to the Lord. 'Proclaim all his wondrous deeds.' Psalm 106 says: 'They who sailed the sea in ships, trading on the deep waters, these saw the works of the Lord and his wonders in the abyss.'[1] If in our bodily ship we shall sail through life unimpaired, and never a storm founder us nor dash us against a rock and shatter our ship into pieces, we shall be able to proclaim the wondrous works of God. And truly a grand miracle it is to sail through this world without a blemish.

'Glory in his holy name.' This is a prophecy concerning the Gentiles: that we are to be and to be called Christians from the name of our Lord, Jesus Christ. 'Rejoice, O hearts that seek the Lord!' Let monks rejoice, for hearts that seek

---

1 Ps. 106.23, 24.

230

the Lord rejoice. If the hearts of those who seek the Lord are full of joy, how much more the hearts of those who find Him? They, indeed, who find Him never let Him go.

'Look to the Lord in his strength.' Before we sought the Lord, we were weak and inconstant; now that our hearts are set on Him, we are strong and brave; if we find Him, how much greater, then, will our perfection be? 'Seek to serve him constantly.' The Hebrews were required to appear before the Lord[2] three times a year. What justice was that? What was there so extraordinary in appearing before God three time a year? In Exodus, the Sacred Scripture was speaking to little ones; here, however, the prophet is urging those who believe in God to seek Him always, as the New Testament bids us that we pray[3] without ceasing.

'Recall the wondrous deeds that he has wrought,' in Egypt, and in the Red Sea, and in the desert.

'You descendants of Abraham, his servants, sons of Jacob, his chosen ones!' If anyone is a descendant but not yet a son, may he heed the message of the Gospel: 'If you are the children of Abraham, do the works of your father.'[4] They, therefore, who are full of pride, are not sons; and if they are descendants, they are servants constituted under the law of fear, not having perfect love which casts out fear.[5] We are sons of Jacob, of him who supplanted his brother and carried off his birthright: 'for many are called, but few are chosen.'[6]

'Wandering from nation to nation.' There are many who think that this refers to the captivity of the Jews. That is not so, however, for the psalmist is speaking of Abraham, that he came out of the land of the Chaldaeans and went into Mesopotamia; from there he went into the promised land, and then into Egypt. 'And from one kingdom to another people.'

---

2 Exod. 23.17.
3 1 Thess. 5.17; cf. Luke 18.1.
4 Cf. John 8.39.
5 1 John 4.18.
6 Matt. 20.16.

We pass through many realms in order to reach the land of promise.

'He let no man oppress them': He did not permit Pharao to harm Abraham in Sara nor Abimelech to harm Isaac in Rebecca. 'And for their sake he rebuked kings.' This, likewise, refers both to Pharao and to Abimelech. 'Touch not my anointed, and to my prophets do no harm.' The psalmist is speaking of the patriarchs themselves. Shame on the Jews, therefore, who say that unless one is anointed with the royal unguent, he cannot be called 'the anointed.' They say that our Lord is not the Christ because He was not anointed with the kingly ointments, but before the law, the patriarchs had not been anointed with royal unguent, yet are called 'the anointed.'[7] The anointed, moreover, are those whom the Holy Spirit anoints; hence, our Lord is justly called the Christ. This they deny and in so doing go counter to the Sacred Scriptures.

'When he called down a famine on the land.' It often happens that what seem to be contradictions take place for the best in the providence of God. If Joseph's brothers had not been jealous of him and sold him, how was he to go down into Egypt? If there had been no famine, how were the patriarchs to go into Egypt and there be recognized by their brother? How was Pharao to be struck by the ten plagues? How were the chosen people to go out from Egypt; how was water to be struck from a rock in the desert; how were the mysteries to come to pass that were performed in the desert in type? We, of course, understand all this in its spiritual signification. If Judas had not betrayed the Lord, how were we to be saved? If the Jews had not crucified Him and been incredulous, how were we to believe? So it was that Joseph went into Egypt to prepare hospitality and food for his brothers. 'He sent a man before them.' This speaks of Joseph

---

7 Cf. *Commentary on Habacuc* 3.13, PL 25.1325 (654); *Commentarioli in ps.* 104.15.

himself. 'Joseph, sold as a slave.' A man, a holy man and well born, is sold.

'They had weighed him down with fetters': because he would not consent to the seductions of the Egyptian woman. 'They had weighed him down with fetters,' but they could not crush justice. When he was sixteen years old, a woman fell in love with him and, although he was at the age that easily surrenders to passion, he refused to yield to evil, for he feared more the danger to his soul. 'The iron pierced his soul.'[8] These were the iron chains of sin that kill the soul; or the versicle may mean that he was in danger, accused of a terrible sin by the wife of his master. The woman was all aflame for him, just as it is written: 'They are all adulterers, with hearts like ovens.'[9] 'Till his word came,'[10] the Word of the Lord Himself who delivered him.

'And the word of the Lord inflamed him.'[11] If he had not been inflamed by the Holy Spirit, he could not have conquered lust. The Spirit of the Lord enkindled him and burned out the fire of lust. 'The king sent and released him.' Historically, it was Pharao who sent and released him; by another interpretation, however, anyone tempted by wanton desire cannot escape sin unless the Lord appear and release him.

'And Jacob sojourned in the land of Ham.' The just man is never a permanent dweller upon earth, but only a pilgrim. 'He greatly increased his people.' About seventy-five souls went down into Egypt, and six hundred came out from Egypt.

---

8 Cf. Ps. 104 (105).18.
9 Cf. Osee 7.4, 6, LXX.
10 Cf. Ps. 104 (105).19.
11 *Ibid.*

HOMILY 32

ON PSALM 105 (106)

LLELUIA, Alleluia.'[1] It is necessary to bear in mind the rule that whenever there are two alleluias in the prescription of a psalm, one marks the end of the preceding psalm; the other, the beginning of the following one.

'Give thanks to the Lord, for he is good.' O you who sin grievously and despair of salvation, and think that because of the magnitude of your sins you cannot obtain pardon, I admonish you—rather the prophet admonishes you—to give thanks to the Lord, for He is good. Great are your sins, but great is the Lord who has pity on you. Confess your sins to the Lord; do penance and do not despair of your salvation, for the Lord is compassionate. Give thanks to the Lord, you who have very great sins. Do not trust in your own strength, but trust in the mercy of the Lord.

'For his kindness endures forever.' Grasp that the psalmist says: 'forever.' 'In the nether world who gives you thanks?'[2] It is not possible for anyone in hell to be sorry for his sins. While you are still in this world, I beg of you to repent. Confess and give thanks to the Lord, for in this world only is He merciful. Here, He is able to compassionate the penitent, but because there He is judge, He is not merciful. Here, He is compassionate kindness; there, He is judge. Here, He reaches out His hand to the falling; there, He presides as

---

1 Cf. Ps. 105 (106).1; cf. *Commentarioli in ps.* 104.1.
2 Ps. 6.6.

judge. Now, I have said all this for the benefit of those who maintain that in hell there is contrition for sin.

'Who can tell the mighty deeds of the Lord?' No one is worthy to proclaim the great deeds of the Father except the Son; no one is able to express the might of the Father except Him who is Himself mighty. He who is Himself omnipotent, who is in the bosom of the Father, is able to tell and proclaim the almighty works of Omnipotens. 'Or proclaim all his praises?' Before our Lord spread abroad the praises of the Father in the Gospel, the Father's praise was unheard of in the world. If taken spiritually, everything that is written in the old law can be understood of the Father.

'Happy are they who observe what is right, who do always what is just.' Right it is for David to utter this prayer. He himself had obeyed the Lord's decrees and had done what was right; but because he did not obey and do justice at all times, he fell; for what does he say? 'Happy are they who observe what is right, who do always what is just,' but be cognizant that to be happy is to do the right at all times. After all, what does it profit a man if for twenty years he preserves continence but afterwards falls? That is the message of the following words of the prophets: 'The virtue which a man has practiced will not save him on the day that he sins; neither will the wickedness that a man has done bring about his downfall on the day that he turns from his wickedness.'[3] Neither should the virtuous man be secure nor the sinner despair of his salvation, for in each of them there should be both fear and hope. 'Who do always what is just.' Our Lord is justice, for He is called the justice of the Lord. Happy is he, therefore, who does what is just, who brings forth Christ. How do we bring Christ forth—or justice? If we live justly, justice is conceived in us, and justice is begotten of us, and we are the mother of justice. Happy and blessed is he who at all times is both father and mother of justice.

---

3 Ezech. 33.12; cf. Letter 54.6, PL 22.553 (285); 122.3, PL 22.1045 (898).

'Remember me, O Lord, as you favor your people.' What blessed David is saying is this: 'I know the old law, O Lord; perfect happiness is not in the old law but in the Gospel; I know that the first people has offended You and that a new people is being prepared who will serve You; I know that Your Son will come, that He will redeem the whole human race, and that they who have been chosen will believe in Him. Because I have been born earlier in the old law, that is why I implore You to reckon me in the reward with Your new people.' Logically, this seems to be the thought. Let us read the versicles with this in mind and we shall find that they agree with our reflections.

'Visit me with your saving help,' with Your Son, when He shall come. 'That I may see the prosperity of your chosen ones.' In other words, grant us fellowship with the apostles, for although we have preceded them in time, they, indeed, precede us in the things of the spirit. What we are asking is that we may see the works of Your tender love that You are going to bring to pass in Your chosen ones. 'Rejoice in the joy of your people.' We are the Lord's people, if only we are truly His people. 'To a people yet to be born,' Scripture says, 'which the Lord has made.'[4] 'And glory with your inheritance': that we, too, may share in the Gospel, we who were made under the old law, for our Father Abraham saw Your day and was glad.[5] Let us see it, too, and rejoice with Your inheritance.

'We have sinned, we and our fathers.' As sons we have followed the example of our fathers; we have participated in their sins. 'For God has shut up all in sin, that he may have mercy upon all.'[6] 'We have committed crimes; we have done wrong.' Pay close attention to what it says. We have sinned with our fathers; we have committed crimes; we have done wrong. Why did not the prophet say: we have acted im-

---

4 Cf. Ps. 21.32.
5 John 8.56.
6 Cf. Rom. 11.32.

piously? It is one thing to be a sinner and do wrong, another
to be impious.[7] A sinner frequently is overcome by the very
weakness of his body, but the blasphemous repudiate God.
Because I am not blasphemous, but a sinner, that is why I
dare to entreat God's mercy.

'Our fathers in Egypt considered not your wonders.' They
saw and yet they did not see; they saw with the eyes of the
flesh, but not with the eyes of the spirit. The prophet did
not say that they did not see, but that they did not understand, for just as our fathers saw wonderful deeds but did not
fathom their mystical significance, even so it is true in reading
the Gospel that one is spiritually blind if he sees and hears
physically to be sure, but without spiritual insight. Blessed,
therefore, are we who have not seen and have believed, rather
than they who have seen but have not believed. They saw
the Red Sea, they saw Pharao drown, and all they understood
was only what they saw. We who did not see him have a
better comprehension. We apprehend the devil in Pharao;
in his army we perceive demons; in the sea we discern baptism. They know from experience the bitter waters at Mara,
and they travel through Mara; but every day we identify those
bitter waters in the baptism of heretics. They mount a bronze
serpent on a pole in the desert. Let the anchorites take heed,
let the hermits who live in the desert give attention. And
what have we done? We, too, have hanged the old serpent in
the desert.

Granted that the Apostle's[8] explanation with reference to
our Lord is not the same as ours. What does he say? On the
cross of the Lord, the devil was suspended and fixed there.
The Lord, yes, was crucified, but the devil died. The Lord
fulfilled the divine mystery and the Victor was visible; the
devil was not visible but was slain spiritually, just as the
Apostle intimates.

---

7 Cf. Homily 1 on Ps. 1, p. 3.
8 Cf. Eph. 2.16; cf. *Commentary on Ephesians* 2.16, PL 26.504 (581).

IVE THANKS to the Lord, for he is good, for his kindness endures forever!' Because He is gracious and forgives sin, for that reason confess your sins to Him. If He were not good, the prophet would not admonish you to confess and give thanks to Him; His kindness is everlasting. Here in this world, He is all clemency; in the next, He is justice. 'For his kindness endures forever.' As long as you are in this world, confess, and give thanks to Him.

'Thus let the redeemed of the Lord say, those whom he has redeemed from the hand of the foe.' The prophet is making a direct reference to the calling of the Gentiles, and their vocation is the mystical theme of the psalm. 'Let the redeemed,' redeemed by the passion of the Lord. 'Thus let the redeemed say': He is Savior, indeed, and Redeemer, and the price of ransom; 'Thus let the redeemed say': He redeems, He pays the price of His blood. Why did He make payment with the price of His blood? To ransom us from the hand of the foe. We were being held captives in the hand of the devil, therefore, the Lord came and redeemed us in order to release us from his grasp.

'Whom he has redeemed from the hand of the foe.' 'To destroy the hostile and the vengeful.'[1] 'Whom he has redeemed from the hand of the foe.' 'The enemy sowed weeds among the wheat,'[2] for the enemy is the devil. 'Whom he has redeemed from the hand of the foe.' The devil is the

---

1 Cf. Ps. 8.3.
2 Cf. Matt. 13.25-30.

foe and he is in possession. He holds us tight within his grip, not because he loves, but because he hates. 'Whom he has redeemed from the hand of the foe.' Great the majesty, great the power of the blood of the Lord that liberated us from the clasp of the devil.

There are, by way of example, some animals that clasp tight to themselves whatever they catch (medical men and naturalists both affirm this) and unless the victim be broken away, it cannot be forced from them, nor do they let go but cling tenaciously to their captive. If, however, oil is applied, all at once, their hold is relaxed, and the creature that had been so securely gripped is suddenly released and completely severed from them. In the same way, the blood of Christ has broken the unyielding clutch of the devil. He did not want to let go of us, but the Lord poured forth His blood as the oil of mercy and through His blood set us free. 'And gathered from the lands.' See how mighty is the hand of the devil! 'Whom He has redeemed from the hand of the foe.' Those whom He rescued from the enemy's hand, moreover, were being held captive by the devil in every land. 'And gathered from the lands.' Throughout the whole world the hand of the devil was holding us in bondage.

'From the rising and from the setting of the sun, from the north and from the sea.'[3] The prophet certainly seems to have indicated four districts—east, west, south, and north— the four quarters of the world, but the psalm does not support this impression. Where it says, 'from the rising and from the setting of the sun,' obviously there are two zones; 'from the north,' that is, from the Little Bear, you see a third zone. 'And from the sea.' The sea, at any rate, is in the west.

Notice, therefore, that the psalmist has named the west twice, but the south not even once. Why did he mention three zones, and not intend to name the fourth? We read in Habacuc: 'God will come from the south, and the Holy One

---

3 Cf. Ps. 106 (107).3.

from the shady mountain.'⁴ God will come from the south.
This refers to the Savior, for God was born in the south.
Bethlehem is located south of Jerusalem, consequently, it
says God will come from the south. But if God will come
from the south, how now does the psalmist say: 'From the
rising and from the setting of the sun, from the north'? No
mention of the south. 'From the rising and from the setting
of the sun.' 'Amen, amen, I say to you, that many will come
from the east and from the west, and will feast with Abraham: but the children of this generation will be put forth
outside.'⁵

'From the rising and from the setting of the sun.' From
heathen lands, of course. 'From the north.' 'The north.'
The strongest of the winds they call, therefore, 'the right
wind.'⁶ 'From the north evil will break out upon the land.'⁷
'The sea.' You meet this term in Numbers and in Exodus and
in all Sacred Scripture; and wherever you hear this expression,
you should understand by it the regional direction of the
west.⁸ That is so, because from the site of Jerusalem, the
sea called the great sea is in the west. Note, therefore, the
divine secrets in Holy Writ. In the passage we are considering, the west is mentioned twice and the south not even once.
Why is that? Because this psalm does not announce the
calling of the Jews, but the calling of the Gentiles. In fact,
what does the psalm go on to say?

'They went astray in the desert wilderness; the way to an
inhabited city they did not find. Hungry and thirsty.' That
you may know that these words foreshadow the call of the
Gentiles and the rejection of the Jews, farther on this same
psalm says: 'He changed rivers into desert,'⁹ thereby indicating
the Jews. 'They went astray in the desert wilderness.' Would

---

4 Cf. Hab. 3.3; cf. *Commentary on Habacuc* 3.3, PL 25.1311 (637).
5 Cf. Matt. 8.10-12.
6 Cf. Prov. 27.16, LXX.
7 Cf. Jer. 1.14.
8 Cf. *Hebrew Questions on Genesis* 13.14, 15, PL 23.1008 (326); *Commentary on Ezechiel* 46.19-24, PL 25.464 (583).
9 Cf. Ps. 106.33.

you have proof that we were formerly in a parched, desert land? 'They went astray in the desert wilderness.' We have identified the waters and designated the rivers. 'The way to an inhabited city they did not find. Hungry and thirsty.' Let us explain how it happened that the Gentiles were in a desert that was scorched and dry, and why, hungry and thirsty, they missed the road to the inhabited city.

From the words, 'they did not find,' it is evident that they were searching. 'The way to an inhabited city they did not find'; they were looking for the way that would lead them to the city; hungering they searched, and thirsting. 'Their life was wasting away within them.' 'They devise a wicked scheme, and waste away their life in scheming.'[10] They are exhausted; they have searched and have gone astray; in their hunger and thirst, they have failed to find the way to the city that was inhabited. There were many, you may be sure, who promised to direct the way that would lead to the city. Socrates promised; Plato promised; Aristotle promised. The woman with the hemorrhage[11] who was suffering a flow of blood sought many physicians, but none was able to cure her. 'The way to an inhabited city they did not find.' The teachings of the philosophers only intensified hunger for truth rather than satisfied it. The woman with the hemorrhage had spent all that she had on doctors; hungering and thirsting, her spirit died within her. But because she had lost everything that she possessed, because her life was wasting away within her, she—the Church gathered from the Gentiles—cried out to the Lord in anguish. Her touch on the hem of His garment was the cry of a believing heart.

'They cried to the Lord in their distress.' 'In my distress I called to the Lord, and he answered me';[12] the Lord gives us gracious hearing when not simply our voice, but our distress, cries out to Him.

---

10 Cf. Ps. 63.7.
11 Cf. Luke 8.43-49; Mark 5.25-35; Matt. 9.20-23.
12 Ps. 119.1.

'From their straits he rescued them.' Because they failed to find the way to the inhabited city, He led them into the right way. He showed them the way, because though formerly they had found roads, they were devious, not direct. 'And he led them by a direct way.' The Way led them by a direct way. The Lord Himself and Savior guided them; the Way led them; He caused them to walk in Him who was both Guide and Way. 'And he led them by a direct way,' that by this way—through the Lord and Savior—they might enter the city of their home, might enter His Church that He had built upon Himself, the Rock, the Way, the Guide.

At this point, we ought to pause and meditate upon the fact that three times the psalm repeats the following verse: 'Let them give thanks to the Lord for his kindness and his wondrous deeds to the children of men, because he satisfied the longing soul'; and later in the psalm are the words: 'Let them give thanks to the Lord for his kindness and his wondrous deeds to the children of men, because he shattered the gates of brass.' Further on, there is again the same doxology; let the intelligent reader find it for himself. Some are saying, I grant, that even a fourth time this praise recurs in order that open honor to the Trinity may be reserved for the Gospels.

The psalm is long and we cannot delay on every versicle, but this much is clear, that it foreshadows the calling of the Gentiles and the rejection of the Jews. Let us beseech the Lord, therefore, that since the first branches were broken off and from the wild olive we were grafted[13] unto the roots of the good olive, we may bring forth good fruits, lest we, too, be pruned as they were. Our Vinedresser looks for fruits. If it is true that He cut off the first branches because they were sterile, we shall undergo the same treatment if we are unfruitful. Fruits, moreover, are not only of the body, but also of the soul, for surely when the body serves the Lord, both the soul and the body are serving God.

---

13 Cf. Rom. 11.17-22.

'Like the earth, parched, lifeless and without water. Thus have I gazed toward you in the sanctuary.'[14] 'For you my flesh pines, O how many ways!'[15] Note that it says: How many ways my flesh pines for You! How does it pine in many ways? Let us not read πῶς ἁπλῶς, but ποσαπλῶς—in manifold or various ways. In all manner of ways is my flesh faithful to You; in fasts, in sleeping on the ground, in troubles, in want and poverty, in hunger, in thirst, in cold. 'For you my flesh pines, O how many ways!' What is it, then, that serves the Lord in many ways? Earth, parched, lifeless, and without water. Grasp what it says: parched, lifeless, and without water. Mark well that this flesh cannot serve the Lord in many ways except when it is barren earth, lifeless and un-watered, when the flesh is parched and dry, when we have become 'like a leathern flask in the smoke,'[16] completely de-hydrated and cured; when our flesh no longer seeks gratifica-tion, but food. When our flesh has dried out and is parched and without humors, it does not look for delicacies, but for food. Moreover, when our arid earth has been irrigated with the waters and rains of delight, it must travail and generate, and the faithful servant brings forth good fruits; but the sinner's earth immediately sends forth thorns.

Why I am saying all this, the prudent hearer understands, for fasting is of great benefit to the Christian soul. It hum-bles the body and with the humiliation of the body, the soul, too, is humbled;[17] but although the body has been reduced to submission, the soul nevertheless suffers its own passions. Now if to the flame of the soul is added the flame of the body, who is able to endure such twofold burning? Prayer frequently extinguishes the fire of the soul, and likewise does trust in the Lord. On the other hand, the control of the fire of the flesh is within our power; when we want to, we can quench the flame of passion. Although we smother that

---

14 Ps. 62.3; cf. Letter 122.1, PL 22.1040 (892).
15 Cf. Ps. 62.2.
16 Cf. Ps. 118.83; cf. Letter 22.17, PL 22.405 (100).
17 Cf. *Commentary on Isaia* 58.6, 7, PL 24.565 (690).

blaze, nevertheless, fire still burns in the soul. I have mentioned this because in the soul there is always the spark of
concupiscence. Just as, if there is a spark of fire in ashes but
nothing to feed it, the spark is there nonetheless but does
not burst into flame; so, too, the spark of fire in our thought
is checked if it is not fanned into flame by the excesses of
the flesh. We all have this spark.

Someone may object. Do not let him; whoever denies it, is
a liar. There is one God, the Creator of all things. He who
created me created you; He who created the general also
created the soldier; He who created the most nobly-born of
senators, created the lowly slave. Circumstances may vary, but
nature is one. Just as we came into the world naked, we pass
out of it naked. On earth we wear different kinds of clothes;
we have different customs; but for those coming into the
world and for those going out of it, the condition is the
same. Why do I say all this? To stress the point that for all
men there is one human nature; but just as all faces are
faces, nevertheless, each one is different. For instance, one
face may have more to it, another less, yet there is only one
face of mankind. In other words, I do not have the face of
man and you that of a lion or some other wild beast. Let
everyone, therefore, heap up his ashes according to the kind
of spark that he knows he has. When we eat, when we take
the more delicate foods, we are feeding that glimmer of fire
that is hiding in our ashes. Let us pray the Lord that this
tiny flame be always in a desert land, lifeless and without
water, and with no kindling whatever for vices. And let us
bless the Lord.

HOMILY 34

ON PSALM 107 (108)

SONG OF a psalm of David.'[1] Song always suggests the work of the mind, but psalm that of the body. To express this distinction more clearly, song implies theory, and the psalm practice in reference to the art. Since, therefore, the title announces a song of a psalm, the second versicle continues logically and correctly with: 'I will sing and chant praise in my glory.'[2]

'My heart is ready, O God; my heart is ready.'[3] I am ready, not only in act, but also in heart and in mind. My heart is ready in desire, my heart is ready in service, in deeds. Because I am ready, not only in heart and in mind, but also in works, that is why I say in the next versicle: 'I will sing and chant praise in my glory.' 'I will sing,' in my heart, that means. 'And chant praise.' Just as the psaltery is composed of many strings and if one should be broken the instrument as such is useless; so, too, in our actions, if we transgress one commandment our psaltery is broken. Hence, the prophet said, I will sing of You and chant praise to You in my glory.

In some codices the wording is, 'in your glory,' but the better reading agrees with the Hebrew text, 'in my glory.' The versicle: 'I will sing, and chant praise, in my glory,' simply means, when I praise You with melody, O Lord, when I sing to You, I render You no favor, but only to myself. As a matter of fact, another psalm says: 'For you have no need

---

1 Cf. Ps. 107 (108).1; cf. *Commentary on Ephesians* 5:19, PL 26.561 (651).
2 Cf. Ps. 107 (108).2.
3 *Ibid.*

of my goods.'[4] What I do, therefore, I do for my own good. Because I serve you, it is to my glory. We fast. Do we thereby give God anything? We do it for our sins. We sleep on haircloth. What are we doing for the Lord in that? Only one thing; we are saving our souls, and that is what He desires. Just as the good and kind doctor rejoices with his patient when he has cured him, so also does our Lord.

'Awake, lyre and harp.' O psaltery, O harp, you were made and fashioned to give praise to God; awake my harp and give praise; why do you lie idle? O monk, you are standing there in body; why is your soul listless, why are you not chanting praises to the Lord? 'Cursed be he who does the Lord's work remissly.'[5] If you are a psaltery, if you are a harp, why are you so mute and not glorifying God? 'I will wake the dawn.' There is no blessing and praising God in darkness, but only in light. I am going to say something startling. Even if we arise in the nighttime, we are blessing God in light. For the Christian, it is never night; for the Christian, the sun of justice is ever rising.

In the foregoing observations, we are quite in agreement with the Jews. According to another interpretation, however, it is the Lord who says: 'My heart is ready, O God; my heart is ready.' I am ready here; I am ready in the future world; I am Savior on earth; I am Savior in heaven; I give eternal life both to angels and to men. 'Awake, lyre and harp.' The Lord is addressing His own body: Psaltery and harp, you that descended into hell and lay at rest, awake and praise the Lord. Be sure that you comprehend what He is saying. Not he who plucks the harp and the psaltery gives praise; but the harp and the psaltery themselves bless the Father; He is God and He is blessed and praised by others, but His body and the human nature that He assumed praise the Lord.

Now, for your satisfaction, not because I am merely airing my opinion, but because the prophet is speaking in the name

---

4 Cf. Ps. 15.2.
5 Cf. Jer. 48.10.

of the Lord, consider what follows. 'I will give thanks to you among the peoples, O Lord': 'the peoples'; in other words, the Jews. 'And I will chant your praise among the nations.' Here, He is speaking of us, for He calls 'the peoples' those who were the first to believe from among the Jews. Note carefully the order: first He praises God among the peoples; after that, among the nations. At first they who believed were of the Jews; later, of the Gentiles.

'For your kindness towers to the heavens.' There is no creature that does not depend upon the loving kindness of God.[6] Every last one of us is in need of God's compassion. Gabriel, Michael, Seraphim, Cherubim, Powers, Dominations, all are holy, indeed, but stand in need just the same of the mercy of their Creator. I am not detracting from the angels, but I am proclaiming their Creator, inasmuch as the angels have themselves given Him glory, freely and gladly.

We may express the thought of this versicle in still another way: Your loving kindness lifts us from earth to heaven 'and your truth to the clouds.'[7] Where are the Jews, where are their followers, they who limit their understanding to the letter only? How does the truth of God reach to the clouds? The Son of God says: 'I am the way, and the truth, and the life,'[8] and He came down to earth and conversed with men.[9] How, then, is the truth of God in the clouds? It is obvious enough that the prophet is referring to the apostles and to the saints; that they are not to rain His rain upon the Jews, but upon the Gentiles, as it is written: 'I will command my clouds not to send rain upon Israel.'[10] In these clouds, therefore, is the truth of God. If the truth of God is in these clouds, by what right do Montanus and the Cataphrygians maintain that what was not revealed to the apostles has been revealed to us?

---

6 Cf. *Against the Pelagians* 2.4, PL 23.562 (744).
7 Cf. Ps. 107 (108).5.
8 John 14.6.
9 Cf. Bar. 3.38.
10 Cf. Isa. 5.6.

'Be exalted above the heavens, O God.' God is not exalted
except above the heavens; He is not exalted above the earth.
When we are worldly, we do not exalt God; but if from
earthly beings we become heavenly beings, then we give
glory to God. Our Lord, when He was on earth, did
not exalt us. Someone may object: You are speaking rather
temerariously, since, indeed, the Lord says Himself in the
Gospel: 'I, if I be lifted up, will draw all things to myself.'[11]
See what He says: When I shall be lifted up to the heavens,
then I will draw all things to Myself. That is a good and
holy thought, true enough, but I see a different meaning.
'When I shall be lifted up, when I shall be crucified, then
I will draw all to myself.' 'That your loved ones may
escape.' O wonderful power of discernment! The Lord is
crucified and lifted up in order that His loved ones may
escape. 'That your loved ones may escape. Be exalted above
the heavens, O God.' Our prayer has been answered; He
has been exalted, and we have been deliverd.

'God promised in his sanctuary,' whether in the temple,
in any one of His saints, in the prophet. He is heard in
Moses; He is heard in the Apostle; and verily, do I say, He
has spoken in His Son. What did God promise? That which
follows: 'Exultantly I will apportion Sichem.' That is why
I am crucified, He says, that I may apportion Sichem. Now
Sichem in our language means 'shoulders.'[12] Shoulders, on
the other hand, imply work; hence, the sense is: the purpose
of My crucifixion is to share My work with My saints. For
this reason I am crucified; that I may place My yoke that is
sweet and My burden that is light upon the shoulders of men.
That You have done, Lord, as You have promised; You have
been exalted and You have divided up Sichem.

'And measure off the valley of tents.'[13] Truly has our Lord
and Savior entered secretly into this valley of tears, into the

---

11 Cf. John 12.32.
12 Cf. *Hebrew Questions on Genesis* 48.22, PL 23.1055 (373); *Commentary on Osee* 6.9, PL 25.871 (67).
13 Cf. Ps. 107 (108).8.

place of our lowliness, that is, into this world. Even though one is a saint in this world, still he does not yet know what it behooves him to know, 'for we know in part and we prophesy in part.'[14]

'Mine is Galaad, and mine Manasse.' Our Lord and Savior rejoices because He has many riches. The meaning of Galaad is 'emigration.' He rejoices because the Gentiles migrated from the nations and came to Him. Manasse means 'from forgetfulness,' consequently, understand that He is saying: That son who took his inheritance and squandered it and forgot all about Me, has remembered Me now; I am calling him Manasse, that is, 'from forgetfulness,' because he has not forgotten but has returned to his Father.

Ephraim is interpreted 'fruitful.' 'Ephraim,' He says, 'is the helmet for my head.' He used helmet here in place of crown, for that which is set upon the head is a crown, and Holy Writ has many different expressions for crown. In one place it has: 'His truth shall compass you with a shield';[15] in another: 'He crowns you with kindness and compassion.'[16] Just as shield in the preceding psalm stands for crown, in our psalm, helmet means crown. Perceive, then, what the psalm says: you have become Galaad; you have become Manasse; you have migrated to the Lord, and after your forgetfulness, you have returned to your Father. Be Ephraim, too; be fruitful, yield good works, and afterwards you will be the Lord's crown.

'Juda, my scepter.' Think of how much glory there awaits the penitent, for the name Judas means 'confession.' 'Moab the caldron of my hope.'[17] A great mystery is learned from these few words. I beg you to pay strict attention, for it will be of profit both to you who are listening and to me who am speaking. The translation of Moab is 'from the father.' AB means 'father'; MO means 'from.' Who is this man 'from

---

14 1 Cor. 13.9.
15 Cf. Ps. 90.4.
16 Ps. 102.4.
17 Cf. Ps. 107 (108).10.

the father'?[18] He who has lost his father, who has deserted
him, who has not returned to him, and who is not worthy to
be called Manasse. Who is this Moab? The enemy of the
Lord from whose race even to the fourth and to the tenth
generation—even to the end of the world—no one will enter
the Church of the Lord. Who is this Moab? He who is born
in a den of darkness from an impure union. From the union
of Lot and his daughters, two sons were born, Moab and
Aman, and Moab is the elder. Notice, therefore, how a
mystery is concealed behind the letter. In darkness, in a cave;
not in the sun, not in the light; hence, Moab is another name
for the devil who is unmindful of his father. Indeed, Absalom
who was the persecutor of his own father, also represents the
devil.

But in what sense is this Moab called the caldron of the
Lord's hope? 'Lebes' means caldron. How is a caldron the
hope of the Lord? Is it believable that Moab, who is interpreted devil, is the caldron of the Lord's hope? In what
sense is he the hope of the Lord? The Apostle says: 'Whom
I have delivered up to Satan that they may learn not to
blaspheme.'[19] The devil is, as it were, the Lord's torturer.[20]
They who do not walk to God in justice are given over to
the devil. Why? That they may be lost forever? Where, then,
is God's clemency? Where is the loving, merciful Father?
Where is He who makes His sun rise on the just and on
sinners alike and sends His rain down on both sinners and
just?[21]

What it means is: I give sinners over to the devil so that
tortured by him they may be converted to Me. Jeremia says
of this: 'What do you see, Jeremia?' 'I see a boiling caldron,'[22]
he replies. You see, meat is put into the caldron; Ezechiel[23]

---

18 Cf. *Hebrew Questions on Genesis* 19.36, PL 23.1017 (335).
19 1 Tim. 1.20.
20 Cf. *Commentary on Joel* 2.22-28, PL 25.973 (199).
21 Cf. Matt. 5.45.
22 Jer. 1.11, 13.
23 Cf. Ezech. 24.

says so. 'And I put meat into the caldron'; that sinners, in other words, may soften and their hardness be converted to the Lord and their stony heart become a heart of flesh, so that where at first there could be no writing because of the hardness of the substance, afterwards there could be because of its softness. 'I will heap up a great bonfire beneath this pot and I shall boil the meat and bones until they lose all their moisture and their filth.'[24] Note what it says later on: 'Thus they shall know that I am the Lord.'[25] Great mercy, a great mystery! Pieces of meat are put into a caldron that the heart of man be melted and he may learn that it is the Lord. There is much for us to learn from Moab and the caldron, but our homily is already too long.

'Upon Edom I will set my shoe.' Edom means 'of earth' and 'of blood.' The God of love and kindness claims, not only heavenly beings, but also those of earth. 'The Philistines have become my friends.'[26] He says this of us who have believed from among the Gentiles.

'Who will bring me into the fortified city?' No one, Lord, for You are He who says: 'The wine press I have trodden alone, and of my people there was no one with me.'[27] 'All alike have gone astray; they have become perverse; there is not one who does good, not even one.'[28] Who, then, will lead Me into the fortified city? No one, Lord, since even Peter who had promised to die for You afterwards denied You. What is this city that is fortified? Hell, where they are shut in, and whence there is no departure. Truly, from that fortress no other except the Lord comes out victorious; that is in truth a fortified city. Moses could not depart from that city; Jacob, likewise, entered it and did not return. Would you know that he did not return? He says to his sons: 'I will

---

24 Cf. Ezech. 24.10, 11.
25 Cf. Ezech. 24.24.
26 Cf. Ps. 107 (108).10.
27 Isa. 63.3; cf. *Against Jovinian* 2.36, PL 23.349 (380).
28 Ps. 13.3.

go down mourning, to my son in the nether world.'[29] He
descended into hell because Paradise had not yet been opened
by the thief. That city is fortified against exit, but it is always open for entrance. 'Who will lead me into Edom,' the
place of punishment and of blood—Edom means bloody—
the place for the slaughter of souls where many are destroyed?
No one descends into hell in triumph save You alone, Lord.

'Have not you, O God, rejected us?' The psalmist did not
say, who is rejecting us, but, who at one time rejected us.
'So that you go not forth, O God, with our armies?' These
words must be read interrogatively: Will You not go into
battle, O God, and lead our armies? You who suffered for
us, why do You not help us? Why do You permit us to be
crushed under the foot of the cruelest of devils? 'So that
you go not forth, O God, with our armies?' Notice the
exact words of the prophet. He did not say, You have gone
forth, but, will You not go forth, O God, with our armies?
The instruction of the prophet is: When we are putting
forth our effort, God helps us. 'So then there is question
not of him who wills, nor of him who runs, but of God
showing mercy.'[30] Do you understand that it says: There is
question not of him who is resting, nor of him who is sleeping, but of God showing mercy? Realize what that means:
there is question not of him who wills, nor of him who runs,
but of God showing mercy. If we neither will nor run, however, God will not come to help us. It is ours to will[31] and to
run, then, He will take pity on us. While the athlete sleeps, he
loses the victory.

'Give us aid against the foe.' The prophet did not say: Give
us aid against delights, but against the foe. 'In my distress
I called to the Lord; and he answered me.'[32] The psalmist
did not say, when I was enjoying delights I called, or while

29 Gen. 37.35; cf. Letter 39.3, PL 22.469 (181).
30 Rom. 9.16; cf. Letter 130.12, PL 22.1117 (989); 133.5 (6), PL 22.1154
   (1033); *Against the Pelagians* 1.5, PL 23.523 (700).
31 Cf. Homily 2 on Ps. 5, p. 15.
32 Ps. 119.1.

I was asleep I called. Do you want to be heard graciously by
the Lord? Be in distress and call to Him, and He will answer
you graciously. Unless one is in distress, he cannot call upon
the Lord for help. 'For worthless is the help of men.' 'Cursed
is the man who trusts in human beings.'[33] No need to interpret this saying from Scripture; the thought is clear to everyone. Someone, for example, has placed his trust in a general,
has set his hopes in a prince, in a father, or a mother; then,
in some trouble or other, suddenly the one in whom he hoped
dies, and gone with him is all his help. Notice that the
psalmist did not say, worthless is the help of that man in
whom one hopes, but vain is his help who sets his hopes
on man.

'Under God we shall do valiantly.' Let us put our trust
in no one save God alone. Do not let us say: If this or that
should happen to me, on what would I live? I answer you:
if persecution should break out, would your resources be any
greater? For the Christian, there is always persecution; nakedness has always been his lot. No one, therefore, ought to take
thought on what he would live; no one should fear; no one
should fret, 'If I grow old, on what shall I live? If my health
breaks down, how shall I live?' You have Christ, and yet you
are afraid? If He feeds the birds of the sky, do you doubt that
He is able to feed you, too? Does the devil feed his men,
and Christ not feed His servants? Does the devil make his
servants judges of this world, and rich men, and is Christ
not able to keep you from becoming a beggar? The devil
gives gold and precious stones, and is Christ not able to
give bread?

Let us cast all anxiety from our hearts and say: 'Under
God we shall do valiantly.' He will be our strength; He will
be our bread; He will be our king. 'It is he who will tread
down our foes.' He crowns; He fights at our side with us;
more than that, He even conquers in us. Why do we say this?
'Under God we shall do valiantly.' Indeed, when we are

---

33 Jer. 17.5.

courageous, it is He who tramples down our enemies. Scripture did not say, He will fight or kill, but He will tread down our foes. He will tread them down in such a way that if it is His will, He may strengthen and glorify them. Let us, therefore, bless God, to whom be glory forever and ever. Amen.

HOMILY 35

ON PSALM 108 (109)

NTO THE END, a psalm of David.'[1] 'Unto the end' is a sign that the message of the psalm pertains not to the present but to the future. If, moreover, the prophet speaks of the future, the prophecy is of Christ.

'O God, be not silent in my praise.'[2] Christ is saying: 'Judas betrayed Me, the Jews persecuted and crucified Me and thought that they were doing away with Me unto the end, but You, O God, be not silent in my praise.' The whole Church throughout the world praises the Lord every day and fulfills the Lord's prayer: O God, be not silent in My praise. Appreciate the dignity of the priesthood! Priests speak, and in priests it is God praising His Son.

'For they have opened wicked and treacherous mouths against me.' Let us reflect upon the traitor Judas and his treacherous malice against the Lord. He comes to the Lord deliberately to betray Him, and calls Him Rabbi,[3] Master. Here, we have a perfect example of the malicious mouth of a sinner, the lips of a treacherous man. In My compassion I want to save him, and I respond to his kiss of greeting, so great is My longing to overcome his malice, but he persists in his treachery and betrays Me. In particular, this is the story of Judas; in general, it is that of the Jews. At the time when they were crying out: 'Crucify him! Crucify him!'[4] their lips were the lips of a sinner condemning their Lord.

---

1 Cf. Ps. 108 (109).1.
2 *Ibid.*
3 Cf. Matt. 26.49.
4 John 19.6.

From the verse that follows you may conclude that the psalmist is speaking of all the Jews, for what does it say?

'They have spoken to me with lying tongues.' I was being crucified for them, and they were hurling insults at Me. My wounds were for their healing and they looked upon Me in derision. 'With words of hatred they have encompassed me.' They had no intention of believing, only of attacking and crushing Me. 'They attacked me without cause.' There is a twofold connotation to the word 'gratis.' It may mean 'without cause': I had committed no crime and, therefore, I was not deserving of their assault. What excuse did they have to fight against Me? Because I had healed their sick? Because I had raised the dead to life? Because I had performed other miracles? Look, how they fought against Him without a single provocation! The second meaning is 'without thanks': They wanted to blot out and destroy My name, and they could not. When a man conspires in hatred against another without success or any satisfaction, he persecutes for nothing.

'In return for my love, they slandered me, but I prayed.' In return for the kindness that I had lavished upon them, they slandered Me. Yet what did I do? I prayed. That is the Lord's weapon; that is our weapon, too, prayer. If ever anyone should persecute us and hate us, let us say likewise: In return for my love, they gave me calumny. But I, what did I do? I prayed. In order to get the better of them? God forbid; does the Lord pray for one in order to vanquish him? Why did He say: 'but I prayed'? What was His prayer? 'Father, forgive them, for they do not know what they are doing.'[5]

'They repaid me evil for good.' When I was hung on the cross, I pleaded for those who were crucifying Me, and they jeered at Me: 'Thou who destroyest the temple, and in three days buildest it up again, save thyself. The Father who

---

5 Luke 23.34.

loveth thee, let him come now and deliver thee.'[6] For their sake I rose from the dead, and they say: 'His disciples came by night, and stole him.'[7] 'Hatred for my love.' Ponder well, O Christian; ponder well, O monk; if the Lord received His deadly conspirator and traitor with a kiss and prayed for those who were persecuting Him, what is our duty toward our brethren?

'Raise up a wicked man against him.' Since I prayed for them on the cross and they saw My wounds and I gave them opportunity to repent, but they are not repentant and do not want Me for their king, let them have the devil as king. They do not want King Jesus; let them have King Barabbas, Barabbas whose name means 'son of the father,' and that means son of the devil. This Barabbas, who was he? A seditious wretch and a robber. Truly, do they have Barabbas for king—even to this day—a rebel and robber, the murderer of the Jews themselves. Barabbas, the thief who reveled in blood, had been imprisoned before the Lord was betrayed. They rejected the Lord, but released Barabbas. From that moment, Barabbas began to hold them in his power; and that demon that had been cast out from the man and from that generation and was wandering about in the desert and could not find a place, took with him seven other devils worse than himself, and entered into the synagogue, and the last state of that man became worse than the first.[8] In fact, before the synagogue of the Jews crucified the Lord, it was certainly sinful, but with only one devil. It crucified the Lord, and immediately eight more devils entered it; hence, the Scripture is fulfilled that said: 'Raise up a wicked man against him.' 'Let the devil stand at his right hand.'[9] Because the devil stood at their right hand, the synagogue had a withered right hand, as it is written in the Gospel.[10]

---

6 Cf. Matt. 27.39-44.
7 Matt. 28.13.
8 Cf. Luke 11.26.
9 Cf. Ps. 108 (109).6.
10 Luke 6.6.

Let us pray that the Lord may stand at our right side,
the devil at our left. It is written in Zacharia: 'Then he
showed me Jesus the high priest standing before the angel
of the Lord, while Satan stood at his right hand to accuse
him.'[11] If the devil is standing on the right hand of the Lord,
how now does the psalm say of Judas: 'let the devil stand at
his right hand'? But notice what it means. The devil stood
at Jesus' right hand in order to accuse Him; in other words, he
wanted to resist His right hand. This psalm, however, does
not mean that the devil wanted to oppose Judas, but that he
had already conquered him. In Zacharia, the devil wants to
contend against Jesus' right hand, but here he is already master
of Judas' right hand.

We must be sure to take into consideration the fact, moreover, that the devil was standing at the right hand of the
Lord to accuse Him at the time when Jesus' garments were
filthy, for Zacharia says: 'Now Jesus was clad in filthy garments.'[12] As long as the Lord Jesus has filthy garments, that
long does the devil stand at His right; as long as He wears
upon Himself our sins, in our sins the devil is His adversary.
But when Zacharia says: 'Take off his filthy garments, and
clothe him in festal garments,'[13] straightway Jesus says to the
devil: 'May the Lord rebuke you, Satan; may the Lord who
has chosen Jerusalem rebuke you!'[14] We have explained all
this because it is written in the psalm: 'let the devil stand
at his right hand.'

'When he is judged, let him go forth condemned.' Do not
let him come into the court of judgment, but let him come
into condemnation, for where there is a judicial investigation,
there is still uncertainty; but where there is condemnation,
the sentence has already been passed and is published. 'May
his plea be in vain.' The repentance of Judas became worse
than his sin. How so? He went out and committed suicide

---

11 Cf. Zach. 3.1; cf. *Against Jovinian* 2.4, PL 23.302 (328).
12 Cf. Zach. 3.3; cf. Letter 53.8, PL 22.547 (278).
13 Cf. Zach. 3.4.
14 Zach. 3.2.

by hanging himself; he who became the betrayer of God
became his own hangman. In regard to the clemency of the
Lord, I say this, that Judas offended the Lord more by hanging himself than by betraying Him. His prayer should have
been repentance, but it turned into sin. You see the heretic
at prayer; you see the Jew praying; you see Manichaeus
pray; even though they fast, even though they pray, nevertheless, their prayer turns into sin.

'May his days be few.' His days decreased, but his nights
increased, for he was taken from life in the midst of his days.
The sun has passed out of his life, and behold for him darkness has intensified. 'May another take his office.' The explanation of this is clearly revealed in the Acts of the
Apostles.[15] Not only does the saying hold true in the time of
Judas, but even today. If Judas lost his office of apostle, let
priest and bishop be on guard lest they, too, lose their minis-
try. If an apostle fell, more easily is it possible for a monk
to fall. Virtue is not lost, even though man falls and perishes.
The Lord continues to lend out His money at interest; if
the man who receives it does not double it, it is taken away
from him and given to another who already has some. The
Lord's money cannot lie idle.

'May his children be fatherless, and his wife a widow.'
Note the mysteries here revealed. Whom do you suppose are
the sons of Judas? The Jews. The Jews take their name, not
from that Juda who was a holy man, but from the betrayer.
From the former, we are spiritual Jews; from the traitor came
the carnal Jews. As a matter of fact, there are two apostles
called by the name of Judas: the eleventh, Judas, the son of
Jacob; the twelfth and last, Judas Iscariot. From that Judas,
son of Jacob, we are called Judaeans; from this Iscariot, they
are called Judaeans. Judas, our father, is called the son of
Jacob, that is, Judas, son of the supplantor, for we have
supplanted the people of the Jews and have received their
birthright. They, on the other hand, are said to be of Iscariot,

---

15 Acts 1.20.

though it is not certain whether the name indicates Judas'
father or his hamlet. Be that as it may, no matter how you
interpret it, Iscariot means money and price.[16] This Judas,
therefore, who was going to betray the Lord and collect the
price, received his name from the word 'price.' Granted, he
did return the ransom to the priests; nevertheless, they condemned him because they did not want to take the money
that was the price of blood.

Mark the inconsistency of the Pharisees and the wretchedness of Judas. If you have purchased the blood of Christ at a
good bargain, why do you not take back your money? If
you do not want to accept the money because it is the price
of blood, you show that it is with injustice and iniquity that
you have spilled blood. Note what they do. They do not
deposit the money in the treasury, but buy a field with it, and
call it Haceldama,[17] or the Field of Blood. Why do they buy
it? To use it as a cemetery for strangers. We are the bene-
ficiaries for whom the field is purchased with the price of
the Lord's blood.

'His wife a widow.' The synagogue which first became the
wife of God, about which He said: 'I gave her a bill of divorce, and I took her back again, and I said to her, Return
to me';[18] that synagogue was divorced by the Savior and
became the wife of Judas, the betrayer. Then what happened?
She did not receive a dowry, but gave a dowry to her husband. That miserable Judas who betrayed the Lord wants,
however, nothing of the vicious dowry, and returns to his
meretricious wife the dowry of sin that he received from her.
What does he say? You displeased your first husband; he
repudiated you and cast you out and gave you a bill of
divorce; I do not want to have you for my wife. You gave
me a price, and you deceived me; and you who have killed
your Lord, have killed me, too. This, then, is my interpreta-

16 Cf. *Commentary on Matthew* 10.4, PL 26.63 (57).
17 Cf. Matt. 27.3–10.
18 Cf. Jer. 3.8–12.

tion of the versicle, for I cannot find anywhere in the Scriptures that Judas had either wife or sons.

'May his children be roaming vagrants and beggars.' Listen carefully, for there are difficulties ahead. From the time of the Lord's crucifixion, from that time, the Jews are constantly on the move; they have no permanent home of their own. Furthermore, Scripture says of Cain: 'Cain went out from the face of the Lord, and dwelt in the land of Naid.'[19] Now the translation of Naid is 'wandering.' Because Cain had been banished from the presence of God, naturally, he dwelt in the land of Naid, became a fugitive. The Jews, too, because they crucified God and their Lord, wander to and fro begging their bread. They are not in their own land, but are dispersed throughout the world. 'Begging' here refers to spiritual riches, for they have no prophets, no law, no priests, no sacrifice; they have become beggars in the true sense.

'May the usurer ensnare all his belongings.' You gave him money, Lord, You gave to Him just as You gave to others, but what did he do with it? He did not wrap it up in a napkin, bury it in the ground, and forget about it. No, indeed, while he held in his charge a talent, the money of the Lord, he accepted a price from the Lord's enemies and sold his Lord. That is why I am warning You, Lord, to exact interest for Your money from that fellow. 'Strangers plunder the fruit of his labors.' The usurer of the Lord obviously has died, and what has happened? 'Strangers plunder the fruit of his labors.' This holds whether we understand in general of all the Jews that they were ravaged by the Romans, or whether, more properly Judas, in particular, was torn asunder by demons—and the people as well.

'May there be no one to do him a kindness, nor anyone to pity his orphans.' At that time the Jews had no one to help them. Answer me, O Jews. You were in Babylonia; you had there prophets, Daniel, Ezechiel; and what were you but idolators? You were in captivity for seventy years and after-

---

19 Cf. Gen. 4.16.

wards came back into your own land. Behold, now four
hundred years have passed; why has no prophet been sent
to you? In those days you were idol worshipers and God took
pity on you. Now, however, you are not worshiping idols;
why has the Lord abandoned you? Just think, four hundred
years ago![20] Then, indeed, you abandoned the Lord and
worshiped idols, but now you have crucified and slain the
Lord. That is why there will be no one to take your part.

'In the next generation may their name be blotted out.' O
prophecy, O divine mystery of prophecy! Before a generation
passes away, their name will be wiped out completely! After
the Passion of the Lord, forty-two years transpired, and that
people met with destruction—forty years constitute a generation. In the forty-second year after the Passion of the Lord,
Jerusalem was destroyed. See how in one generation their
name was blotted out! In this destruction, nevertheless, there
is also the compassion of the Lord. The Jews crucified Him
and for forty-two years He gave them opportunity to repent.
I am simply saying that He destroyed them forty-two years
later, for not one of those who crucified the Lord survived.
Judas is cursed, that in Judas the Jews may be accursed.

'May the guilt of his fathers be remembered by the Lord.'
They sinned in the desert and He forgave them; now He
imputes to them the sins they then committed, for they
have crucified the Lord. Or let us interpret this verse in
another way. He imputes to them the cruelty of their mur-
derers, and forgives them nothing. 'Let not his mother's sin
be blotted out.' Who is the mother of Judas? Jerusalem that
rejoices in blood, that kills the prophets and the Lord Himself.

'Because he remembered not to show kindness.' Learn how
great is the graciousness of the Lord! He sees Judas coming
with the guards and officers; He sees him coming with clubs,
and offers him a kiss. He comes to betray, and the Lord
offers him a kiss, so that he who has no fear of the Master
may be vanquished, indeed, by kindness.

20 Cf. Letter 129.7, PL 22.1106 (975).

'But persecuted the wretched and poor.' 'Who, although he was rich, he became poor for our sakes.'[21] The Lord calls Himself a pauper and a beggar; who, then, has any right to glory in his wealth? Be comforted, you who are poor, the Lord is poor with you. 'And the brokenhearted, to do them to death.' What does it mean to do the brokenhearted to death? The same as He said in the Gospel: 'My soul is sad, even unto death';[22] and again: 'Father, if it is possible, let this cup pass away from me.'[23] Or it may mean: I was grieving, and I was in deep sorrow for My persecutors because they refused to repent. I was hanging on the cross and with My blood I washed away their stains, and they refused to do penance. This was My grief, this My brokenheartedness, that I was unable to save those who were persecuting Me.

'Rescue me; for I am wretched and poor.' The Lord says He is poor in order to comfort the poor. He became a poor man with men that no one might despair of salvation because of his poverty. 'My heart is pierced within me.' Note: My heart is torn in anguish. He utters a similar cry in another psalm: 'I am troubled and cannot speak,'[24] I am troubled in my human nature. It is a mark of great virtue and strength to rise above affliction and control anger, wherefore the Apostle says: 'Be angry and do not sin.'[25] Are you angry? You are a man. Anger finds no lodging in you? You are a Christian.[26]

'I am swept away like the locust.' I had come to protect My people and I said: 'Jerusalem, Jerusalem! thou who killest the prophets, and stonest those who are sent to thee! How often would I have gathered thy children together, as a hen gathers her young under her wings.'[27] I had come as the

---

21 Cf. 2 Cor. 8.9.
22 Matt. 26.38.
23 Matt. 26.39.
24 Ps. 76.5.
25 Eph. 4.26.
26 Cf. Letter 12, PL 22.346 (27); 79.9, PL 22.731 (506); 130.13, PL 22.1118 (989).
27 Matt. 23.37.

hen to shelter them, but they received Me with hatred and
malice. I had come as a mother, and they, as it were their
own slaughterer, slaughtered Me. 'I am swept away.' How is
that? They persecuted Me; they rejected Me. They drove
Me out of Nazareth, I went into Capharnaum; they drove
Me from Capharnaum; I went into Bethsaida, and they drove
Me out of there. I went into Jerusalem; I wanted to stay with
My people, and from there they drove Me out. They treated
Me just as if I were a swarm of locusts! What did I do? Was
I angered? Did I defend Myself? Did I curse them? Did I
abandon them? No, not any of that did I do. What did I
do? I prayed for them.

'My knees totter from my fasting.' Find comfort, O monk,
in your fasting, since even the Lord fasted. I maintain that
when the monk fasts, he becomes stronger from the fast;
when his knees tremble from fasting, then is he strongest.
'My flesh is wasted for want of oil.'[28] I seem to be saying
something very difficult, and I am following a literal interpretation to edify my listeners, for the strict sense edifies me, too.
It is good to fast; it is good to shun pleasures. Before I take
up the spiritual sense, I am going to pause a moment longer
over the literal. The man who says he does not eat rich
foods, keeps far away from the other pleasures. This much
I have said because of the words: 'my flesh is wasted for want
of oil.' I have given the ordinary interpretation. This is,
however, what I think it means. Oil is a symbol of brightness;
oil is, as it were, the food of light. Accordingly, from Me the
Jews also have received oil; they have received life; they have
received light. Lest anyone think that oil is used here to
represent mercy, know that in Hebrew oil signifies understanding.

'Is wasted,' not in joy, but in sadness; not that I may be
found more beautiful, but that I may appear more loathsome.
That is why Scripture says: 'We have seen him, and there

---

28 Cf. Ps. 108 (109).24.

was no stately bearing in him.'[29] Why? Because His flesh
has become wasted for want of oil. There was nothing ap-
pealing about His body, only about His spirit. When we
fast, when our faces are pale from fasting, when we are
loathsome to look upon, let us realize that it is then that
we appear more beautiful to Christ. Soldiers that are heart-
free from fasting are the soldiers that Christ loves. Fasting
is our food and means of our subsistence. How so? Because
in fasting there is victory, and in victory, triumph. The
Apostle did not glory in his abundance, but in his infirmity;
'For when I am weak, then I am strong.'[30]

'I am become a mockery to them.' Indeed, they called me
a Samaritan and scoffed: 'By Beelzebub, the prince of devils,
he casts out devils.'[31] 'Is not this the son of Joseph the car- /
penter, and his brethren and sisters, are they not all with
us?'[32] Again: 'Thou who destroyest the temple, and in three
days buildest it up again.'[33] And once more: 'Let us see
whether Elias is coming to save him.'[34] He was calling Eli,
Eli,[35] which means, My God, My God, and they thought He
was calling upon Elias. See the ignorance of the Jews! Was
the Son of God begging help from Elias? 'When they see me,
they shake their heads.' Why did they shake their heads in
derision? Because they had already shaken the dust from
their feet.

'Save me, in your kindness.' In the Gospel, on the other
hand, He says: 'I have the power to lay down my life and
take it up again,'[36] and: 'No one takes it from me.'[37] Then
how is it that He begs for mercy? He pleads for mercy and He
grants mercy; as man He begs, and as God He gives.

---

29 Cf. Isa. 53.2.
30 2 Cor. 12.10; cf. Letter 3.5, PL 22.334 (12).
31 Luke 11.15.
32 Matt. 3.55-58.
33 Mark 15.29.
34 Matt. 27.49.
35 Matt. 27.46.
36 John 10.18.
37 *Ibid.*

'And let them know that this is your hand; that you, O
Lord, have done this.' What is this that He is saying: 'And
let them know that this is your hand, that you, O Lord, have
done this'? Let the Jews perceive that they have not prevailed against Me, but that it is Your will that I suffer. Besides, I desired to suffer; that is why I say in My human
nature: 'To do your will, O my God, is my delight.'[38] It was
Your will and Mine that I suffer; not their plottings and
power did it, but You and I desired it. You, in truth, struck
Your Shepherd, and the sheep have been scattered, as it is
written in Zacharia: 'Strike the shepherd that the sheep may
be dispersed.'[39] That I suffer was Your will and Mine also.
What You desired, I also desired. It was necessary that scandal
come, but woe to the man through whom it comes![40]

'Let them curse, but do you bless.' That goes on to this
very day:[41] they curse in the synagogue; the Lord blesses in
the Church. 'May my adversaries be put to shame, but let
your servant rejoice.' They rise up against Me, but I, Your
servant, rejoice. How am I Your servant? Because He 'though
he was by nature God, did not consider being equal to God
a thing to be clung to, but emptied himself, taking the
nature of a slave.'[42]

'Let my accusers be clothed with disgrace.' It is of great
profit to us to understand exactly what we are saying here.
The compassionate and merciful God is evident in the words:
'Let my accusers be clothed.' He does not say, let them
perish; He does not say, let them be destroyed forever; but
what does He say? Let them be clothed with shame; that is,
let them realize their error and be ashamed and persevere
in their repentance. He who is covered with shame is close
to salvation, for when one is sincerely disturbed and in con-

---

38 Ps. 39.9.
39 Cf. Zach. 13.7.
40 Cf. Matt. 18.7; cf. *Commentary on Matthew* 18.7, PL 26.134 (138).
41 Cf. *Commentary on Isaia* 5.18, 19, PL 24.86 (81); 49.7, PL 24.467 (565);
   52.4-7, PL 24.498 (604).
42 Phil. 2.6, 7; cf. Letter 108.18, PL 22.893 (709).

fusion, he begins to repent. Ponder deeply, O monks, if ever
you have anything against your brother, you must never fail
to beseech God in his behalf. The Lord is crucified and He
prays for those who are crucifying Him. Moreover, if you
should hear an abusive word, do not persist in your anger.
'Do not let the sun go down upon your anger.'[43]

'Let them wear their shame like a mantle.' The mantle
is a kind of double cloak; in fact, in Hebrew it is called
MAIL. It is double because it folds twice around the body.
Therefore, I say to You, Lord: My enemies are the Jews;
they have conspired in hatred against Me, crucified Me, heaped
evils of all kinds upon Me, blasphemed Me; forgive them,
since I who have suffered intercede for them. What do I
ask for them? Let them blush and be covered with confusion and so be saved. They are naked; they have lost My
tunic. Grant them confusion, grant them shame, and let them
be wrapped in a double mantle of shame and confusion; do
not let their disturbance be onefold but twofold that they
may do penance all the more. He does not say this against
the Jews, but in their behalf. He is their Creator and ours;
He has not altogether uprooted them. Do you want proof?
Peter was one of them; Paul was one of them; all the apostles
were from them. We have been grafted upon their root;
we are the branches, they the root. We must not curse our
roots; rather we ought to pray for them. We who have
been grafted upon the root, let us pray the Lord that just
as the branches have been saved, so may the root be also.
Perhaps someone is raising the objection: Do you pray for
the Jews, for blasphemers? Yes, I pray the Lord in their
behalf, for if He has pity on His persecutors, how much more
will He be merciful to me?

'I will speak my thanks earnestly to the Lord.' This is said
after the Resurrection and foretells the Church that is to come.
'In the midst of the throng I will praise him'; not in Judea

---

43 Eph. 4.26.

alone, but in the whole world, in the Church, I will praise
You.

'For he stood at the right hand of the poor man.' The devil
stood at the right hand of Judas, but the Lord stood at my
right hand. 'To save my soul from those who would condemn me.'[44] My soul, He says, He will save. Again in another place, He says: 'My soul is sad even unto death.'[45]
Anyone who is sad has the capacity for sympathy. The in-
sensible soul is unperceptive and without feeling; it has no
understanding nor sorrow. Where there is grief and sorrow,
there is human affection and emotion. If He was sorrowful,
if He grieved because of His sorrow, He had emotions, for
grief is an emotion. Consequently, if they want to say to us:[46]
'We say that He did not have human emotions or affections
so that there would be no question of sin in Him,' let us
give them this answer: 'Did He have a body just as ours, or
did He not?' If they say, 'He had,' let us answer back, 'Then
He also had the passions of our body.' Everyone understands
what I mean. If, however, they deny that He had the passions or appetites of the body, then we are compelled to
answer that He had no body; but let us assure them: 'Just
as He had a true body like ours, but did not have the sins
of the body, so also did He have a true soul, but did not
have the sin of the soul.' Let us, therefore, acknowledge and
give thanks that He had a true body and a true soul, for if
the Lord did not assume human nature in its totality, then He
did not redeem mankind. If He assumed the body only, but
not the soul, He saved the body, but not the soul. But we
want our soul to be saved far more than our body; hence, the
Lord assumed both body and soul to redeem both body and
soul, to redeem the whole man just as He made him.

If, however, they insist that the Lord did not assume a
human soul in order not to sin, and believe that whoever

44 Cf. Ps. 108 (109).31.
45 Matt. 26.38.
46 Cf. Letter 84.3, PL 22.745 (524); 98.6-8, PL 22.797-798 (590-591); cf.
Homily 88 on the Birth of the Lord.

has a human soul cannot control it, let us ask them: 'Did John the Baptist have feelings and emotions or did he not? When he was in the desert, did he commit sin?' Surely, they will answer that he did not. In fact, our Lord says: 'Amen I say to you, among those born of women there has not risen a greater than John the Baptist.'[47] Did Peter have feelings and emotions, or did he not; and the other holy apostles? If, then, the apostles controlled their human inclinations, did the Lord fear to take on a rational, intelligent, sensible soul lest He be dominated by it? All the while that they want to give glory to the Lord, they rob Him of honor. How do they dishonor Him? They imply that the Lord fears what the apostles did not fear. Let us give thanks to the omnipotent God and say: In Your human soul You had no sin; and: 'The prince of the world is coming, and in me he has nothing.'[48] Help us, O Lord; just as You overpowered the devil in Your human soul, vanquish the devil in ours, too, so that just as You created us a whole man, You may redeem us a whole man. You are Creator; You are Master; You are Lord; You are He who suffered for us, who live and reign forever and ever. Amen.

---

47 Matt. 11.11.
48 John 14.30.

HOMILY 36

ON PSALM 109 (110)

THE LORD SAID to my Lord: "Sit at my right hand." A psalm of David.'[1] It is David who is speaking, a prophet, a holy man, a king. What is the king saying? What does the king and prophet say? 'The Lord is my Lord.' The Savior has revealed the meaning of these words in the Gospel when He asked: 'If the Christ is the Son of David, how then does David in the Spirit call him Lord?'[2] Notice, therefore, that He is saying: If He is David's son, as you say, how does David in the Spirit call Him Lord? Someone may ask: Is He, therefore, not the son of David? The Lord was interrogating the Pharisees because they were acknowledging Christ simply as the son of David.

I am directing the same question to the Jews and to Photius: If Christ is the Son of David, how, then, does David call his own son, Lord? On the other hand, for the benefit of him who admits that the Lord is God and the Son of God— for example, Manichaeus, who denies that Christ is the Son of David—in his presence I shall prove that Christ is the Son of David. Now to us, He who is the Son of God is also the Son of David; there is not one Son and another son; I do not make two persons, one in God and another in man; but He who is the Son of God is Himself also the Son of David. 'The Lord said to my Lord: "Sit at my right hand." ' In the Hebrew, the first title of Lord is written in those

---

1 Cf. Ps. 109 (110).1.
2 Cf. Matt. 22.43.

characters that are reserved for God alone,[3] but the second title of Lord is written with letters ordinarily respectful in polite address, as, for instance, a master is called lord by those who serve him, and as kings are called lords.

Understand, then: 'The Lord said to my Lord' to mean, to the Lord to whom is given the command to be seated. God does not sit; He who has assumed a human body sits; hence, He who is told to be seated is man, the Incarnate Word. This we affirm against the Arians and in contradiction to those who say: The Father, who gives the command to be seated, is greater than He who receives the command. All the Gospels proclaim the Person in His human nature; no need to stop for proof now, since anything and everything less than divinity is referred to the man, is referred to the flesh. Now we turn our attention to the psalm.

'The scepter of your power the Lord will stretch forth from Sion.' 'Scepter.' The Hebrew text does not so much employ the word for rod as the word for scepter, the symbol of royal power. 'The scepter of your power the Lord will stretch forth from Sion,' 'for from Sion shall go forth instruction, and the word of the Lord from Jerusalem.'[4] 'Rule in the midst of your enemies.' The psalmist did not say, kill your enemies, but what? Rule in the midst of Your enemies. Bring it to pass that Your enemies who had been strangers become Your friends. 'Rule in the midst of your enemies,' Your enemies of whom it is written in the sixty-seventh psalm: 'The tongues of your dogs will have their share of your enemies.'[5] These are the enemies who were under a foreign power. Now, however, the prayer of David is: rule over Your enemies; deign to be Lord of Your enemies.

'With you is the beginning in the day of your strength, in the brightness of the saints.'[6] This versicle is very obscure. Let us ponder the day of the Lord's strength, so that when

3 Cf. *Commentarioli in ps.* 109.1.
4 Isa. 2.3.
5 Cf. Ps. 67.24.
6 Cf. Ps. 109 (110).3; cf. *Commentarioli in ps.* 109.3.

we know the day, then, we may know what beginning this is, and how this beginning is with Him and has been with Him; as this same beginning in the day of His strength is also in the brightness of the saints. This beginning that is with the Lord in the day of His strength, I say, then, is with Him in order that His saints may be in splendor. 'With you is the beginning in the day of your strength': 'In the beginning was the Word, and the Word was with God, and the Word was God. He was in the beginning with God.'[7] The Father is the beginning, but the Son also is the beginning, for beginning does not have a beginning; if it has another beginning, it has ceased to be the beginning. Whatever, therefore, we attribute to the Father, we attribute also to the Son, for if the Father is in the Son, and the Son in the Father, and all things of the Father are of the Son, and all things of the Son are of the Father, the beginning of the Father is also the beginning of the Son.

What the passage means, therefore, is this: At the time of Your Passion when You cried out: 'Father into your hands I commend my spirit,'[8] and You uttered these words in Your state as man, You were not praying as weak man, for with You was the beginning, with You was divinity. You were praying for help in order that, when You had received it, You might give it to Your saints, and they might be resplendent.

The notion of 'receiving that You might give' should not be a scandal to anyone; it is expressed in accordance with the human nature of the Son, for if He has assumed the body of man, necessarily He takes upon Himself the language of man. Christ is man, and truly man; we say this because of the Incarnation. Since, if He is man by virtue of His human nature, you see His body and you are not scandalized; why, then, is it such a wonder to you if He speaks in the manner of man? If, however, the meanness of a body scandalizes

---

7 John 1.1, 2; cf. Letter 108.10, PL 22.885 (698).
8 Luke 23.46.

you, if the cross, the injuries, the blows, and the scourging, and all the wrong of the cross, if that is scandal to you, revert to the beginning, to the divine generation, and do not be scandalized, for the Father says to the Son: 'From the womb before the daystar, I have begotten you.'[9] Are you surprised if our Lord and Savior, who truly assumed a human nature, speaks as man does, when God the Father who did not assume a human nature says in the manner of man: 'From the womb before the daystar, I have begotten you'? I do not have a womb, but I cannot indicate My Fatherhood in any other way except to use human language.[10] 'From the womb before the daystar, I have begotten you.' 'From the womb'; from My substance. 'From the womb.'

Listen, Eunomius; listen, Arius. If the Lord is a creature, if He is something that has been fashioned, does the craftsman beget his own work? Does the craftsman call his work his son? A carpenter makes a bench; has he begotten it from his womb? Does he say to it: From my womb, I have begotten you, O bench? By no means. What does he say? I made you with my hands. When the womb is specified, however, a son is signified and not an adopted son, even though the adopted also are called sons. 'To as many as received him he gave the power of becoming sons of God.'[11] This psalm, however, actually specifies that He begets a Son from the womb, from His nature, from His own vitals, from His own substance. 'From the womb,' clearly means from the marrow of His Godhead. Everything whatsoever the Father is in divinity, He has given to the Son whom He has begotten: 'From the womb before the daystar, I have begotten you.'

'Before the daystar.' The rhetorical figure in this phrase is the one called συνεκδοχή in Greek, and by the grammarians

---

9 Cf. Ps. 109 (110).3.
10 Cf. Letter 65.5, PL 22.626 (377).
11 John 1.12.

ἀπὸ μέρους τὸ πᾶν,[12] for the expression, 'before the daystar,' mentions by name one creature, but includes all. When the psalmist says, 'before the daystar,' let us understand, 'before the moon, before the sun, before every creature.' From the womb before the daystar, I have begotten You. 'Before the daystar.' Before the daystar that is seen in the world, true light was begotten; hence, another psalm says: 'In your light we see light.'[13] This remark is addressed to the Father: O Father, in the light of the Son we see light, the Holy Spirit. 'From the womb before the daystar, I have begotten you.'

'The Lord has sworn, and he will not repent.' The Lord has sworn. The Lord made a solemn promise, not to Him who was begotten before the daystar, but to Him who was born of a virgin after the daystar. 'You are a priest forever, according to the order of Melchisedec.' It is superfluous for us to attempt the interpretation of this versicle, since the holy Apostle has discussed it amply in his Letter to the Hebrews, for this is that Melchisedec without father, without mother, without origin.[14] Furthermore, it is very carefully explained there why he is without father, without mother, without birth; and all ecclesiasts agree that 'without father' means according to the flesh, 'without mother,' according to God. Let us, therefore, restrict our comments on: 'You are a priest forever, according to the order of Melchisedec,' simply to a consideration of why he said 'according to the order.'

'According to the order': You will be priest in no wise according to the Jewish sacrifices, rather in the line of Melchisedec. Just as Melchisedec, the king of Salem, offered bread and wine,[15] even so shall You offer Your Body and Blood, true bread and true wine. This is our Melchisedec who gave us the divine sacrifice that we have. It is He who

---

12 Cf. *Commentary on Isaia* 14.2, PL 24.160 (176); *on Jona* 2.2, PL 25.1131 (405); *on Matthew* 12.40, PL 26.85 (83).
13 Ps. 35.10; cf. *Commentarioli in ps.* 35.10.
14 Heb. 7.3.
15 Cf. Gen. 14.18; cf. Letter 46.2, PL 22.484 (200).

said: 'He who eats my flesh and drinks my blood';[16] according to the order of Melchisedec, He gave us His sacrament.[17]

'The Lord is at your right hand.' I see something new here. In the beginning of the psalm, we find: 'The Lord said to my Lord: "Sit at my right hand"'; now the psalmist says: 'The Lord is at your right hand.' If He is sitting at the right hand of the Father, how, on the contrary, is the Father sitting at the right hand of the Son? 'The Lord said to my Lord: "Sit at my right hand,"' obviously means that the Son sits at the right hand of the Father; 'The Lord is at your right hand,' means that the Father is sitting at the right hand of the Son. I am saying all this to make clear that the Son is equal to the Father.

There is much to be said on this subject. In the case of sinners, the devil is standing at their right side; but that is another matter for discussion. Whoever is a sinner has the devil standing at his right hand. Someone is raising the objection: How, then, in Zacharia is the devil said to stand on the right hand of Jesus, the Son of Josedec? 'And Satan stood at his right hand.'[18] How in Zacharia is it written that the devil stands at the right hand of the Savior? You appreciate that this is a problem. At the time that the devil stood at the right hand of the Savior, 'Jesus,' Holy Writ says, 'was clad in filthy garments.'[19] He was wearing our sins; He was wrapped up in the folds of our vices; that is why the devil was standing at His right side.

'He will crush kings on the day of his wrath.' 'All these have been delivered to me.'[20] 'In a moment of time,' Scripture says the devil 'showed him all the kingdoms of the world.' The kingdoms of the world, the devil shows Him, and what does he say? 'To me they have all been delivered; if thou

---

16 John 6.55.
17 Cf. Letter 73.3, PL 22.678 (442); *Hebrew Questions on Genesis* 14.18, PL 23.1011 (329).
18 Cf. Zach. 3.1.
19 Cf. Zach. 3.3; cf. *Against Jovinian* 2.4, PL 23.302 (328).
20 Cf. Luke 4.5, 6.

wilt worship before me, the whole shall be thine.'[21] 'On the
day of his wrath,' on the day of conflict and strife, He will
crush kings.

'He will do judgment on the nations.' Notice the contrast:
kings are crushed; nations are judged. 'Heaping up corpses.'
Our Lord ascended the cross, and as a result many fell away
in disgust. 'He is destined for the fall and for the rise of many
in Israel, and for a sign that shall be contradicted.'[22] 'Heaping up corpses,' He will heap corpse upon corpse, not of
believers, but of those who have not believed the herald
apostles. Moses, too, sent scouts into the world; and because
the people did not believe the messengers, they fell while
in the desert. Even to this day, the bodies of nonbelievers
fall in the death of the desert of this world. 'He will crush
heads in the land of many.'[23] He will heap up corpses of
nonbelievers; He will crush heads of those who waver, of
those whose faith is imperfect. He will crush heads in the
land of many, but not in the land of all; for if it had said
'of all,' there would be no hope for us. 'Of many,' Scripture
says, to signify that there may be room for others to survive.

'From the torrent by the wayside he will drink.'[24] Who will
drink of the wayside torrent? He to whom it was said: 'The
Lord said to my Lord: "Sit at my right hand"'; He who
heard: 'You are a priest forever, according to the order of
Melchisedec'; He who crushed kings on the day of His wrath;
He who passes sentence on the nations, who stacks up
corpses, who crushes heads in the land of many. What else
will this One do? He will drink from the torrent by the
wayside. Let us examine the way first, that afterwards we
may consider the torrent by the wayside. Now the way is the
way of this world, the way on which He walked. In fact, it
is written in the Gospel: 'Come to terms with thy opponent

21 Cf. Luke 4.6.
22 Cf. Luke 2.34.
23 Cf. Ps. 109 (110).6.
24 Cf. Ps. 109 (110).7.

quickly, while thou art with him on the way.'[25] In other words, while you travel through this world, you are hastening on the way to Him who is the true way; hence, Psalm 118 says: 'Happy are they whose way is blameless.'[26]

Happy are they who pass through this life blamelessly, and through this world; hence, the Priest in the line of Melchisedec, because He came in the way of the world and walked in our way, drank also of the torrent that was in the world. A torrent does not have natural or running waters; its waters come from rains, floods, storms, tempests. A torrent is never found on the mountains, but always in valleys, in downhill and steep places. The torrent becomes pregnant with foreign waters, and is swollen and in labor as it rushes on. 'From the torrent by the wayside he will drink.' A torrent's water is never clean but always muddy. This is said because the waters of this world are always turbid, always full of tempests.

Would you know how it is that He has drunk of a troubled torrent? He said Himself: 'My soul is sad, even unto death';[27] and the Evangelist says: 'He began to be saddened and exceedingly troubled.'[28] Our Lord, then, drank of the troubled waters from the torrent of this world, sad waters, waters that had no joy. He took up the chalice and filled it from the floods of the world, and because the waters were muddy, He prays: 'Father, if it is possible, let this cup pass away from me.'[29] He drank of the torrent of this world, not in His own home, but on the way, hastening to another place. He drank of the wayside torrent; He drank of the torrent because it was on the way. 'From the torrent by the wayside.' If the Lord drinks of the torrent of this world, how much more do His faithful servants? Would you like evidence that saints always drink of the torrent?

Another psalm says: 'Our soul has passed through a tor-

---

25 Matt. 5.25; cf. Luke 12.58.
26 Ps. 118.1.
27 Matt. 26.38.
28 Matt. 26.37.
29 Matt. 26.39.

rent.'[30] 'From the torrent by the wayside.' We have discussed the significance of the torrent; we may even say with the assurance of Sacred Scripture: 'Our soul has passed through a torrent.' Would you like to hear of another torrent? When Jezebel was persecuting the holy prophet Elias; when he received food and for forty days made his way through the desert: 'He was in the desert,' Scripture says, 'and he drank of the torrent Carith.'[31] Now you who are hearing about the torrent of this generation, do not lose hope, for it often happens that the torrent dries up. The flood looks swollen, indeed, threatening with many waters, but almost overnight, it dries up if only you endure it patiently.

Back now to Elias, for he drank water in the desert when he was in deep sorrow and in dire want. He had fled from Judea; see how full of fear he was? He had quitted Judea and made for Mount Sinai; because Jezabel was in dread pursuit of him, he had drunk of the torrent Carith. Nevertheless, because he persevered to the end, the waters of the torrent dried up. Because the water of the torrent failed, the Lord said to Elias: 'Arise and go to the widow in Sarephta of the Sidonians.'[32] See, there, how Elias also drinks of the torrent?

But the Lord and Savior Himself drinks the cup of the torrent Cedron; for that is where Scripture records He was when His enemies came to arrest Him. 'They came,' it says, 'beyond the torrent to arrest him.'[33] Notice how lowly is the place of the torrent, how rough and rugged it is. Cedron in Hebrew means 'darkness,' so you see that the torrents of this world are in darkness. The Lord, as we were saying, is betrayed; He is not betrayed on the Mount of Olives nor in the temple, but in the torrent, and in the torrent of 'darkness,' Cedron, for all who hate the light, love the darkness.

---

30 Cf. Ps. 123.5.
31 Cf. 3 Kings 17.4-6.
32 Cf. 3 Kings 17.9.
33 Cf. John 18.1; cf. *Hebrew Questions on Genesis* 26.17, PL 23.1029 (346); *Commentary on Ecclesiastes* 1.7, PL 23.1070 (389-390A).

'From the torrent by the wayside he will drink.' Because, moreover, the Lord drank of the torrent and tasted death, the Father 'has exalted Him and bestowed upon Him the name that is above every name.'[34] Logically, then, the psalmist says: 'From the torrent by the wayside he will drink,' and because He drank of the torrent by the wayside: 'therefore will he lift up his head.' And what does He say? 'I, if I be lifted up from the earth, will draw all things to myself.'[35] He was lifted up and He has lifted us up. His head has been exalted, but the heads of the dragon have been crushed and smashed beneath the waves of the sea.[36]

'Therefore will he lift up his head.' The psalmist did not say, 'His head is lifted up,' implying that it is lifted up by someone else, but He who had humbled Himself, lifted Himself up. He says in the Gospel: 'I have the power to lay my life down, and I have the power to take it up again.'[37] 'Therefore will he lift up his head.' He who is head of all has lifted up Himself; or, more accurately, He lifted up His head; not, He lifted up Himself; He lifted up His head, for He has always been erect. When, however, the psalm says, He lifted up His head, it really means, He lifted up our head, the heads of us who were lying prostrate on the ground; He lifted up the heads of us who were bent over and unable to look upwards at the sky, only down at the ground. Would you be convinced that He lifted up the head of man?[38] He released that woman[39] whom the devil held in bonds; He lifted up the head of her who had been bent over all her life, and she adored Him, to whom be glory forever and ever. Amen.

---

34 Phil. 2.9.
35 John 12.32.
36 Cf. Ps. 73.13, 14.
37 John 10.18.
38 Cf. *Commentarioli in ps.* 109.7.
39 Cf. Luke 18.11-13.

HOMILY 37

ON PSALM 110 (111)

WILL GIVE THANKS to the Lord with all my heart.' If David were not single-hearted and sincere, he would not have said, I will give thanks to the Lord with all my heart; not only with his lips, but with all his heart.

'In the company and assembly of the just. Great are the works of the Lord.' Of the just, he says, of those who at first were sinners, but are now just. Is it not cause for wonderment when, moreover, we behold the elephant and the camels on the one hand, and the fly and the mosquito on the other, all with the same mobility, breath of life, and members?

'He has given food to those who fear him.' He fed Elias when he was hungry; He rained down manna in the desert for the Jews, and fulfilled the Scripture: He has given food to those who fear Him. This interpretation accords with the literal sense. The food that He gave, however, was the Bread which came down from heaven;[1] with this He feeds us if we are worthy. How many martyrs there are, indeed, who have been consumed with hunger and are now with the Lord!

'Holy and awesome is his name'; holy to the saints, terrible to sinners. 'The fear of the Lord is the beginning of wisdom'; there is no wisdom in those who do not fear the Lord, or, they who have no wisdom have no fear.

'His praise endures forever.' Because 'alleluia'[2] is inscribed in the title, naturally the psalm closes with a doxology, for the translation of alleluia is, praise the Lord.

1 John 6.41-59.
2 Cf. *Commentarioli in ps.* 104.1; Homily 32 on Ps. 105, p. 234; 56 on Ps. 146, p. 400; 58 on Ps. 148, p. 416.

HOMILY 38

ON PSALM 111 (112)

'Happy the man who fears the Lord.' I have told you frequently that all interpretations in the name of the just man point to Christ. If the saints are types prefiguring the Savior, the truly holy man, for example Isaia, is a type of the Lord and Savior, and so, too, are Joseph, David, Solomon, and the rest of the saints. Now the happy man who is being described in this psalm is a just man in truth, but this just man is a type of the true just Man. 'Happy the man who fears the Lord.' So much for the distinction we have made in the psalm. Let us now say of the just man: 'Happy the man who fears the Lord.'

Psalm 111 is arranged alphabetically in the same manner as Psalm 110. The first versicle begins with the Hebrew letter ALEPH: 'Happy the man who fears the Lord'; the second with BETH: 'who greatly delights in his commands'; the third with GIMEL: 'His posterity shall be mighty upon the earth'; and so on to the twenty-second and last letter of the Hebrew alphabet, THAU. With the help of your prayers, let us direct our attention to individual versicles.

'Happy the man who fears the Lord.' These are the opening words of the psalm; not yet does the psalmist say, Happy the man who loves the Lord. Fear is the mark of beginners; love, indeed, of proficients since 'perfect love casts out fear.'[1] The psalm, therefore, is speaking of the neophyte, of the soul setting out on the road to sanctity. Let us note the sequence of the psalm. 'Happy the man who fears the Lord.'

---

1 John 4.18; cf. Letter 82.3, PL 22.737 (514); 133.6, PL 22.1154 (1034).

What does the man do who fears the Lord? Does he heed the word of God? Is he learned in the law? No, that is not what the psalmist says. What does he say? 'Who greatly delights in his commands.' The man who fears the Lord, the happy man, cheerfully obeys the commands of the Lord; He loves His commands with a deep and strong love. Grasp what that means. The psalmist did not merely say, he complies with the Lord's commands, for many obey out of fear and do not gain their reward.[2] The man who fears hell, and for that reason does not commit fornication, does not receive as great a reward as he who serves the Lord faithfully through love, but the man whose will is in the law of God wills what God wills; he ardently desires to accomplish the will of God. In the same way that one thirsts in the midday heat, this loyal servant thirsts and longs to obey the commands of the Lord. He bears great love always in fulfilling the Lord's will. He does not merely do His bidding, he wills it, not just in passing but with all the ardor of his heart.

The third versicle is: 'His posterity shall be mighty upon the earth.'[3] I who have obeyed God from my own choice am worthy to become the father of saints. We shall be brief in our remarks in order to keep our sermon within bounds. 'The upright generation shall be blessed.' May the Lord grant that you, too, who are listening to me, be an upright generation.

'Wealth and riches shall be in his house.' Wealth and riches. Do we imagine that we have here a reference to the wealth and riches of the world? Is that why one fulfills the will of God and obeys His commands, to obtain the riches of this world? Surely, one does not serve God with devotion unless he despises the wealth of the world. 'Wealth and riches shall be in his house.' The Apostle has clearly indicated the wealth of those who believe: 'Are you not my

---

2 Cf. Homily 1 on Ps. 1, p. 3.
3 This is actually the second verse of Ps. 111 (112).

crown of glory?'[4] 'And riches.' These are the riches to which
the same Apostle refers when he says: 'because you have been
enriched in all knowledge.'[5] 'His generosity shall endure
forever.'[6] The prophet did not say, His generosity endures
for a generation, and then comes to an end; no, but that His
bounty shall continue without end.

'He dawns through the darkness, a light for the upright.'
Once upon a time we were in darkness; we were sitting in
darkness and in the shadow of death, but as Isaia attests,
light has shone upon us;[7] 'He is gracious and merciful and
just.' Mark the two attributes: merciful and just. If you are
a sinner, do not despair of pardon; the Lord is merciful. If
you are proud and presume upon the mercy of God, be careful; He is also just. 'He is gracious and merciful and just.'
Notice the wisdom of the psalmist: justice is single, mercy
twofold. 'He is gracious and merciful and just.'

'Well for the man who is gracious and lends.' Because the
Lord is gracious and kind, and the just man imitates his
Lord, he, too, should be kind and merciful. 'Well for the
man who is gracious and lends.' Is anyone under the impression that the psalmist is referring to gold and silver and
money? The just have had so little of the goods of this world
that instead they received food from others. Does it follow,
then, that if I have nothing to give away, I am no longer just?
If I do not give alms, am I excluded from the number of the
just? Not at all, for how many holy people have engaged in
almsgiving and have fallen from sanctity! The perfect have
not given alms; they have had none to give.[8] To have no
part in almsgiving is a reproach to the man of possessions;
but the man who possesses nothing from which to give alms
is free. He gave as much as ever he would desire to give
because he gave by vow. Yet the saints do have a source of

4 Cf. 1 Thess. 2.19.
5 Cf. 1 Cor. 1.5.
6 Cf. Letter 75.4, PL 22.688 (454).
7 Cf. Isa. 9.1.
8 Cf. *Life of Hilarion* 18.

almsgiving. Peter says: 'Silver and gold I have none, but what I have, that I give thee. In the name of the Lord Jesus, arise and walk.'[9] Which is greater, to give a man money or to make the weak strong and the cripple straight?

'Well for the man who is gracious and lends.' What kind of alms are these? What is it that the just man lends? The answer is revealed in the next versicle: 'Who conducts his words with justice';[10] not he manages his gold and silver, or his money with justice, but he conducts his words with justice. This is compassionate kindness, for the saintly man teaches holiness to others who are not holy. 'Who conducts his words with justice.' Now we see what kind of money is graciously lent. The real meaning of, 'he conducts his words with justice,' is found in the Gospel where we are warned not to throw our pearls before swine.[11] In other words, one should know what to give and to whom to give; one should be able to discriminate. So it is that the faithful servant says: 'Within my heart I treasure your promise, that I may not sin against you.'[12] I did not give Your words to those to whom it was pleasing to give them; I did not cast Your holy one to the dogs; I did not give Your pearls to swine. Great, therefore, is the responsibility of him who expounds the word of the Lord.

There is much for discussion in this psalm, but since time prohibits, let us bless the Almighty Lord; and he who has such coin, may he give to those who have not; and may those who are without receive it in all joy. May the Lord grant to me, also, the grace to possess these riches that I may give them to those who have not, and to those who have that they may the more abound; and may the blessedness of the just man be mine both in speaking and in heeding. 'Happy is he who speaks to attentive ears.'[13] What good is there for

---

9 Cf. Acts 3.6; cf. Letter 22.32, PL 22.418 (117).
10 Cf. Ps. 111 (112).5.
11 Matt. 7.6; cf. Letter 84.3, PL 22.746 (525).
12 Ps. 118.11.
13 Cf. Sirach (Ecclus.) 25.9.

me to speak if another does not accept my words? What benefit for me to pour forth wine if immediately that wine is spilled and wasted? You recall that in the Gospel[14] water is put into jars, and it turns into wine and is preserved lest it be wasted. Let us, therefore, attend diligently to the words of God to whom be glory forever and ever. Amen.

---

14 Cf. John 2.7-10.

HOMILY 39

ON PSALM 114 (116A)

HAVE LOVED the Lord because he will hear my voice in supplication.'[1] The psalmist did not say, I shall love, but I have loved. He does not promise to love, but testifies that he has loved. 'I have loved.' Why have I loved? Because the Lord will grant gracious hearing to my entreaty. I have loved expresses time past; the granting of my request, however, is in the future. Indeed, he did not say, I have loved because the Lord has so graciously answered my prayer, but I have loved because the Lord will attend my plea.

'Because he has inclined his ear to me.' Because we are little and lowly and unable to lift ourselves up to Him, the Lord stoops down to us and in His compassionate kindness deigns 'to hear us. In fact, because we are men and cannot become gods, God became man and inclined Himself, as it is written: 'He inclined the heavens and came down.'[2] 'Throughout my days I will call upon him.'[3] Here, the question naturally arises, how does one call upon the Lord in the daytime and not pray to Him in the nighttime? Further, why does another psalm say: 'At midnight I rise to give you thanks,'[4] since it is the practice of the saints to pray during the night? And still another psalm says: 'During the hours of night, lift up your hands towards the sanctuary, and bless the Lord.'[5] What, then, does our psalmist mean

---

1 Cf. Ps. 114 (116A).1.
2 Ps. 17.10.
3 Cf. Ps. 114 (116A).2.
4 Ps. 118.62.
5 Ps. 133.1, 2.

when he says: 'Throughout my days I will call upon Him'?
He did not say, I have called, but I will call—in the future.
While we are in the present world, we call upon the Lord
in the night; in the future world, we invoke the Lord in
the daylight; hence, the psalmist said: 'Throughout my days';
it is nighttime for sinners, but daytime for me.

'The pains of death encompassed me.'[6] It seems to me that
the pains of death are evil thoughts. When the soul enter-
tains foul thoughts, it has a longing to sin; when it is in
labor with sin, death is at hand. 'The snares of the nether
world seized upon me.' O what unhappy, wretched, miserable
creatures we are, for sin is ever ready to ensnare us! If sins
are always on our trail, let us run so fast that they will never
overtake us. There is, moreover, this difference between the
pains of death and the perils of hell: the pains of death
are evil thoughts; the perils of hell are evil deeds. To
theorize is one thing, however; action—or practice—is another. In the latter, there is grief and anguish; in the former,
there is danger and the proximity of death.

'I fell into distress and sorrow.' This is a new slant. The
prophet does not say, 'I found rest,' or 'I found satisfaction.'
If he had said, 'trouble came upon me; sorrow caught up
with me,' there would be no problem. Instead, what does
he say? 'I fell into distress and sorrow.' Looking for trouble,
as it were, he fell right into it, for one does not find unless
one seeks. The saint does not look for rest, but for tribulation; he knows that 'tribulation works out endurance, and
endurance, tried virtue, and tried virtue, hope. And hope
does not disappoint.'[7] This is parallel to what Jeremia says:
'I have called upon tribulation and misery,'[8] 'for,' he says,
'your bitter word was to me joy and gladness';[9] in this world
I desire nothing but tribulation that I may have happiness
and repose in the next. That is why, he says, I now bear

6 Cf. Ps. 114 (116A).3.
7 Rom. 5.3-5; cf. Letter 130.7, PL 22.1112 (982).
8 Cf. Jer. 15.15.
9 Cf. Jer. 15.16.

with bitterness, that afterwards I may have all sweetness. The
people of the Lord coming out of Egypt came into Mara which
means 'bitter,' and from Mara, into Sinai which means
'temptation.' Again Jeremia says: 'I sat alone because I was
filled with bitterness.'[10]

'O Lord, save my life!' Neither Greek nor Latin can do
justice to the Hebrew idiom. Instead of 'O' the Hebrew text
has ANNA.[11] 'Anna,' moreover, means 'I beg and entreat.'
What it says here, then, is: 'I beseech You, Lord, save my
soul.' The prophet is not giving way to sentiments of awe,
but to prayers of entreaty,[12] for he is in serious trouble and
affliction. 'Gracious is the Lord and just; yes, our God is
merciful.' Prick up your ears, sinner, the Lord is merciful;
but, be careful, for the next words say He is also just. If you
have sinned much, heed that the Lord is merciful; if you are
careless, heed that He is also just. The Lord, nevertheless,
seems to be equally merciful and just, ten parts, for example,
merciful and ten parts just—to put it clearly for the sake
of the less learned. One might say: If my sins were weighed
on a scale, I could not possibly have as much good as evil;
but this psalm says that the Lord is merciful and just—
merciful in regard to sinners, just in regard to the good; my
sins are becoming very heavy, and so the Lord's mercy gains
the victory. The psalmist, therefore, posited justice once
and mercy twice. 'Merciful.' This attribute could apply to
the past as well. 'God is merciful,' says the psalmist, to make
it known that He is always merciful.

'The Lord keeps the little ones.' If a great man puts on airs
and is puffed up with pride, the Lord is not his keeper; if anyone thinks himself very important, the Lord has no pity for
him; but if one humbles himself, the Lord takes pity on him
and protects him. Holy Writ says of this: 'Look at me and
the children, whom the Lord has given me';[13] and again: 'I

---

10 Cf. Jer. 15.17, LXX.
11 Cf. Letter 20.3, PL 22.377 (66).
12 Cf. Letter 20.5, PL 22.378 (67).
13 Isa. 8.18.

was brought low, and he saved me.' We understand 'I was brought low and he saved me' in two ways: either I sinned and He saved me; or when I was proud, He humbled and saved me.

'Return, O my soul, to your tranquillity.' Since it says return to your tranquillity, the soul possessed tranquillity before it lost its peace and serenity. No one returns except to that state or place where he was before. The Lord created us good and of His own choice placed and left us all with Adam in the Garden of Paradise. Because, however, we fell away from that state of happiness through our own decision, and came into the valley of tears, the just man is urging his soul to return thither whence he fell.[14] 'Return, O my soul, to your tranquillity.' This is the place of tribulation; this, the land of fighters; this, the place of tears, where no one walks with security. Everywhere there is danger; if one is in the desert, there are scorpions; if one is in the city, the destructive eye of the meretrix spells his doom; if he is on the sea, there are robbers and pirates. I say this in its figurative sense, of course, for to be slain by bandits is not now a danger to the man of holiness since martyrs, indeed, have won the victory with their blood.

'Return, O my soul, to your tranquillity, for the Lord has been good to you.' It means, return, O my soul, into Paradise, not because you are worthy, but because of the kindness of the Lord. Your going out from Paradise was the work of your own vice; your return, however, was of the compassion of the Lord. Let us, also, say to our own soul: Return to your tranquillity. Our tranquillity is Christ our God. If ever we are in great straits and our thoughts are ready to capitulate to sin, let us cry out: Return, O my soul, to your tranquillity.

'He has freed my soul from death.' The prophet has not yet returned to Paradise, but he has already returned, he says, to safety. He said before: 'Return, O my soul, to your tran-

---

14 Cf. Letter 22.19, PL 22.406 (102).

quillity'; and now as one who is secure: 'For he has delivered
my soul from death.' When did He snatch my soul from
death? My God suffered for me; for me my God was crucified, and I exclaim: 'O death, where is thy victory? O death,
where is thy sting?'[15] 'My eyes from tears.' I cried for grief
so that I may laugh for joy; I mourned that everlastingly
I may rejoice. The man who does not weep in the present
world will shed tears in the next. 'Blessed are they who
mourn, for they shall be comforted.'[16] In contradiction to
the world we say: 'Woe to you who laugh now! for you shall
mourn and weep.'[17] 'My feet from stumbling.' Because my
feet were not set firmly upon the rock: 'I almost lost my
balance; my feet all but slipped.'[18] My feet were saved from
stumbling. Why? Because my soul returned to its tranquillity.

'I shall please the Lord in the land of the living.'[19] People
think that I am a just man, the psalmist is saying, I who have
no good works; people think that I am a saint, I who have
no good words. So says David and the saints, and the apostles,
too, for no sinner utters such words. What does the just man
say? I have neither good works nor good words, and I pass
for a holy man, and I am praised by men; but I know my
conscience, I know with what kind of thoughts my heart is
tossed hither and thither; I know how many inordinate desires
take hold of me, and: 'I see another law in my members,
warring against the law of my mind and making me a prisoner
to the law of sin.'[20]

That is why I cry: 'Unhappy man that I am! Who will
deliver me from the body of this death?'[21] Therefore, I pray:
'Cleanse me from my unknown faults! From wanton sin

---

15 I Cor. 15.55.
16 Matt. 5.5.
17 Luke 6.25.
18 Ps. 72.2.
19 Cf. Ps. 114 (116A).9; cf. *Commentarioli in ps.* 114.9.
20 Rom. 7.23; cf. Letter 133.8, PL 22.1157 (1036).
21 Rom. 7.24.

especially restrain your servant.'[22] From wanton sin. It is not my will to conceive sin; I do not want to entertain bad thoughts, and yet I do; I do not want to entertain evil and, like a captive against my will, I am drawn into evil reflections. Because it is not in my power either to think or not to think evil, that is why I declare: Surely they are wanton sins that come into my heart, but since I cannot seem to avoid them, I plead: 'Cleanse me from my unknown faults.' Unprovoked they come, but because I harbor them, I beg the Lord: 'From wanton sin especially restrain your servant.' Why am I saying all this? Because the prophet said: 'I shall please the Lord'; not 'I please,' but 'I shall please,' for no matter how much I strive here, I cannot be a perfect man, a just man. Consequently, the Apostle also says: 'We know in part and we prophesy in part,'[23] and: 'We see now through a mirror in an obscure manner.'[24]

We have drawn out this sermon to such length precisely to emphasize the point that in the present world no one is able to be perfectly just, not David, nor the apostles, nor any one of the saints. 'No one is clean from sin, not if he lived for but a single day.'[25] Since the apostles and saints have not dared to say, 'we are saints,' neither have they dared to say, 'I please,' but 'I shall please.' The prophet promises for the future what he confesses he has not done in the past: 'I shall please the Lord.'

Where shall I please Him? 'In the land of the living.' This land is the land of the dead; the other, the land of the living. Since David, too, was on this earth and actually in the land of promise, when he says: 'I shall please in the land of the living,' he recognizes this world not as the land of the living, but as the land of the dead. Would you like to know

---

22 Ps. 18.13, 14; cf. *Against the Pelagians* 1.12, PL 23.527 (705); 32; PL 23.550 (730).
23 1 Cor. 13.9.
24 1 Cor. 13.12.
25 Cf. Job 14.4, 5; cf. *Against the Pelagians* 1.32, PL 23.549 (729); *Against Jovinian* 2.2, PL 23.296 (323).

this land of the living? The Lord tells us in the Gospel: 'I am the God of Abraham, and the God of Isaac, and the God of Jacob,'[26] and they were dead. But what follows this statement? 'Not the God of the dead, but of the living.' Accordingly, then, what does the just man say? 'I shall please the Lord in the land of the living,' in the land of Abraham, Isaac, and Jacob; in other words, when I am truly in the bosom of Abraham, then, shall I please the Lord.

---

26 Matt. 22.32.

HOMILY 40

ON PSALM 115 (116B)

BELIEVED, THEREFORE have I spoken.'[1] In the Hebrew psalter Psalms 114 and 115 are integral parts of the same psalm. Why, then, did the prophet say, I believed, therefore, I spoke? What was it that you believed? What did you say? The first of these psalms closes with the words: 'I shall please the Lord in the land of the living.'[2] With that in mind, the prophet says now: 'I believed, therefore have I spoken.' What did I believe? That I shall be pleasing to the Lord in the land of the living; that is what I believed; that is why I spoke. What was it that I said? 'I am humbled.'[3] O profound understanding of divine utterance! I believed, he says, that I shall please the Lord, that I shall be an angel, that I shall be in heaven; and I was not proud, I was not exalted, rather was I exceedingly humbled. It is because of God's great mercy that I shall be in the land of the living. I know myself very well, clay and ashes; therefore, I say: 'I am humbled indeed.' What boast is there to clay and ashes?

'I said in my alarm, "Every man is a liar!" '[4] The Hebrew text varies a little: 'I said in my alarm, "Every man is a lie!" ' for the meaning of the word, ZECAM, is lie. I shall please the Lord in the land of the living; but I know that, as far as my body is concerned, I am nothing. There is no truth in our substance; there is only shadow and in a certain sense a lie—

---

1 Cf. Ps. 115 (116B).10 (1); cf. 2 Cor. 4.13.
2 Cf. Ps. 114 (116A).9.
3 Cf. Ps. 115 (116B).10 (1).
4 Cf. Ps. 115 (116B).11 (2); cf. *Commentarioli in ps.* 115.11.

I mean in our corporeal being, not in the soul. What the prophet is saying, is this: I shall please the Lord in the land of the living; still, as I reflect upon human life and ponder over all the different species of error, I do not find truth in this world. How can I, for: 'we know in part and prophesy in part.'[5] That is why I say: Everything we see, everything we grasp with the intellect is a lie. How is it a lie? 'Lie' is used here in the sense of a shadow, as it were, a phantom, as another psalm says: 'A phantom only, man goes his ways.'[6] In this same connotation, our psalmist says, in accordance with the Hebrew, every man is a lie, meaning that every man is a phantom.

We shall also give the Septuagint interpretation for someone may be objecting: What has Hebrew to do with me? I go along with the Church. 'I said in my alarm, "Every man is a liar!" ' Is David telling the truth or is he lying? If it is true that every man is a liar, and David's statement 'Every man is a liar' is true, then, David also is lying; he, too, is a man. But if he, too, is lying, his statement: 'Every man is a liar,' consequently is not true. Whatever way you turn the proposition, the conclusion is a contradiction. Since David himself is a man, it follows that he also is lying; but if he is lying because every man is a liar, his lying is of a different sort.[7]

You have an example here of the syllogisms of philosophers. In fact, the Aristotelian syllogism is constructed on just such a pattern. Accordingly, you say—speaking to another: If you are lying and in your very fact of lying are speaking true to form, you are, therefore, lying. Just look at how this statement turns into a contradiction! What after all does it say? O you, who are speaking with me, if you lie and speak truly by lying, by that very fact you are lying, and in the same proposition one may be speaking truly and lying at

---

5 1 Cor. 13.9.
6 Ps. 38.7.
7 Cf. *Commentary on Ephesians* 1.22, 23, PL 26.494 (569).

the same time. That is precisely the reason why the Apostle says: 'See to it that no one deceives you by philosophy and vain deceit, according to human traditions, according to the elements of the world.'[8] By their clever art and deception, philosophers have made the great discovery of how in the same utterance one may be speaking truly and telling a lie. Let us maintain, however, that David spoke the truth when he said that every man is a liar. As long as we are men, we speak falsehood; when we are gods, we shall cease to be liars. 'For since there are jealousy and strife among you, are you not carnal, and walking as mere men?'[9] 'I said: You are gods, all of you sons of the Most High; yet like men you shall die, and fall like any prince.'[10] The man of holiness, then, becomes a god; and when he is a god, he ceases to be man and no longer utters lies. What is it that the Apostle says in this regard? 'For God is true, and every man is a liar.'[11]

Let us interpret: 'I believed, therefore have I spoken,' in another way. When a teacher instructs a student, unless he himself believes what he is teaching, he cannot teach the other; hence, the prophet is saying that first he believed and from the fullness of his belief taught others. 'I am humbled indeed.' Because I obtained this favor from God, I was not elated with pride; knowledge did not inflate me; but what did I do? I was deeply humbled. That is why I who taught with speech was also able to teach with humility. 'I said in my alarm, "Every man is a liar."' As I was teaching my student, the prophet says, and meditating upon heavenly contemplation and pondering over divinely inspired truths, I realized that all that man knows is a lie, for what truth can there be in this world, when our life is as a shadow[12] upon the earth. If the teacher confesses that every man is a liar,

---

8 Col. 2.8.
9 1 Cor. 3.3; cf. Letter 22.4, PL 22.397 (91).
10 Ps. 81.6, 7.
11 Rom. 3.4; cf. *Against Jovinian* 2.31, PL 23.342 (373); *Against the Pelagians* 3.14, PL 23.612 (799).
12 Cf. 1 Par. 29.15.

how much less must the student plume himself and be im-
pressed with his own importance?

'How shall I make a return to the Lord, for all the good he
has done for me?' I said before: I shall please the Lord in the
land of the living; I believed that and, therefore, I spoke, and
I was humble indeed, and I said: Every man is a lie; every
man is a shadow; every man is a phantom. In return for the
great favor and honor of pleasing the Lord in the land of
the living, what have I worthy to give Him? I am clay; I am
ashes. He promised me that I shall please Him in the land of
the living; He made me a teacher; I believed, therefore, I
spoke. What have I that is fitting to give Him in return for
such favor and kindness? Whatever I give Him is already
His; rather than giving, I am returning. I have nothing else
to give Him except to shed my blood for Him, except to die
a martyr for Him. This is the only fitting return: to give
blood for blood, that redeemed by the Savior, we may rejoice in spilling our blood for Him.[13]

'The cup of salvation I will take up, and I will call upon
the name of the Lord.' The Hebrew text has: 'I will take the
cup of Jesus.' That is also the interpretation of the angel:
'And thou shall call his name Jesus, for he shall save his
people.'[14] The cup, then, of Jesus I will take up. What is
Jesus' cup? 'Father, if it is possible, let this cup pass from
me,'[15] and: 'Can you drink of the cup of which I am about to
drink?'[16] He continues, saying: 'Of my cup you shall indeed
drink.'[17] Now why have I stressed this? That you may appreciate that the cup is the passion of martyrdom.[18]

Martyrdom is a grand thing. Why? Because the martyr gives
back to the Lord what he received from Him. Christ suffered for him and he suffers for the name of Christ. We said

---

13 Cf. Letter 22.39, PL 22.423 (123).
14 Matt. 1.21.
15 Matt. 26.39.
16 Matt. 20.22.
17 Matt. 20.23.
18 Cf. *Commentary on Matthew* 20.22, PL 26.148 (155).

that the martyr has nothing else to give to the Lord, and that the Lord reckons it as equality because He knows that His servant has nothing else to give Him. Where is the likeness? God suffered for men; the Lord, for the servant; the Just, for the sinners. Where is the equality? For the very reason that the servant has nothing else to give the Lord, God in His compassion accepts martyrdom as of equivalent value. It is, for example, as if some rich man were supporting a certain poor man, and this same rich man should happen to come along with his family and by chance enter the house of the poor man. The poor man has nothing to give him and his family and his horses, but only says to him, 'Enter into the house of your client,' thus showing his affection and good will. There is nothing else a poor man may give, nothing more a poor man may do; he is like that widow who put the two mites in the treasury. 'The cup of salvation'—or of Jesus—'I will take up.' This martyrdom is not of my strength, he is saying, but of the grace of God; hence, I cannot drink of it unless I call upon the name of the Lord. It is Jesus who triumphs in His martyr; in His martyr, it is Jesus who bears the crown.

'Precious in the eyes of the Lord is the death of his faithful ones.' In view of this revelation, let the Jews tell us what they mean by saying that every human body is unclean. According to the law, if a Jew dies—whether a prophet or any holy man—no matter who touches him, even if it be a priest, he is unclean until evening. This is specifically written in the law.[19] Let us say to them in reply: If the body of the dead is unclean, how now does the psalmist say: Precious in the eyes of the Lord is the death of His faithful servants? If the body of the dying saint is precious, how is it unclean? This verse, therefore, refers to the evangelist and foreshadows the martyr.[20]

'O Lord, I am your servant.' I have on a previous occasion

---

19 Cf. Num. 19.11-14.
20 Cf. *Commentarioli in ps.* 115.15.

drawn your attention to the fact that in Psalm 114 where it says: 'O Lord, save my life!'[21] the Hebrew text has ANNA, which means, 'I beseech' or 'I entreat.' Likewise, in this psalm, the Hebrew reads: 'I entreat you, O Lord, for I am your servant.' 'I am your servant.' Servant seems to imply a lowly office. It is of great dignity and merit to be a servant of the Lord, and not a servant of sin. Because men are not my masters, because sin is not my lord—for sin does not reign in my mortal body[22]—I am Your servant. A privilege sublime! Scripture, in fact, says of Moses: 'Not so with my servant Moses!'[23] Abraham and Isaac and Jacob are called servants of the Lord. The Apostle, too, begins his letter: 'Paul, the servant of Jesus Christ.'[24]

'You have loosed my bonds. To you will I offer sacrifice of thanksgiving.' Supreme happiness, indeed, it is to approach the Lord thus with conscience undefiled. Every saint who dies a natural death, even if he is a saint who has fulfilled the corporal works of mercy, performed miracles, cast out devils, still does not approach the Lord without concern; his conscience trembles when he beholds the Lord. Nevertheless, the martyr, even though he has sinned after baptism, is cleansed by the second baptism of martyrdom and goes to the Lord in utmost confidence. 'You have loosed my bonds.' 'In the meshes of his own sin everyone will be held fast';[25] in my martyrdom, however, You have broken the bonds of my sins, and of my bonds You have woven for me a crown of victory, for: 'where the offense has abounded, grace has abounded yet more.'[26] 'To you will I offer sacrifice of thanksgiving.' After martyrdom, where does one offer sacrifice? In the land of the living. I will sacrifice to You, the prophet says, a sacrifice. What kind of sacrifice? Will it be a goat or

---

21 Ps. 114.4.
22 Cf. Rom. 6.12.
23 Num. 12.7.
24 Rom. 1.1; cf. *Commentary on Titus* 1.1, PL 26.590-591 (688).
25 Cf. Prov. 5.22.
26 Rom. 5.20.

a calf? No, those were Jewish sacrifices and are now over and past. I will offer to You a sacrifice of praise and thanksgiving, the thanksgiving of the martyrs. Now just as the martyrs praise the Lord chastely in the land of the living, even so monks who sing praise to the Lord day and night should have the same chastity as the martyrs, for they, indeed, are also martyrs. What the angels do in heaven, the monks do on earth.

'My vows to the Lord I will pay in the presence of all his people.' What are the prayers of the martyrs? What are the prayers of those who love the Lord? 'I took hold of you and would not let you go.'[27] I will adore the Lord whom in the Gospel I have found crucified, whom in heaven I shall behold reigning with the angels. 'In the presence of all his people.' Read the Book of Daniel.[28]

---

27 Cf. Cant. 3.4.
28 Cf. Dan. 7.27; 12.1.

HOMILY 41

ON PSALM 119 (120)

ET US TURN to the psalm that is read after the one hundred and eighteenth psalm. Psalm 118, by the way, is constructed, as we have more than once indicated, on the pattern of the alphabet and is, therefore, alphabetical in form. It begins with ALEPH and goes on down to the last Hebrew letter THAU, with successive groups of verses beginning with successive letters of the alphabet. There are twenty-two Hebrew letters, and the verses are composed in octaves corresponding to the letters of the alphabet. The first eight verses, for example, begin each with the letter ALEPH. When this octave comes to an end, another begins with BETH as the first letter of each of its eight verses. A third group of eight verses follows, each starting with GIMEL, the third letter. Thus, Psalm 118 is alphabetical in structure. Now, if we intended to read a letter, we cannot read it unless we know the characters in which it is written, in like manner we cannot understand the Scriptures without first knowing the alphabet. Psalm 118, then, is alphabetical in form and moral in character and contains instruction for our life.[1] Since there is no time at the present to discuss the entire psalm, let us rather review the first of the gradual psalms which opens with the words: 'In my distress I called to the Lord, and he answered me.'

These gradual psalms, as you have heard me say often enough, are called songs of ascent because in them we mount step by step to greater heights. Time does not permit us now

---

1 Cf. *Commentarioli in ps.* 111.

300

to investigate all the degrees of ascent and to determine just what step we take in each psalm to arrive at the summit. For the present, let us limit our discussion to the first ascent, passing over the mystical reason for fifteen steps, as frequent repetition of the same matter grows wearisome to an audience. Mystical in significance are, likewise, the fifteen days the Apostle remained with Peter in Jerusalem[2] to confer with him over both covenants, the septenary [i.e., of the synagogue?] and the octonary [i.e., of the Church?].[3] There is ever so much that could be said. 'In my distress I called to the Lord, and he answered me.' Let anyone who is still on the lowest step fix his gaze on the highest step, the fifteenth. He who is on the fifteenth step is already in the vestibule of the temple. This is the temple that we now see in ruins, for it sinned against its Lord. What did the Lord say? 'Arise, let us go from here.'[4] Again what in another place? 'Your house is left to you desolate.'[5] The Lord has left the temple; it has fallen in ruins. This temple, as I was saying, has fifteen steps encircling it. We can see some of their fragments;[6] count them, and you will see that it is so.[7] The Levites and the priests used to stand on one or other of these steps, each according to his rank. The chief priest, for instance, stood on the first step, that is, on the fifteenth step from below; on the second step stood the different degrees of priests. On the third, were the minor priests; on the fourth, the Levites, but among the Levites there was great distinction, the least of this order being on the lowest step.

Consider for a moment how this earthly temple is a figure of the heavenly temple. 'For star differs from star in glory. So also with the resurrection of the dead.'[8] Happy the man

---

2 Cf. Gal. 1.18; cf. *Commentary on Galatians* 1.18, PL 26.354 (395); Letter 53.2, PL 22.541 (271).
3 Cf. *Commentary on Ezechiel* 40.24-28, PL 25.388 (484).
4 John 14.31.
5 Matt. 23.38; cf. *Commentary on Ezechiel* 11.22, 23, PL 25.101 (112).
6 Cf. *Commentary on Isaia* 38.4-10, PL 24.392 (470).
7 Cf. Letter 36.5, PL 22.455 (163).
8 1 Cor. 15.41, 42.

who has merited to be on the fifteenth step in the heavenly Jerusalem and in the temple! Because that height is so sublime and is, I think, the place of the apostles and the holy martyrs, let us pray that we may merit to be at least on the lowest step of the temple of the Lord. They all stand on different steps, to be sure, but in unison they sing one psalm of praise and thanksgiving to the Lord. Places vary, but the praise of the Lord is one. That is the heavenly Jerusalem we have been describing, but for the present, we have been placed in this world to be disciplined, I presume, every day of our lives. One of us is on the first step; let him not be discouraged of attaining the second. The man on the second, let him not lose hope for the third. Happy the martyrs of whom many merited to ascend from the last steps to the very top. We who live in this world cannot ascend all at once from the lowest to the highest step, yet neither must we be satisfied to remain on the first step, but must ever strive to mount higher. Let not the man on the lowest step lose courage of reaching the top; nor should the man on the top yield to a complacent security, for it is possible for him to fall all the way down to the bottom. I think this is the meaning of Jacob's ladder,[9] when Jacob fled Esau, his brother.

'He came,' Scripture says, 'into Bethel, and placed a stone under his head and slept there.'[10] Consider our ascetic: he was running away from a very cruel man; he was fleeing his brother, and he found help in a stone. That stone is Christ; that Stone is the support of all those who suffer persecution, but to the unbelieving Jew, it is 'a stone of stumbling, and a rock of scandal.'[11] 'Jacob saw there a ladder set up on the ground with its top reaching to heaven; and in heaven the Lord [leaning upon it] ἐπιστηριγμένον αὐτῇ. And he saw angels ascending and descending.'[12] Note: he saw angels ascending; he saw Paul ascending; he saw angels descending;

---

9 Cf. Letter 7.3, PL 22.340 (19); 53.8, PL 22.546 (277).
10 Cf. Gen. 28.11.
11 1 Peter 2.8.
12 Cf. Gen. 28.12, 13.

Judas, the betrayer, was falling headlong. He saw angels ascending—holy men going from earth to heaven; he saw angels descending—the devil and his whole army cast down from heaven. It is very difficult, indeed, to ascend from earth into heaven. We fall more easily than we rise. We fall easily; it requires great labor, a great deal of sweat to climb upwards. If I am on the lowest step, how many more are there before I reach heaven? If I am on the second, the third, the fourth, the tenth, what benefit to me unless I reach the top? Grant with me that this ladder has fifteen rungs. I climb as high as the fourteenth, but unless I reach and hold the fifteenth, what profit to me to have mounted the fourteenth? If I should arrive at the fifteenth and then fall, the higher my ascent, the greater my descent.

Now meditate upon the mystical significance of the ladder: it requires great pain, severe effort, to climb from earth to heaven. Would you know what these steps are? What the first one is? I think the first step is fasting, for it is still quite close to earth; we are withdrawing from earth, beginning to ascend; nevertheless, we are still thinking of material things, still preoccupied with the care of the body. Someone may be saying: 'Why should I be concerned with fasts? My only anxiety is the purity of my soul in the presence of the Lord; there are many who do not fast and are saints.' I do not agree with that. If Paul the Apostle, a vessel of election, chastised his body and brought it into subjection, lest after preaching to others, he should be rejected,[13] if he says: 'I see another law warring against the law of my mind and making me prisoner,'[14] and after that: 'Unhappy man that I am! Who will deliver me from the body of this death?'[15] If he fears the lures of the body, are we then safe? If he says: 'when I am weak, then I am strong,'[16] the weakness of the body is the vigor of the soul. Why am I stressing all this?

---

13 Cf. 1 Cor. 9.27; cf. Letter 22.5, PL 22.397 (91); 108.1, PL 22.879 (691).
14 Cf. Rom. 7.23.
15 Rom. 7.24.
16 2 Cor. 12.10; cf. Letter 3.5, PL 22.334 (12).

Because abstinence is the first step. Let us not leap to the conclusion, however, that if we fast we shall ascend at once into the kingdom of heaven; fasts do not necessarily lead up to the kingdom of heaven, though without them, we shall not arrive there. Alone they are of no worth; with other things they are. Why do I say this? Because fasting is, as it were, the foundation and [the support] ὑποστήριγμα, of those who are mounting to greater heights.[17]

The second step is the true renouncement of the world, and consists in aiming at nothing of this world, in despising everything that is of earth. Somebody may ask: Detachment, then, is the second step? Yes, the second. It is nothing, however, to give up the things of the world; to renounce vice, that is the noble thing! If I should fast—if I am on the first step; if I should give away all my possessions—if I am on the second step; what does it profit me if I am quarrelsome, if I give way to anger, if I criticize and malign, if I am envious?

There is nothing great in renouncing the world; there are greater vices that must be repudiated. Someone else may declare: But that is difficult, severe, hard. That is exactly why it is a great thing, because it is difficult. Christ's athlete is not crowned unless he has entered the contest and competed according to the rules.[18] Do not give up hope though the climb is arduous, and difficult, and engenders despair. Do not lose confidence, O man; the Lord is up there on the fifteenth step. He is watching over you; He is helping you. If you are on the first step, and the [passage] diábēma between the first and the fifteenth seems insurmountable, do not look down at the steps, but look up at the Lord. Attend exactly to what the Scripture says. Holy Writ did not say, I saw the Lord standing on the fifteenth step; it is not possible for us to reach the Lord while He is standing and erect. Mark what it does say: Jacob saw Him leaning over the ladder. Just realize what that means: from where He was standing,

17 Cf. Letter 130.11, PL 22.1116-17 (988).
18 2 Tim. 2.5.

He stooped down and lowered Himself that we might ascend.[19] The Lord stooped down; for your sake He humbled Himself; climb up, therefore, with safety and confidence.

This man of ours who is now on the first step is not in distress, for he has already withdrawn from the source of affliction; he has already set his foot on the first rung. He is not saying: Now I am in trouble, now I am crying out in prayer; but because he is on the first step, he reflects back upon what he has suffered. What, however, does he say? 'In my distress I called to the Lord, and he answered me.' This versicle does not seem to have a hidden meaning; it is short, yet it does express three thoughts of equal importance.[20] What is the psalmist saying? When I was in distress, one thought; I called, and after the call, what happened? He answered me. In one verse, former sorrow, a prayer for help, and a gracious answer. He did not say: When I was carefree, when I was happy, I called, but when I was in distress. 'You ask,' says Scripture, 'and do not receive, because you ask amiss.'[21] 'In my distress I called to the Lord, and he answered me.' What was His answer? He caused me to stand on the first step. But in comparison to the fifteen steps, what is so triumphant about the first step? I have renounced the things of the world, but I have not yet reached the top. I ought not, therefore, to feel safe; on each step, I must beg God for help.

'O Lord, deliver me from lying lip, from treacherous tongue.' This applies to all heretical sects; it applies to the Jews, the Arians, the Manichaeans, and all the other promoters of heresy. When an Arian asserts that the Father is greater, the Son less, what are we to say? Lord, deliver me from lying lip and treacherous tongue. When Manichaeus proclaims—and his ilk—: 'The Lord has not risen in the reality of a body, for to convince you that His body was not

---

19 Cf. Letter 54.6, PL 22.553 (285); 108.13, PL 22.888 (702); 118.7, PL 22.966 (798).
20 Cf. *Commentarioli in ps.* 119.1.
21 James 4.3.

real He came in through closed doors,' what should we answer? Lord, deliver me from lying lip and from a treacherous tongue.

Greater by far are the wounds of the tongue than those of the sword. The sword kills the body, not the soul; the tongue kills the soul. The tongue is a bad business, a great evil: 'So the tongue also is a little member, but it boasts mightily.'[22] Read in the Letter of St. James how much evil the tongue can cause. The tongue knows no middle way; either it is a great evil or a great good; a great good when it acknowledges that Christ is God, a great evil when it denies that Christ is God. Let no one, therefore, harbor the illusion and claim: I have not committed sin in act; if I sinned, I sinned with my tongue. What more monstrous sin is there than blasphemy against God? Yet it is the tongue that is sinning. Why did the devil fall? Because he committed theft? Because he committed murder? Because he committed adultery? These are certainly evils, but the devil did not fall because of any of these; he fell because of his tongue. What was it that he said? 'I will scale the heavens; above the stars I will set up my throne, I will be like the Most High!'[23] Monks surely, then, have no right to think they are safe and say: We are in the monastery and so we do not commit serious offenses; I do not commit adultery; I do not steal; I am not a murderer; I am not guilty of parricide; and so of all the rest of the big vices. But the devilish sins are those of the tongue. It is outrageous to detract from my brother; I am killing my brother with my tongue, for: 'Everyone who hates his brother is a murderer.'[24]

Listen to what Solomon says: 'Death and life are in the power of the tongue.'[25] 'In the power of the tongue,' do you see how much evil there is in the tongue? It has power, for

---

22 James 3.5.
23 Cf. Isa. 14.13, 14; cf. Letter 133.1, PL 22.1148 (1025); *Against the Pelagians* 3.14, PL 23.11 (799-800); Letter 61.4, PL 22.605 (351).
24 1 John 3.15; cf. Letter 13, PL 22.346 (27).
25 Prov. 18.21.

what does he say? 'In the power of the tongue.' It is no slight
fault to malign a brother, to be unable to keep silence, to go
from cell to cell slandering others. I am a sinner; he is a
sinner; what has that to do with you? Take heed about
yourself lest you fall. Why do you take pleasure in another's
fall? If I fall, will you remain standing? Granted it is my
downfall, but the fall of your brother ought to be your fear,
not your joy. He fell. Are you glad or are you sorry? Answer
me. A brother has fallen into sin; either you rejoice or you
are sorry. If you are glad, does one rejoice in the misfortune
of another? If you are sorry, why do you go about gossiping?
Why do you tell others? Let God see your sorrow, and let
the brother himself perceive it; do not let other brethren hear
about it. 'O Lord, deliver me from lying lip, from treacherous
tongue.'

'What shall be given to you, or what shall be meted out
to you, to a deceitful tongue?'[26] The reply of the Holy Spirit
to the prophet's plea: 'O Lord, deliver me from lying lip,
from treacherous tongue,' is: 'What shall be given to you,
or what shall be meted out to you, to a deceitful tongue?'
His answer means: You who say: 'O Lord, deliver me from
lying lip, from treacherous tongue,' what do you want given
to you? And after it has been given you, what more do you ·
want meted out to a treacherous tongue? Grasp the full
import of what He says. He did not say, 'against' a deceitful
tongue, but 'to' a deceitful tongue. If He had said against a
deceitful tongue, He would seem to be referring to an adversary. Note the mystical meaning: the prophet, or rather the
faithful servant who has been placed on the first step—I am
speaking very simply for the sake of the simple—what does
he say? 'O Lord, rescue my soul from lying lip, from treacherous tongue,' for example, from my enemy who is slandering
me. What does the Lord answer? He did not say: 'What
shall be given to you or what shall be meted out to you, against
a deceitful tongue?' In other words, He did not ask: What

26 Cf. Ps. 119 (120).3.

do you desire Me to do for you against your enemy? But
what did He ask? 'What shall be given to you or what shall
be meted out to you, to a deceitful tongue?' He did not say
'against' a tongue, but 'to' a tongue.

Realize what that means: 'to a deceitful tongue'; to your
tongue, not your enemy's. If an enemy slanders you, he does
you no harm; you slay yourself if you slander others. By way
of example, if a brother blackens me, what harm does he do
me? If he should call me a murderer, and adulterer, a scoun-
drel, a liar, what wrong does he do me? He is doing one of
two things certainly: either he is telling the truth or he is
telling a lie. If he is telling the truth, what he has said does
not hurt me; but the fact that I have really committed the act,
that does. If, however, he is lying, his lie does not injure me,
but it kills the soul of the one uttering it. Unhappy men
that we are, what miserable creatures! When we have an
enemy and think that we are doing something against him,
all the while we are doing it against ourselves. We disparage
him; we go hither and thither talking about him to everybody.
Do we think that we are hurting him? We are doing nothing
to him, but we are killing our own souls because we are
lying. 'A lying mouth slays the soul.'[27]

'What shall be given to you, or what shall be meted out to
you, to a deceitful tongue?' Just as if the good physician
were to say: What do you want put upon this diseased tissue,
this wound? What salve do you want me to apply? Just as
one might ask a wounded person: What is to be given you
or what is to be applied to the wound that is causing you
such suffering? The Lord is asking that question, not because He does not know, but in order to teach the one who
is praying how he ought to pray.

'Sharp arrows of the mighty with fiery coals of the desert.'[28]
'Sharp arrows of the mighty.' Now the prophet, in turn, is
answering the Lord and telling Him what his petition is.

---

27 Wisdom 1.11.
28 Cf. Ps. 119 (120).4.

Because the Lord had asked: 'What shall be given to you, or what shall be meted out to you?' now he makes known his request. This, Lord, is what I am asking: sharp arrows of the Mighty with fiery coals of the desert. Be sure you comprehend his petition. Nothing is able to expel the deadly venom of my tongue and its back-biting except Your arrows which make a solitude of my tongue. My tongue is all swollen; it is filled with poison; unless Your arrows pierce and lance it, the poison cannot escape. We must give you an example of this. If in the body there is a wound that has become infected and cancerous and is filled with pus, unless it is opened, there is no way of removing the pus. Then, when the pus is discharged, unless the wound is cauterized, it fills up again with poisonous matter. We see now what the psalmist means. Because my tongue is swollen with pus and poison, first wound it with Your arrows that the pus may be released; then apply Your burning coals of fire, so that all the evil in it may be burned out and it may become a desert waste.

Now look at what the psalmist says: 'Sharp arrows of the mighty, with fiery coals of the desert.' I would that this burning coal of desolation were given to us! I would that we, too, might exclaim: 'Was not our heart burning within us while he was speaking on the road and explaining to us the Scriptures?'[29] Isaia says to Babylon: 'You have coals of fire; sit upon them; they will give you relief.'[30] The apostles, too, before they received the Holy Spirit, had tongues still infected with a few human tumors; that is why the Holy Spirit descended in the form of fire and settled, as it were, upon their tongues[31] to burn out of them any remaining impurity.

Here is another example. When Isaia had seen the Lord seated high upon a lofty throne, what does he say? 'Woe is me, because I am in sorrow; because I am a man of unclean lips, and I dwell in the midst of a people that hath unclean

---

29 Luke 24.32.
30 Cf. Isa. 47.14, 15, LXX; cf. *Against Rufinus* 2.7, PL 23.449 (496).
31 Cf. Acts 2.3.

lips.'[32] Pay attention to his exact words: Woe is me because of my unclean lips. After that, what does he tell us? Because his lips were soiled, one of the Seraph is sent to him, and the Seraph taking a burning coal from the altar touches with it Isaia's lips and tongue and purifies his mouth. Then, what does the Seraph say? 'See,' he said, 'now that this has touched your lips, your tongue is purged.'[33] Then immediately, what does the Lord say? 'Whom shall I send? Who will go for us?'[34] O divine secrets of Scripture! As long as his tongue was treacherous and his lips unclean, the Lord does not say to him: Whom shall I send, and who shall go? His lips are cleansed and straightway is he appointed the Lord's spokesman; hence, it is true that the man with unclean lips cannot prophesy nor can he be sent in obedient service of God. 'With fiery coals of the desert.' Would to heaven this solitude were granted us, that it would clear away all wickedness from our tongue, so that where there are thorns, where there are brambles, where there are nettles, the fire of the Lord may come and burn all of it and make it a desert place, the solitude of Christ.

'Woe is me that my sojourn is prolonged!'[35] This is the plaint of the lover of Christ[36] who wants nothing of the body, who is detached from the world and longs for heaven. Unhappy man that I am because my exile is prolonged. When we are sick, when we are tossing with fever, when we fear death is at hand, when we are flinging out our arms, when we are full of dread, when we are begging for respite, we cannot utter these words. This holy man was in the vigor of health, he was not sick, and what is his complaint? 'Woe is me that my sojourn is prolonged!' As long as we tarry in this bodily tent of ours, we are wanderers away from the Lord.

---

32 Cf. Isa. 6.5; cf. *Commentarioli in ps.* 119.4; *Against the Pelagians* 3.14, PL 23.612 (799).
33 Cf. Isa. 6.7.
34 Isa. 6.8; cf. Letter 18.14, PL 22.370 (57).
35 Cf. Ps. 119 (120).5.
36 Cf. Letter 22.40, PL 22.424 (124).

Alas for me because my wandering is prolonged! 'My sojourn,' not my dwelling. 'My sojourn,' for in the present world we have no lasting dwelling place; we are pilgrims. That is why the Apostle says: 'as strangers and pilgrims.'[37] 'I am but a wayfarer and a pilgrim.'[38] Woe to me that my exile is prolonged! What the psalmist means is: As long as I am in this body, I am unhappy. Who of us could say that? If we are octogenarians, we are afraid to die; if we are centenarians and sick besides, still we cling to life and beg for respite. Why do we do that? Because sin gnaws at our conscience. We know that if we leave our body, we are going not to Christ, but to hell. On the contrary, what does the Apostle say? 'I desire to depart and to be with Christ.'[39] Give me freedom from anxiety, for after death I am going to be with Christ; even now I long to die. So our psalmist, because he is one who loves the Lord, cries: Unhappy man that I am, because my sojourn is prolonged!

'That I dwell amid the tents of Cedar!' Cedar in our language means darkness.[40] Meditate, therefore, upon what it means. In what kind of place are we? In what kind of world are we? I dwell amid the tents of Cedar. Long have I been in darkness; long have I been in the body of this death. 'All too long have I dwelt.' Mark what the saintly man is saying: Even if I have lived only ten years, all too long have I dwelt in exile. What happiness, after all, is there in the things of the world that can compare with the happiness of heaven? There is much to be said here, but it is time our sermon were drawing to its close.

'With those who hate peace. When I speak of peace, they are ready for war.' Miserable men that we are, we cannot hold our tongue; we cannot refrain from vilifying our brothers. If anyone offends us, we put on a friendly face, but

---

37 1 Peter 2.11.
38 Cf. Ps. 38.13; cf. Letter 108.1, PL 22.879 (691).
39 Cf. Phil. 1.23; cf. Letter 3.5, PL 22.334 (12).
40 Cf. Letter 39.3, PL 22.468 (180); 108.1, PL 22.878-79 (690); *Against Jovinian* 2.36, PL 23.349 (380).

we have the venom of resentment in our heart. We are called monks, even though we are not all that we ought to be. We pray at the third hour, at the sixth, at the ninth; we say vespers at sunset; we rise in the middle of the night; then we pray again at cock-crow. How constantly we are being roused to the devout services of God: the third hour, the sixth, the ninth, vespers, midnight, dawn, early morning.[41] We do all this, and yet it does not occur to us that if we harbor enmity against our brother, our prayer is vain.

What does the Gospel have to say about this? 'If thou art offering thy gift at the altar, and there rememberest that thy brother has anything against thee.'[42] Our Lord did not say, 'if you have anything against your brother,' but, 'if your brother has anything against you.' This seems to be imposing upon us a kind of injustice, for if the Lord had said, if you have anything against your brother, it was within our control that we did. But what does He actually say? 'If you remember that your brother has anything against you.' I make this reply to the Lord: 'Lord, it is not within my control[43] if my brother has anything against me. I have nothing against him. If he has something against me, how am I responsible? Why do You refuse to receive my gift and why do You say: "If you are offering your gift at the altar, and there remember that your brother has anything against you, leave your gift and go to be reconciled with your brother, and then come and offer your gift?" Look, I have nothing against him; if he has something against me, how does that apply to me?'

The Lord answers you: Wicked servant, I know your soul; you have nothing against your brother? You have nothing? You love him? Why, then, do you not want him to be saved? If you love him, go, ask him not to hold anything against

---

41 Cf. Letter 22.37, PL 22.421 (121); 107.9, PL 22.875 (686); 108.19, PL 22.896 (712).
42 Matt. 5.23; cf. *Commentary on Matthew* 5.23, PL 26.38 (27); Letter 82.2, PL 22.737 (514); 13, PL 22.547 (28).
43 Cf. *Against the Pelagians* 2.11, PL 23.570-71 (753).

you, and to think of his salvation. But you show that you
do not love him, because you are not interested in his salvation. Go to him, plead with him, throw yourself at his feet,
implore him day and night; say to him: 'I have left my gift
at the altar, on account of you I cannot offer a sacrifice.' In
compunction, he regrets his past conduct, and what does he
say? If this man on his knees before me does not offer his
gift, if I who have been beseeched do not forgive, what am I
going to do? This is precisely why the Apostle exhorts us to
give food and drink to our enemies, 'for by so doing thou
wilt heap coals of fire upon his head.'[44] Someone may raise
the objection, 'That is the sort of thing enemies do; and so
I am being kind to my enemy only to heap coals of fire upon
his head?' That is not what it means. If he does you a wrong
and in return you do him a good, then you will be heaping
coals of fire upon his head; in other words, you are curing
him of his vices and burning out his malice in order to convert him to repentance.

Think over the words of the holy prophet: 'All too long
have I dwelt with those who hate peace.' He did not say,
with those who did not want peace, but who hated peace.
They hate peace, but I love those who hate peace. On that
account the Apostle also says: 'If it be possible, as far as in
you lies, be at peace with all men.'[45] Let us plead with our
brother if he is our enemy; let us beg of him even twice, and
three times, and seven times. 'Lord, how often shall my
brother sin against me, and I forgive him? Up to seven times?'
'I do not say to thee seven times, but seventy times seven,'[46]
and that means four hundred and ninety times! If we should
care to keep a record, from morning until evening, we could
not possibly commit as many as four hundred and ninety
sins.[47] Yet what does the Lord say? If he sins seventy times

44 Rom. 12.20; cf. Homily 22 on Ps. 93, p. 174; cf. *Against the Pelagians*
1.30, PL 23.548 (728).
45 Rom. 12.18; cf. Letter 82.2, PL 22.736-37 (513).
46 Matt. 18.21, 22.
47 Cf. *Commentary on Matthew* 18.21, 22, PL 26.137 (142).

seven times in a day and begs your pardon, forgive him. But you say: He is not sorry down deep in his heart, he is lying. Let us leave that judgment to God; he implores me, he beseeches me; if he is not telling the truth, God knows. I hear the voice, Christ understands the heart; I accept what I hear, let Christ accept what He knows. Besides, think of your reward; he lies, you accept it as truth; it is death for him and for you salvation.

Why have I spoken at such length? Because in monasteries, and especially among monks living together in communities, there are apt to be these serious faults. The fact, furthermore, does not embarrass us, it does not even grieve us. We have left mothers, parents, brothers, sisters; we have given up wives and children; we have given up our countries; we have left our homes; we have left behind the nurseries in which we were born and reared; we have left servants with whom we grew up to manhood; we have come into a monastery; all these things we have given up in order that in the monastery we may quarrel with our brothers over some silly trifling object! We have given up our property, abandoned our country, renounced the world; and in the monastery, we quarrel over a reed pen! If I hear a bitter word, I cannot bear it; it lodges in my heart; it is engraved on its very core for ten or fifteen days; it cannot be removed. I speak to the brother who had hurt me; I promise peace with my lips and hold the poison of resentment in my heart. Very often my eyes and face reveal what is going on in my heart. When our heart has received a deep wound from another, we cannot meet his eyes directly; our face and eyes are as the mirror of our soul. What does Scripture say about this? 'Could not even greet him';[48] the tongue could not falsify what the heart concealed. I am saying this both for your benefit and mine; I am not instructing you in this matter merely to exhibit myself as if I were one already secure. It is because

---

48 Gen. 37.4.

of this verse that I have felt compelled to make these remarks. A mighty evil is the tongue.

'O Lord, deliver me from lying lip, from treacherous tongue'—not from another's tongue, but from my own. Another's tongue does not injure me; my own is my enemy. Deliver me; deliver me from my own tongue. My tongue is a sword and it is slaying my soul. I think that I am harming my enemy; I do not realize that I am killing myself. My adversaries may contradict me when I speak to them, but I shall speak peace. Their spirit may be hostile, but let our spirit be that of peacemakers. It is written in Paralipomenon: 'The sons of Israel came to fight with peaceful heart.'[49]

Does one go to fight with a peaceful heart? Peace is the might of Christians: 'the peace of Christ which surpasses all understanding.'[50] Blessed the peacemakers, not only those who restore peace among the quarrelsome, but those who establish peace in themselves. Blessed the peacemakers. If others engage in strife and I intercede and bring peace to them, yet do not have peace in my heart, what benefit to me that they are at peace? 'Blessed are the peacemakers, for they shall be called children of God.'[51] Blessed the peacemakers who speak peace to those who hate peace. Blessed the peacemakers. Christ is peace. Since Solomon represents Christ, and Solomon means peaceful, Christ our Lord is peace. As He was going to heaven, He left us His standard, saying: 'My peace I give to you, my peace I leave with you.'[52] Let us guard carefully the gift Christ has given us; let us preserve peace, and it will preserve us in Christ Jesus, to whom be glory forever and ever. Amen.

---

49 Cf. 1 Par. 12.38; cf. Letter 112.2, PL 22.917 (738).
50 Cf. Phil. 4.7.
51 Matt. 5.9; cf. *Commentary on Matthew* 5.9, PL 26.35 (24).
52 Cf. John 14.27; cf. Letter 13, PL 22.547 (28).

HOMILY 42

ON PSALM 127 (128)

APPY ARE THEY who fear the Lord.'[1] What is the reward of those who fear the Lord? What is their
crown? Let us see what their glory is, what their
reward. 'Happy shall you be, and favored.' I have already
granted their happiness; now I am inquiring into its nature.
What is the happiness of the man who fears the Lord? 'Your
wife shall be like a fruitful vine in the recesses of your home;
your sons like olive plants around your table.'[2]

I think that in the merciful kindness of Christ, we all fear
the Lord. Then do we not have this happiness? It is written
that he who fears the Lord has a special happiness,[3] namely:
'Your wife shall be like a fruitful vine in the recesses of
your home; your sons like olive plants around your table.'
The man who has only one son, therefore, and the man who
has two sons is really not happy? What does it say? 'Your
sons like olive plants around your table.' Unless, therefore,
we have so many sons that they fill the places around our
table, shall we not have the happiness of the one who fears
the Lord? Isaac was not so blessed, for he had only two sons;
one the wicked Esau for whom it were better had he never
been born, the other, Jacob. Do you take it for granted, therefore, that he had no happiness because one son could not
encircle his table? According to such reasoning, virgins do
not fear the Lord. Why, then, does it say that he who fears

---

1 Cf. Ps. 127 (128).1.
2 Cf. Ps. 127 (128).3.
3 Letter 22.21, PL 22.407 (104); 123.13, PL 22.1054 (910); *Against Jovinian*
1.22, PL 23.252 (272).

the Lord rightly understands what it means to be happy? 'Your wife shall be like a fruitful vine in the recesses of your home; your sons like olive plants around your table.' John did not possess that kind of happiness, neither the Evangelist nor the Baptist, for both were virgins. This happiness was not Paul's either who says: 'For I would that you all were as I myself.'[4] You gather by now that 'wife and sons' must be understood spiritually; otherwise, without a spiritual interpretation, we must admit that angels do not possess such happiness, for they do not have children. Let us go back, therefore, and reread the verses in order.

'Happy are they who fear the Lord.' In the same way that one cannot say: 'My portion is the Lord,'[5] and still claim another portion in this world, one does not fear the Lord if he fears anything else apart from the Lord. The Savior says in fact: 'Do not be afraid of those who kill the body but cannot kill the soul, but rather be afraid of him who is able to destroy both soul and body in hell.'[6] You see, then, that he who does not fear the Lord, fears something other than the Lord.

What are the marks of the man who fears the Lord? The stamp of those 'Who walk in his ways.' There are many ways, and the many ways lead to the one Way, wherefore it says in Jeremia: 'Stand beside the ways of the Lord, and ask for the eternal pathways; find the one way, and walk it.'[7] Notice that it says: 'Stand beside the pathways of the Lord, and ask for the eternal paths of the Lord, and find the one way; and then walk it.' Through many ways, we find the one Way. This same thought occurs in the Gospel[8] under another form and figure in the parable of the merchant who had many pearls and sold them and bought a single pearl of great price.

---

4 Cf. 1 Cor. 7.7; cf. Letter 48.4, PL 22.496 (215); *Against Jovinian* 1.8, PL 23.232 (249).

5 Lam. 3.24.

6 Matt. 10.28.

7 Cf. Jer. 6.16. Cf. Homily 23 on Ps. 95, p. 183; Letter 54.11, PL 22.555 (289).

8 Cf. Matt. 13.46; Letter 54.11, PL 22.555 (289); 66.8, PL 22.644 (399).

'Stand beside the pathways,' that is, be in possession of many
pearls; stand in the pathways and ask for the eternal way
of the Lord. Beautiful eternity! Let us not imagine that
with the advent of Christ, the law and the prophets have
come to an end, but mark well: Stand beside the pathways;
do not put complete trust in one way to the exclusion of
many; but stand beside the pathways and inquire about the
eternal paths of the Lord. Ask for the eternal paths of the
Lord; ask what Jeremia said, what Isaia, Ezechiel, what the
rest of the prophets said. Ask for the paths. The meaning
here of paths is expressed better by the Greek tríbous[9] for
'semita' is used to denote a path that has been worn down
by the tread of feet. Now this is what the prophet has in
mind, search for the paths—tríbous—that the Lord made with
His own feet, inasmuch as the Lord also walked these paths.
When, moreover, you have examined carefully the eternal
paths of the Lord and through them have found the one
Way, who says: 'I am the way, and the truth, and the life,'[10]
walk that Way. Study the divine secrets of Holy Writ. See
how much mystical connotation there is in the simplest words
of Scripture, in such words as ways and paths, in law and
prophets. Note especially, too, that the prophet did not say,
walk, but stand; do not disregard the law or the prophets.
Nevertheless, when you have found the paths of the law and
the prophets, through their ways walk the one Way.

'For you shall eat the labors of your hands.'[11] Many commentators, not understanding this passage, have translated
it:[12] 'You shall eat the labors of your fruits.' As a matter of
fact, the Latin copies have: 'You shall eat the labors of your
fruits,' but in the Hebrew text, we read: 'You shall eat the
labors of your hands.' Who, indeed, eats the labors of his
fruits? Certainly, it must be understood the other way
around, for one eats the fruit he has won from his toils and

---

9 Cf. *Commentary on Jeremia* 6.16, PL 24.725 (886).
10 John 14.6.
11 Cf. Ps. 127 (128).2.
12 Cf. Letter 34.5, PL 22.450 (158).

not the toils of his hands. We accept, therefore, the other interpretation, for it can be said more truly that one eats the fruit of his labors and not the labors of fruits. Because the Hebrew has: 'You shall eat the labors of your hands,' I think the Greek translators of the Septuagint made a good rendition here. Actually, the word for hand in Hebrew is IAD; this passage of Scripture, however, does not have IAD, but CAPH. CAPH, furthermore, is translated karpós, not karpós —fruit—but karpós meaning some part of the hand,[13] because karpós in Greek means 'arthra,' or joint. So much for the translation. The labors of your hands, therefore, you shall eat, 'for what a man sows, that he will also reap.'[14] 'See the man and his recompense.'[15] We, too, shall eat what we have earned from the work of our hands. By the word 'hands,' works are to be understood: 'For you shall eat the labors of your hands.'

Somebody may raise the question of whether we are going to eat after the resurrection, for Scripture says of the happy man: 'You shall eat the labors of your hands.' My answer is quite simple. Man is composed of two substances: one of the soul, the other of the body; the soul is immortal, the body mortal. What is mortal necessarily requires food that is mortal; what is immortal, the soul, requires immortal food. Would you have proof that the soul has its own food? Our Lord and Savior says so when He was eating: 'My food is to do the will of him who sent me.'[16] Would you know what foods the soul has? The prophet tells us himself: 'Taste and see how good the Lord is.'[17] Just as the body dies unless it is given its proper food, even so does the soul if it is not given spiritual food. Why am I making such a point of this? Because there are some who insist on saying, I have no need for Sacred Scripture; the fear of God is enough for

13 *Ibid.*
14 Gal. 6.7.
15 Cf. Isa. 62.11, LXX.
16 John 4.34.
17 Ps. 33.9.

me. That is, therefore, precisely why we affirm that just as there are foods for the body, so there are, likewise, foods for the soul, namely, the Sacred Scripture.

'Your wife shall be like a fruitful vine in the recesses of your home.' It is Solomon who says that he longed to make wisdom his bride.[18] In another place, he says again of wisdom: 'Love her, and she will embrace you; embrace her and she will preserve you.'[19] Let us, too, take her for spouse; let us hold her in our arms; let us never let her go from our embrace, never let her escape from our arms. If this bride is always in our embrace, we shall beget sons from her, not daughters, but sons.[20] That is what it says right here: 'Your sons like olive plants around your table.' Why could it not say your daughters, or why not [children] tà tékna sou, so that masculine and feminine might be understood? But it says, 'your sons'; he who has wisdom for wife, does not beget daughters from her, but sons. There is nothing soft, nothing delicate, nothing tender, nothing effeminate in his mind or heart. Do you think it is for any other reason that the saints are recorded to have had not daughters, but sons?

Let us read Genesis, for there the order of generation is preserved. Abraham the holy patriarch had a wife, Sara, and a concubine, Agar; later he had Ceture. From two wives, he procreated sons, not daughters. Let us turn to Isaac. Isaac also had two sons; he did not have daughters. He was a saint, indeed, with nothing of softness in him, nothing tender and effeminate; he was all virility, every bit of him, and hard, too. Blessed Jacob has twelve patriarchal sons, and one daughter, Dina, meaning law-suit, dispute, strife.[21] In a word, he had one daughter and twelve sons, and on account of that one daughter, many a war broke out in Sichem. Never had Jacob said [except for Dina], 'I fear you have made

---

18 Cf. Wisdom 8.2.
19 Cf. Prov. 4.6, 8; cf. Letter 52.3, PL 22.528 (256).
20 *Commentary on Ecclesiastes* 2.8, PL 23.1080 (400); *Commentary on Isaia* 66.7, PL 24.657 (805).
21 Cf. *Hebrew Questions on Genesis* 30.21, PL 23.1034 (352).

me loathsome.'[22] In speaking of Levi and Simeon, he exclaims: 'Simeon and Levi, never be in their assembly, my spirit!'[23] Why does he say that? Because the men wanted to plead the cause of a woman. Why have I labored this point? Because the saints did not have daughters, but sons only. I am telling you something new, new to the uninformed, but to those who read the Scriptures, and read carefully, it is what they already know. Jacob had twelve sons, patriarchs: Ruben, Simeon, Juda, Levi, Issachar, Aser, and the rest of the twelve. Read the lists of generation and no where will you find that any one of these twelve patriarchs had a daughter, but all sons. I am going to tell you something, lest perhaps it escape you. Aser did have a daughter, Sara. Jacob had twelve sons and one daughter; likewise, among the twelve patriarchs, one had only one daughter.

Why have I stressed all this? Because it is necessary that in Holy Writ we discern the spiritual sense of sons and daughters. 'Your wife shall be like a fruitful vine in the recesses of your home.' 'As a fruitful vine.' A fruitful vine has many clusters of grapes, even so our wife, our bride, wisdom who is our spouse. We also find written in another place of Scripture: 'O my sister, my bride, come.'[24] Lest you associate anything base with the concept of bride, the word sister is adjoined to preclude any dishonorable love. Come, my sister: love is something sacred and for that reason I call you sister. My bride: I call you my bride that I may have a wife, and from you, my wife, beget sons in number, sons as many as the clusters of grapes on the vine. Now, as the vine has many different clusters and only one root, but spreads its shoots far and wide, thither and hither, and the shoots themselves bring forth their own fruits; and as these fruits are in clusters, one larger and one smaller, some seeds are greater, others are less; so also from wisdom, who is our wife, if we shall never

---

22 Cf. Gen. 34.30.
23 Cf. Gen. 49.6.
24 Cf. Cant. 5.1; cf. *Against Jovinian* 1.30, PL 23.265 (286).

let her go, many clusters will be engendered—many virtues,
many holy resolutions, many noble deeds.

'Your children like olive plants around your table.' We
read in another psalm: 'And wine to gladden men's hearts,'[25]
and again, in the Canticle of Canticles: 'Come brethren,
drink deeply of love.'[26] Wine to cheer the heart of men. The
wine of the flesh does not cheer the heart of man, but overpowers it and produces madness; it is written, in fact, that it is
not for kings to drink wine.[27] The Apostle, too, writes that
it is good not to eat meat and not to drink wine;[28] yet we
are told that wine gladdens the heart of man. This means,
however, spiritual wine, by which, if one drinks, he immediately becomes inebriated. All of you, in order to detach yourselves from your possessions and your parents, your sons
and relations, drank wine, and it began to inebriate you;
you became mad for the sake of Christ. Does it not seem to
you inebriation—spiritual madness—to scorn pleasures, to
seek out the dregs of the people, to shun the city, to pursue
solitude with zeal, to despise affections, to ignore a kinsman,
and to know Christ only? The apostles had been inebriated
with this kind of wine; hence, it is said of them: 'They are
full of new wine,'[29] for they had not been intoxicated by the
old law, but by the Gospel. I think that was Noe's kind of
intoxication.

'Your children like olive plants.' Our sons are compared
solely to olive plants. The prophet did not liken them to the
old olive, but to the new, the olive plants. Just as in the
reference to the inebriation of the apostles, Scripture does
not say they are full of old wine but of new wine; so here
they are like olive plants, new olives, fresh and strong in the
youth of the Gospel, new olive plants full of light.

---

25 Ps. 103.15.
26 Cf. Cant. 5.1.
27 Cf. Prov. 31.4.
28 Cf. Rom. 14.21; cf. Letter 22.8, PL 22.399 (94); 54.10, PL 22.555 (288);
   79.7, PL 22.729 (504); 108.1, PL 22.879 (691).
29 Acts 2.13.

It is the nature of olive oil to season food, to feed a flame, to refresh the body almost to newness after a long, weary journey; in fact, the worn and weary practically regain their former vigor after anointing with oil. Do you think that Scripture specifies wine and oil in this psalm arbitrarily? No, it could never substitute honey, nor any other spice, nor any other tree, only the vine and the olive. These are the healing remedies of our life, the vine and the olive, wine and oil. In wine there is severity; in oil, there is compassion. It is pertinent to recall that the man who had been wounded on his way coming down from Jerusalem to Jericho, a Samaritan— a guardian—received no medication save wine and oil. Wine, the austerity of the commandments; wine, the astringent, that any bad fluid may be boiled down and burned out. Since, moreover, human frailty is unable to bear the truth—'if you, O Lord, mark iniquities, Lord who can stand?'[30]—we could not live if the Lord were only just; hence, to His justice, to His wine, is added the oil of clemency.

'Behold, thus is the man blessed who fears the Lord.' We have been speaking at great length; let us hasten the end. 'The Lord bless you from Sion.' From this Sion? If so, how does another prophet say: 'Sion shall become a plowed field'?[31] The Lord, too, says: 'Jerusalem, Jerusalem! thou who killest the prophets, and stonest those who are sent to thee!'[32] When He had drawn near Jerusalem and had seen the city, He wept over it,[33] but when He wept, surely He wept because it was going to fall into ruins, to perish. In fact, what does He say? 'Arise, let us go from here';[34] and again: 'Your house is left to you desolate.'[35] When, therefore, the psalmist says: 'The Lord bless you from Sion,' he does not mean this Sion that we see so desolate; the very gates, the very plain

---

30 Ps. 129.3.
31 Jer. 26.18.
32 Matt. 23.37.
33 Cf. Luke 19.41.
34 John 14.31.
35 Matt. 23.38; cf. Letter 46.4, PL 22.485 (201); 58.3, PL 22.581 (320).

and the ruins, bespeak the wrath of God. Even if we are
ignorant of the facts, our very eyes proclaim their witness
to the wrath of the Lord. 'The Lord bless you from Sion.'
Sion means watchtower; Jerusalem symbolizes vision of peace.
If our soul had a watchtower, if it were high aloft, if it gave
no thought to the things of earth but only to things of
heaven, if our soul possessed the vision of peace, if Christ who
is true peace dwelt in it, He would bless us with happiness.
If Christ shall dwell in us, we shall be Sion, and we shall
be Jerusalem.

'May you see your children's children.' I am preaching to
you. If I have taught you anything from my sermon, I have
looked upon my sons; if you have taught others, I have seen
the sons of my sons. Let us pray the Lord that we may have
sons, that we may have grandsons, that our progeny be always more numerous.   Let us hasten to procreate such sons.
That is a holy union. I am telling you something strange;
without wife, many such sons are born. 'Peace be upon
Israel!' Israel means, 'man seeing God,' therefore, 'Peace be
upon Israel,' means 'upon those who discern God.' If my
mind always has the vision of God, if I always see Christ, I
shall not see others. Whoever has Christ within him, has
peace within him. 'Peace I leave with you, my peace I give
to you.'[36] Granted there are many persecutions, granted that
many are being persecuted, nevertheless, the man in whom
Christ dwells, always has Christ.

---

36 John 14.27; cf. Letter 13, PL 22.347 (28).

HOMILY 43

ON PSALM 128 (129)

UCH HAVE THEY oppressed me from my youth, let Israel say, much have they oppressed me from my youth.' Twice the psalmist repeats his complaint: much have they persecuted me; time and again from my youth they have persecuted me. If, however, I have begun to serve the Lord in middle life—at about forty, for instance—obviously, I cannot say that they have oppressed me from my youth. Nevertheless, what am I saying? They have tormented me from my youth; they have wounded me from my youth; they have trampled upon me from my youth. What, moreover, does he say who begins to serve the Lord from boyhood and is assaulted almost constantly by the devil and his angels, yet is never vanquished? 'Much have they oppressed me from my youth; yet they have not prevailed against me.' Christ's 'athlete is not crowned unless he has competed according to the rules,'[1] unless he has accepted and sustained the challenge, unless his face is black and blue from the fray and bathed in blood. Discolored bruises deserve a crown; suffering and pain merit joy.

'Much have they oppressed me from my youth.' This versicle belongs to the Lord's virgin and to the monk who began to serve the Lord from boyhood, but I, who began to serve Him at forty or fifty, how can I say: 'Much have they persecuted me from my youth'? Let the virgin, therefore, say this and the monk, too, who possesses integrity of body

---

1 Cf. 2 Tim. 2.5.

and spirit. But what does it mean? Why have they fought against me so much from my youth? Somebody may challenge me: 'O monk, how have demons and the devil fought against you?' True, my assailants seemed to be men, but in men I recognized the devil. Let us be on guard, therefore, not to give way to anger against our persecutors, but let us grieve and lament for them because it is another who is acting through them. If a man possessed by the devil should come along and strike me with his fists and kick me with his heels, should I not be roused to fury against him? No; he strikes me with blows; but I grieve and weep for my assailant, for I realize that he is being struck more piteously by the one working in him than I who receive the stinging blow from his hand. As often, then, as we suffer anything and endure temptations, let us recognize that it is the devil and his spirits who are breeding in men temptations against us. Someone may say: Prove your claim from Sacred Scripture, for we must not make an assertion unless it has been adduced from and confirmed by Scripture. Judas was a traitor, but Satan had entered into him and had betrayed him into treachery. When the wife of Putiphar caught hold of Joseph, her servant —the mistress, the servant; the wealthy woman, the young pauper; the citizen, the stranger—she was clinging to him but the saintly man apprehended the devil gripping him by her hands.

Now why am I saying all this? So that when we suffer anything at all from men, we may not yield to anger against them, but rather weep for them and perceive that it is the master of deceit forging his lies in them. 'Much have they oppressed me from my youth; yet they have not prevailed against me.' They have tormented me with base thoughts; they have provoked me to irascibility. If I have entertained evil thoughts, if I have yielded to temptation, if I have carried out any evil design, if the passion of anger has conquered me and I have wronged a brother, I cannot say, 'they have not prevailed against me,' because they have.

'Upon my back sinners have wrought.'[2] Watch carefully what Scripture says. The saint is an athlete and 'he is not crowned unless he has competed according to the rules.'[3] You know, of course, that there are many different kinds of athletes: some are wrestlers; others vie in contests of all sorts;[4] some compete in discus throwing; others race in the stadium. The Apostle says, furthermore, that he runs in a race so as to obtain the crown;[5] and in another Letter: 'Forgetting what is behind, I strain forward to what is before.'[6] Listen again to the psalmist: 'Upon my back sinners have wrought.' It has always been my way of running, and I have run that way always, to prevent my opponent from ever getting ahead of me and to keep him always safely behind. He has never met me face to face, for he cannot endure the light of my eyes, but he is always in pursuit of that part of me that is blind, that has no eyes. 'Upon my back sinners have wrought.' Whenever anyone slanders a brother, he is machinating behind his back. Upon my back sinners have forged their lies, but I was ignoring their traps. They plotted against me behind my back, but I kept my gaze fixed upon heaven. They piled up their snares against me, but I was consumed with a longing to behold the crown.

'Long did they continue their iniquity.'[7] Why did the psalmist say: 'Long did they continue their iniquity'? If I have sinned, and afterwards repented, my state of iniquity is brief; but if I commit sin, as often as I sin the cord of my transgressions lengthens proportionately. Scripture says, therefore, in another place: 'the snares of the wicked are twined about me';[8] note: 'the snares of the wicked are twined about me.' And elsewhere: 'in the meshes of his own sin

---

2 Cf. Ps. 128 (129).3.
3 2 Tim. 2.5.
4 Cf. *Commentary on Amos* 1.1, PL 25.992 (224).
5 Cf. 1 Cor. 9.26.
6 Phil. 3.13.
7 Cf. Ps. 128 (129).3.
8 Ps. 118.61.

he will be held fast.'⁹ Just think of what that means: everyone is caught in the meshes of his own sins! These cords of
sins cannot be intertwined unless I have committed many
sins. If I commit one sin, it is not so much a cord as it is a
strand. If there is just one strand, it is easily broken and
cannot hold nor bind, but if I commit many sins and my
wickedness is prolonged, from many sins—just as from many
strands—a cord is formed which binds firmly and is not
easily broken. What has prompted me to say this? It was
suggested by the versicle: 'Long did they continue their iniquities.'

'The just Lord has humbled the pride of sinners.'¹⁰ Understand what this means. The psalmist did not say the Lord
has destroyed sinners; if he had said that, no one could be
saved; we are all sinners. What does he say? 'The just Lord
has humbled the pride of sinners'; they who are both sinful
and proud, for 'God resists the proud, but gives grace to the
humble.'¹¹ Therefore, does He humble the pride of sinners
to the ground.

---

9 Prov. 5.22; cf. Letter 48.21, PL 22.510 (233).
10 Cf. Ps. 128 (129).4. Cf. *Commentarioli in ps.* 128.4.
11 James 4.6; 1 Peter 5.5; cf. Prov. 3.34; cf. Letter 76.1, PL 22.689 (455).

HOMILY 44

ON PSALM 131 (132)

REMEMBER, O LORD, for David all his meekness.'[1] There are many commentators who conclude from the words of the Gospel: 'Son of David, have mercy on us'[2]—the cry of the blind man sitting on the wayside at Jericho—that this David, whose name means 'strong of hand,' refers to the Lord Savior.[3] If, however, we accept their judgment, we are doing violence to our intelligence, for if the words: 'Remember, O Lord, for David all his meekness,' refer to Christ, how, then, does Christ say as of another: ' "Till I find a place for the Lord, a dwelling for the God of Jacob." Behold we heard of her in Ephratha, we found her in the fields of the wood'?[4] Furthermore, what is the meaning of: 'For the sake of David your servant, reject not the plea of your anointed'?[5] The order of exposition in the psalm does not admit of such interpretation, for if David is Christ, as they think, we begin our process of deduction thus: For the sake of Christ your servant, reject not the plea of your Christ. I am opposing this consideration to those who construe David in this passage as Christ—not that we would deny that David is a type of Christ, in conformity with the Scriptural texts; but that in this particular instance such exegesis does not make sense.

How it happens that they make this blunder, I shall ex-

1 Cf. Ps. 131 (132).1.
2 Matt. 20.30.
3 Cf. *Commentary on Galatians* 5.22, PL 26.449 (512).
4 Cf. Ps. 131 (132).5, 6.
5 Ps. 131 (132).10.

plain to you. Because it is written: 'Remember, O Lord, for
David all his meekness,' and the Lord says in the Gospel:
'Learn of me, for I am meek and humble of heart,'[6] they,
with pious sentiment, indeed, but no less with error, interpret David here as Christ and apply his meekness to
Christ. Consequently, let us expound this psalm in its reference to David, in order that we may discern Him more
truly as the Christ who derives His origin from David. Besides, take note of the sequence in the psalm. Since, undoubtedly, this is one of the great psalms, and we have already said much, we shall have to compress our thoughts into
concise remarks that the prudent hearer, from what we have
said, may on his own comprehend what we must leave unsaid.

'How he swore to the Lord, vowed to the God of Jacob.'[7] In
the Hebrew text, there is not the word ὡς equivalent to our
Latin 'sicut,' nor is the meaning such; but instead there is ὅς
or the Latin 'qui,' and the meaning is: 'Remember, O Lord,
for David all his meekness, *who* swore to the Lord, *who* vowed
to the God of Jacob.' I do not think that this discrepancy is
as much a fault of the Septuagint translators, as I think it is
an error on the part of the scribes.[8]

'I will not enter the house I live in.' David is saying here:
I seek no other resting place save Christ who will be born of
my seed, whom You promised would be born of my posterity.

'I will give my eyes no sleep, my eyelids no rest, nor rest
to my temples, till I find a place for the Lord, a dwelling for
the God of Jacob.'[9] Many exegetes think that this foreshadows
the Church, but to me it seems to refer not so much to the
Church, as to holy Mary. It even says: 'Behold we heard of
her in Ephratha; we found her in the fields of the wood.'[10]
Let us read Sacred Scripture, and day and night let us ponder
over its every syllable, every letter; let us analyze and discuss

---

6 Matt. 11.29; cf. Letter 82.1, PL 22.736 (513); 76.1, PL 22.689 (456).
7 Cf. Ps. 131 (132).2.
8 Cf. *Commentarioli in ps.* 131.
9 Cf. Ps. 131 (132).4, 5.
10 Cf. Ps. 131 (132).6.

it. Someone may say that here 'Ephratha' stands for Bethlehem. To be sure we read in Genesis: 'He came into Bethlehem, that is, Ephratha.'[11] This is said of Jacob when his wife Rachel died in Ephratha. Let us look into the origin of the name Ephratha. It is written in Paralipomenon that Maria, the sister of Moses and Aaron, had married a man by name, Or—not Ur, but Or. By reason of this marriage the right order is defined and expressed as follows: 'Mary, the sister of Moses and Aaron, that is, Ephratha.'[12] You will find this in Paralipomenon. This, then, is the source of the name Ephratha in our psalm. Perhaps some one questions the derivation because it is so novel, but I refer such a one to the authority of the Book.

'Behold we heard of her in Ephratha.' The Hebrew text has 'him'[13] instead of 'her,' calling attention to Him who is to be born of the descendants of David: 'We heard of him in Ephratha': because these words point to Mary. We also may understand simply that Ephratha is said for Bethlehem, and Christ is to be born in Bethlehem. Happy, indeed, the place celebrated so long before its time in the song of the prophets! True, all the places are holy and venerable, where Christ was born, where He was crucified, where He rose from the dead, and where as victor He ascended into heaven, but this place is fittingly more venerable. Just think of the compassionate kindness of God! Here, a poor little Child is born, an Infant is laid in a manger: 'because there was no room for them in the inn.'[14] O monks, the Lord is born on earth, and He does not have even a cell in which to be born; there was no room for Him in the inn. The entire human race had a place, and the Lord about to be born on earth had none. He found no room among men; He found no room in Plato, none in

---

11 Cf. Gen. 35.19; cf. *Hebrew Questions on Genesis* 35.19, PL 23.1042 (360); Letter 108.10, PL 22.885 (698); cf. *Commentary on Michea* 5.2, PL 25.1197-1198 (489-490).

12 Cf. 1 Par. 4.4; 2.19; 2.50, 51; 6.3; cf. Josephus, *Jewish Antiquities* 111.4 (Loeb).

13 Cf. Letter 108.10, PL 22.885 (699); *Commentarioli in ps.* 131.6.

14 Luke 2.7; cf. Letter 14.11, PL 22.354 (37).

Aristotle, but in a manger, among beasts of burden and brute animals, and among the simple, too, and the innocent. For that reason the Lord says in the Gospel: 'The foxes have dens, and the birds of the air have nests, but the Son of Man has no where to lay his head.'[15]

---

15 Luke 9.58.

EHOLD, HOW GOOD it is, and how pleasant, where brethren dwell at one!' The psalmist mentions two qualities of the common dwelling of brethren, good and pleasant. Martyrdom is good, but it is not pleasant, for it consists in suffering and sorrow; in torture there is always pain, and in pain there is certainly no pleasure. 'Behold, how good it is, and how pleasant.' On the other hand, sensuality is pleasant. Eating rich foods, for example, seems to be pleasant, for it may incite sensual desire. The prophet, then, has predicated two attributes, possibly contradictory—good and pleasant—which he has reconciled into one characteristic: Behold how good and how pleasant. 'Pleasant where brethren dwell at one'—brothers in mind and heart, not in body. Esau and Jacob were brothers, and their living together was the cause of their discord; hence, 'brothers' here does not mean brothers in the flesh, but brothers in the spirit, brothers in the sense that the Savior implied when He said to the women: 'Go take word to my brethren.'[1]

'Behold, how good it is, and how pleasant, where brethren dwell at one!' This psalm is truly the psalm of convents and monasteries. It may even be applied to the churches, although, because of the great diversity in personal interests on the part of the members, there does not in the Christian assembly appear to be the same degree of harmony. Actually, what kind of fraternity do we find there? Usually, one mem-

---

1 John 20.17; cf. *The Perpetual Virginity of Blessed Mary* 15, PL 23.208 (222).

ber is in a hurry to go home, another to the circus; another,
all the while he is in church, is planning how he will invest
his money. In the monastery, however, there is one aim and,
as it were, one soul. 'Behold, how good it is, and how pleasant, where brethren dwell at one'—truly good, truly pleasant.
We have lost one brother, and behold how many we have
gained! My brother, a layman, (I am not speaking of myself,
but for each of you) does not love me as much as he loves
my property. Spiritual brothers, on the other hand, who assuredly have no use for their own possessions, are not looking
for another's. We read in the Acts of the Apostles that 'the
multitude of the believers were of one heart and one soul. And
they had all things in common.'[2] In truth did they possess all
things in common, for they had Christ in common. We have
touched on many points, but we must hasten to the rest of
the psalm.

'It is as when the precious ointment upon the head runs
down over the beard,. the beard of Aaron.' Oh, if only there
were time to explore together each verse; even a day would
not suffice! We have read in Exodus[3] the account of how oil
is prepared for the anointing of the priest; we have read, too,
of the different kind of balm used to anoint kings. There
was still another unguent for prophets. What more is there
to say? All these oils of unction were different, each with its
own spiritual symbolism. Do we have the proper reverence
for sacramentals? After a leper has been cleansed—when
he has been sprinkled with hyssop and the blood of a hen,
and a hen has been set to wander in the desert—he also has
his own proper ointment. Nothing is ever made sacred except
by anointing. It is with this in view that young maidens say
in the Canticle of Canticles: 'Your name is a spreading per-
fume: we will run after you in the odor of your ointments.'[4]

'It is as when the precious ointment upon the head runs

---

2 Cf. Acts 4.32.
3 Cf. Exod. 3.
4 Cf. Cant. 1.2, 3.

down over the beard, the beard of Aaron.' Aptly said: 'upon
the head.' It 'runs down over the beard.' The beard is the
sign of manhood, for by this sign nature has distinguished man
from woman. It is, therefore, a token of virility.[5] The head
symbolizes divinity, that is, the Godhead; the beard designates
man. 'Until,' Scripture says, 'we attain to perfect manhood,'[6]
that is, Christ. Now see what the prophet means when he says:
'It is as when the precious ointment.' Just as the blessing of
precious ointment from the head—that is, from the Hermon
of divinity—runs down over the beard, runs down upon the
perfect man who is Christ, from that beard the same precious
balm runs down afterwards to the collar of His robe; even
so the blessing and the dew of Mount Hermon runs down
over Mount Sion. 'Ointment' here, therefore, means the same
as 'blessing.' 'You love justice and hate wickedness; therefore
God, your God, has anointed you with the oil of gladness
above your fellow kings.'[7] Attend closely to what it says:
you love justice and hate wickedness. It is not enough to
love justice, but you must hate wickedness. What is the
reward of such virtue? God, your God, has anointed you
with the oil of gladness above your fellow men. This is said
to Christ: You have been anointed that You may anoint
others. You have been anointed with the oil of gladness
above Your fellow men, above Your apostles. You possess
the font of unction; they, the drops.

'It is as when the precious ointment upon the head.' May
the Lord give to us also this precious ointment of divinity
that came down upon the beard, that is, upon the perfect man
Aaron, Aaron the priest. The name Aaron, moreover, means
'of the mountains';[8] this priest is not of the valleys, but of
the mountains. 'The beard,' the psalmist says, 'of Aaron.'
Because from the head the oil of unction came down upon

5 Cf. *Commentary on Isaia* 7.20, PL 24.112 (114); *on Ezechiel* 5.1-4, PL
25.52 (49).
6 Eph. 4.13.
7 Ps. 44.8.
8 Cf. *Letter* 78.11, PL 22.706 (477).

the beard, from the Word of God it came down upon man whose human nature He deigned to assume.

What benefit to us is this beard that has been anointed and this perfect man? Let us look into their effects upon us. 'Till it runs down upon the collar of his robe.' If we are Christ's robe, we clothe His nakedness with our faith. Behold Him hanging naked upon the cross, a stumbling-block to the Jews and to the Gentiles foolishness;[9] nevertheless, He is robed in our faith, in our acknowledgment and praise. Noe[10] lay naked in his tent and his nakedness was exposed; the elder son laughed but the younger covered him. Why am I saying all this? Just to teach you that we are the robe of Christ. I am going to tell you something new; really not new, but from Sacred Scripture. We are the robe of Christ; when we have clothed Him with our confession of faith, we, in turn, have put on Christ. It is the Apostle[11] who says that Christ is our robe, for when we are baptized we put on Christ. We both clothe and are clothed. Would you like to know in what manner we clothe the Lord? We read in Jeremia:[12] 'Go buy yourself a linen loincloth; wear it on your loins, and go to the Pharat; there hide it in a cleft of the rock. Obedient to the Lord's command, I went to the Pharat and buried the loincloth. After a long interval, again I went to the Pharat, and the loincloth was rotted, good for nothing. Then the message came to me from the Lord.' Listen very carefully. 'As close as the loincloth,' Jeremia says, 'clings to your loins, so had I made this people cling to me, says the Lord.' Why have I drawn this out to such length? To prove to you that the faithful are the garment of Christ.

'Till it runs down upon the collar of his robe: it runs down over the beard, the beard of Aaron.'[13] This is not the

---

9 Cf. 1 Cor. 1.23.
10 Cf. Gen. 9.21-25.
11 Cf. Gal. 3.27.
12 Cf. Jer. 13.1-9.
13 Cf. Ps. 132 (133).2.

time to discuss the priests' vestments.[14] The high priest alone
had eight different varieties. It would take too long now to
discourse on the ephod, on the tunic; too long to describe the
rational [breastpiece of decision], the illuminations and per-
fections [Urim and Thmmim]; the little chains, the girdle, the
breeches; the fringes, the tassels shaped like a pomegranate,
the little bells; the virtues requisite of the priest entering the
Temple of the Lord and the Holy of Holies. If we wish to
be a part of the priestly vestment, we are either the super-
humeral—the ephod—that our works may be good works and
that we may carry the commandments of Christ upon our
shoulders; or surely we ought to be the under tunic which is
a straight linen garment fitting close to the body. It is not
loose nor flowing, but clings tight to the body. You perceive,
therefore, that the interior man, the under tunic, is very intimately united to the body. If a man is truly the rational—
λόγιον—he is in no other place than in the heart. Notice the
order: whoever is a rational, and is λόγιον and is 'ratio' is
established firmly in the heart. It is possible, however, for
one to have wisdom, to have λόγιον, yet lack the power of
expression. The true priest, therefore, must have λόγιον,
and he must have δηλώσεις or the power of communication,
that he may bring forth and impart to others what he conceives in his mind and heart. Yet all these powers are vain
if chastity has not been a precaution and an adornment.
There is a girdle, therefore, that girds the loins; it binds
and mortifies.

In the next place, Scripture says the priest must have
breeches, a covering of the thighs, in order that our shameful
and unbecoming parts may be purified and mortified by this
kind of loincloth. Lastly, we must have a long garment
reaching to our feet as if to adorn them. This tunic is em-
broidered with different kinds of flowers; there are pomegranates and even tassels. I think that it was this tassel that

---

14 Cf. Exod. 28.4-42; cf. Letter 64, PL 22.607-622; 29, PL 22.435-441;
    Against Jovinian 2.34, PL 23.346 (378).

the woman with the hemorrhage touched and was healed.[15]
Consider, finally, that on the hem of the tunic there were little
bells in between the pomegranates, and these tiny bells tinkled
every time the priest entered the sanctuary. The bells and the
pomegranates represent the different virtues, each of which
has its own special sound; the tinkling of the bells, likewise,
announces the departure of the priest when he leaves the
sanctuary. We promised to be brief, and here we have spoken
at length! Yet whether we eat or whether we drink, we do all
in the name of the Lord![16]

'It is a dew like that of Hermon, which comes down upon
the mountains of Sion.' The dew of Hermon. We have read
in a certain apocryphal book[17] that when the sons of God were
coming down to the daughters of men, they descended upon
Mount Hermon and there entered into an agreement to
come to the daughters of men and make them their wives.
This book is quite explicit and is classified as apocryphal.
The ancient exegetes have at various times referred to it,
but we are citing it, not as authoritative, but merely to bring
it to your attention. 'It is a dew like that of Hermon, which
comes down upon the mountains of Sion.' I have read about
this apocryphal book in the work of a particular author who
used it to confirm his own heresy. What does he say? He
says: The sons of God who came down from heaven upon
Mount Hermon and coveted the daughters of men are angels
descending from the heavens and souls that desired bodies
since bodies are the daughters of men. Do you detect the
source of the teachings of Manichaeus, the ignorant? Just as
the Manichaeans say that souls desired human bodies to be
united in pleasure, do not they who say that angels desired
bodies—or the daughters of men—seem to you to be saying
the same thing as the Manichaeans? It would take too long
to refute them now, but I merely wanted to indicate the

15 Cf. Matt. 9.20-23.
16 Cf. 1 Cor. 10.31.
17 Cf. Henoch 6.5-8; cf. Gen. 6.2, 4.

coincidence, as it were, of the book that opportunely confirmed their dogma.

Hermon in our language means ἀνάθημα,[18] or condemnation. The dew of the Lord, therefore, was formerly upon the Jews who later were cursed; and that blessing, which at one time descended upon an anathematized people, later descended upon Mount Sion, that is, upon the Church. We are of the Church if we believe the truth of Christian teaching, acknowledge Christ. We are in a church, but how many saints there are in the desert; how many who are not part of a congregation; or not in a Christian assembly, who abide, nevertheless, in the Church of Christ. If, as I was saying, we are in the Church, if we possess the faith of the Church, of the apostles, of Christ, the truths of Christian teaching, we are the mountains of Sion. We do not want to be among the valleys of Sion, we want to be mountains of Sion. Sion, indeed, has her valleys; she has plains, too. The sinner is a valley of Sion, not a mountain. Someone may interpose: 'You are giving us your own opinion.' Let us call upon the testimony of Isaia when Sion had fallen into sin, in which after many visions, the prophet mentions one against Idumea, one against Moab, one against Edom and the sons of Ammon, and lastly: 'A vision of the valley of Sion.'[19] Because Sion had descended from sublime faith, she fell recklessly from the mountain into the valley.

Before all else, then, let us flee from the valleys of Sion and come to the plains; from the plains, let us go to the hills, from the hills up the mountains; let us follow Christ in the mountains since our brother like a gazelle or a young stag comes leaping over the hills, springing across the mountains.[20] In truth, Christ after the Resurrection did not ascend into heaven from the valley but from the mountain. Unless we are mountains of virtue, we cannot ascend into heaven. There

---

18 Cf. *Commentarioli in ps.* 132.3.
19 Cf. Isa. 21; 22.1, LXX.
20 Cf. Cant. 2.8, 9.

assuredly—in the mountains of Sion, in the virtues, in the confession of faith, in the truth of the word of God—there is blessing and 'life forever.' Christ is our life. He who confesses Christ receives life everlasting. Amen.

HOMILY 46

ON PSALM 133 (134)

OME, BLESS THE LORD, all you servants of the Lord.'
This is the last psalm in the songs of the steps.[1] The
first of these gradual psalms opened with the words:
'In my distress I called to the Lord, and he answered me.'[2]
In the second, the psalmist had begun his ascent with: 'I lift
up my eyes toward the mountains';[3] on the third: 'I rejoiced
at the things that were said to me';[4] on the fourth: 'To you
I lift up my eyes, who are enthroned in heaven.'[5] Notice how
gradually he mounted step by step, always ascending to something more sublime. Even if it were our desire, it would take
too long to quote the first verse of each of the psalms, the beginning of each of the steps. The prophet reached the thir-
teenth psalm, rather he arrived at the twelfth, and there,
after all the other virtues, he placed humility. Vain, indeed,
are our virtues if they are not crowned with the humility of
the Lord, for what did the prophet declare? 'O Lord, my
heart is not proud, nor are my eyes haughty.'[6] Then, because
he has given evidence of his humility, he asks for the coming
of Christ. What does he say? 'Remember, O Lord, for David
and all his meekness';[7] and a few verses further on: 'For the
sake of David your servant, turn not away the face of your

---

1 Cf. *Against Jovinian* 2.34, PL 23.346 (378).
2 Ps. 119.1.
3 Ps. 120.1; cf. Letter 7.3, PL 22.340 (19).
4 Cf. Ps. 121.1.
5 Ps. 122.1.
6 Ps. 130.1; cf. Letter 22.27, PL 22.413 (111).
7 Cf. Ps. 131.1; cf. Letter 76.1, PL 22.689 (456); 82.1, PL 22.736 (513).

Christ.'[8] After he had received Christ, after he had received
the faith of Christ, he gathers the Church together, and what
does he say? 'Behold, how good it is, and how pleasant,
where brethren dwell at one!'[9]

Since now the brethren have come together as one, and the
Church of the Lord has been assembled, what is the counsel
of the last psalm? 'Come, bless the Lord, all you servants of
the Lord'; because it is good and pleasant for brethren to
dwell united, and together you have formed a community:
'Come, bless the Lord.' Praise Christ now after His coming,
for in Him you have come together; now bless Him in the
last psalm of ascent, for you have gathered together on the
summit of the virtues. Before you reached the top, the fifteenth step, you were not able to bless the Lord, but I say
to you now: 'Come, bless the Lord.'

When one says 'Come,' the invitation is just as definite as
if one were pointing at you with his finger. Come, bless the
Lord. Who are to bless the Lord? All the servants of the
Lord; you who are not the servants of sin, but the servants of
the Lord. Do we deem it of little account to say, I am a
servant of the Lord? To merit that title is the height of ex-
cellence. Just as one vindicates his honor, as it were, by saying, I am the servant of the Emperor—and no one dares to
approach the servant of the Emperor—even so it is of infinite dignity to call oneself the servant of the Lord. The
Apostle glories in the servitude of the Lord and writes at
the beginning of his Letters: 'Paul servant of Christ.' Similarly of Moses, Scripture says: 'But it is not so with my
servant Moses, for I speak to him face to face!'[10] Think of
what that means: I have spoken to others in visions and in
allegories, but not so to My servant Moses; with him I have
spoken face to face!

---

8 Cf. Ps. 131.10.
9 Ps. 132.1; cf. *The Perpetual Virginity of Blessed Mary* 15, PL 23.208
    (222).
10 Cf. Num. 12.7, 8; cf. Homily 40 on Ps. 115, p. 293.

Let us pose an example. Let us say that there is a very wealthy lord; he owns an estate and he has servants who minister to him. But do the servants who work on the grounds have as great confidence in their lord as the servants who attend him daily? The servant who sees the face of his master and waits upon him enjoys a great privilege. Furthermore, when the other servants who never come into the presence of their lord want something from him, they entreat their fellow servant to intercede for them. Why have I expatiated on this? Our Lord Jesus Christ has a great household. He has those who minister to Him in His presence, and He has others who serve Him in the fields. Monks and virgins, I think, are they who attend their Lord personally; laymen are the members of the household who are at work in the fields. If the workers in the field are in need of anything, what do they do but ask the others to approach the Lord for them. The honor of those who see the face of their master every day is, however, equalled by their punishment if they neglect their duty to him. Wicked servants are apt to be in greater fear of their master as long as they are on the farm or on the grounds because, naturally, they do not see him; if, however, they begin to see him every day, they make light of him, and familiarity breeds arrogance. We must be careful, therefore, not to permit ourselves from custom to esteem lightly the goodness of our Lord.

Praise the Lord, all you servants of the Lord, who are not the servants of sin but the servants of the Lord; all you servants of the Lord who have one Lord only, God; all you servants of the Lord who are not governed by anger, who are not swayed by passion, who are not ruled by other sins. They who are not under the dominance of vice are under the dominion of the Lord. 'All you servants of the Lord.'

Thus far there seems to be no problem, but note that the prophet stipulates a condition. It is not enough to be a servant of the Lord, unless the servants are themselves standing. There are some, for example, who stand, others who fall

prostrate; some who sit, others who lie down.[11] Those, of
course, who are falling, who are sitting, who are prone, are
not able to praise the Lord; you that are standing, praise
Him. Someone may object: There are others who stand;
there are many churches, many congregations; who, then,
are standing? Are the Arians standing? The Eunomians and
the other heretics call Christ by name; are they, therefore,
standing?

To avoid any misunderstanding about this liberty to praise
the Lord, mark that the prophet says: 'Who stand in the
house of the Lord,' 'in order that,' as the Apostle says, 'until
I come thou mayest know how to conduct thyself in the
house of God, which is the Church.'[12] The Church does not
consist in walls, but in the truths of her teachings. The
Church is there where there is true faith. As a matter of
fact, fifteen and twenty years ago, all the church buildings
belonged to heretics, for heretics twenty years ago were in
possession of them; but the true Church was there where
the true faith was. You bless the Lord, therefore, who are
the servants of the Lord. 'Unseemly is praise on a sinner's
lips!'[13] Praise the Lord, you that are servants of the Lord,
you that are both serving and standing. 'Who stand': 'He set
my feet upon a crag,'[14] says David; and to Moses the Lord
says: 'Then you stand here near me.'[15] 'God arises in the
divine assembly';[16] you stand, therefore, not anywhere, but in
the house of God. 'In the courts of the house of our God.'[17]

In the Hebrew scrolls, these words are not found in this
psalm but in the following one.[18] What is their context there?
'Praise the name of the Lord; praise, you servants of the Lord
who stand in the house of the Lord, in the courts of the house

---

11 Cf. Homily 1 on Ps. 1, p. 3; Homily 14 on Ps. 81, p. 102.
12 Cf. 1 Tim. 3.15.
13 Sirach (Ecclus.) 15.9.
14 Ps. 39.3.
15 Cf. Deut. 5.31; cf. Letter 21.15, PL 22.386 (77).
16 Ps. 81.1.
17 Cf. Ps. 134.2.
18 Cf. *Commentarioli in ps.* 133.1.

of our God.'[19] Now just because that psalm contains the verse: 'Who stand in the house of the Lord, in the courts of the house of our God,' a certain scholar was of the opinion that, likewise, in this psalm to the versicle, 'who stand in the house of the Lord,' should be added, 'in the courts of the house of our God.' The interpretation of the text: 'In the courts of the house of our God,' as well as the distinction between house and courts, will be discussed at a later time when the next psalm is read.

'During the hours of night, lift up your hands toward the sanctuary, and bless the Lord.' 'The whole world is in the power of the evil one'[20] and 'our wrestling is not against flesh and blood, but against the world-rulers of this darkness.'[21] It is in harmony with this thought that the Apostle says: 'The night is far advanced; the day is at hand.' This world is night; the future world is the true day; so the Apostle says: 'The night is far advanced; the day is at hand. Let us walk becomingly as in the day.'[22] Let us live our lives in the same way now as we are going to live in the day, that is, in the future world. 'During the hours of night, lift up your hands toward the sanctuary.' Whether we will it or not, we are in the night; as long as we are in this world, we are in the hours of the night. The night has darkness, the darkness of the sins of men. This is the sense in which you are to comprehend the meaning of: 'During the hours of night, lift up your hands toward the sanctuary.' While you are in this world, while you are in the nights, lift up your hands. Do not let them down, but lift them up, raise them up with Moses. If you lift up your hands, Amalec is conquered; if you lower them, Jesus is vanquished.

While you are reflecting upon this thought, meditate upon the mystery that is hidden within it. If we lift up our hands, Jesus triumphs; if we lift up our hands in good works,

19 Ps. 134.1, 2.
20 1 John 5.19.
21 Cf. Eph. 6.12.
22 Cf. Rom. 13.12, 13.

through our good works, Christ overcomes the devil. Hands, moreover, connote works, whereupon it is written: 'The word of the Lord came by the hand of Aggai';[23] 'the word that came by the hand of Jeremia the prophet.' To be sure, the word of the Lord does not come by the hand but by the mouth, but grasp the mysticism of Scripture. God does not come because of words, but because of good works.[24] The homicide, for all that, acknowledges Christ, but the Lord does not come to him; his hands are not worthy of His coming. Accordingly, it is written in another place: 'Death and life are in the hand of the tongue.'[25] Does the tongue, then, have hands? Tell me, why does it say: Death and life are in the hand of the tongue? Consider what that means. God does not hear the tongue, nor does He hear words, but He heeds works, that words may be translated into works. That is why the last of the gradual psalms exhorts us: 'During the hours of night, lift up your hands toward the sanctuary.' Lift up your hands, the prophet says, because Jesus also lifted them up on the cross.

'During the hours of night, lift up your hands toward the sanctuary.' Why did he deliberately add, 'toward the sanctuary'? You see heretics lifting up their hands, and heathens and the Jews likewise. They even give alms. If they see a poor man, they reach out their hand to him. When the Jew gives alms, does it not seem to you that he is lifting up his hand? He certainly raises his hand, but not toward the sanctuary, for he does not acknowledge Christ. You, however, who are in the house of the Lord, who stand in the house of the Lord, in the courts of the house of our God, who are the servants of the Lord, to whom I had said: 'Behold, how good it is, and how pleasant, where brethren dwell at one':[26] be sure that when you lift up your hands you raise them toward the

---

23 Cf. Ag. 1.1.
24 Cf. *Commentary on Aggai* 1.1, PL 25.1389 (738); on *Ecclesiastes* 4.5, PL 23.1099A (420).
25 Cf. Prov. 18.21.
26 Ps. 132.1.

sanctuary, that you acknowledge Christ, and whatever you do, you do for Christ.

Virtues differ in accordance with the motive and nature of the person performing the act. A Christian, for example, gives alms, a pagan also and a Jew and another Christian, a holy man. You will find some Christians giving alms in order to be honored by men. When a poor beggar comes up to them, such Christians first look all around and, unless they catch sight of a witness, they do not give their money. If that kind of person is alone, his hand is cramped even more than ever;[27] he does not give willingly. O you Christian, a pauper begs you for money, why do you refuse him in secret[28] but give to him in public? If you seek God as your witness, why do you look around for human eyes? Your alms-giving in the presence of the unsophisticated looks like real almsgiving, but in the presence of God it is a wrong; you are doing an injury to your brother, for you wish to show him up as a beggar in the presence of others. When we have the opportunity of giving, therefore, let us give not as from our own substance, but as from Christ's; we ought not give as to a beggar, but as to a brother. We give him material things; he gives us spiritual; the pauper gives more than he receives. We give him bread that will be consumed that same day; in return for the bread, he gives us the kingdom of heaven.

That is why I exhort that whatever we do, we do it in a sanctuary; that whatever we do, we do for the sake of Christ. There are many heathens who give alms; if they see anyone with a hand cut and torn, or someone with a cancerous and decaying foot, immediately their whole soul is in pain, the human soul is overwhelmed by a natural sense of pity. What does such a one say? If I were in his place, what would I do in such misery? I could be very easily in his condition, and who would help me out? Surely, I ought to give him alms

---

27 Cf. *Against the Pelagians* 2.11, PL 23.572 (754).
28 Cf. Matt. 6.2-4; cf. Letter 22.32, PL 22.418 (117).

so that someone may give to me if ever I am in a similar state. Yes, this pagan gives bread to the pauper; but in the poor man he does not pity the pauper, he pities himself. This mercy is not the compassionate kindness of Christ, but his own feeling of self-pity. Whatever we do, therefore, let us do it for the sake of Christ; let us do it in holiness. 'Whether we eat or drink, let us do all in the name of Christ.'[29]

We read the Scriptures; we commit the psalms to memory; we master the Gospels; we expound the prophets; but we must not do this so as to win praise and glory in the presence of our brothers, but to please Christ, that His word may resound from our lips. Men and monks, and even women, often vie with one another in committing Holy Writ to memory, and the more they learn by heart the better they think they are. He who truly has learned more is the one who does more; besides, what you are committing to memory, I am putting into practice. My works preserve the sacred writings more truly than your discourse that rings hollow. 'During the hours of night, lift up your hands toward the sanctuary.' Lift up your hands, raise aloft the standard of the cross. During the hours of night, lift up your hands toward the sanctuary; and when you have lifted them to the holy places, and performed holy deeds, let Christ be as the adornment of your good works.

'And bless the Lord.' Along with this, the Apostle, likewise, says: 'Lift up pure hands everywhere,'[30] and bless the Lord. Whatever you do, present it to the Lord. Let hands be raised in prayer; let lips resound with Christ. During the night, lift up your hands; give alms to the poor; and praise the Lord; give thanks to the Lord, who gave to you that you may share with your brother. When you give, thank Christ in greater measure than your brother thanks you. The poor render us great service. Almsgiving atones for sins that we have not been able to wash away otherwise. What does

---

29 1 Cor. 10.31.
30 Cf. 1 Tim. 2.8.

Scripture say in this regard? 'Water quenches a flaming fire, and alms atone for sins.'[31] The effects of almsgiving are similar to those of baptism; just as baptism remits sin, even so almsgiving atones for sins. Just as water extinguishes a fire, so does almsgiving extinguish sin; the fires of hell have been kindled for sins; almsgiving quenches them.

'May the Lord bless you from Sion, the maker of heaven and earth.' You bless the Lord, and the Lord blesses you, 'from Sion,' from the watchtower, from the Church, from true Christian doctrine, from devout faith. May the Lord bless you from Sion. The Holy Spirit speaks these versicles, or rather the prophet utters them in the Spirit. What does he say? O you who have mounted fifteen steps to the top, who have done this and this, you who bless the Lord, who during the hours of night lift up your hands toward the sanctuary and bless the Lord, receive your reward. May the Lord bless you from Sion. What you have given, receive back. You have given alms, you have performed virtuous deeds; from God you shall obtain a reward and a blessing. 'May the Lord bless you from Sion,' from Sion: from the heavenly Jerusalem; in the mother of the first born,[32] where the joys of the future are; where the archangels are; where the rest of the heavenly powers are; where the apostles, the prophets, the saints, the martyrs are; where throngs of angels and saints follow the Lamb wherever He goes.

John, too, beheld the holy city coming down out of heaven, built upon foundations of precious stones and having twelve gates.[33] The city itself was pure gold; it had golden walls, and it had streets made of all kinds of precious stones. In this city, Christ reigns; in this city, the inhabitants themselves are both dwellers and gates, both houses and dwellers. Would you know how they are houses? Christ dwells in them; Christ moves about in them. 'I will dwell,' He says, 'and move

---

31 Sirach (Ecclus.) 3.29.
32 Cf. Heb. 12.23.
33 Cf. Apoc. 21.10-21.

among them.'³⁴ Think of the saintly soul, how ineffable it
is; it holds Christ whom heaven is not large enough to contain! See what He says? 'I will dwell,' He says. It is possible,
moreover, for Him to dwell within a narrow space: 'I will
dwell, and move among them.' Wherever He moves about,
certainly it is a spacious house in which He walks. 'You are
the temple of God,' He says, 'and the Holy Spirit dwells in
you.'³⁵ Let us make ready our temple, that Christ may come
and take up His abode in us, that our soul may be Sion, that
it may be a watchtower, that it may be set up upon the heights,
that it may be ever up, never down. We read in Zacharia the
prophet: 'the angel who spoke in me, said to me.'³⁶ If the
angel spoke in the prophet, does not He who dwells in us
possess us much more intimately as dwelling places and as
companions with whom to hold deep converse?

'May the Lord bless you from Sion, the maker of heaven
and earth': if you are a saint, 'the maker of heaven'; if a sinner, 'the maker of earth.' He made both heaven and earth.
For the present, let us stay with the literal sense. The prophet
uttered this verse to discriminate between idols and the true
God. Let the gods who did not make heaven and earth, he
said, perish from the earth, 'but the Lord made the heavens.'³⁷
So much for the literal interpretation; now for the spiritual.
Just as it is said to the sinner: 'Dust you are, and unto dust
you shall return,'³⁸ so, likewise, to the saint: heaven you are,
and unto heaven you shall return. Why have I stressed all
this? To prove that saints are heaven. 'The heavens declare
the glory of God, and the firmament proclaims his handiwork.'³⁹ 'You waters above the heavens, let them praise the
name of the Lord.'⁴⁰ 'Heaven is the heaven of the Lord.'⁴¹

---

34 2 Cor. 6.16.
35 Cf. 1 Cor. 3.16; cf. *Against Jovinian* 2.19, PL 23.328 (356).
36 Cf. Zach. 1.9.
37 Ps. 95.5.
38 Gen. 3.19.
39 Ps. 18.2.
40 Ps. 148.4, 5.
41 Ps. 113B.16.

'The maker of heaven and earth.' Granted we are earthly, granted we move about on earth, nevertheless, our residence is in heaven;[42] there we have our citizenship. 'The maker of heaven and earth.' Even though you are a sinner, do not be discouraged; the Lord is all powerful. Many of earth have become heaven, and many of heaven have become earth. Unhappy Judas was heaven, and he became earth. Paul the Apostle was earth when he was persecuting the Church; he confessed and became heaven. It behooves one who is of heaven not to feel secure, nor ought he who is of earth lose hope of life.

When Jacob was in flight from his brother, in Mesopotamia he came to Luza, and there to rest, Scripture says, he placed a stone under his head.[43] The stone under his head was Christ. Never before had he put a stone under his head, only at the time when he was escaping from his persecutor. When he was in his father's house, and as long as he was in his father's house and enjoyed the comforts of the flesh, he had no stone at his head. He departed from his home, poor and alone; he left with only a staff, and immediately that very night he found a stone and placed it at his head. Because he had a pillow of that kind upon which to rest his head, think of the vision he saw. 'He dreamed that a ladder was set up on the ground with its top reaching to heaven; angels were ascending and descending on it.'[44] He saw angels descend from heaven to earth and others ascend from earth to heaven. Would you know that the stone at Jacob's head was Christ, the cornerstone? 'The stone which the builders rejected has become the cornerstone.'[45] That is the stone that is called Abenezer in the Book of Kings. That stone is Christ. The name Abenezer, moreover, means 'the Stone of Help.'[46] 'Jacob woke

---

42 Cf. Phil. 3.20; cf. Letter 14.3, PL 22.348 (30); 16, PL 22.359 (43); 60.3, PL 22.591 (333).
43 Cf. Gen. 28.11; cf. Letter 123.15, PL 22.1056 (912).
44 Cf. Gen. 28.12; cf. Letter 118.7, PL 22.966 (798).
45 Ps. 117.22.
46 1 Kings 4.1; 7.12; cf. Letter 78.11, PL 22.706 (477).

from his sleep,'[47] Scripture says, and what did he say? 'This is the house of God.' What did he do? 'He poured oil over the stone.' Unless we penetrate the spiritual mystery of Holy Writ, what reason is there that he should anoint the stone?

---

47 Cf. Gen. 28.16-22.

HOMILY 47

ON PSALM 135 (136)

IVE THANKS to the Lord, for he is good.'[1] Despite these words, heretics maintain that there is no repentance, but the prophet urges us to confess our sins, for God is good. Blessed, therefore, is he who acknowledges that he is a sinner just as the Apostle does: 'I am not worthy to be called an apostle, because I persecuted the Church of God.'[2] If the Apostle makes such a confession, how much more should the sinner? Scripture says, moreover: 'The just man accuses himself when he begins to speak.'[3] If the just man is prompt to accuse himself, how much more should the sinner be?

'Give thanks to the God of Gods.' The prophet is referring to those gods of whom it is written: 'I said: You are gods';[4] and again: 'God arises in the divine assembly.'[5] They who cease to be mere men, abandon the ways of vice and are become perfect, are gods and sons of the Most High.

'Give thanks to the Lord of lords.' This refers to the Son, and 'God of gods,' to the Father. We give thanks, therefore, to the Father and to the Son, for the Father is in the Son and the Son in the Father.

'Who alone does great wonders.' First the prophet said, give thanks to the God of gods; and then to the Lord of lords; now, because he mentioned two persons, he says: 'Who alone

---

1 Cf. *Commentarioli in ps.* 135.1.
2 1 Cor. 15.9.
3 Cf. Prov. 18.17; cf. *Against the Pelagians* 1.13, PL 23.527 (705).
4 Ps. 81.6.
5 Ps. 81.1; cf. Letter 22.4, PL 22.397 (91).

does great wonders,' in order to offset any misconception of
two gods. It is written, moreover: 'Only one God from whom
all things; and one Lord Jesus, through whom are all things,
and we through him!'[6]

'Who made the heavens in wisdom.' These are the heavens
that declare the glory of God,[7] that are clothed in the image
of the heavenly, not in the image of the earthly.[8] In wisdom,
'in intellectu,' in 'Christ, the power of God and the wisdom
of God':[9] so wisdom actually declares in the Book of Proverbs:
'When he established the heavens I was there.'[10]

'Who established the earth upon the waters.'[11] Even though
earth is said to rest upon the waters—is poised upon the seas—
nevertheless, He established and cònfirmed our earth in baptism. The psalmist did not say that He raised up or exalted
our earth, or that He caused it to ascend into heaven. Baptism remits sin, and, as it were, releases the soul from prison;
it cannot, however, bestow the kingdom of heaven,[12] for if
one does not enter through faith and good works, he cannot be
sure of salvation.

'Who made the great lights.' If we follow the letter, the
psalmist is speaking of the stars. Although they appear to
us small, nevertheless, they are of great magnitude. If, for
example, we should ascend a high mountain and gaze down
upon a man in the valley below, he would look like a tiny
speck and be indistinguishable; so, likewise, the stars are
mighty, but from their altitude, they seem little to us. The
same star that is seen in Britain is visible everywhere else
in the world. This versicle, by the way, is directed to those
to whom the Lord said: 'You are the light of the world.'[13]

'Who split the Red Sea in twain.' The Hebrews claim that

---

6 Cf. 1 Cor. 8.6.
7 Cf. Ps. 18.2.
8 Cf. 1 Cor. 15.49.
9 Cf. 1 Cor. 1.24; cf. Letter 53.4, PL 22.543 (274).
10 Prov. 8.27.
11 Cf. Ps. 135 (136).6.
12 Cf. *Against the Pelagians* 1.22, PL 23.539 (719); 3.1, PL 23.596 (781).
13 Matt. 5.14.

the Red Sea was divided into twelve parts; that would be one for each tribe. It is said to be red, moreover, from blood.

'But swept Pharao and his army into the Red Sea.' Well said, 'swept,' for He swept off Pharao's sins, but Pharao did not repent; and on that account he died. With similar import He says to Jerusalem: 'Shake off the dust.'[14]

'Who smote great kings.' First, He smote Pharao, who is a symbol of the devil, and in like manner, struck his army.

'Who remembered us in our abjection.' The psalmist did not say that He was mindful of us in our wisdom, in our wealth, in our learning, but that He remembered us in our humility. Granted those are excellent sources of power; nevertheless, unless one has humility, he is not acceptable to God. 'God resists the proud, but gives grace to the humble.'[15]

'And he redeemed us from our foes.'[16] He did not say, He set us free, but He redeemed us—with His blood, of course.

'Who gives food to all flesh.' Consider with me the elephant, the camel, the cow, the stag—and these are great quadrupeds —how every single one of them has a face with eyes, nose, a mouth, and also, feet. Then, on the other hand, ponder over the tiny creatures, like the fly, the ant, the flea; and in these minute beings, consider their eyes, their nose, their mouth, their feet, and how like they are to the greater animals; and in your meditation give glory to God, for He it is who gives food to all of them. Or we may guide our reflections by the text: 'I will remove the stony heart, and replace it with a natural heart';[17] a yielding heart with which to submit to the law of God;[18] for unless one bends his stiff neck he cannot receive the food and the bread that came down from heaven; he cannot pray: ' "Give us this day our daily bread,"[19] the bread that is of Your substance.' The Hebrew Gospel ac-

---

14 Isa. 52.2.
15 James 4.6.
16 Cf. Ps. 135 (136).24.
17 Cf. Ezech. 11.19.
18 Cf. *Commentary on Ezechiel* 11.17-22, PL 25.100 (111).
19 Matt. 6.11; cf. *Commentary on Matthew* 6.11, PL 26.44 (34).

cording to Matthew reads: 'Give us this day tomorrow's bread,' in other words, the Bread that You will give us in Your kingdom, give us this day.

HOMILY 48

ON PSALM 136 (137)

BY THE STREAMS of Babylon we sat and wept when we remembered Sion.' If one has never been sick, he does not appreciate the value of health.[1] The cripple does not know the strength of feet that are sound; the blind man does not realize the power of vision. This is all by way of introduction, for the psalm says that we sat down by the streams of Babylon and wept when we remembered Sion. The meaning of Babylon is confusion; hence, Babylon is a figure of this world. It is the sinner, therefore, that fell from Paradise and entered the valley of tears, the Babylon of this world—rather, it is the prophet in the person of the fallen— who says: 'By the streams of Babylon,' the streams, I say, of Babylon. When you see someone who has been very beautiful lose his beauty in sickness, and his bloom and vigor wither and decay, he is passing away just like the river with the ebb and flow of its waters, as new waters rise again and again, and in their turn vanish. It is the same with this world, because only for the moment or the hour are we rich or strong or beautiful, and after a short while all vanishes as the waters of the stream that flow away and are gone. So there we sat and wept because we remembered Sion. Even though we have fallen from Paradise through our own fault, nevertheless, we are mindful of our former happiness; we never forget it. In point, here is the parable of the man who was coming down from Jerusalem to Jericho,[2] Jericho that signi-

---

1 Cf. Letter 66.1, PL 22.639 (393); 122.1, PL 22.1039-40 (891).
2 Luke 10.30-37.

fies 'moon or the ever-changing'—which, moreover, is understood to mean this world—and fell in with robbers, and a Samaritan took him and healed him with oil and wine, mingling mercy with austerity.

'On the aspens of that land we hung up our harps.' The aspen is by nature unproductive, and they say that if anyone drinks a potion made from the flower of this tree, or eats of it, he will become sterile.[3] Well, that is where we hung up our harps. Now the body of man is a harp. Just as the shepherd's pipe is composed of many reeds but sends forth one harmonious tune, even so, we have our own musical instrument on which to play, and by means of it, through works, we offer a tune, a song, a hymn to God. By analogy, too, through our sense of hearing, through smell, taste, sight, and through all our faculties, we offer a hymn and a song to the Lord as from a single instrument. They tell us, in addition, that the aspen does not have roots; that if a branch is broken off and planted near water, it begins to grow green at once. So, too, the sinner, granted that he has sinned, granted that he has fallen, nevertheless, if he is near water, that is, if he reads the Sacred Scriptures and listens to the divine word from a holy man, his soul revives and he is converted unto repentance.

'Though there our captors asked of us the lyrics of our songs.' The evil spirits that deceived us and led us into captivity, now make sport of us as they hiss in mockery: 'Pledge to us your word of faith, and do it just as you used to sing a song to God when you were in Jerusalem.'

'How could we sing a song of the Lord in a foreign land?' This is the answer of those who had been trapped into sin, and they demand: How shall we sing the Lord's song in a foreign land, we who are fixed in sins, who have fallen from Jerusalem into Babylon? One cannot praise the Lord if he

---

3 Cf. *Commentary on Zacharia* 14.16, PL 25.1537 (932); *on Isaia* 15.3-9, PL 24.233 (268); 44.1-6, PL 24.435 (525); cf. *Commentarioli in ps.* 136.2.

is unfaithful, for it behooves the sinner to lament his sins, not sing to the Lord.

'If I forget you, Jerusalem, may my right hand be forgotten!' It is because he has sinned and fallen that he remembers Jerusalem and his former life, and he resolves: 'If I ever forget you and think no more of you, may the power of my right hand—my works—perish.' Notice that the prophet did not say left hand but right, for we do not work with the left. Do you want to be always in the memory of the Lord? Do the works of the right hand.

'May my tongue cleave to my palate if I remember you not'; may I lose completely the faculty of speech and power of action if the memory of You is not ever present in my heart.

'Remember, O Lord, against the children of Edom, the day of Jerusalem.' The name Edom means earthly and bloody. Who, therefore, is Edom if not the devil? Mark what it says. It is Adam who is speaking: Lord, remember how the devil-serpent deceived me and drew me—the devil-serpent recognized in Nabuchodonosor—and thrust me out of Paradise? Remember, O Lord, and pay him back; let him feel the punishment that in his malice he has brought upon me, drawing and dragging me into Babylon and into the midst of the Assyrians.

'O daughter of Babylon, you miserable one.'[4] The daughter of Babylon is the soul that is ever restless, always in confusion, never settled; full of imperfection and sin, it is truly miserable. 'Happy the man who shall repay you the evil you have done us!' Happy the man who will repay her measure for measure: she drove me out of the Garden of Paradise; through abstinence I lead her back to that very place; she ensnared me into fornication; through chastity I lead her back into Jerusalem; from vice, back into virtue. I do not treat her as an enemy; I treat her as a friend.

'Happy the man who shall seize and smash your little ones against the rock!' The 'little ones' are evil thoughts. I saw

---

4 Cf. Ps. 136 (137).8; cf. *Commentarioli in ps.* 136.8.

a woman, for instance; I was filled with desire for her. If I do not at once cut off that sinful desire and take hold of it, as it were, by the foot and dash it against a rock until sensual passion abates, it will be too late afterwards when the smoldering fire has burst into flame. Happy the man who puts the knife instantly to sinful passion and smashes it against a rock! Now the Rock is Christ.[5]

5 Cf. 1 Cor. 10.4; cf. Letter 22.6, PL 22.398 (92).

HOMILY 49

ON PSALM 137 (138)

I WILL CONFESS to you, Lord, with all my heart.'[1] The nature of a wound determines the medication to be applied. Just as the body has wounds of various kinds, so also the soul has its passions and its wounds, and we must do penance in proportion to the nature of our sin. If a man makes confession of all his sins, he is acknowledging his sins to the Lord wholeheartedly. If, for example, someone has committed fornication and he confesses only that and is avaricious, or irascible, or a slanderer, or blasphemer, and is full of faults and vices, his confession is not sincere. The man who repents for all the sins and passions of his soul is the man who is able to say: I confess and give thanks to You, O Lord, with all my heart. 'For you have heard the words of my mouth.'[2] This verse is not found in the Hebrew text. Nonetheless, what it means is: In my confession I have poured out my whole heart, O Lord; I have confessed all my sins and faults, for I have not admitted merely one sin to You, and You have listened to me graciously.

'In the presence of the angels I will sing your praise.' Just think of the promotion of that penitent! After confession and repentance, he merits to sing with the angels! He who sings is no longer doing penance but is giving thanks and benediction. 'I will worship at your holy temple.' If that is the temple that we now see desolate at which one must worship, then, for the Jews worship is over, for that temple

---

1 Cf. Ps. 137 (138).1.
2 *Ibid.*

361

has been destroyed. No, the psalmist's temple is the holy
and heavenly Jerusalem.

'Because of your kindness and your truth.' May the sinner
heed the word, 'kindness,' but may the just man, and the
proud man hear the word, 'truth.'

'You will build up strength within me';[3] my soul, burdened
with its many troubles, You will fill with courage.

'All the kings of the earth shall give thanks to you, O Lord.'
The kings of the earth are those who reign over sin; consequently, they who govern sin shall give thanks. The prophet
is certainly not referring to the kings of this world, for it is
written: 'The king's heart is in the hand of the Lord.'[4] Do
you for one moment suppose that the heart of Julian the
Apostate was in the hand of God? God forbid! Or of Nero or
of Maximianus and Decius, the persecutors? God forbid! No,
he is speaking of those who have control over sin, who, because their heart is in the hand of God, have conquered the
vices and passions of their soul and thereby prevail over sin.
'When they hear the words of your mouth,' when they keep
and safeguard your commandments.

'They shall sing in the ways of the Lord.'[5] The philosophers
of this generation did not sing in the ways of the Lord, but
we sing in the ways of the Lord, for we sing in the way of
Moses and Isaia and Jeremia, and from their paths, we
arrive at the way that says: 'I am the way.'[6]

---

3 Cf. Ps. 137 (138).3.
4 Cf. Prov. 21.1.
5 Cf. Ps. 137 (138).5.
6 John 14.6.

HOMILY 50

ON PSALM 139 (140)

ELIVER ME, O Lord, from the evil men.' In no way does the devil succeed so well in deceiving us as he does through the agency of men; it is from treachery of this kind that the prophet prays for deliverance.

'Who devise evil in their hearts.' He is warning us against heretics.

'The venom of asps is under their lips,' for their words, friendly enough on the surface, are full of deadly poison.

'By the wayside they have laid snares for me'; they have tried to set a trap for me in Holy Scripture by adducing proof more apparent than real.

'I say to the Lord, you are my God.' These are words that only a saint may claim, a man who is not dominated by sin, a man who bears witness that 'my portion is the Lord.'[1]

'Give me not up, O Lord, to the wicked from my desire.'[2] Scripture affirms: 'that anyone who even looks with lust at a woman has already committed adultery with her in his heart';[3] hence, the prophet prays: Deliver me not, O Lord, to the devil through lust of mine, but judge me well by my deeds, not by my desires.

'Those who surround me lift up their heads; may the mischief which they threaten overwhelm them.'[4] Just as a serpent that sees someone coming to strike it instinctively makes a coil

---

1 Lam. 3.24.
2 Cf. Ps. 139 (140).9.
3 Matt. 5.28.
4 Cf. *Commentarioli in ps.* 139.10.

363

of its entire body to conceal and protect its head,[5] even so these heretics hide themselves in the winding utterances of Aristotle and the other philosophers and so shield and defend themselves. The man of the Church, however, with the cross as a staff unwinds the coil, discloses the head hidden within its recesses, and there strikes at it. In other words, he draws proof from the Sacred Scriptures and disseminates it.

'The upright shall dwell in your presence.' What is the presence of God if not Christ, 'who did not consider being equal to God a thing to be clung to'?[6]

---

5 Cf. *Commentary on Matthew* 10.17, PL 26.66 (60).
6 Cf. Phil. 2.6.

HOMILY 51

ON PSALM 140 (141)

LORD, TO YOU I call; hearken to me.'[1] Moses was standing his ground in the midst of his people, and Pharao, marching in pursuit, was almost upon him; on all sides he was straitened. It was then that he cried out to God and instantly God said to him: 'Why are you crying out to me?'[2] All the while that Moses was praying in silence, God was hearing him. Scripture, however, does not record what he said, only that he cried. The blood of martyrs, too, constantly cries out to the Lord and He listens graciously. The Lord declared to Cain: 'The voice of your brother's blood cries to me';[3] and in the Apocalypse of John, the souls of the just that were under the altar were crying to the Lord: 'How long, O Lord, dost thou refrain from avenging our blood?'[4] Let us not fail in passing to consider that the souls of the just are an altar to the Lord. 'Hearken to my voice when I call upon you.' Take note, O Lord, of what I am asking of You. I am not begging for carnal pleasure, nor for gold, nor for the things of this world, but I am pleading for mercy; wherefore the prophet says: Hearken, do not let my plea go unheard; I am not asking anything amiss.

'Let my prayer come like incense before you.' May my prayer rise up to You directly; there is nothing in it that is mean, nothing malicious, nothing that is the work of the devil. Incense, moreover, represents the prayers of the saints.

1 Cf. Ps. 140 (141).1.
2 Cf. Exod. 14.15.
3 Gen. 4.10.
4 Cf. Apoc. 6.10; cf. *Against Vigilantius* 6, PL 23.359 (392).

We know this from the Apocalypse where the twenty-four elders were holding vessels of incense and saying: 'These are the prayers of the saints.'[5] 'The lifting up of my hands, like the evening sacrifice.' Lifting up of the hands draws attention to the Lord, and in the elevation we behold the Creator. Notice, however, that the prophet did not say 'the extension of my hands.' Extension is not the same as elevation; it is, in fact, quite the opposite—stretching forth of one's hands to the back or to the sides, to sins or imperfections, even as the Lord says: 'When you spread out your hands, I close my eyes to you.'[6] 'Like the evening sacrifice,' of the eleventh hour, means that I lift up my hands in the New Testament. The Apostle says, furthermore: 'Lift up your hands in prayer.'[7] Then, there is Moses; when he lifted up his hands, Jesus was winning; when he put them down, Jesus was losing. If I interpret Holy Writ in its historical, or literal, sense, Moses has his hands down; if, however, I understand the Scriptures spiritually, Moses has his hands on high.

'O Lord, set a watch before my mouth.' 'Death and life are in the power of the tongue';[8] and again: 'I tell you, that of every idle word men speak, they shall give account on the day of judgment.'[9] The prophet prays, therefore, that his words may not be vain, but holy and pleasing to God. 'A guard at the door of my lips.' He is asking for a guard round about his lips like the rampart of a castle, that he may never capitulate to sin. It is Jeremia who says: 'Death has come up through our windows.'[10] We have, moreover, five windows: sight, hearing, taste, smell, and touch. If I look at a woman to lust after her, I have already committed adultery in my heart, and death has come through my window of sight. If the sound of the harp or the organ or the pipe enervates me,

---

5 Cf. Apoc. 5.8.
6 Cf. Isa. 1.15.
7 Cf. 1 Tim. 2.8.
8 Prov. 18.21.
9 Matt. 12.36.
10 Jer. 9.20; cf. Letter 22.26-7, PL 22.412 (110); *Against Jovinian* 2.8, PL 23.310 (337).

death has entered my soul through the sense of hearing.
Again, if I touch something soft and supple, and wantonness
breaks down the resistance of my flesh, death has entered
through touch, and so on down the line. The prophet prays
earnestly, therefore, that a sentry be placed around all his
senses, that his whole household be fortified against the in-
vasion and conquest of his adversary the devil. St. Peter
writes: 'Our adversary the devil, as a roaring lion, goes about
seeking someone to devour.'[11] Not ordinarily does the devil
make his attack through grave faults but through slight ones,
that in some way or other he may gain admittance, win his
victory, and ultimately impel his man to greater vices. Not
through fornication or avarice, but through lesser sins, he
secures an entrance.

'Let not my heart incline to evil words, to make excuses in
sins.'[12] O unhappy race of men! We seek excuse for sin by
saying, 'Nature got the better of me,' and all the while it has
been in our power to sin or not to sin. We are always justi-
fying ourselves and saying: I did not want to sin, but lust
overwhelmed me; that woman came to me; she herself made
the advances; she touched me; she said this or that to me,
she called me; and while we ought to be doing penance and
crying, 'Lord, I have sinned,' we excuse ourselves instead,
and yoke sin to sin. We all have the same kind of body,
but with our own particular difficulties. 'God is not a respecter of persons.'[13] Would you know that we have the same
bodies as the saints? Paul the Apostle says: 'I see another
law in my members, warring against the law of my mind and
making me prisoner to the law of sin that is in my members';[14]
and again: 'But I chastise my body and bring it into subjection, lest perhaps after preaching to others I myself should
be rejected.'[15] Later, he says: 'Unhappy man that I am! Who

---

11 Cf. 1 Peter 5.8; cf. Letter 14.4, PL 22.349 (31); 22.4, PL 22.396 (90).
12 Cf. Ps. 140 (141).4; cf. Letter 55.3, PL 22.562 (297).
13 Acts 10.34.
14 Rom. 7.23.
15 1 Cor. 9.27; cf. Letter 125.7, PL 22.1076 (937).

will deliver me from the body of this death?'[16] We all have our own struggles, therefore, and it is in proportion to his struggles that each one receives his reward.

'With men who are evildoers.' The general understanding of these words is,[17] incline not my heart to men that are evildoers: 'I will not communicate with the choicest of them.'[18] Just as the Lord has His chosen saints, so does the devil have his elect. Think of the chief heretics and you will have no doubt about his chosen band. If the prophet had said 'the choicest' without the determinant 'of them,' there would be reason for doubt; as it is, he is excluding the elect of God. 'I will communicate' has two interpretations: I may either be in agreement, or I become a second member, and, therefore, unclean. You know, surely, that Scripture calls the number two unclean. The Apostle says: 'That of both, that is, of the two men, he might create one new man':[19] two men, the interior and the exterior; in other words, remake a base man into a holy one. Remember, also, Noe took into the ark with him seven clean animals, but of the unclean animals, two.[20]

'The just man shall correct me; that is kindness; and shall reprove me.'[21] 'Whom the Lord loves, he chastises; and he scourges every son whom he receives.'[22] Happy the man who is chastised in this life, for: 'the Lord will not ‚punish twice for the same thing.'[23] Mighty is the wrath of the Lord when He is not angry with us here, for, then, He reserves us like a calf for slaughter. In fact, He says to Jerusalem: 'Many are your sins and many your iniquities, but I will not be

---

16 Rom. 7.24; cf. Letter 22.5, PL 22.397 (91).
17 Cf. *Commentary on Matthew* 5.22, PL 26.38 (27).
18 Cf. Ps. 140 (141).4.
19 Cf. Eph. 2.15.
20 Cf. Gen. 7.2; cf. Letter 22.19, PL 22.406 (103); 48.19, PL 22.509 (231-32); 123.12, PL 22.1054 (909).
21 Cf. Ps. 140 (141).5; cf. Letter 125.19, PL 22.1084 (946).
22 Heb. 12.6; cf. Letter 68.1, PL 22.652 (410).
23 Cf. Nah. 1.9, LXX; cf. *ibid.*

vexed with you.'[24] In other words, when you were only an
adulteress, I loved you with a jealous love; but when you
had many lovers, I despised you, and I will not be vexed with
you. In this same way, a man is jealous of his wife when
he loves her; but if he is not jealous, he hates her and does
not imitate the words of Him who says: 'I will punish their
crime with a rod,'[25] but, 'I will not punish your daughters for
their harlotry.'[26]

'The just man shall correct me; that is kindness; and shall
reprove me.' Consider in this connection any teacher or
father or doctor. If a physician should notice infected and
decayed tissue in a body and say, 'What concern is that of
mine?' you would conclude rightly that he is cruel; but if
he should excise the infected tissues and cauterize the wound,
he is compassionate, for he is saving the life of a man. Likewise, a teacher, if he dismisses a lad and does not exact
obedience from him, hates him; if, on the other hand, he
disciplines him and the remedy cures him, his apparent
severity turns out to be clemency. Achab, too, was censured
by the Lord when he killed Naboth and took his vineyard
and spilled just blood. Elias, the prophet, was sent to him
to say: 'Thou hast slain. Moreover also thou hast taken possession.'[27] Immediately his conscience smote and tormented
him; he bowed his head and walked with eyes downcast; and
this is an impious king robed in purple. Afterwards, Scripture says, he went about wearing haircloth under his royal
attire, and God seeing him said: 'Because Achab hath humbled
himself for my sake, I will not bring evil against him.'[28] Just
realize the power of haircloth, and of fasting, and how much
blood is washed away by humble tears! This, then, is the
proper way to wear haircloth and the proper way to fast,
that no one may observe it. 'Shall correct' may be under-

24 Cf. Ezech. 16.42; cf. *ibid.*
25 Ps. 88.33.
26 Osee 4.14.
27 3 Kings 21.19.
28 Cf. 3 Kings 21.29; cf. Letter 147.9, PL 22.1202 (1093).

stood in two different ways: either he will rebuke or he will instruct.

'Let not the oil of the sinner fatten my head.'[29] 'O my people, they who call you blessed, mislead you.'[30] The praise of heretics, the balm with which they anoint the heads of men and promise them the kingdom of heaven,[31] fattens the head with pride. In Scripture, moreover, anything fat is reprehensible, as it says: 'So Jacob ate his fill, the darling grew fat and frisky; he became fat and gross and gorged.'[32] The manna of the angels, on the other hand, is refined and delicate.

'For my prayer will still be against the things with which they are well pleased.'[33] This means: They, indeed, raged in their madness; but I continued to pray for their conversion. 'Their judges driven against the rock were swallowed up,'[34] just as another passage in Scripture says: 'Happy the man who shall seize and smash your little ones against the rock!'[35] 'But the rock was Christ.'[36] 'The little ones' are trifling thoughts before they grow into ones of serious consequences. Even heretics, although they seem to despise the simplicity of the Church, as compared to Aristotle and Plato; when they turn to the Scriptures, are swallowed up immediately by the Rock, that is, by Christ, and are converted to Him. 'Swallowed up' stands for victory, as the Apostle says: 'Death is swallowed up in victory! O death, where is thy victory? O death, where is thy sting?'[37] He calls this swallowing up, victory, the victory that is his in engulfing death.

---

29 Cf. Ps. 140 (141).5.
30 Cf. Isa. 3.12; cf. Letter 125.19, PL 22.1084 (947); *Against the Pelagians* 2.24, PL 23.589 (773); 3.16, PL 23.614 (801).
31 Cf. *Commentary on Aggai* 1.11, PL 25.1398 (749); *on Ecclesiastes* 9.8, PL 23.1140 (463).
32 Cf. Deut. 32.15.
33 Cf. Ps. 140 (141).5.
34 Cf. Ps. 140 (141).6.
35 Ps. 136.9; cf. Letter 22.6, PL 22.398 (92); 130.8, PL 22.1114 (985).
36 1 Cor. 10.4; cf. Letter 22.6, PL 22.398 (92).
37 1 Cor. 15.54, 55; cf. *Against John of Jerusalem* 36, PL 23.406 (446); Letter 124.5, PL 22.1064 (921).

'They heard how powerful were my words.'[38] The Lord Himself says: They who came to Me were won over, and they delighted in My words and were converted to Me in My Church. 'As when a clod of earth.'[39] Anything thick and gross is but one degree from earth, and the soul that sins is clinging to earth. From the beginning, the Lord made everything fine and delicate; everyone is coarsened, therefore, by his own vice and is reduced to earth. A wound in the body, for example, is swollen and hard and full of pus, but when the doctor lances it, the swelling goes down, it heals, and the body is restored to its former condition, as it was when first created; hence, the prophet says: 'As when a clod of earth is broken up upon the ground.'

'So our bones are strewn by the edge of the nether world';[40] and in the twenty-first psalm the Savior says: 'all my bones are scattered.'[41] A literal explanation of this does not square with history since Christ was crucified only, but when you see Arius and Eunomius outside the Church, realize that the bones of the Lord are strewn by the edge of the nether world. Bone, because it is strong, typifies the greater and promising men who are seduced by the loquacity, philosophy, and contentions of heretics.

'Keep me from the trap they have set for me.' Heretics or demons are forever setting traps for us. Vice is certainly the next door neighbor to virtue.[42] A trap is set for me in almsgiving if I stretch out my hand in order to be seen by men and, while appearing to do a good work, I fall into imperfection and sin. If I give away an undergarment to a brother for the benefit of those who are looking on, a demon has laid a snare for me. Nets are stretched and traps are set wherever the hunter discovers tracks of the deer. The deer, by the way,

---

38 Cf. Ps. 140 (141).6.
39 Cf. Ps. 140 (141).7; cf. *Commentarioli in ps.* 140.7.
40 Cf. Ps. 140 (141).7.
41 Cf. Ps. 21.15.
42 Cf. *Against the Luciferians* 15, PL 23.178 (188); *Against the Pelagians* 3.11, PL 23.608 (794).

symbolizes the saints, for the deer is a noble animal, has great antlers and kills serpents; hence, another psalm says: 'Who made my feet swift as those of hinds.'[43] They say that deer, by the breath of their nostrils, have the power to draw forth serpents from their coverts and feed upon them.[44] These same serpents—I mean the demons—place snares for us, therefore, in the very path in which we are striving to walk, that is, in the virtues, in almsgiving, that we may perform these acts to be seen by men and win their vain applause, in fasts, in prayer, in haircloth that we may show off ourselves. The man who wears haircloth ought to be lamenting his sins and not pluming himself in the sight of others. 'From the snares of evildoers': that I may not commit offense.

'Let all the wicked fall into his net.'[45] In the previous verse, the prophet said: 'Keep me from the trap they have set for me,' alluding to the snares of many; now, however, he is referring solely to the trap of one: 'Let all the wicked fall into his net.' Even as the Lord lets down the net and catches a great multitude of fish, and has His apostles as fishermen gather and bring to Him those who through them have faith in Him; so, too, the devil has demons who are subject to him, and who ensnare men and lead them to him. 'I am alone until I go over.'[46] Jeremia says: 'I sat alone because you filled me with indignation,'[47] meaning, I was full of contrition. Alone: clean, not the unclean second number. Moses says: 'I must go over to look at this remarkable sight.'[48] If he does not go over, that is, if he does not escape all vice, he cannot behold the great marvel. Remarkable, indeed, was that sight, for the bush was ablaze, yet did not burn; the thorns were

43 Ps. 17.34.
44 Cf. *Commentary on Jeremia* 14.5, PL 24.770 (938); Letter 130.8, PL 22.1114 (985).
45 Cf. Ps. 140 (141).10; cf. *Commentarioli in ps.* 140.10.
46 Cf. Ps. 140 (141).10.
47 Cf. Jer. 15.17.
48 Cf. Exod. 3.3.

burning, but the thorns were sins. Isaia was cleansed at this fire, for that was the coal that was on the altar and that touched his lips. The prophet David, too, remembered this coal: 'Sharp arrows of the mighty, with fiery coals that lay waste.'[49] This is the coal that lays waste; it desolates and purifies.

---

49 Cf. Ps. 119.4; cf. *Against the Pelagians* 3.14, PL 23.612 (799).

HOMILY 52

ON PSALM 141 (142)

F UNDERSTANDING for David. A prayer when he was in the cave.'[1] The title of this psalm agrees with history and refers to the time when David fled Saul into the wilderness of Engaddi and hid himself in a cave. Saul, unaware of David's hiding place, also entered the cave in order to take care of his needs, I presume,[2] but, because the words: 'Of understanding for David' are part of the superscription, it is necessary to take into consideration, also, the spiritual significance of the psalm. Accordingly, this psalm of David is accepted for certain in the name of the Lord; Saul appears as the devil and the cave becomes this world. The devil, furthermore, does not discharge any good into this world, but only dung and corruption. Then, too, the cave symbolizes this world because its light is very imperfect when compared to the light of the future world, albeit the Lord, on coming into this world as light, brightens it up considerably. That is why the Apostle, in relation to the Father, speaks of Him 'who is the brightness of his glory.'[3] Now just as David entered the cave in his flight from Saul, the Lord, too, has come into this world and has suffered persecution.

'My complaint I pour out before him.' Without the least reserve the prophet cries: I pour out my whole heart to the Lord, like a man who shows his wound to the physician and tells him of all his sufferings so he may prescribe a remedy.

---

1 Cf. Ps. 141 (142).1.
2 1 Kings 24.4; cf. 1 Kings 22.1.
3 Cf. Heb. 1.3.

'Before him I lay bare my distress.' This is the kind of tribulation the Apostle welcomes, the tribulation that, when numbered with the others, works out hope; hope, moreover, does not disappoint.[4]

'When my spirit is faint within me.' If the evil spirit that strangled Saul does not withdraw from us, the Lord cannot watch over our paths. What are these paths of the just? Justice, good works, integrity, chastity, continency, and all the other kindred virtues.

'In the way along which I walk they have hid a trap for me.' Vices are next door neighbor to the virtues.[5] In whatever path a man is determined to walk, traps are set for him: in fasting, in almsgiving, or in any other good works.

'I look to the right to see, but there is no one who pays me heed.' If we construe the psalm in the name of the Lord, it is the Lord Himself who is saying: All My disciples abandoned Me and fled. One only remained, Peter who had promised: 'Even if I should have to die with thee, I will not deny thee,'[6] yet he is the one who denied his Lord. Because Peter repented, however, the Lord said: I look to the right to him, and did not say: I look to the left.

'I have lost all means of escape': when He was apprehended by the Jews. 'There is no one who cares for my life.' Indeed, they were all shouting: 'Crucify Him, crucify Him.'

'Attend to my cry, for I am brought low indeed.' Unless a man has been humbled, the Lord does not grant him gracious hearing. What avail for salvation are words of prayer when the man who utters them is stiff-necked with pride—if we really understand that the Lord says: 'Learn from me, for I am meek and humble of heart'?[7]

'Rescue me from my persecutors, for they are too strong for me.' They who fight against us have more strength than we. They are the chiefs of this world.

---

4 Cf. Rom. 5.3-5; cf. Letters 108.18, PL 22.894 (709).
5 Cf. Homily 51 on Ps. 140, p. 365.
6 Matt. 26.35; cf. Letter 42.2, PL 22.478 (192).
7 Matt. 11.29; cf. Letter 76.1, PL 22.689 (456).

'Lead me forth from prison, that I may give thanks to your name': from the prison of this body.[8] 'That I may give thanks': that I may glorify with praise, like the Lord's: 'I praise thee, Father.'[9] 'The just wait for me, until you reward me.'[10] The Lord is saying: The apostles wait for Me, until I shall rise again from the dead.

---

8 Cf. *Against John of Jerusalem* 7, PL 23.376 (413).
9 Matt. 11.25.
10 Cf. Ps. 141 (142).8.

HOMILY 53

ON PSALM 142 (143)

LORD, HEAR my prayer.' Modest words, full of humility and compassion. 'Hearken to my pleading in your truth.'[1] These are the words of a man who trusts. 'In your truth,' in Your Christ, of course: 'I am the way, and the truth, and the life.'[2] 'In your justice answer me.' Here, likewise, in Your Christ; I place no trust in myself, but I seek the mercy of Your truth and justice.

'Enter not into judgment with your servant.' How clearly the prophet reveals his trust in the loving kindness of Christ when he says: Do not summon Your servant to trial before You. Here, someone seems to be passing judgment in the presence of God and the prophet, in terms of the versicles in the fiftieth psalm: 'That you may be justified in your sentence, vindicated when you condemn.'[3] For no other reason does God enter into judgment but that He may punish justly. Thus Cyrus, the king of the Medes and the Persians, acted in the case of the king of the Armenians when his people violated the bonds of friendship. Cyrus conquered the king and took him prisoner, and at his trial had the Armenian's own kindred and wife and sons present to join in judgment to insure the fulfillment of justice either in punishment or acquittal.[4] 'For before you no living man is just.' 'The God of Abraham, and the God of Isaac, and the God of Jacob. Now he is not the

---

1 Cf. Ps. 142 (143).1.
2 John 14.6; cf. *Against Jovinian* 2.2, PL 23.296 (322).
3 Ps. 50.6.
4 Xenophon, *Cyropaedia* 3.1.

God of the dead, but of the living.'[5] Not even the patriarchs
are just in the sight of God; 'the stars are not clear in his
sight.'[6]

'For the enemy pursues me.' No need for clarification here;
anyone knows it is the devil. 'He has crushed my life to the
ground': formerly I had wings and I could fly; now, however,
the enemy has pursued and captured me, and has bound my
feet and hands. I am like a bird caught by a man, as good as
dead without the freedom of its wings. So, the psalmist says,
did the consciousness of my sins hold me captive.

'He has left me dwelling in the dark, like those long dead.'
Like those long dead, yet not actually dead. How so? Because
he is contrite of heart. If, however, anyone sins and does
not repent, then, he is long dead; he is not merely like those
dead, but is actually dead. That is what the enemy has taken
for granted is my condition: that I am not doing penance for
the sins that he prompted me to commit. 'My spirit is faint
within me.' 'First tell your sins that you may be acquitted';[7]
again: 'If you do penance for your sins, you shall live.'[8] 'My
heart within me is appalled,' because I know that I have
sinned.

'I remember the days of old.' I recall the days that are past
and how confident I was, but now for me it is all black night.

'I stretch out my hands to you.' Bound by the enemy,
there was nothing else I could do but repent of my sins and
lift my hands to You in supplication. 'My soul thirsts for
you like parched land.' Just as the earth becomes parched
with drought and craves the rain, even so my soul longs and
thirsts for You its God.

'Hasten to answer me, O Lord, for my spirit fails me.' My
soul is faint within me, my body has failed me; only my spirit
is left and it, too, is crushed. Come quickly to my assistance;

---

5 Cf. Luke 20.37, 38.
6 Job 25.5.
7 Cf. Isa. 43.26, LXX; cf. *Against the Pelagians* 1.13, PL 23.527 (705).
8 Cf. Ezech. 18.21.

Lord, have pity on me. 'Show me the way in which I should walk.' Show me Your Christ who said: 'I am the way.'[9]

'May your good spirit guide me on level ground.' Here, the impious Arians quote Scripture at us and say: ' "Good Master, what shall I do to gain eternal life?" But Jesus said to him: "Why dost thou call me good? No one is good but God only." '[10] If, therefore, the Son is not good but only the Father, the Father is greater than the Son. Very well. According to your own mode of thinking, impious Arian, who is greater, the Son or the Holy Spirit? Obviously, you say: The Son. But in this psalm, the Son is saying: May Your good Spirit guide me on level ground. If, therefore, as you say, the Spirit is good who is less, how much more is the Son good who is greater, namely, Christ? Now this is how the Gospel intends it: 'One of the Scribes coming up to test Him says, "Good Master." But Jesus says, "Why do you call me good, and yet do not acknowledge Me?" '[11] It is the same as one tempting his bishop whom he despises who says to him, 'Bishop'; and the Bishop answers, 'To you I am not the bishop; you may leave my presence.' Besides, have you not read in some other place in Holy Writ: 'The good shepherd lays down his life for his sheep'?[12] What more is this than the Son has done who was incarnated for our sake and suffered? Nine months He was in the womb of the Virgin, and descending from His majesty, He was slaughtered. He was in a cradle; He suffered Himself to grow and develop gradually at man's pace; to be beaten with rods, and struck with blows, and crucified. What more than this?

---

9 John 14.6.
10 Luke 18.18, 19; Mark 10.17, 18.
11 Cf. Luke 10.25; Matt. 22.35.
12 John 10.11; cf. *Commentary on Matthew* 19.17, PL 26.141-142 (148).

HOMILY 54

ON PSALM 143 (144)

VEN THOUGH we have preached at length on the Gospel, nevertheless, for the sake of those who do not know Latin, we must make a few comments on the psalter, that some may not go away starving while others are well satisfied. Since, moreover, the psalm is long and we would be here a whole day if we lingered over each verse, we ought to reflect briefly upon a few thoughts, rather than spend our time unfolding the meaning of words.

'Blessed be the Lord, my God, who trains my hands for battle.'[1] One who attempts a brief explanation of Holy Writ forfeits all grounds for praise; nevertheless, those who listen do retain something from the exposition. 'Blessed be the Lord, my God, who trains my hands for battle, my fingers for war.' Let us lift up our hands in prayer without distractions, without contentions,[2] and on every occasion, for when we raise our hands to God, our prayer is our weapon against the devil. 'Who trains my hands for battle, my fingers for war.' Prayer is our harp, prayer our cither; to its accompaniment, we sing our hymn to God.

'My mercy and my refuge, my stronghold, my deliverer, my protector.'[3] With such titles as these the psalmist addresses God whose names are as many as His kindnesses. 'Who subdues people under me.' These words may be uttered in the name of Christ with reference, of course, to His Incarnation;

---

1 Cf. Ps. 143 (144).1.
2 Cf. 1 Tim. 2.8.
3 Cf. Ps. 143 (144).2.

they may be said also by the apostles. In like manner, the
abbot in the monastery gives thanks to God and says: Blessed
be the Lord, my God, who subjects people to me, for they
are not subject to me, but to You; they obey me that they
may serve You.

'Lord, what is man, that you notice him; the son of man,
that you take thought of him?' This same reflection occurs in
the eighth psalm: 'What is man that you should be mindful
of him, or the son of man that you should care for him?'[4]
Lord, what is man that You notice him? The psalmist is
speaking here of the frailty of the body and of human weakness, and what does he say? If you consider his flesh, what is
man? If you consider his spirit, he is noble. Let us by no
means scorn the flesh,[5] but let us reject its works. Let us not
despise the body that will reign in heaven with Christ.
'Flesh and blood can obtain no part in the kingdom of God';[6]
no, not flesh and blood of themselves, but the works of the
flesh. 'Flesh and blood can obtain no part in the kingdom
of God.' How, then, are they going to reign together with
Christ; how shall we be seated together in heaven in Christ?[7]

'Lord, what is man, that you notice him; the son of man,
that you take thought of him?' The prophet is giving thanks
to God and this is the import of what he says. As far as man's
human estate is concerned, he is nothing. 'Vanity of vanities!
all things are vanity!' said Ecclesiastes.[8] If all things are
vanity, heaven, too, is vanity, and so are the angels. If
heaven and the angels are vanity, how much more vain is
man? If the angels are vanity, if heaven is vanity, why has
God fashioned vanity? Vanity, yes, in comparison to God,
but in itself, not vanity.[9] Lord, what is man that You notice
him, that You have deigned to notice him? Sublime happi-

---

4 Ps. 8.5.
5 Cf. *Commentary on Isaia* 52.2, 3, PL 24.497 (603).
6 1 Cor. 15.50; cf. *Against John of Jerusalem* 36, PL 23.406 (446).
7 Cf. Eph. 2.6.
8 Cf. Eccles. 1.2; cf. Letter 48.14, PL 22.503 (224).
9 Cf. *Commentary on Ecclesiastes* 1.2, PL 23.1065 (385).

ness of man, to know his Creator! That is the very distinction
that separates us from brutes and beasts—that we recognize
our Creator; brute beasts have no understanding. By the
very posture and constitution of his body, man seeks his
Maker. Animals, for the most part, have their eyes fixed on
the ground, and their belly is there where their eyes are;
our eyes are raised to heaven, so that even if our mind should
become darkened, we would, despite our reluctant eyes, behold
the heavens.

'Man is like a breath; his days, like a passing shadow.'
Truly, our days are like a shadow. I was an infant; I was a
lad; I was an adolescent; I was a youth; I was a mature man;
I reached middle life; then, before I realize it, I am an old
man. Death creeps up on old age. I am changing every day,
and I do not perceive that I am nothing. Never for a moment
do we mark time as we pass through life, but we are always
either growing or shrinking. Man, then, alters from moment
to moment; all unaware of it he is dying. As an old man,
I recall my infancy: what I was, what I did, how I played,
how I ran about hither and thither; now I see myself weighed
down under too great a burden. 'His days like a passing
shadow.' Our life is a shadow; it does not seem to have any
substance. What existence it does have quickly passes away.
Because, therefore, man is so miserable, because he is so
weak, what is our entreaty? For what do we plead? What
does the prophet say here? For what does he pray?

'Incline your heavens, O Lord, and come down.' You cannot
save this worthless thing that is man, unless You Yourself
assume his worthlessness. 'Incline your heavens, O Lord, and
come down.' Your wandering sheep cannot be cured of its
waywardness unless You carry it upon Your shoulders. 'Touch
the mountains, and they shall smoke.' 'Amen I say to you, if
you have faith like a mustard seed, you will say to this mountain, "Remove from here"; and it will remove.'[10] That was
said in reference to the boy that was possessed. The moun-

10 Matt. 17.19.

tain that they could not remove is written of in Jeremia: 'Give glory to the Lord, your God, before it grows dark; before your feet stumble on the darkening mountains.'[11] Now why have we said all this? Because of the words of the psalm: 'Touch the mountains and they shall smoke,' mountains that dominate the earth, mountains that are haughty with pride, that say: 'The rivers are mine; it is I who made them.'[12] 'Touch the mountains and they shall smoke.' The prophet did not say, 'they shall burn,' but 'they shall smoke.' May they be marked by the sign of their punishment, not by divine resplendence and sublimity.

'Flash forth lightning, and put them to flight.' Note that the prophet did not say: You will destroy them, but, You will scatter them. We read in Genesis that when they were building the tower of Babel, God says: 'Come, let us go down, and there confuse their language so that they will not understand one another's speech';[13] it is for their own good that they be scattered.

'Reach out your hand from on high.' 'Who would believe what we have heard? To whom has the arm of the Lord been revealed?'[14] Reach down Your hand from above; Lord, incline Your heavens and come down. This is said to the Son: Incline Your heavens and descend. How, now, does the psalmist say: Reach out Your hand from on high? Granted He is on earth; He, nevertheless, reaches out His hand from heaven; for He does not depart from there. 'Deliver me and rescue me from many waters.' Because You have descended, inclined the heavens, reached down Your hand from on high, and deigned to assume a human body, and many have believed in You, in the place of one water, there have begun to be many waters. You may observe that many different heresies have spread throughout the world. 'Deliver me and rescue me from many waters': rescue me from many

11 Jer. 13.16.
12 Cf. Ezech. 29.9.
13 Cf. Gen. 11.7.
14 Isa. 53.1.

waters, and show me the living fountain. There is only one baptism: 'one faith, one Baptism.'[15] Deliver me from many waters, for these waters do not generate Your sons, but the sons of strangers. Then the psalmist continues: 'Rescue me from many waters, from the hands of alien children,'[16] for they are not Your children that are born in many waters, but the children of aliens.

'Whose mouths swear false promises.' They assure themselves of knowledge, and yet they set their mouth against their Creator. 'They set their mouthings in place of heaven,'[17] whose mouths swear false promises. Their science is the science of false promises. 'While their right hands are the right hand of iniquity.'[18] The prophet denounces both their mouths and their hands, their science and their works: 'Whose mouths swear false promises' pertains to their science; 'Their right hands are the right hand of iniquity,' to their works. They say they are right-handed, but they are all left-handed. Their right hand is the hand of iniquity and not of equity. Of their left hand, Scripture says: 'Let the devil stand at his right hand.'[19] The man who has that kind of right hand—the right hand of iniquity—has the devil standing at his right hand.

'O God, I will sing a new song to you'; a new man, a new song. To You, my God, I will sing a new song. 'Sing to the Lord a new song.'[20] How appropriately the psalmist said, I will sing, and not, I sing. His promise is for the future, for how well he realizes that the present life is a contest, not a canticle. An army never sings unless it is on its way to victory; consequently, I am not free to sing in the present combat. When I win the victory, then, I shall sing. 'With a ten-stringed lyre I will chant your praise.' Then, I will stretch

---

15 Eph. 4.5.
16 Cf. Ps. 143 (144).7.
17 Ps. 72.9.
18 Cf. Ps. 143 (144).8.
19 Cf. Ps. 108.6.
20 Ps. 95.1.

out both hands and on such chords I will sing to You. My prayer is Your psaltery.

'You who give victory to kings.' To which kings? 'The king's heart is in the hand of God.'[21] The heart of Julian, the persecutor, of Nero, of Decius, are their hearts in the hand of God? No, the hearts in the hand of God are those who govern their body, who bring it into subjection and compel it to servitude, lest preaching to others they themselves should be rejected.[22] These are the kings of whom Wisdom says in Proverbs: 'He gives kingship to kings.'[23]

'Deliver me; and rescue me from the hands of alien children.' These versicles are a repetition of those above. 'Whose mouths swear false promises while their right hands are the right hand of iniquity. Whose sons are like new plants well-nurtured in their youth.'[24] Deliver me from the hands of alien children. Let us see what kind of sons heretics have: Whose sons are like new plants in their youth. Note very carefully what follows about heretics.

'Their daughters clothed with finery, adorned like a temple. Their garners full, overflowing with every kind of store. Their sheep fruitful, thronging in their going forth; their oxen fat. There is no breach in the walls, no passage, no outcry in their streets. They have called the people happy, for whom things are thus.'[25] Heretics say this. What do I say? 'Happy the people whose God is the Lord.' Let us take each versicle separately and briefly examine it with the help of your prayers. 'Whose sons are like new plants well-nurtured in their youth.' Their crop is not old but new; it is not from the old law, nor from the prophets nor apostles, but from new teachers. Their sons are like new plants well-nurtured in their youth. They are ever youths. Granted that

---

21 Cf. Prov. 21.1; cf. Homily 9 on Ps. 75, p. 62; Homily 49 on Ps. 137, p. 361.
22 Cf. 1 Cor. 9.27.
23 Cf. Prov. 8.15.
24 Cf. Ps. 143 (144).12.
25 Cf. Ps. 143 (144).12-15.

many heresies are old, nevertheless, since they change daily and are discovered anew each day, they are new; even though they are old stories, because their doctrine is retold, they are new. As a matter of fact, heretics are not content with the errors of ancient teachers; they must find new ones. Their sons are like young saplings. Now, what does Holy Writ say about the Church on the fear of the Lord? 'Happy are all who fear the Lord, who walk in his ways!'[26] What does it say about those who walk in His ways? 'Your sons like olive plants around your table.'[27] These sons are around the table of Christ, not away from it. No girls are mentioned, only sons. Heretics, on the other hand, have daughters, also; the weaker sex, the delights of pleasure. 'Their daughters clothed with finery'; their speech is full of adornment, but its sense is sordid. In Holy Writ, thoughts and reflections are always spoken of as sons, words as daughters. See, now, what the psalmist means? Their ideas, their sons, are new; their words —of the heretics—are borrowed from worldly wisdom and well ordered; their speech is facile and elegant. 'Their daughters clothed with finery.' Indeed, do their words seem apt, but because they are daughters, not sons, they are without strength or force. 'Adorned like a temple.' A neat saying, 'like a temple'; they do not have the true Church, but only an image of a church.

'Their garners full, overflowing with every kind of store.' They are well stocked for debate. If you refute them in one proof, they turn to another. If you contradict them by Scripture, they take refuge in Aristotle; if you rebut them in Aristotle, they by-pass to Plato. Their garners are full, overflowing with every kind of store. 'Garners' is well chosen because it implies a wealth of material ready for use. The heretics possess storehouses, for they have words hoarded for disputation. On the other hand, churchmen are undesigning; they do not anticipate their arguments. They open their

26 Cf. Ps. 127.1.
27 Cf. Ps. 127.3.

mouths and the Lord fills them just as He promised: 'Open wide your mouth, and I will fill it';[28] 'do not be anxious how or what you are to speak; for what you are to speak will be given you in that hour.'[29] You see, we do not have storehouses all stocked up, but our plenty abounds at that moment.

Someone may ask, what proof have you that the saints do not have granaries? 'Look at the birds of the air: for they have neither storehouses nor granaries. Yet your heavenly Father feeds them.'[30] Monks, especially, are birds of this kind; they do not have storehouses or depositories, but they have the Lord of provisions and storehouses, Christ Himself. They do not have granaries, but the Lord of granaries; they do not have the wealth of the devil, but they have the poverty of Christ. What does the devil say? 'All these things are mine. I will give them to thee, if thou wilt fall down and worship me.'[31] What does Christ say to His followers? 'He who doth not sell all that he hath, and give to the poor, cannot be my disciple.'[32] The devil promises a kingdom and wealth in order to destroy life; the Lord promises poverty in order to preserve it. We do nothing so very great if we renounce our possessions; Christ left His Father and the kingdom of heaven for our sake. Let no one think me blasphemous because I said He left His Father. I am speaking in terms of the Christian dispensation, in terms of His mission, in accordance with which He says: 'The Father who sent me is greater than I.'[33] God is not sent; God is not made subject; He does not serve; but the Divine Dispensation is sent. If God is everywhere and all things are in God, how is God sent to anything, since all things are of God? Christ, I say, was made a pauper for us. Why have we said all this? Because it says here in the psalm: Their garners full, over-

---

28 Ps. 80.11.
29 Matt. 10.19.
30 Cf. Matt. 6.26; cf. Letter 22.31, PL 22.417 (116).
31 Cf. Matt. 4.8, 9.
32 Cf. Matt. 19.21; Luke 14.33; cf. *Against Jovinian* 2.6, PL 23.307 (333).
33 Cf. John 14.28.

flowing with every kind of store. Quite right, 'overflowing' with superabundance. They eructate from gorging themselves and perish; from fasting, we win salvation.

'Their sheep fruitful.' They have many sons, for the number of heretics is legion. 'Their sheep fruitful.' Osee, the prophet, says: 'Give them, O Lord! give them what? Give them an unfruitful womb, and dry breasts!'[34] For whom are these words intended? For the teachers of heretics who plume themselves in the number of their disciples. 'Their sheep fruitful, thronging in their going forth.' The psalmist did not say, in their coming in, but in their going out, for they are not coming into the Church, but going out of it. 'They have gone forth from us, but they were not of us, for if they had been of us, they would surely have continued with us.'[35] 'Thronging in their going forth'; every day they are going forth from the Church. 'Thronging in their going forth.' What does the psalmist say about the Church? 'All glorious is the king's daughter as she enters.'[36] 'Their oxen fat.' Pharao in a dream saw fat Egyptian oxen. 'Their oxen fat.' The Israelite people are slender; the Egyptians are fat. You should see the teachers of heretics doing nothing but ogling their treasures. They gaze fondly at their possessions and scorn Christ the pauper. 'Their oxen fat.' Well said, 'fat oxen'; 'their god is the belly, their glory is in their shame.'[37]

'There is no breach in the wall, no passage.' Do these words seem obscure to you: 'There is no breach in the wall, no passage, no outcry in their streets'? Rarely do you find an inexperienced heretic, for all heretical teachers are trained in secular science. They have not the nets of the apostles, but they possess the little chains of dialectics. 'There is no breach in the walls, no passage.' Whenever they engage in disputation, whenever they begin to argue with you, their words are so concise, so compressed in masterly language,

---

34 Osee 9.14; cf. Letter 133.11, PL 22.1159 (1040).
35 1 John 2.19.
36 Ps. 44.14.
37 Phil. 3.19.

that it is difficult to escape their cogency. When they hold you tied up in their syllogisms and, as it were, weave a web of them and build a wall about you, you cannot break down the wall nor break through the web, and there you are a prisoner. Their walls are without breach, without exit, and when they keep you imprisoned in their gyrations, you are not on the narrow way that leads to life, but on the broad way that leads to death.[38] 'No outcry in their streets.' Jesus cries out and calls, saying: 'If anyone thirst, let him come to me and drink.'[39] Jesus' outcry is in the narrow way, not in the avenues of the heretics.

'Happy the people for whom things are thus.' Many in their ignorance think that this sort of happiness is theirs. Christian simplicity is ours; we have no desire for Platonic eloquence, we want only the apostolic simplicity of fishermen. This simplicity holds a net; it has muddy feet and working hands, hard and calloused from work. 'Happy the people whose God is the Lord'; happy the people who possess Christ in the place of all riches. The others have sons and daughters; they have granaries, fruitful sheep, fat oxen, sleek and well built. We, on the contrary, do not have their multitudes, but we know and have experienced that saying in the Gospel: 'Where two or three are gathered together for my sake, there am I in the midst of them.'[40] Do not be afraid, little flock,[41] for it has pleased God to dwell in your midst. Monks have no right to say: 'Look at the great crowds, the cities are filled, the whole world is filled; but do you think no one is saved except the monk in the monastery? Just look at the multitudes; but are we only to be saved?'[42] When such thoughts tempt and trouble you, listen to the Lord saying: Do not be afraid, little flock, because it has pleased your Father to dwell among you.

---

38 Cf. Matt. 7.13, 14.
39 John 7.37.
40 Matt. 18.20.
41 Cf. Luke 12.32.
42 Cf. Letter 125.17, PL 22.1082 (944); 58.5, PL 22.582-83 (322).

We have read in the Gospel[43] how two thousand swine perish because one soul is saved. Why do I say all this? To prove that the soul of one saint is more precious than an infinite number of sinners. From the whole world He chose twelve apostles. One of twelve deserted; eleven remained loyal. The cross came; they fled; one remained—Peter, one with One. This one himself fled, and would that he had! He denied Christ. We may say, then, that the entire human race was lost. Because it had perished, the complaint of the Lord crucified is: 'The wine press I have trodden alone, and of my people there was no one with me.'[44] Then was the psalm fulfilled: 'Help, O Lord! for no one now is dutiful.'[45] 'There is none who does good, no not even one.'[46] He who had promised: 'Even if I should have to die with thee, or be imprisoned, I will not deny thee,'[47] denied Him. Why am I making such a point of all this? Because it behooves the monk not to look at the crowd of sinners, but to reflect upon the way of life and the fewness of the saints. The whole of Judea was led into captivity. Nabuchodonosor had come, and thousands of men were displaced into Babylonia as prisoners. Jeremia alone was left praising God and they threw him into a muddy cistern;[48] nevertheless, the soul of this one man was more precious than that of all the people. Would you know what one man can do? Jesus, son of Nave, was alone, although the whole world was inhabited. There were, to be sure, countless multitudes, but he was alone. Alone he commanded the sun and the moon, and they stood still; a man gives an order, and heaven gives heed. Heaven listened to him because he was listening to the Lord. Jeremia was in captivity, but there were, also, with him great numbers of

---

43 Mark 5.2-14.
44 Cf. Isa. 63.3; cf. *Against Jovinian* 2.36, PL 23.349 (380).
45 Ps. 11.2.
46 Rom. 3.12; cf. Ps. 13.1; cf. Letter 60.3, PL 22.591 (333).
47 Cf. Mark 14.31.
48 Cf. Jer. 38.6.

exiles. What does he say? 'I sat alone, because you filled me with indignation.'[49] How were you alone in the city? I say, I was alone because I had no one with whom to share my purpose.

---

49 Cf. Jer. 15.17; cf. Letter 128.2, PL 22.1097 (962).

HOMILY 55

ON PSALM 145 (146)

RAISE THE LORD, O my soul.' The title of this psalm is: 'Of Aggai and Zacharia.'[1] In the first place, we should know that this title is not found in the Hebrew text, but in the Septuagint translation. We should say a word, however, about the superscription, 'Of Aggai and Zacharia,' that appears in the popular edition. Because the restoration of Jerusalem is implied in the verse: 'The Lord shall reign forever; your God, O Sion, unto generation and generation,'[2] some exegetes are of the opinion that the psalm refers to the restoration of Jerusalem that took place under Aggai and Zacharia.

'Praise the Lord, O my soul.' The psalmist did not say, 'Praise, O my body,' but 'Praise, O my soul,' because he condemned the body, but because he censured the works of the flesh.[3] 'Praise the Lord, O my soul.' The soul is earnestly encouraging itself, just as if David were to say: Praise the Lord, O David, even so the soul says: Praise the Lord, O my soul. 'I will praise the Lord in my life.'[4] Notice that the soul is urging itself strongly and responds to its own exhortation. What does it say? It says to me: O my soul, praise the Lord. I answer: I will praise the Lord in my life. In my present state, I cannot give praise; I am oppressed with sins. Whenever I attempt to open my lips to praise God, the consciousness of my sins seals them shut. 'I will praise the Lord in my

1 Cf. Ps. 145 (146).1, LXX.
2 Cf. Ps. 145 (146).10.
3 Cf. Homily 54 on Ps. 143, p. 380.
4 Cf. Ps. 145 (146).2.

life.' Rightly did the psalmist say, 'I will praise,' and not, 'I praise.' When I shall be with my Lord, then, I will praise Him in my life. Now I am in death, I cannot utter praises. In my life, I will praise. Our life is Christ; let us praise the Lord in life. 'I will sing praise to my God while I live.' Just realize what that means: when we perform deeds of justice, we are alive; when we sin, we cease to be. There is much we could say, but our sermon must hurry along.

'Put not your trust in princes, in the sons of men, in whom there is no salvation.'[5] To everyone in general the prophet says: Put not your trust in princes, not in emperors, not in governors, not in judges of this world. Do not trust in princes. Who are princes? The sons of men. Who are sons of men? Those for whom there is no salvation.

'When his spirit departs he returns to his earth.' When he has returned to his earth, what happens? 'On that day his plans perish'; all the self-reliance of princes vanishes; all their plans perish. Do not trust in princes. Many have put their trust in a prince. Today, he is; tomorrow, he is no more.[6] Today, an army marches before him; tonight, he lies in his grave. After so much power, so much splendor, no time intervenes; in but a moment, Christ does His work. 'In the sons of men, in whom there is no salvation.' Who are princes? Sons of men. If men themselves are nothing, what are their sons? 'When his spirit departs.' Whose? Man's. 'When his spirit departs.' The psalmist used 'spirit' here for 'soul.' 'Father, into thy hands I commend my spirit.'[7] When his spirit departs he returns to his earth; not that the spirit returns to earth, for the spirit is not of earth; the spirit takes flight, and man returns to his dust. On that day, all his plans perish. We ourselves, who are not princes, how much we plan today and say: 'I shall do it tomorrow; I will pull down my barns, and build them up again tomorrow.' To me the

---

5 Cf. Ps. 145 (146).3.
6 *Commentarioli in ps.* 145.2, 3.
7 Luke 23.46.

words apply: 'Thou fool, this night do they demand thy soul
of thee; and the things thou hast provided, whose will they
be?'[8] This is said of those who set their hopes in princes.
What does it say of the saint?

'Happy he whose help is the God of Jacob.' 'Some are
strong in chariots; and some in horses; but we call upon the
name of the Lord, our God.'[9] They have many more helpers;
still they are but princes; they are but men; they fall to their
destruction. We have one helper and He has the power to
save. 'Whose hope is in the Lord, his God.'

Let us turn our thoughts to the three boys in the fiery
furnace in Babylonia, and listen to what they say when
Nabuchodonosor summons them before him and compels
them to worship Bel. What is their answer to Nabuchodonosor? 'King, there is no need for us to defend ourselves before
you in this matter. If our God whom we serve can save us
from the white-hot furnace, may he save us! But even if he
will not, know, O king, that we will not worship the statue
which you set up.'[10] Look at their faith! We believe, it says,
that He is able to save us; but if perchance our sins prevent
Him, we still believe in Him who wills not to deliver us. We
do not believe in this life, but in the future life; nor do we
believe in Him in order to escape burning here, but in order
to escape passing from this fire into another fire. Go ahead,
then, prepare your furnace; this heat, this fire, is our purga-
tion. Happy he whose help is the God of Jacob! Do not miss
the significance of the words, 'whose help.' 'And because of
their unbelief, he did not work many miracles there.'[11] God
is our helper. While we labor with determination, He de-
livers us and works together with us; when we are slothful,
supine, irresolute, He does not set us free.

'Whose hope is in the Lord, his God.' Felicitous word,
'hope'; even if He does not liberate us in the present, not-

---

8 Luke 12.20; cf. Letter 127.11, PL 22.1094 (959).
9 Cf. Ps. 19.8.
10 Cf. Dan. 3.16-18.
11 Matt. 13.58.

withstanding, there is hope for the future. 'Who made heaven and earth.' He is the God who made heaven and earth, 'The sea, and all that is in them.' In comparison to heaven and earth and the sea, we men in our creaturehood are as the ant or the flea. Does it stand to reason that He who created heaven and earth does not have the power to save man whom He made?

'Who keeps truth forever.'[12] If we are crushed by falsehood and deceit, let us not grieve over it; the Lord is the guardian of truth for all eternity. Someone has lied against us, and the liar is given more credence than we who are telling the truth. We must not despair; the Lord keeps faith forever. Aptly said, 'keeps.' He keeps truth and keeps it in His own treasury; He pays back to us what He has stored away for us. 'Who keeps truth forever.' Christ is truth; let us speak truth, and Truth will safeguard truth for us. 'Secures justice for the oppressed.' Even if justice delays its coming, do not give up hope; 'it will surely come,'[13] and bring salvation. 'Secures justice for the oppressed.' May our conscience testify only that we are suffering unjustly. May we be always conscious that we are not suffering on account of our sins and that we are not guilty of the charge brought against us.

'Gives food to the hungry.' Here is instruction in the very letter of the words; even in their simplest sense they edify the listener. 'Look at the birds of the air: they do not sow, or reap; yet your heavenly Father feeds them.'[14] 'Gives food to the hungry,' to the hungry, not to the belching. Let, then, the monk who does not have food receive it with confidence; he who is filled to eructation should not take any. You know that you are hungry, that you have no food; if you hunger and are in want and someone should give you food, by taking it you are rendering a greater kindness than that bestowed upon you. If, however, you have food and are not hungry,

---

12 Cf. Ps. 145 (146).6.
13 Cf. Hab. 2.3.
14 Cf. Matt. 6.26.

you ought not take it from the hungering for the sake of
your own satiety. Take what you need and not anything to
save; take a garment to cover your body, not to put away.
'Gives food to the hungry.' So much for the literal interpretation.

Now let us consider another meaning. Let us hunger for
Christ, and He will give us heavenly bread: 'Give us this
day our daily bread.'[15] They who pray thus are hungering;
it is they who long for this Bread. He who prays: Give us
this day our daily bread, surely prays in hunger. 'Gives food
to the hungry.' Someone is of the opinion that the prophet
is referring to the heavenly Bread of the Sacrament. We,
indeed, accept such exegesis, for it is truly the Body of Christ
and truly the Blood of Christ. Let us, however, push the interpretation a little further. The Bread of Christ and His
Body is divine utterance and heavenly doctrine. Now whoever receives this bread and receives it with abundance, what
happens to him?

'The Lord sets captives free.' If this bread, the divine word
and heavenly doctrine, refreshes our soul, it releases our feet
immediately from their shackles. 'The Lord sets captives
free.' Lazarus had been in bonds, and the Lord said: 'Unbind
him.'[16] The Lord unbinds the fettered. The daughter of
Abraham for eighteen years suffered the fetters of a bent back;
He loosed her from her bonds and she looked straight up at
the heavens. Note the Gospel: 'Behold, there was a woman
who for eighteen years had had a sickness caused by a spirit;
and she was bent over and utterly unable to look upwards.'[17]
Because she had an infirmity caused by a spirit, she was unable
to lift up her head. 'The Lord sets captives free.' Works also
are shackles, since, indeed, the same sins that bend down our
necks bind also our feet. The man that is fettered cannot
run in the stadium of Christ, for his feet are weighted down

---

15 Matt. 6.11.
16 John 11.44.
17 Luke 13.11; cf. Letter 147.9, PL 22.1202 (1092).

with shackles that pin him to the ground; fetters fasten us to earth. 'The Lord sets captives free.' Note the order. He gives food to the hungry: first, we hunger; next, we receive food. When He has assuaged our hunger, He unshackles our feet. When we begin to walk with freedom, what follows?

'The Lord gives sight to the blind.' Mark that if the psalmist were speaking of the organically blind, he would have said: The Lord gives sight to the blind. That, however, is not what he actually said. According to the Hebrew and Greek truth, what did he say? 'The Lord makes the blind wise.'[18] If he were speaking of the eyes of the body, he would have said: The Lord gives sight to the blind; in fact, his words were: The Lord makes the blind wise. 'If you were blind,' the Lord says, 'you would not have sin.'[19] Our heart grows blind from the darkness of sins. Foolishness and stupidity are the darkness of our eyes. When, therefore, we have been refreshed in our hunger, and our feet have been released from their fetters, then, with the eye of our heart, we begin to see the light that we had at sometime lost, and we grow in wisdom. When, finally, we have become truly wise, what follows?

'The Lord raises up those that were bowed down.' Even if you are lying prostrate, be at peace; the Lord is reaching out His hand. 'The Lord loves the just.' I see two points for consideration here: He loves and He protects. He who loves, loves, as it were, his own; he who protects, protects one who is in danger. 'The Lord loves the just.' The just and perfect man the Lord loves, but He watches over the stranger who has not entered the service of the Lord.

'The Lord protects strangers; the fatherless and the widow he sustains.' This verse, even in its literal sense, is profitable for meditation. He sustains the fatherless and the widow. O martyr, you who are a prisoner and are pouring out your blood for Me, do not be anxious for your children, for your

18 Cf. *Commentary on Isaia* 54.15, PL 24.527 (641).
19 John 9.41.

wife; they have Me in your place. Now, for its spiritual message. He sustains the fatherless and the widow: the fatherless, who lost God the Father through sin; the widow, the soul that has lost Christ, its Spouse. Note that the psalm did not say He protects, He saves the fatherless and the widow; but He sustains them, if the soul returns to the Father, if it comes back to the Spouse.

'But the way of the wicked he will destroy.'[20] The prophet did not say He will destroy sinners. This is in agreement with the words of the first psalm: 'The way of the wicked vanishes.'[21] If Christ is the way of the just, the way of the wicked is the devil, but the way of the wicked He will destroy. The way, then, of all the wicked is the devil; him He will destroy, but He will preserve us who were walking in the midst of that way but now do so no longer.

'The Lord shall reign forever.' When the way of sinners shall vanish, then, the Lord will reign forever. The prophet did not say, He will reign in the present world, but forever. As long as the way does not vanish, Christ does not reign in us; as long as the way of the wicked does not vanish, Christ does not reign in us. As long as our feet walk in the path of the devil, Christ does not reign in us. I give way to anger against my brother without cause,[22] I am walking in the way of the devil; Christ does not reign in me. I malign the reputation of my brother; I am going the way of the devil; Christ does not reign in me. In whatever kind of sin I walk, I am walking the devil's way and Christ is not reigning in me. My mind is vain and preoccupied with distractions of all sorts. I am in one place and my mind is wandering all over the world. It hunts for angels; it settles on kings; it captures an army; it embraces the world; of one monk, however, it does not take hold.

Why am I saying this? For the benefit of those who wander

---

20 Cf. Ps. 145 (146).9.
21 Ps. 1.6; cf. *Commentarioli in ps.* 145.9.
22 Cf. *Against the Pelagians* 2.5, PL 23.565 (747).

over the whole world and cannot settle down in one place. 'Your God, O Sion, from generation to generation.'[23] 'Your God, O Sion.' We have frequently mentioned that usually Sion typifies a watchtower, or the Church, or a soul contemplating God. 'Your God, O Sion, from generation to generation': in the first generation, of the Jews; in the second, of the Gentiles. In all of Holy Writ, and in all of the psalms, generation unto generation symbolizes two peoples. We may, however, express the verse differently: Your God will reign forever, O Sion, in this generation and in the generation to come. May Christ reign in us. 'Do not let sin reign in your mortal body.'[24] 'The king's heart is in the hand of God.'[25] May we be kings; may we govern our body and bring it into subjection, and may our heart be in the hand of Christ. To whom be glory forever and ever. Amen.

---

23 Cf. Ps. 145 (146).10.
24 Rom. 6.12.
25 Cf. Prov. 21.1.

HOMILY 56

ON PSALM 146 (147A)

RAISE THE LORD, because a psalm is good.'[1] The title of Psalm 146 is 'Alleluia.' Those who are unfamiliar with the Hebrew language, are wont to inquire into the significance of the word 'alleluia' when it appears in the title of a psalm. This particular psalm has 'alleluia' not only in its title but also in its prelude. Where our text says, 'Praise the Lord,' the Hebrew says, 'alleluia.' Among the Hebrews, God has as many as ten names; He is called Sabaoth, Saddai, Eloim, El, even Jao, and Eser Jaia. Along with others, there is also the name Ja, the meaning of which is 'invisible.' As the Hebrew for our word praise is 'allelu,' the Hebrew psalm has, 'allelu Ja,'[2] in the same way that it would say: allelu Sabaoth, allelu Saddai, allelu Eloim. As a matter of fact, Theodotion, one of the translators, in his attempt to produce a literal translation, says, αἰνεῖτε τὸν Ἰά. Why have we made such a point of this? So that we may know that alleluia is the title and theme of this psalm: Praise the Lord. Since we have digressed, meditate on this explanation in your hearts; otherwise, we shall have to prolong our sermon.

'Praise the Lord, because a psalm is good.' The prophet did not say, a good psalm, but a psalm is good in the absolute sense; it is a good thing to sing a sacred song. To sing, not with the voice, mind you, but with the heart. How many there are who have good voices but because they are sinners, their singing is bad. He sings well who sings in his heart,

---

1 Cf. Ps. 146 (147A).1.
2 Cf. Letter 26.3, PL 22.430 (132); cf. *Commentarioli in ps.* 146.1.

who sings to Christ in his conscience. 'It is fitting to praise
him in joyful song.'³ It is fitting to praise Him with joyful
song, not with the voice, but with a good conscience. In such
wise, Noe, too, offered holocausts 'and the Lord smelled the
sweet odor.'⁴ There is much more to be said, but we must
touch lightly upon the high points and indicate the thought,
rather than dwell on the broader meaning of the words.

'The Lord rebuilds Jerusalem; the dispersed of Israel he
gathers.' How Jerusalem is rebuilt and the banished exiles
are brought home again has already been told. Since, moreover, these two versicles have been explained and we must
not build on another's foundation, let us move on to the
rest of the psalm to learn just how Jerusalem is restored,
for the prophet has given us a description in the remaining
verses.

'He heals the brokenhearted.' You see now how the rebuilding of Jerusalem takes place: The broken heart is
mended. 'A heart contrite and humbled, God does not
spurn.'⁵ 'And binds up their wounds.' You wound your
heart and the Lord binds up your wounds. The Samaritan,
who was on his way down from Jerusalem to Jericho, bound
up the wounds of the torn and bruised man he found lying
in the road. He is the one to whom the Scripture fittingly
applies:⁶ 'And binds up their wounds.' It refers also to those
who are penitent, but of the unrepentant, Scripture says,
their wounds 'are not drained, or bandaged, or eased with
salve.'⁷

'He tells the number of the stars.' What literal connection
is there between, 'binds up their wounds' and 'he tells the
number of the stars'? Well, since He healed the brokenhearted and bound up their wounds, after their wounds had
been healed, He changed them into stars. 'He tells the

---

3 Cf. Ps. 146 (147A).1.
4 Cf. Gen. 8.21.
5 Cf. Ps. 50.19.
6 Cf. *Commentarioli in ps.* 146.3.
7 Isa. 1.6.

number of the stars.' 'The number.' Many, indeed, had
sinned; many there are whom He has healed. 'He tells the
number of the stars.' He does not tell the number of the
wounded, but the number of those who have already become
stars; God tells the number only of those who are worthy of
Him. 'He calls each by name.' He speaks of Lucifer and Orion,
of the stars that we see in the sky, and it is certainly understandable, for God is wonderful who made heaven and earth
and all that they contain. Let us on our part make an effort
to understand this daily occurrence in such a way that it may
be for our gain. 'He calls each by name.' Would you like
to know how stars are made from the brokenhearted? It is
written in Genesis that God led Abraham outside and showed
him the stars and said to him: 'So shall your posterity be.'[8]
He calls each by name. He calls Abraham from Abram;
he was Abram in Chaldaea, but in heaven he is called
Abraham. When he is made a star, his name is changed to
Abraham. He who formerly was Saul, later in heaven is
named Paul. John and James are the sons of thunder;
thunder is certainly in the heavens. Thus the stars are
numbered; the number of the saints is endless; Christ alone
is without number.

'Great is our Lord, and mighty in power; to his wisdom
there is no limit.' Mighty in power: 'Christ the power of
God and the wisdom of God.'[9] There is no limit to His
wisdom; Christ is wisdom. To Wisdom alone there is no
limit.

'The Lord sustains the lowly.' What stars are these? The
Lord sustains the lowly. The humble have changed into
stars. 'The just shall shine bright like the stars,'[10] says Daniel.
'The wicked he casts to the ground.' Note the distinction:
the angels fall to the ground; men hasten to heaven. The
Lord sustains the lowly; meekness He summons to heaven;

---

8 Gen. 15.5.
9 1 Cor. 1.24.
10 Cf. Dan. 12.3; cf. Letter 53.3, PL 22.542 (273).

pride He lays low in the dust; the wicked He casts to the ground.

'Sing to the Lord in confession.'[11] This David fulfilled; he who had given us an example of justice, gave us also an example of penitence. By his repentance he taught us how we ought to repent. See how the holy prophet benefits us, not only in his justice, but also in his sin! 'Sing praise with the harp to our God.' Not a single chord of the virtues should be broken; all the chords should sound together in concert. 'Sing praise with the harp to our God.' The harp has many strings; if one is broken, it cannot play. So, too, the holy man; albeit he is a saint, if he be lacking in one virtue he cannot give voice to his song.

'Who covers the heavens with clouds.' This heaven that we behold cannot be covered over with clouds, but there is another heaven, and there are other clouds. 'Your truth to the clouds.'[12] Does this mean that the truth of the Lord reaches to those clouds that are quickly scattered by the blowing of the wind? The truth of God is Christ: 'I am the way, the truth, and the life.'[13] Is the truth of Christ, therefore, in those clouds that have no substance in themselves? Is it possible for truth to be where the wind has the power to disperse and to destroy? 'I will command the clouds not to send rain upon them,'[14] that is, upon the Jews. The clouds are the prophets; the Lord commanded them to rain no rain upon Israel. The word of prophecy has turned to us. If clouds collide, they produce thunder and lightning. 'Who covers the heavens with clouds.' Why did the prophet say that He covers the heavens with clouds? If the clouds are the prophets and the apostles, how does He cover the heavens with the apostles and prophets? The heavens represent divine mysteries. Since, then, divine mysteries are called 'the heavens,' the clouds conceal the divine message from the

---

11 Cf. Ps. 146 (147A).7.
12 Cf. Ps. 35.6.
13 John 14.6; cf. *Against Jovinian* 2.2, PL 23.296 (322).
14 Cf. Isa. 5.6.

unworthy. Anyone who is unworthy is unable to comprehend divine doctrine; for him it is covered over with clouds.
'Who provides rain for the earth.' The earth needs rain;
unless our earth receives the rain which is the fountain of
divine instruction, it does not yield fruit. When earth holds
the moisture of that doctrine, what is the result?

'Who makes grass sprout on the mountains.' If the psalmist
were speaking of mere grass, certainly, it is more apt to grow
in the valleys than in mountainous places, for wherever rain-
fall is more plentiful, the growth is more luxuriant. From
the mountains, waters flow down into the valleys, the better
for the grass to grow.

'Who gives food to the cattle.' The Scriptures that we read,
discuss, hold in our hands, are called mountains. Scripture
calls Abraham a mountain, Jeremia a mountain, Isaac a
mountain, the prophets holy mountains. These mountains
contain grain and grass. If you are man, you receive grain
from them; if you are cattle, you receive grass. 'Man and
beasts you save, O Lord.'[15] If you are a brute beast, you
receive grass; if you are man, you receive grain. Salvation is
yours according to your faith. 'Who makes grass sprout on
the mountains, and gives food to the cattle.' If you are man,
in the Sacred Scriptures you receive spiritual understanding;
if you are a beast of burden, you receive only the letter as
does the Jew.

I see an important point here. God who has been praised
with such meet praises is drawn down to His meaner creatures: 'to the young ravens when they cry to him.' If the
prophet had reference to birds, surely, he would name the
eagles or the vultures. 'To the young ravens when they cry
to him.' No other bird is mentioned by name except the
young ravens, and not the ravens themselves, but their young.
The raven is not saved; but the young born of it are saved.
We are the young ravens, for we are born of idolatrous

---

15 Ps. 35.7.

parents.[16] We read in Solomon: 'The eye that mocks a father or scorns the speech of his mother, will be plucked out by the ravens in the valley.'[17] It did not say the young of the ravens, but the ravens themselves, for he who is a raven cannot be saved. A raven is sent forth from the Ark and does not return. During the flood, it is in the Ark with the rest of the creatures; after the flood, happily it is cast out. In other words, when it is calm and peaceful, the raven cannot be in the Ark of God. When there is a storm or deluge, the raven is there in the midst of it; the calm returns and the raven is in flight. Who are these ravens? Who are the young ravens? I think the black ravens that always prey upon the carcasses of the dead, that always stir up quarrels with their raucous voice, are demons; and those enslaved by demons are just like the ravens and even take on their color. So, as we were saying, our parents, who were the slaves of idols and demons, were ravens, for ravens hover about only where there are filth, dung, and carcasses of the dead. We who are born of ravens do not look for dead bodies, but for the dew. Young ravens, they say, live on dew; that is what biologists tell us.

Would you like to know another mystery about ravens? Elias, whose name means Lord God; Elias, that is, our Lord and Savior, suffered persecution from the Jews, and received food from the ravens, the people of the Gentiles. 'To the young ravens when they cry to him.' If you cry, you are a young raven; if you are silent, you are an old raven. 'To the young ravens when they cry to him.' We read in the prophet: 'Everyone shall be rescued who calls on the name of the Lord.'[18] If we apply this without reserve to ravens, will they also be saved? Answer, O Jew, you who follow only the letter of the word. You say that these ravens are really ravens; you do not interpret spiritually but carnally when

---

16 Cf. *Against Vigilantius* 7, PL 23.361 (394).
17 Cf. Prov. 30.17.
18 Joel 3.5.

you maintain that our verse is written about ravens. If it is written about the young ravens, and it says here: 'To the young ravens when they cry to him,' and: 'Everyone shall be rescued who calls on the name of the Lord,' will the young ravens, therefore, also be saved on the day of judgment? We, then, are the young ravens, and we cry to Him and are saved. In fine, Paul the Apostle wrote to the Church of saints, to those who call upon the name of the Lord.[19]

'In the strength of the steed he delights not.' We promised to be brief, but necessity constrained us to expound more at length. We lied, then, but it was a very useful lie. Would that Herod had lied and sworn a false oath. We, as I say, promised less and have given more because of your prayers. The hour bids me be silent, but the greatness of the mysteries compels me to speak. 'In the strength of the steed He delights not.' I hear a horse and the neighing of horses, and I cannot pass them by. It is written in the psalter: 'Useless is the horse for safety';[20] and in another place of Holy Writ: 'Horse and chariot he has cast into the sea.'[21] It was of precept for the king of Israel not to breed horses.[22] Solomon, moreover, who procured chariots from Egypt,[23] became the victim of passion. 'In the strength of the steed he delights not'; 'Horse and chariot he has cast into the sea.' 'Lustful stallions they are, each neighs after another's wife,'[24] says Jeremia. In horses of that sort, God, to be sure, does not delight. We have commented on the horse. 'Horse and chariot he has cast into the sea.' We have indicated the nature of the horses; let us now identify the riders. I think the horses are men, sinners, and the horsemen are the demons that ride them. If ever, then, it is our experience to have brother turn persecutor, to have one who is called brother maltreat

19 Cf. 1 Cor. 1.2.
20 Ps. 32.17.
21 Exod. 15.1.
22 Cf. Deut. 17.16.
23 Cf. 3 Kings 10.26-29.
24 Jer. 5.8; cf. Letter 123.13, PL 22.1054 (909); *Against Jovinian* 2.37, PL 23.351 (382); *Against Vigilantius* 2, PL 23.356 (389).

us as an enemy, we may know that he is a horse. He is the
horse, but the devil is his rider that smites us with a spear.
The horse runs and the devil smites; the horse is driven and
goaded by spurs and rages madly against its will.

'Nor is he pleased with the legs of men.'[25] Notice that it
did not say, with the head of men, or with the hands, but
with the legs, which are downward. 'Nor is he pleased with
the legs of men.' Legs, just as thighs, usually connote inordinate desire. In fact, even in Ezechiel, God, upward from
what resembled His waist, seemed like electrum; from His
waist downward, like fire.[26] Whatever is above is gold; whatever is below is ready for the purgatory of gehenna. 'Nor is
he pleased with the legs of men.' Let us consider this passage
in its literal sense. Since the psalmist had said: 'In the
strength of the steed he delights not,' and had described man
as a warrior, it seems to me that here, where he said, 'nor
with the legs,' he is not designating legs, but periknēmídas
[covering for the leg]. We see, therefore, that whatever covers
the legs does not please God, but that which is above does.
God is not pleased with strength; He is not pleased with the
legs of men but with his fear. Strength is not pleasing; fear
is. He brings down the warrior, He elevates the beggar; He
exalts the humble, He casts down the proud.

'The Lord is pleased with those who fear him.' One fear
casts out many fears. Would it not be better to fear one in
order not to fear many, than to fear many in order not to
fear one? 'With those who hope for his kindness.' They trust
not in their own words, but in the compassionate kindness of
the Judge. Praise the Lord, for it is good to sing His praise;
salvation is for those alone who have hope in his loving kindness. To whom be glory forever and ever. Amen.

25 Cf. Ps. 146 (147A).10.
26 Cf. Ezech. 1.27, 28; cf. *Commentary on Ezechiel* 1.27, PL 25.30 (21).

HOMILY 57

ON PSALM 147 (147B)

LORIFY THE LORD, O Jerusalem; praise your God, O Sion.' We have just heard the venerable priest declare in his sermon that the Jews had been abandoned because of their transgression of the law. How, therefore, does Scripture say: 'Glorify the Lord, O Jerusalem, praise your God, O Sion'? Then, too, what about the verse that follows?

'He has strengthened the bars of your gates.' Is it of this Jerusalem that the prophet is speaking? Of this Sion? Praise your God. Why? Because He has strengthened the bars of your gates. There are no gates; how, then, are the bars in good condition? 'He has blessed your children within you.' What is this blessing of Him who said: 'Your deserted house shall be left to you'?[1]

'He has granted peace in your borders.' Where peace has been granted, what peace has been upset by war? 'With the best of wheat he fills you.' Does Jerusalem have the best of wheat?[2] Answer, O Jew; does Jerusalem have the best of wheat? If it does not, then sheer necessity compels you to a spiritual interpretation that will determine your view of the rest of the psalm. Glorify the Lord, O Jerusalem, Jerusalem, the vision of peace;[3] Sion, praise your God. Sion signifies a watchtower.[4] Now see what 'Glorify the Lord, O Jerusalem,' means. Wherever there is the vision of peace, wherever there

---

1 Cf. Luke 13.35.
2 Cf. Homily 13 on Ps. 80, p. 93.
3 Cf. Letter 46.3, PL 22.485 (201).
4 Cf. Letter 75.1, PL 22.686 (452).

is contemplation of God, there should also be the praise of God. Therefore, O Church, glorify the Lord; because you have begun to believe in Him and to possess peace, you have also begun to see peace, Jerusalem, the vision of peace. You, who were formerly the slave of idols, have become the servant of God; therefore, glorify your God. Because you are truly in possession of knowledge and have become Sion—citadel of contemplation—praise the Lord. In other words, O Jerusalem, you give glory; O Sion, you give praise; you, O ecclesiastical soul, you, O Church. Do not let the heretics praise, nor the synagogue, but you give praise. Why? Because He has strengthened the bars of your gates.

'The Lord loves the gates of Sion more than any dwelling of Jacob.'[5] We have spoken of the prophets as the gates of Sion, so since we know they are called that, let us see what the bars of the gates are. The prophets in truth are the gates of the Church; we cannot enter the Church except through them. Manichaeus tried to enter without the gates and could not. Marcion rejects the Old Testament, but without it, he has not been able to enter the New. We, on the other hand, accept the prophet-gates, and through them make our entrance. Still, let us see what the bars of the gates are. Many robbers, many thieves conspire to enter through the gates. 'All whoever have come before me were thieves and robbers.'[6] Oh, if only the Lord would grant me the privilege of being a bar in the gates of Sion! If any heretic dared to force a way through those gates into the divine economy of the Gospel, I would stand astride them and prevent him. 'He has strengthened the bars of your gates.' 'He has strengthened.' Give me any churchman trained in divine Scripture. Let Eunomius come, let Arius come and try to adduce anything from the prophets against us, does not our churchman stand firm as a bar? Does he not refute them with the fixed firmness of a bar? 'He has strengthened the

---

5 Cf. Ps. 86.2.
6 Cf. John 10.8.

bars of your gates.' Neatly said, 'strengthened'; whenever you
see a man of the Church in debate, do not imagine that it is
he who is debating; no, He who gives strength to him is
carrying on the disputation.

'With the best of wheat he fills you.' 'Unless the grain of
wheat fall into the ground and die, it remains alone, but if
it die it brings about the salvation of many.'[7] Our Lord, the
grain of wheat, has fallen into the ground and has multiplied
us. This grain of wheat is very fertile, full of marrow, rich,
fruitful. 'With the best of wheat he fills you.' Happy the
man who perceives the richness of this grain. We have read
the Sacred Scriptures. I think the Gospel is the body of
Christ; Holy Writ, His teaching. When He says: 'He who
does not eat my flesh and drink my blood,'[8] although the
words may be understood in their mystical sense, nevertheless, I say the word of Scripture is truly the body of Christ
and His blood;[9] it is divine doctrine. If at any time we
approach the Sacrament—the faithful understand what I
mean—and a tiny crumb should fall, we are appalled. Even
so, if at any time we hear the word of God, through which
the body and blood of Christ is being poured into our ears,
and we yield carelessly to distraction, how responsible are we
not for our failing?

He fills you with the best of wheat. The divine word is
exceedingly rich, containing within itself every delight. Whatever you desire is found in it, just as the Jews recount that
when they were eating manna each one tasted the kind of
food he liked. If, for example, he was hungry for an apple,
or a pear, or grapes, or bread, or meat, the taste of the manna
corresponded to his longing. We, in the flesh of Christ, which
is the word of divine doctrine, or the interpretation of the
Sacred Scriptures, receive manna in accordance with and in
proportion to our desire. If you are a saint, you will find

---

7 Cf. John 12.24, 25; Letter 54.16, PL 22.559 (293).
8 Cf. John 6.54.
9 Cf. *Commentary on Ecclesiastes* 3.13, PL 23.1092 (413).

refreshment; if a sinner, anguish. With the best of wheat He fills you; He does not lose a single fragment. He has blessed your children within you; 'To as many as received him he gave the power of becoming sons of God.'[10]

'He has granted peace in your borders'; or, as in another psalm: 'In peace is his abode.'[11] 'Peace I leave with you, my peace I give to you,'[12] 'My peace'; not as the world gives peace, for the peace of the world is our warfare. 'My peace I give to you.' Wage war with the world, and you will have My peace. 'He has granted peace in your borders.' The man, therefore, who is not at peace with his brother, is not in the borders of Jerusalem. Someone may say, What shall I do? My brother does not want to be reconciled; am I, therefore, outside the borders of Jerusalem? 'As far as in you lies, be at peace with all men,'[13] Scripture says. 'With those who hate peace, I speak of peace';[14] you be at peace; if another is angry, the conflict is his and through his struggle peace is born for you. Would you like to know how there is both war and peace? Unhappy Judas came only to betray the Lord, and the Lord offered him the kiss of peace. Judas chose to beget war from that kiss.

'He sends forth his command to the earth.' Answer, O Jew. If the psalmist was speaking of grain when he said: 'With the best of wheat he fills you,' how, now, does he mean: 'He sends forth his command to the earth'? 'In the beginning was the Word.'[15] This Word is sent in the flesh; 'the Word was made flesh, and dwelt among us.'[16] 'He sends forth his command to the earth.' At that time was fulfilled the prophecy: 'The earth has yielded its fruits.'[17] 'He sends forth his command to the earth.' He is speaking of evangelical

---

10 John 1.12.
11 Cf. Ps. 75.3; cf. Letter 125.14, PL 22.1080 (942).
12 John 14.27.
13 Rom. 12.18.
14 Cf. Ps. 119.6, 7.
15 John 1.1.
16 John 1.14; cf. *Against Jovinian* 2.29, PL 23.341 (371).
17 Ps. 66.7.

preaching, of the teachings of the apostles; in fact, the very next words are: 'Swiftly runs his word!' In every land is heard His word, and in the whole world the teaching of the apostles. One man, poor, already old, preached the Gospel from Jerusalem round about as far as Illyricum,[18] and 'swiftly runs his word!' Because, too, the word has sped swiftly from Jerusalem all the way to Illyricum, the Word itself said, through Paul the Apostle: 'I wish to go to Spain, too.'[19] Mark well the swiftness of the Word; it is not satisfied with the East; it desires to speed to the West.

'He spreads snow like wool; frost he strews like ashes. He scatters his hail like crumbs.' Note the difficulty, the real obscurity, of the words: 'Before his cold the waters freeze.' Whose cold? It does not say, but the psalmist continues: 'He sends his word and melts them.' This refers to Him of whom the psalmist had said: 'He sends forth his command to the earth'; He sends His Word. Who sends? God the Father. 'The Word was with God, and the Word was God.'[20] We have mentioned the Father and the Son; we cannot believe in a twofold number unless the Trinity be completed. 'He lets his breath[21] blow and the waters run.' Where the Father and the Word of God is, there at once is the Holy Spirit.

Let us go back and review the psalm in sequence. With the best wheat He fills you; He sends forth His command to the earth; swiftly runs His word! What follows unexpectedly? 'He spreads snow like wool.' The word of the Lord that runs swiftly is spread like snow, and the snow itself is like wool. Just think of the merciful kindness of the Lord! The food of the Lord is changed for us into a garment. John had said of the Lord Savior: 'Behold the lamb of God, who takes away the sin of the world';[22] and Isaia: 'He shall

---

18 Cf. Rom. 15.19.
19 Cf. Rom. 15.24.
20 John 1.1.
21 Cf. Ps. 147 (147B).18.
22 John 1.29.

be led like a lamb to the slaughter.'[23] Of this lamb, therefore, and of this sheep, is the wool that is like snow. Isaia says: 'Though your sins be like scarlet, they may become white as snow.'[24] 'Cleanse me of sin with hyssop, that I may be purified; wash me, and I shall be whiter than snow.'[25] 'He spreads snow like wool.' Take away, O Lord, my uncleanness; take away whatever there is of baseness. Grant Your snow, Your purity, to the minds and hearts of Christians. Unless You cleanse us with the snow of Your purity, we cannot wear Your garment. Christ is our garment. If we want to possess Christ as our garment, let us be pure as snow.

'Frost he strews like ashes.' The Latin word used here, 'nebulam,' is a very poor translation, for the Greek word homíxlē follows the concept in the Hebrew text that is expressed by the Latin 'pruinam,' hence, the reading: 'Frost he strews like ashes.' He teaches us and makes us a garment white as snow, and when He has clothed us in His own garment, then He gives us nourishment. 'Frost he strews like ashes.' Mark: 'like ashes.' Do you want to be clean? Do penance. 'For I eat ashes like bread, and mingle my drink with tears.'[26] Do you see now how He strews His frost like ashes? Wonderful mutation of things! From ashes snow is made; from repentance cleanliness is effected.

'He scatters his hail like crumbs.' Just as His bread is broken up into morsels, in the same way hail is broken up into crumbs of ice. Hail is like frozen water;[27] hail and water, therefore, have the same difference as water and ice, for water pours, but hail is formed of crystals compressed and clinging together into one solid mass. Whenever water freezes, it crystallizes; consequently, since we cannot take the meat of the divine word in its totality, it is broken up so that we

23 Cf. Isa. 53.7.
24 Isa. 1.18.
25 Ps. 50.9.
26 Ps. 101.10.
27 Cf. *Commentary on Ezechiel* 1.22-27, PL 25.29 (20).

may partake of it in small pieces.[28] This is an obscure point and the difficulty of interpretation does not warrant us to speak more fully.

'Before his cold who shall stand?'[29] Whose cold? Some say of hail; others, with truth, say of God. To me, too, it seems that the words: 'Before his cold who shall stand,' refer to God. Of God, I say, 'Who is able to endure His cold?' What torments does Holy Writ tell us are prepared for sinners? Nothing is hotter than hell-fire, yet gehenna itself is icy. Gehenna consists of fire, but if anyone grows cold enough, he is sent into the fire of hell. It is written: in the last days the 'charity of the many will grow cold.'[30] Whoever becomes cold like that is sent into the fire. May the Lord grant that no cold ever creep into our hearts. We do not commit sin except after charity has grown cold. Furthermore, what does the Apostle say? 'Be fervent in spirit';[31] 'our God is a consuming fire.'[32] If God is fire, He is fire in order to drive out the cold of the devil.

'Aquilo is the iciest of the winds, though it is called by an honorable name.'[33] Nicely said, 'is called'; it assumed that name of itself, since the north wind is not honorable.[34] If anyone's soul should grow cold, as cold as the north wind; if the warmth of charity should ever grow cold in our heart; if one should sin, should chill, should die—attend very carefully to what I am saying—if one should grow cold, if one should die, [God is a consuming fire]. It is the nature of the dead to be cold; of the living to be warm. If anyone, then, should grow cold and die, God will send His Word and melt him. May the Lord grant that our frigidity, too, may thaw, that this crystal of ice be dissolved and melt. 'He sends his word, and melts them.'

---

28 Cf. *Commentary on Isaia* 48.20-22, PL 24.463 (560).
29 Cf. Ps. 147 (147B).17.
30 Matt. 24.12.
31 Rom. 12.11.
32 Cf. Deut. 4.24.
33 Cf. Prov. 27.16, LXX; Jerome *'dexter vocatur.'*
34 Jerome *'sinister est.'* Cf. Letter 78.4, PL 22.702 (472).

Give me any sinner who has no regard for God, who has no heat, but is thoroughly frozen and dead; if at the word of God he is roused to compunction and begins to repent and the hardness of his heart is softened, at that moment are the words fulfilled: 'He sends his word and melts them.' The Father sends; the Word is sent; the Holy Spirit is given. 'He lets his breath blow.' 'Be fervent in spirit.' Cold is not expelled except by the heat of the Holy Spirit. Where are the Eunomians, the Arians, the Macedonians who say: 'We do not rank the Holy Spirit with the Father and the Son'? God the Father sends; the Word is sent; but the cure is not complete, except by the breath of the Holy Spirit. 'He lets his breath blow and the waters run.' 'Waters.'[35] What was hard previously is now made soft. He, who before could render justice to no one, is now a disciple.

Since we have spoken at such length and the remaining verses of the psalm are explicit enough, let us pray the Lord that any hardness in us may soften, that our sins be purged, that we may become as fire, so the chill of the devil—whatever there is of it in our hearts—may be expelled so that we may grow warm with the Holy Spirit. There is, of course, also a heat that is evil. 'They all burn with adultery, their hearts like an oven for baking cakes.'[36] But that heat is banished by the heat of the Holy Spirit. To whom be glory forever and ever. Amen.

---

35 Cf. Ps. 147 (147B).18.
36 Cf. Osee 7.4, LXX; cf. Letter 130.10, PL 22.1116 (987).

HOMILY 58

HERE IS A DOUBLE 'alleluia' in the title of this psalm, and many suppose that the two alleluias constitute the title. We ought to know, however, that one alleluia marks the close of the preceding psalm and the other the beginning of this. We must learn the rule that all psalms that commence with an alleluia, also end with an alleluia.[1] Many are of the opinion that a subjoined alleluia indicates the beginning of another psalm, but that is not so, for the psalm that opens with alleluia, likewise, closes with an alleluia. Why am I drawing your attention to this matter? So that you may know why there are two alleluias at the head of this psalm.

'Praise the Lord from the heavens, praise him in the heights.' To praise God, human nature alone does not suffice; the heavens, too, join in His praise. 'Praise the Lord from the heavens.' The psalmist did not mean, praise, O heavens; but, you who are in heaven give praise, you who dwell in heaven: thrones, dominations, powers, seraphim, cherubim, and 'every name that is named, not only in this world, but also that which is to come.'[2] 'Praise the Lord from the heavens.' You who are in the heights, praise Him in the heights. You who are on high, praise the Most High. He did not say this to the lowly and those established below, but to you who are on the summits.

'Praise him, all you his angels.' Do you notice the order of

---

1 Cf. *Commentarioli in ps.* 104.1.
2 Eph. 1.21.

the angels? First named are the thrones; thrones are seats. Let us not suppose that they are chairs upon which God remains seated; but that they are some heavenly powers upon which God always sits as if in His own chariot. 'Praise him, all his angels.' All His angels. Let him who is an angel give praise; he who is a demon cannot. 'Praise him, all you his hosts.' Because we have summoned the angels to the praise of God, and I, a man, cannot know the names of all the angels, I say in general: Praise Him, all His heavenly hosts. Thus far the psalmist calls upon invisible creation: Praise Him, you who are unseen, who are not visible to the human eye. Now he comes to His creatures that we do see with our own eyes.

'Praise him, sun and moon.' Take note, heathens; note well, Manichaeans. The sun gives praise, it does not receive it. 'Praise him, sun and moon.' You call the sun god. Just watch and see how much praise precedes that of the sun. Praise from the heaven; praise in the heights; give praise all you angels; praise, all you hosts. Your god with its praise is fifth in order. 'Praise him, sun and moon.' The psalmist did not say, moon and sun, but sun and moon; the greater light praises first. Mark well the order of the visible universe: Praise Him, sun; after the sun, the moon; after the moon, all the stars. 'All the stars,' not only the morning star, not only the greater stars, but let the lesser equally praise the Lord.

Someone may raise the question: How do the sun and moon and stars praise God? In that they do not depart from the duty and servitude that is theirs. Their service is the praise of God. Sublime honor is yours, O human soul. The sun and the moon and the stars hasten in their course to serve you. Angels, thrones, dominations do not need the sun, nor the moon, nor the stars, for they are in heavenly abodes beyond the sun and the moon. Sun, moon, and stars exist for our sake; they serve us. It is the Apostle who says that creation itself groans and travails to be delivered into the freedom of the sons of God.[3] When, moreover, the sons of God shall attain glory, creation itself also will be delivered from its slavery.

Someone may ask: How is the sun in slavery and how is it set free? In what way, the moon; in what way, the stars? The sun is liberated that it may not look upon the Jews, that it may not look upon the heathens, upon those who are blaspheming its Lord. It beholds parricides; it looks upon homicides; yet it is always obeying the command of Him who issued it: 'for he makes his sun to rise on the just and the evil.'[4]

'Praise him, all you stars and light.'[5] Someone may wonder: What light is there without the sun, without the stars, without the moon? We may answer, the light between night and day or between day and night, because that is a time of light without the sun, although there are many who believe that this light is but the resplendence of the sun. So the prophet says: 'Praise him, all you stars and light.' Just as he had said of invisible creation: 'Praise him, all his hosts'; even so of visible creation, he may say: Praise Him, everything that shines.

'Praise him, you highest heavens.' We speak of many heavens. Paul says, in fact, that he was caught up to the third heaven.[6] Know, then, there is so much brightness that there is a heaven of heavens. From here on, the rest of the psalm refers to visible creation.

'For he spoke and they were made.'[7] For God to have commanded is to have created; the command is creation. He spoke, and they were made, according to that which is written in Genesis: God said, and God created; that is, God the Father gave the command; God the Son created. Someone may say: He is the greater who gives the command, and He is the less to whom it is given. That is what the Arians, the

---

3 Cf. Rom. 8.22, 21.
4 Cf. Matt. 5.45.
5 Cf. Ps. 148.3.
6 2 Cor. 12.2; cf. Letter 51.5, PL 22.523 (249).
7 Cf. Ps. 148.5.

Eunomians, and the Macedonians maintain. I answer you, O heretics, in accordance with your own reasoning. You say, the Father is greater because He gives the command, and the Son is less because He is commanded by the Father. If this is in accord with human understanding, answer me: Is it greater to command or to create? I say, 'Let a house be made,' and another builds the house. There is nothing great in uttering the words; it is difficult to build the house. He is greater, therefore, who creates than he who gives the command. But that is impious irreverence, for the Son is not greater than the Father. It is just as blasphemous to believe this of the Son against the Father, as it is to believe it of the Father against the Son. 'For he spoke and they were made: he commanded and they were created.' One nature both commands and creates; God gives the order, God fulfills it. A painter bids a painter paint, and the painter paints what he has bid be painted.

'He established them forever and ever; he gave them a duty which shall not pass away.' Great your honor, O man, and great your misfortune. The sun runs its course for you; the elements serve you; and you ignore your Creator. 'He gave them a duty which shall not pass away.' He gave the sun a duty; and see how many years the duty imposed by God has persisted unchanged. It has been so constant that human observation has been able to note its course. 'He gave them a duty which shall not pass away.' He has prescribed for the moon that it wax and wane through a period of thirty days. Does the moon ever change its course? In heaven, God's order is obeyed, and on earth it is not. He has fixed the limit of the sea that it may not go beyond its shores; the sea surges, swollen with billows, and again recedes, mindful of God's decree. The entire universe heeds God and remembers His injunction; man alone does not remember. We pray, therefore, in the Lord's prayer: 'Thy will be done on earth, as it is in heaven.'[8] As in heaven the angels obey You, and

---

8 Matt. 6.10; cf. *Commentary on Matthew* 6.10, PL 26.44 (34).

creation serves You, so even may man serve You. O unhappy race of mankind! God has come down to you, since you are unwilling to ascend to heaven. It is not enough for you to reject Him, but you kill Him; you murder, you crucify, you blaspheme, you scourge. It does not satisfy you to slay; but you do not repent that you have slain.

The psalmist has spoken of the invisible and the visible in the heavens; now he comes to the visible on earth. Mark carefully the order of praise: first, the invisible; then, the visible divided into two groups, the heavenly and the terrestrial. He has spoken of the heavenly; now he speaks of the earthly.

'Praise the Lord from the earth.' Since the angels have given praise, since heaven has praised, let earth also praise. Let us see who of earth are first to praise God. 'You sea monsters, and all depths; fire and hail, snow and mist, storm winds that fulfill his word; you mountains and all you hills, you fruit trees and all you cedars; you wild beasts and all tame animals, you creeping things and you winged fowl.' After all these, what does the prophet say? After the sea monsters, the creeping things, fire, hail, wild beasts and tame animals, what follows? O man, you who think you are so great, of you he speaks next—and not of ordinary man, but of men who are the mightiest among men.

'Let the kings of the earth and all peoples, the princes and all the judges of the earth,' and then: 'Young men too, and maidens, old men and boys, praise the name of the Lord, for his name alone is exalted.' How many mysteries these verses contain! Heavenly beings, the non-visible, the visible, have praised the Lord; now the psalmist descends to the earthly, and first of all he rouses the sea monsters and the unfathomable depths to the praise of God. 'Where the offense has abounded, grace has abounded yet more.'[9] You who were at

---

9 Rom. 5.20.

first a sea monster, who hissed[10] with venom of serpents; O you who were an abyss, with clouds gathered above you, grasp what he says. Where there are sea monsters, there is venom; where there are depths, there are clouds and darkness. Do not despair, O you who were a sea monster, you who were full of darkness, and did not dare to praise God; repent of your sins, and at that instant you are converted to God. Granted that sea monsters are not mentioned in the Hebrew text, but THANNINIM[11] is there instead, which in Hebrew signifies a huge sea animal of the species of whale. This sea animal, moreover, they say is enormous in size; hence, this is the monster in the great deeps of the sea.

Let us discuss the literal interpretation first. Watch what it says. Praise, you creatures in the sea; and give praise, you creatures not in the sea; sea monsters and all the depths— from the part, the whole συνεκδοχικῶς.[12] Next comes fire. Note the harmony of discord; water and fire praise the Lord simultaneously. 'You sea monsters and all depths; fire.' Everything that generates from water generates also from fire, that is, from moisture and heat; neither can fire generate alone without moisture, nor moisture without fire. Nothing is so contrary as moisture to heat and heat to moisture; yet, by the will of God, these contraries harmonize in our birth.

'Hail, snow and mist, storm winds that fulfill his word.' There is much I would like to say to you, but we cannot tarry over single words. 'Hail, snow and mist, storm winds'; everything we see in this world ministers to us. Creeping things and depths, fire, hail, snow, mist, storm winds, all seem to be without reason, yet they serve us. Yesterday there was a storm, and it certainly seemed like a contradiction to us; it was cold and damp; there were rains; but that which at the time appears to be at cross-purposes, is really for our

---

10 Cf. *Against Jovinian* 1.4, PL 23.224 (241); Letter 130.16, PL 22.1120 (992).
11 *Commentary on Isaia* 27.1, PL 24.307 (361); 43.16-22, PL 24.432 (621).
12 Cf. Homily 36 on Ps. 109, p. 270; *Commentary on Isaia* 14.2, PL 24.160 (176); on *Jona* 2.2, PL 25.1131 (405); on *Matthew* 12.40, PL 26.85 (83).

benefit, for it brings forth fruit for us. Understand, then,
what the psalmist means: they are all creatures that fulfill
the word of God. Blush with shame, O man, creeping
things and depths,. snow, rain, and storms obey the word of
God, and you do not.

'You mountains and all you hills.' Mountains do not
change into hills, nor valleys into mountains; they preserve
their own nature. 'You fruit trees, and all you cedars.' You
see a tree that is almost withered up, all its leaves are gone,
and suddenly when spring arrives, it sends forth a bud, it
brings forth fruit for you. The tree bears fruit for you,
but you bear no fruit for God. 'All you cedars.' Follow the
example of the cedar. Cedars stretch to reach the heights as
if they were hastening to heaven; it is for you to imitate the
non-rational tree. 'You wild beasts and all tame animals.'
They do not change their nature; all creatures keep their
order, except man alone to whom all are subject. 'You
creeping things and you winged fowl.' Earthly creatures do
not leave earth for heaven, nor heavenly beings for earth;
they serve you.

Someone may say: You are following history; you are not
speaking allegorically. If you are giving us the historical
sense, why do depths and snow and hail praise God first, and
fruit trees and the rest of irrational creation second, and
last of all man? Let us read Genesis and we shall see that
all creatures glorify God in the order of generation and
creation, for there it is written that God gave existence first
to living beings that are in water, next those on land, then
the birds of the air, and after that He made one man. Consequently, that .which He made first, should praise the Lord
first. But there is another meaning. O man, all these things
that I have mentioned, for whose sake did God make them?
Wild beasts, creeping things, fruit trees, winged birds, all
these give praise to God by the very fact that they do not
change their nature. 'He gave them a duty which shall not
pass away.' Do, therefore, as the creatures that serve you.

God made them to serve you; He made you to serve Him. They obey you; follow their example and serve God just as they serve you; it is through God that they serve and obey. To whom be glory forever and ever. Amen.

HOMILY 59

THE ONE-HUNDRED-FORTY-NINTH PSALM has been read which begins with the words: 'Sing to the Lord a new song.' The venerable priest has explained that Psalms 95 and 97 have this same introduction. The ninety-fifth psalm is entitled: 'A song for David himself, when the house was built after the captivity,'[1] and alludes to the house of Christ that is built after captivity, that is, after repentance for sin. Since, therefore, he has given us an excellent interpretation of the opening verse of our psalm: 'Sing to the Lord a new song'—that it is a new people that sings a new song—let us run quickly through the rest of it.

'Let Israel be glad in their maker.' Let them be glad who discern God, for the meaning here of Israel is 'perceiving God.' 'Let the children of Sion rejoice in their king.' Children of the Church, children of a new people, let them rejoice in their king, in Christ, who reigns over them. Just listen to how lightly we are striking only the high tones!

'Let them praise his name in choir.'[2] Wherever there is a choir many voices blend into one song. In the same way that separate chords produce a single effect, so, too, do separate voices harmonize as one. In other words, when the faithful gather together, they form the Lord's choir. Let them praise His name in choir; where there is dissension, where there is jealousy, there is no choir. 'Let them praise his name in choir, let them sing praise to him with timbrel and

---

1 Cf. Ps. 95.1; 96.1, LXX.
2 Cf. Ps. 149.3.

424

psaltery.'³ May this choir of ours have song; may it have timbrel and psaltery. Let us crucify our bodies for Christ and sing to God with a timbrel of this kind.

'Let them sing praise to him with timbrel and psaltery.' A timbrel is not made of flesh but of skin, and as long as we are carnal, we are not timbrels. You cannot make a timbrel unless you remove all the flesh and draw the skin tight; a timbrel cannot contract; the membrane must be stretched taut. Let not sin contract us, but justice expand us. We must hasten on over the rest of the psalm. Let them sing praise to Him with timbrel and psaltery. What we sing in choir, let us play on the psaltery. The psaltery is a kind of musical instrument that is quite similar to a harp, but not identical with it. You pluck the strings of a harp downwards, but the psaltery upwards. The common term for psaltery is polyphthongum. So much for that. The prophet, therefore, bids us sing a new song to the Lord, not downwards on the harp, but upwards, on the psaltery.

'For the Lord loves his people, and he exalts the meek to victory.'⁴ 'Blessed are the meek, for they shall possess the earth.'⁵ If, then, the Gospel says: Blessed are the meek—that is, the patient—for they will possess the earth; and this psalm says: He exalts the meek to victory; and they are the meek who will possess the earth; that being the case, this earth is not downwards, but upwards. What are the words of the psalmist? 'He exalts the meek to victory.' Certainly, if these meek were to be in possession of the earth, that is, downwards, he would not say, God 'exalts.'

'Let the faithful exult in glory.' In what glory? 'Awake, O my glory; awake, psaltery and harp; I will wake the dawn.'⁶ In glory: 'For the Spirit had not yet been given, seeing that Jesus had not yet been glorified,'⁷ that is, He had not yet

---

3 *Ibid.*
4 Cf. Ps. 149.4.
5 Matt. 5.4.
6 Cf. Ps. 107.3.
7 John 7.39.

been crucified. Scripture says: The Spirit had not yet been given because Jesus had not been glorified, meaning that He had not been crucified. 'Let the faithful exult in glory.' Why am I stressing this point? Because the psalmist says: Let the faithful exult in glory, but I say: let the faithful exult in the cross. 'But as for me, God forbid that I should glory save in the cross of our Lord Jesus Christ.'[8] Behold the prophecy had been fulfilled in the voice of the Apostle. 'Let the faithful exult in glory.'

'Let them sing for joy upon their couches.' 'Every night I flood my bed with weeping; I drench my couch with tears.'[9] That is the cry of the sinner, of the penitent, but the words here: 'Let them sing for joy upon their couches,' apply to the saints, to the just. Who of us sings for joy upon his couch? Who is there who does not struggle with his flesh? When I keep watch over myself upon my couch, I am not singing for joy; I am struggling; I do not sigh for the kingdom of heaven, but I wrestle with the flesh. I drench the fire of lust with my tears, and put it out. That is why the psalmist says: 'Every night I flood my bed with weeping; I drench my couch with my tears.' Tears extinguish the flames of my bed burning with lust. Happy are they of whom it says: 'Let them sing for joy upon their couches.'

'Let the high praises of God be in their throats.' To be sure, he who cries out does not cry out in his throat, but with his lips; I mean, of course, one does not call aloud with the throat but with the lips. How, then, does it say here: 'Let the high praises of God be in their throats'? 'Crying in our hearts, "Abba! Father!" '[10] The voice that cries to God does not come from the lips, but from the heart. In fact, the Lord says to Moses: 'Why are you crying out to me?'[11] Certainly Moses had not spoken a word.

'Let two-edged swords be in their hands.' They who sing

8 Gal. 6.14; cf. Letter 22.27, PL 22.412 (110).
9 Ps. 6.7; cf. Letter 108.15, PL 22.891 (706); 122.1, PL 22.1040 (892).
10 Rom. 8.15.
11 Exod. 14.15.

for joy upon their couches—this means the saints surely,
perfect men—what else do they have? 'Let two-edged swords
be in their hands.' 'Two-edged swords.' The swords of the
saints are two-edged. We read in the Apocalypse of John—
which, by the way, is read in the churches and is accepted,
for it is not held among the Apocrypha but is included in
the canonical writings[12]—as I was saying, it is written there
of the Lord Savior: 'Out of his mouth came forth a sharp
two-edged sword.'[13] Mark well that these saints receive from
the mouth of God the two-edged swords that they hold in
their hands. The Lord, therefore, gives the sword from His
mouth to His disciples; a two-edged sword, namely, the word
of His teachings; a two-edged sword, historically and allegorically, the letter and the spirit; a two-edged sword that
slays adversaries and at the same time defends His faithful.
'A two-edged sword.' This two-edged sword has two heads:
it speaks of the present and of the future world; here, it
strikes down adversaries; above, it opens up the kingdom of
heaven.

Why do saints carry such swords? 'To execute vengeance
on the nations.' O if I could but carry this two-edged sword
so that I might be able to execute vengeance upon the nations, that I might be able to slay various heathens, that I
might be able to kill Arius, Eunomius, Manichaeus, and
destroy every last heresy! But grasp that it says: 'To execute
vengeance on the nations.' So that they may be killed? So
that they may perish? It does not say that. 'Punishments on
the peoples.' Punish the peoples in order to save them, in
order to save those whom evil teachers have seduced. It is not
possible to liberate them, however, without first putting their
teachers in chains, so the next verse continues right along.

'To bind their kings with chains.' Do you want to liberate
the nations? Bind up the teachers. 'To bind their kings.'
The psalmist did not call them teachers, but kings, for they

---

12 Cf. Homily 1 on Ps. 1, p. 3.
13 Apoc. 1.16; cf. Letter 14.2, PL 22.348 (29).

hold sway over sin and misery. 'To bind their kings with chains.' Well said, 'with chains'; that the teachers may not have freedom to run about, that they may not mislead the many, but that chained together, they may be forced to stand still. 'Their nobles with fetters of iron.' 'Their nobles.' You should hear them say in the presence of heretics: This man is learned; that one performs wonders; this one casts out devils. The saints of the Lord, who carry two-edged swords, swords of two heads—the Old and the New Testament— bind fast those teachers and fetter their feet with iron to prevent them from running. 'Their nobles with fetters of iron.' They fetter but do not kill or destroy them. They chain their hands together and lead their captives to the Church. These chains are made of links of scriptural proof while I join testimony to testimony. These chains are unbreakable because they are not made of single links, but are intertwined back and forth. 'A three-ply cord is not easily broken.'[14] Now why is all this done?

'To execute on them the written sentence.' What is the written sentence? That they, who had first rejected the Lord, later return to Him through repentance. The written sentence: that they release their captives; that those whom they had bound, whom they had led in chains from the Church, they may afterwards set free in the Church. 'To execute on them the written sentence.' I shall state this more simply. 'To execute on them the written sentence,' in other words, to judge them according to the manner prescribed in the Sacred Scriptures.

'This is the glory of all his faithful.' Certainly, that is not glory where there is gold, silver, gems, garments of silk. The man who possesses the sword of Holy Writ, what else does he need? Mark what it says: 'This is the glory of all his faithful.' Let us beg the Lord that this glory may be ours; that the sword coming forth from the mouth of our Savior may provide our hands with a weapon, and that we may be able

14 Eccles. 4.12.

to say: 'Blessed be the Lord, my God, who trains my hands for battle, my fingers for war.'[15] The man who carries this long saber has no fear of the sword of the world. He who possesses this weapon is not afraid of the world's. I am telling you something novel. Very often, it is the sword of this world that confers the other sword; frequently, it happens that the one provides us with the other. If we are not afraid of the one, we receive the other. Let us, therefore, give thanks to Him who has that sword, and bless Him forever and ever. Amen.

---

15 Cf. Ps. 143.1.

The indices to this volume will be combined with the indices of the second volume of this work which will be published at a later date.

CPSIA information can be obtained
at www.ICGtesting.com
Printed in the USA
LVHW092141041218
599292LV00001B/64/P